AMERICAN INDIAN
LACROSSE

AMERICAN INDIAN

THOMAS VENNUM, JR.

SMITHSONIAN

INSTITUTION

PRESS

WASHINGTON

AND LONDON

LITTLE BROTHER OF WAR

LACROSSE

Copy Editor: Jan McInroy
Supervisory Editor: Duke Johns
Designer: Linda McKnight

Library of Congress Cataloging-in-Publication Data

Vennum, Thomas.
American Indian lacrosse : little brother of war / Thomas Vennum.
    p.   cm.
  Includes bibliographical references and index.
  ISBN 1-56098-301-9 (cloth). — ISBN 1-56098-302-7 (pbk.)
  1. Lacrosse—History.   2. Indians of North America—Games.
3. Indians of North America—Rites and ceremonies.   I. Title.
E98.G2V46   1994
796.34'7—dc20   93-29968

British Library Cataloguing-in-Publication Data is available

Manufactured in the United States of America
01 00 99 98 97   5 4 3 2

For permission to reproduce illustrations appearing in this book, please correspond
directly with the owners of the works, as listed in the illustration credits. The Smithsonian Institution Press does not retain reproduction rights for these illustrations individually, or maintain a file of addresses for photo sources.

On the cover: Detail from George Catlin's *Ball Play of the Choctaw—Ball Up*.
Color lithograph from *North American Indian Portfolio*, plate 23 (London, [1844]).

Contents

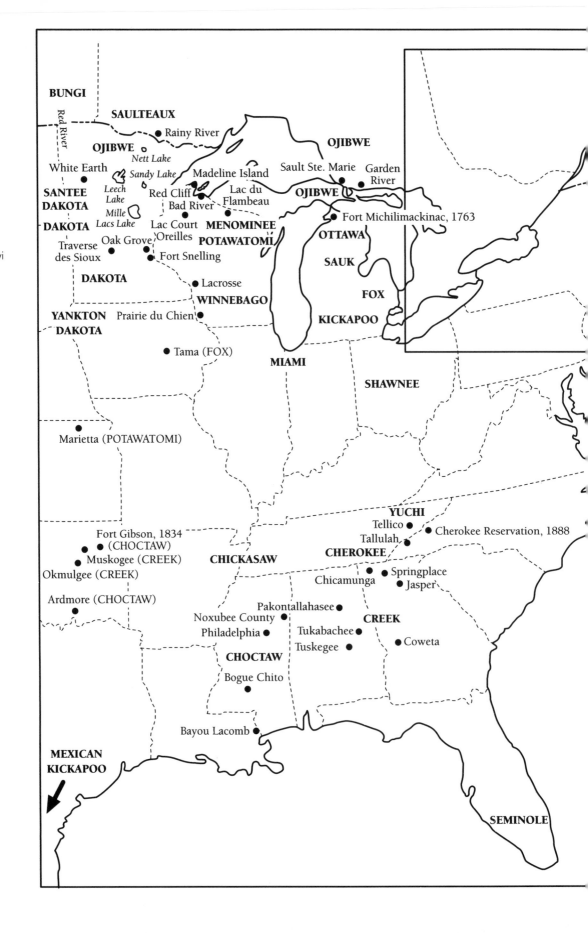

LOCATIONS OF TRIBES AND COMMUNITIES MENTIONED IN THE TEXT

This map shows the regions generally occupied by tribes that played lacrosse and the communities referred to in the text. Dates correspond to the location of sites in the narrative chapters. Because the time span covered in the text is more than three and a half centuries, tribal locations on the map should be accepted as rough approximations. The location for some tribes, such as those in the southeast, shows their general area of occupation at the time of European contact. Many have since changed their location, having been removed by the federal government and settled on reservations away from their original homeland. Historical forces induced others to move voluntarily. The Ojibwe, for instance, were at the east end of Lake Superior when Europeans first encountered them, but under the pressure of the fur trade they gradually moved west and north. For the most part, they now live on reservations in the area around the west end of the lake.

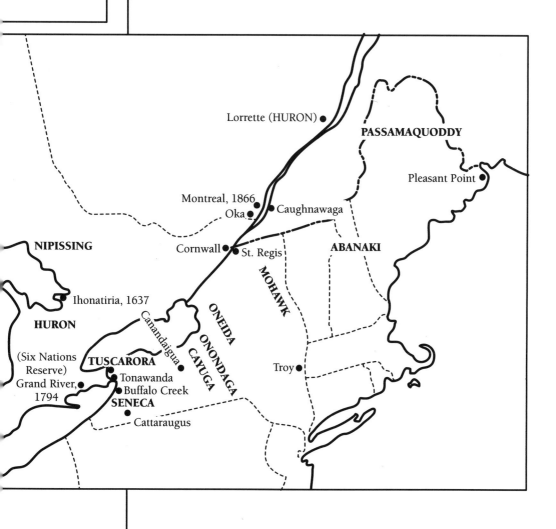

Acknowledgments

Of the many who contributed to this book, I wish to thank in particular the following: Cheryl Anderson, Joallyn Archambault, Franklin Basina, Frank Benedict, Owen Benedict, Kendall Blanchard, Brandon Bristol, Freeman Bucktooth, Jr., Joe Callahan, Andrew Connors, Mary Kay Davies, Bill Fenton, Ray Fogelson, Lucy Fowler-Williams, Tom Garland, Ives Goddard, Daniel Goodwin, Ellen Green, Conrad Heidenreich, Don Heldman, Rick Hill, Fred Hoxie, Ansley Jemison, Duke Johns, Vic Krantz, the Lacrosse Foundation, Mark LoBello, Linley Logan, Kent Lyons, Rex Lyons, Jan McInroy, Linda McKnight, Cesare Marino, Peter Nabokov, John Nichols, David Noble, Emmett Printup, Guha Shankar, Daphne Shuttleworth, Roy Simmons, Jr., Jay Stevens, Bill Sturtevant, Lori Taylor, Leland Torrence, Bill Truettner, Joan Wolbier, and Hanni Woodbury. I owe a special debt to my former student Edward Brown, who has inspired me from the beginning with his love of sports and his passion for writing.

Preface

A dual purpose had brought me to Philadelphia that late May week-end in 1992. The National Collegiate Athletic Association (NCAA) men's field lacrosse championship play-offs and postgame socializing would occupy the bulk of my time, but my trip had a more impor-tant mission. Just across the street from the playing field on the University of Pennsylvania campus, where Syracuse would do battle with Johns Hopkins and North Carolina would struggle with Prince-ton, was the University Museum, the repository of the object that I sought. Locked in a drawer of the collections division, out of public view, rested a hickory lacrosse stick made by a Cayuga Indian in southeastern Ontario nearly two centuries ago. I had read of this stick and seen photos of it in the museum's publications. Immersed in the study of American Indian lacrosse, I kept returning to my notes on this item for compelling reasons; I now needed to see the artifact firsthand to confirm a suspicion.

The setting was a familiar one. As a researcher I was accustomed to examining historical objects in museum vaults, where musical instruments that no longer sound are stored and pieces of now extinct games remain in boxes. The curator located by index card the appropriate drawer and then disappeared to find it. Soon I heard the familiar squeaking of an examination cart coming toward me. There was the lacrosse stick that I was so intrigued with (Figure 1), laid out in its protective plastic covering like some corpse in a body bag, with a museum identification tag tied to its protruding handle as though it were a cadaver's toe. Removing the covering, I gingerly picked up this contraption of wood and rawhide. Accession information described the stick as having been played with before 1845 by the grandfather of the Cayuga Indian from whom it was obtained in the

Figure 1 • A pre-1845 Cayuga lacrosse stick that belonged to the grandfather of Alexander T. General of Six Nations Reserve, Ontario.

1930s. But this stick showed none of the signs of wear that are usually apparent on old wooden lacrosse sticks—none of the nicks and scratches that are typical on pieces used in Indian games of the past. Nor was there the usual dark patina that developed over time on a stick's handle, where its owner's sweaty hands grasped it. Close examination of the webbing revealed that the twisted rawhide still had small hairs attached; such hairs would have quickly worn off in play.[1] My suspicion seemed confirmed: I concluded that this particular Cayuga lacrosse stick had never made it onto the field!

And for good reason. Of the hundreds of lacrosse sticks that I have examined, this Ontario hickory crosse—one of the oldest surviving—is by far the most extraordinary piece of sports equipment that I know of. Its elaborate carving indicates that some talented Cayuga more than a century and a half ago must have devoted days to meticulously incising the decorations. While the stick's construction conforms generally to the type used by the Cayuga as well as other Iroquois until about 1860, the craftsman went beyond simply producing a utilitarian stick to create a work of art. The butt end (Figure 2a), usually left plain or, at the most, terminating in a sort of knob, was painstakingly carved to represent a human hand clutching a ball—the cardinal violation in lacrosse. Beneath the wrist on a band around the circumference are four animals in relief, followed by two human hands clasped in a handshake.

The shaft continues with intricate geometric designs in chip carving, a well-known technique in American as well as Iroquoian carving of the period. Beyond the graceful bend of its crook, at the very end, is another unusual detail. Ordinarily such a stick would have an incision about half an inch from the tip, like that on a hunting bow to secure its string. On old lacrosse sticks the incision anchors one end of the outermost string; here, however, the stickmaker terminated the crook by carving a dog's head (Figure 2d), cleverly designed so that the outermost string is made to come out of the animal's mouth. The dog's nose protrudes beyond the mouth, forming the small hook that on most Iroquois sticks of the period was used to catch the webbing of an opponent's stick and jerk it out of his grasp. Such a priceless Cayuga artifact would surely *not* have been taken onto the field and exposed to potential damage from the violence of the game. This lacrosse stick had some ritual significance, enough to have remained a carefully preserved family heirloom—at least for three generations, until it was sold or given to some inquisitive anthropologist who had wandered onto the reservation.

But what do the carvings themselves tell us? Researchers have speculated on their meanings. One suggested that the butt end represents "holding the ball as securely as though in the hand." But to

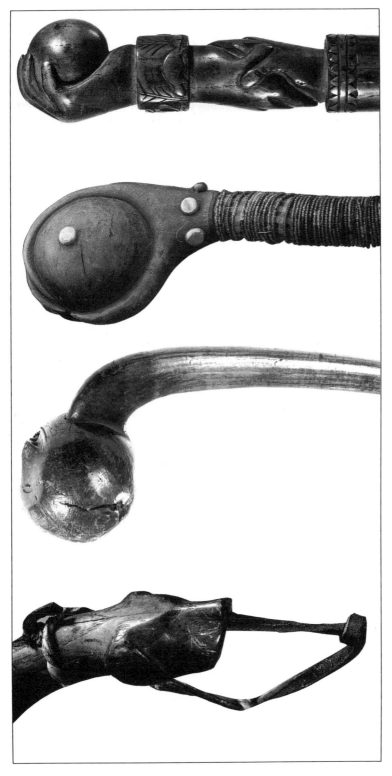

Figure 2a • Detail of the butt end.

Figure 2b • Ball end of Ojibwe ceremonial war club, possibly from the Lac Court Oreilles Reservation, c. 1900 (?) and probably carried in dances by a former warrior. The ball is clutched by eagle talons.

Figure 2c • Ball-headed war club of the Ojibwe, carved and painted to resemble a human head. It belonged to "Medicine Sky," a Lac du Flambeau warrior, who received instructions in a dream that he would kill an enemy with it, which he did on a raiding party against the Dakota.

Figure 2d • Detail of tip of the Cayuga stick's crook.

touch the ball with the hand is a clear violation in all forms of lacrosse. The clasped hands, others said, might signify the friendly nature of the game, but my study has taught me that the Indian game was often anything *but* friendly. The dog's head was viewed by some as perhaps symbolizing "the stick in pursuit of the ball like a coursing hound," but traditional Indian attitudes toward dogs make me suspicious of that theory.[2] While dogs were often mistreated, they were also considered to have a sacred function, acting as intermediaries between the human world and the spiritual world in many rituals (see Appendix A, No. 10). Long ago, in the Iroquois new year or midwinter ceremony, for instance, it was the custom to sacrifice one or two white dogs. They were first strangled carefully so as to avoid breaking any bones; their purity was thereby retained. The bodies were then suspended on a pole for a period of time, and finally they were burned. White dogs were rare; unblemished, they were believed to serve as proper messengers from the people to the Great Spirit. The special position of the dog in Iroquois ceremony would suggest that ultimately some deeper meaning must lie behind the dog's head and the rest of the carving; if we could decode that meaning we might gain clues to the place of lacrosse in American Indian culture.

As I struggled to interpret these Cayuga decorations, I was reminded of the beginnings of my fascination with Indian lacrosse, a somewhat surprising departure for someone trained in music. Some years ago, when I was researching drum making among the Ojibwe people of northern Wisconsin, I was struck by the strong resemblance of one type of Ojibwe drumstick to the Ojibwe lacrosse racquet (Figure 3). The drumstick was constructed just like the lacrosse stick, except that it was much smaller and lacked the rawhide thongs crossed at the head that kept the ball cradled. Further, both the drumstick and the lacrosse racquet looked very much like a type of war club common to many tribes, including the Ojibwe and nations of the Iroquois—one that terminated in a ball (Figure 2b). That these material objects shared an identical shape seemed to express some ancient, hidden relationship or ritual among music, game, and warfare beyond the objects' simple functions of pounding drums, throwing balls, or clubbing enemies.

In native languages of southeastern tribes lacrosse was called "brother to war," or "little brother of war," and most historians writing on the sport stressed its violent nature. A new interpretation of the Cayuga stick was in order: If correctly read, the meanings encoded in the decorations concerned warfare, not friendly competition. The object itself, although shaped like a lacrosse stick, was not intended to be played with; rather it was meant to symbolize certain

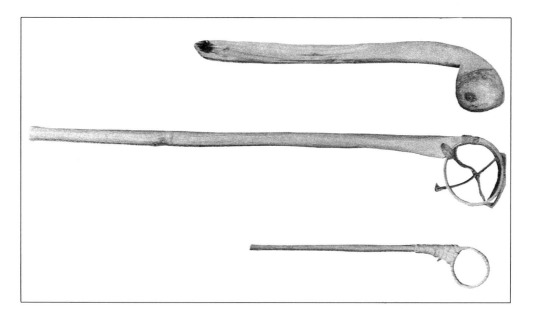

beliefs relating the game to battle. As such, the Cayuga lacrosse stick is an icon of war.

Figure 3 • Ojibwe war club (Garden River Reserve), lacrosse stick (Red Cliff Reservation), and drumstick (Bad River Reservation) in the author's collection.

The hand clutching the ball makes the statement that this curved piece of wood is as much a weapon of combat as a tool for play. It was common for the ball end of war clubs to be carved as though held in the mouth of some animal, like a snake, or in the talons of a bird of prey, like the eagle (Figure 2b). In the days of Indian warfare, when such ball clubs were used to dispatch an enemy, the symbolism associated with the club had it that the bird's claws (or the animal's mouth) *released* the ball, which flew through the air, struck the enemy's head, and killed him. In a variation of this type of war club, the ball was carved to represent a human head (Figure 2c), which (symbolically) would fly off the club's handle and strike down the enemy.

Flying heads are equated with airborne balls in a number of Iroquois legends that incorporate lacrosse game episodes. In one story, a flying head pursues a family, seeking to destroy them. The head is caught and thrown into a vat of boiling bear grease, where it burns to death. To give thanks for their safety, the mother of the family insists that it is their duty to sponsor a lacrosse game. The head, says the mother, will serve as the ball (see Appendix A, No. 11). This symbolic equation of heads with lacrosse balls has led one writer to speculate that lacrosse might even have evolved from an ancient sport in which games were played using the heads of battle victims as balls![3] But if the human hand carved on this lacrosse stick holds an implement of war, ready to release it, what of the friendly handshake beneath it?

It, too, points toward warfare. At the beginning of the nineteenth century, the great Seneca prophet Handsome Lake emerged to found the Longhouse religion among the Iroquois and promote peace. All former acts of violence, including warfare and anything associated with it, were expressly forbidden by his teachings. Handsome Lake outlawed many former rituals connected with the warpath, among which was a very old rite called the Clasping Hands Dance, a type of war dance engaged in by warriors to strengthen themselves and serve as protective "medicine" before going on the warpath.[4] The hand shaking during the dance apparently signified a sort of male bonding to shield the group in action. The dance appears to have continued after Handsome Lake's edicts, but in a modified form that omitted the handclasp. Therefore its presence carved in relief on the shaft of the lacrosse stick says, in effect, "In the game we continue to wage war on our enemies"—a sort of secret emblem reinforcing the warfare/lacrosse analogy.

As I returned the stick to its protective plastic covering and left the museum, I could not shake its impact on me. Within this century-and-a-half-old piece of carved hickory that I had just held was embedded the whole story of lacrosse, as its originators, the American Indians, conceived of the game. Now a popular, rapidly growing spring athletic activity of major American schools in the United States and Canada, the game was just beginning to stir in such unlikely places as Eastern Europe and Japan. But how much did today's many players know about the Indian game? Were they aware that it was a surrogate for warfare, that long before Europeans arrived in North America, tribes settled territorial disputes with lacrosse games? And how much of the ritual and ceremony so characteristic of Indian lacrosse has survived in the non-Indian game?

My contact with the Cayuga stick made the NCAA play-offs that weekend come particularly alive for me. Everything about the games seemed to strike parallel chords, taking me back into history, to long before mid-nineteenth-century Canadians adopted lacrosse from the Mohawk Indians. When the phalanx of Syracuse Orangemen surged onto the empty field to the cheers of a roaring crowd, I thought back to the account of the English traveler Basil Hall in 1828, who could hear the approaching shouts and war whoops of an Alabama Creek team that he knew would emerge from the woods at any moment. As the players on the Penn field began to scrimmage among themselves, tossing the hard rubber ball back and forth from their plastic-stamped, aluminum-shafted sticks, I recalled Ojibwe

elders from Lake Superior telling me of games from their youth—
how the hard wooden ball carved from the charred knot of a tree was
perforated by two holes so that it would make a whistling scream as it
careened toward their heads, and how each man made his own stick
of white ash and decorated it with symbols that had personal meaning. As the NCAA teams crowded around their coaches for final
instructions, I remembered the many passages I had read about
Cherokee conjurers preparing their players not only by giving special
game instructions but also by rubbing protective ointments on them
and scratching them with rattlesnake fangs until they bled. As the
university players donned their helmets, I could see Choctaw players
of a century ago tying into their hair feathers from birds of prey,
known for their keen eyesight. The feathers, it was believed, enabled
the player to see the ball better. And as the two centermen crouched
for the face-off, I thought of Lewis Henry Morgan's description of
Iroquois centerfield players before 1850, who, straining and pushing
when the stuffed deerskin ball was dropped between their sticks,
would lift the ball off the ground until it was freely tossed in one
direction or the other.

To penetrate the Indian game, one must enter a world of spiritual belief and magic, where players sewed inchworms into the
innards of lacrosse balls and medicine men gazed at miniature lacrosse
sticks to predict future events, where bits of bat wings were twisted
into a stick's netting, and where famous players were (and are still)
buried with their sticks. The magic is still there in the Indian game,
but it is just under the surface, easily overlooked by the unsuspecting. During the Cherokee Fall Festival in North Carolina, I once
watched the Wolftown Wolves beat the Wolftown Bears. Although
the field was surrounded by carnival rides and food concession
stands, little had changed in the Cherokee game since 1888, when it
was described and photographed by James Mooney, who must have
come by wagon on a dirt road to get there. Each team still marched
abreast in line by degrees to midfield, letting out ritual war whoops
and yells as they faced their opponents and laid down their sticks to
be counted.

At the conclusion of the Cherokee game, in keeping with tradition, the teams were "taken to water," an ancient ritual meant to
cleanse and restore them from their warlike condition during the
game. To get to the Oconaluftee River, now mostly hidden by
motels, the teams, barefoot and wearing only trunks, were led to the
busy two-lane road—their only impediment in reaching the stream.
The traffic was bumper to bumper, as tourists crawled along in their
cars admiring the panoply of Great Smoky Mountains fall foliage,
impervious to these native players, sweaty and fresh from the game.

No car seemed willing to let them through. Finally the frustrated team managers, each carrying the two traditional willow sapling goalposts with leaves still at their tops, simply moved out into the middle of traffic, where they firmly and defiantly planted the saplings in front of cars, forcing them to stop. A passageway thus formed, the two lines of players walked abreast across the road and down the bank to the river. There they dipped their sticks in the sacred waters of the Oconaluftee, considered especially powerful at this time of year, for the falling leaves had added their medicine to the water and darkened it. Their managers said Cherokee prayers in a centuries-old rite, but the Indian players went unnoticed by two white fly-fishermen scarcely fifteen yards downstream.

Sitting in the Franklin Field bleachers, I watched the punishing action on the field as Syracuse seesawed its way to victory over Johns Hopkins in the oppressive heat. A large thermometer had been placed on the sidelines to remind the shaded fans how uncomfortable the players must have been. No cool, clear waters of the Oconaluftee to remove the sweat and grime of the game here, and the Schuylkill was too distant, blocked by a freeway and probably too polluted anyway. A bruised Hopkins player, fresh from battle, was being examined by the team physician; two centuries ago some Indian "doctor" had bathed a center fighter's wounds at the end of the field with herbal decoctions of powerful plants. A broken Syracuse plastic chin strap was being replaced; a hundred years ago some Cherokee player had replaced torn webbing on his stick with cords of twisted groundhog skin that he had prepared at the final "stripping-off place" on the long ceremonial march to the field. Unknown to the players, coaches, and fans that day, the story of how it all began was just across the street, back in its plastic covering, locked in a drawer.

Carrier Dome, Syracuse University, 21 May 1989

The two centermen crouch to the ground, straining their thighs as they dig in for the face-off. So far it has been a one-sided game in the NCAA quarterfinals, with Syracuse comfortably holding Navy to a single goal. In the stands, Freeman "Bossy" Bucktooth, Jr., reaches his arm around his two young sons, Tyler and Drew, while he points toward the field. "Watch how Gary is positioning himself. See how he keeps shifting to stay in front of his man? He's gotta be ready in case the centerman can draw the ball out to where he can pick it up." At work earlier in the week Bossy was offered two free tickets, even though it meant driving all the way into the suburbs west of Syracuse to retrieve them. But the effort was worth it. Finally, his boys, now six and eight years old, would get a chance to see the Gait brothers in action during the intense postseason play-offs. Back on the Onondaga Nation Territory, Bossy is the boys' coach, and because Indians grow up playing the box version of lacrosse, he particularly wants to show them how the Gaits have been able to infuse the field game with box skills brought to Syracuse from British Columbia. Recent rule changes have encouraged the Canadian twins to display their uncanny talent with behind-the-back passes and shots. Maybe this flashy new style of play will inspire more Indian kids to stay with the game in hopes of someday being recruited by a Cornell, Nazareth, or Hobart coach.

Less than a minute into the second period the Gait brothers are engaged in one of their favorite tricks, the hidden ball deception. (Bossy has heard that Cherokee Indians were also fond of hiding the ball; some of them put it in their mouths, provoking their opponents to choke them to dislodge it.) Gary Gait has quietly slipped the ball to his brother and then begun a mad dash downfield as if to score, artfully behaving as though he is cradling the ball in the empty pocket of his stick. He moves around quickly, shooting glances side to side as if checking out Navy's defensive positions. By this time all eyes, including the goalie's, are on Gary as he cuts to the right. The goalie is drawn to the right side of the net, leaving Paul, who still has the ball, a wide-open shot. He slams in the ball, giving Syracuse a 5–1 lead.

Bossy is getting slightly annoyed with his kids. Drew left ten minutes ago to go to the men's room, and Tyler is pestering his father once again for soda money—it will be his second. Are they getting spoiled? he wonders. Bossy, who got his nickname early for being the neighborhood bully (he was always big for his age) remembers that his parents' friends would say he earned the name because he always got his way at home. Maybe I *was* spoiled, thinks Bossy, but that's not going to happen with my boys. His "strict but gentle" policy seems to be working well at home, where he requires his sons to help him move lumber piles as he builds his family's new home. The boys' reward will be a small swimming pool behind the house.

Scanning the Carrier Dome, Bossy marvels at the opulence of this gigantic new athletic facility. He has heard that the strips of Astroturf are zip-locked and that special machines can quickly roll them back to expose the wooden basketball floor. His eyes wander over the sea of white faces in the crowd. We're probably the only "'Skins" here, he thinks. There certainly were none on the playing field or the benches. At halftime he took the boys on a brief tour of the Dome. He wanted them to see the trophy room at the end of the indoor stadium. At least a few team pictures had to show a dark-skinned player or two. The room was locked.

Both boys are back, and the referee blows his whistle, igniting the face-off. Like two gladiators, the centermen struggle to gain possession of the ball, and suddenly the Syracuse player pops the ball in the direction of one of his wingmen. Throwing his upper body in front of his Navy opponent, the wingman easily scoops the ball and dodges around him, looking for a fast break. Upfield he spots John Zulberti open and dishes him the ball. Taking the Navy defenseman one-on-one down the side, Paul Gait rolls to the middle, where he is left wide open as Zulberti flips him the ball. He fakes to the right, throwing the goalie off guard, and effortlessly fires into the net to score with a behind-the-back shot.

Bossy marvels at the exceptional stickwork of these Canadian Syracuse recruits. He wishes that more of the kids back on the "rez" could afford the price of a ticket to see this sort of action. The Gaits, rapidly becoming idols to young American lacrosse players, have injected new life into the field game. Sure, there are still plenty of conservative, old guard coaches who resent the fancy new "hot-dog" style of performance and will continue to train players in traditional overhand passing and scoring. Bossy himself has his young players practice these skills, but once they have mastered the basics, he will begin to train them in both left and right backhand shots. That's why he holds special "fun practices," having his charges use nothing but behind-the-back and between-the-legs stickwork, which provokes lots of laughter and general horseplay. His goal is to develop versatility in these young athletes, so that they will be prepared later to adapt to either field or box conditions. Maybe someday, ten years or so down the road, he might be sitting here in the Carrier Dome watching his own sons, the Bucktooth brothers, as Orangemen lacrosse greats.

On the sidelines, Bossy spots Syracuse coach Roy Simmons, Jr., his silver hair setting off the blue baseball cap with the bright-orange SU emblem. He recalls how, fifteen years earlier, Simmons approached him as he came off the field from a game at Lafayette High School, to which Onondaga kids were bussed daily. Although at that time Indians made up only a quarter of the school's population, their participation in lacrosse far exceeded that of the non-Indian locals. Bossy attributed this to their coach, Gordie Ohrstrom. Although not a lacrosse player himself, Ohrstrom knew the game thoroughly, and, most important, he understood how to work with Indian people. After Ohrstrom's death from leukemia, Indian participation in the sport at the high school dwindled steadily, and today there are no Onondagas on the team at all. Bossy is acutely aware of that fact; it was one of the motivating forces that caused him to start training youngsters on his reservation. He devotes all his spare time to bringing the three- to six-year-old Peanuts to the next level, the seven- and eight-year-old Tykes, then finally to the nine- and ten-year-old Novices.

When Simmons introduced himself that day and attempted to recruit Bossy for Syracuse, he was unaware that the powerful young attackman was only a Lafayette junior. Bossy recognized the Simmons name at once as part of a coaching dynasty that was making lacrosse history: Roy's father had trained the great Jim Brown, on the same team as Oren Lyons, a Faithkeeper of the Onondaga, an artist, and the current coach of the Iroquois Nationals. Flattered by Simmons's offer, Bossy nevertheless postponed it for a year, feeling that he needed to finish high school in order to survive the academic load he would face at Syracuse University. Ultimately he played for Simmons for only two seasons (1974–75) before he decided to leave the university. Looking back, he felt that a combination of poor preparation for college study and an inclination to work more with his hands than his head had been responsible for his leaving. He chose instead to pursue first jewelry making, then construction, which was his present profession. Still, his experience at Syracuse prompted him to encourage his young players to think as much about their long-range goals as about their immediate involvement with the sport of their ancestors. When they assembled for practice, Bossy would throw them the question "What's the strongest part of your body?" Invariably the kids would reply, "Your legs" or "Your back," whereupon he would correct them, saying, "You're all wrong. It's your brain." He knew that education was the only chance that reservation kids had to escape the endless cycle of Indian poverty and its attendant social problems; it was the only way they would be able to achieve a meaningful future.

As Syracuse maintains its edge over Navy, Bossy turns to his sons. "Do you guys think you might ever be playing on that field?" It's good for them to see two brothers leading Syracuse to victory. Although there are currently no Iroquois Indian players on the team—

• 3

Emmett Printup, a Tuscarora now playing professionally, was the last—the Onondaga reservation has traditionally provided Syracuse with talented players, many of them brothers. Ron and Oliver Hill played for Simmons when Bossy entered the university, and Lavern and Ron Doctor before them. Since Bossy left, there have been other Iroquois—goalie Travis Solomon, midfielder Mark Burnam, and attackman Greg Tarbell. But Bossy guesses now that it will be four or five years before another Onondaga will don the lacrosse uniform of the Orangemen.

In the final period, with four goals in a row, Syracuse has a comfortable lead, and the team clearly has a good chance of walking away again with the NCAA championship (as the Orangemen will for three consecutive years). Watching the Gait brothers is reason enough for Bossy to attend as many games as possible. He remembers the first time he saw the now famous ''Air-Gait'' tactic: Gary Gait literally flies over the crease behind the goal and, with a windmill-like swing of his arm, tucks the ball in the top of the goal while airborne. No goalie has yet developed an adequate defense against that maneuver.

The image of Gary Gait scoring a goal while in mid-air makes Bossy suddenly recall the legendary Indian story of the lacrosse game between the birds and the land animals, which the airborne creatures were said to have won. When he was a small child he heard elders relate the tale on long winter evenings, and his father told him a version of it when the four-year-old boy first took up lacrosse. At that time he used to go with his father, who played for the Onondaga lacrosse club, when they competed against other Iroquois Indian nations. When he was little, he had trouble understanding how birds could actually play lacrosse; now he sees the legend as an allegory, drawing attention to the amount of time the ball is in the air and not on the ground. But he is beginning to ponder the playing techniques of his ancestors. Is it possible that they, too, took to the air to score and that somehow it became recorded in legend?

By the time Bossy and his sons exit the interstate at Nedrow, the excitement of the game in the Carrier Dome has subsided, and the talk has shifted to tomorrow's practice. The team has been invited to the nation's capital in late June to take part in the Smithsonian Institution's annual Festival of American Folklife. There, representing the Onondaga [Nation], they will play demonstration lacrosse matches over a two-week period against their counterpart Novices from the Tuscarora Reservation, another nation of the Iroquois, located north of Buffalo. Bossy has not yet selected the final roster of the players who will come to be known as ''the Washington bunch'' (Figure 4). The Tuscarora players are being chosen and coached by Emmett Printup, who, unlike Bossy, finished his study at Syracuse, went on to play professional indoor box lacrosse for the Washington Wave, and is now coaching at Niagara-Wheatfield High School.

While Bossy's sons are trying to pry out of him the names of those he is considering for the honor, he turns onto the winding, unlit roads of the reservation, and his thoughts turn

Figure 4 • Coaches and players of "the Washington bunch" between games on the National Mall for the Smithsonian Institution's 1989 Festival of American Folklife. Left to right: Murray Stout, Drew Bucktooth, Freeman "Bossy" Bucktooth, Jr., Calvin Hill, Averill Bucktooth, David Stout, Dustin Hill, Jeff Powless, Bruce Hill.

as well to other matters. He passes their beat-up old outdoor lacrosse box, where he regularly holds practice, even in rain or snow. As a kid Bossy spent most of his spare time here in informal reservation "pickup" games (Figure 5). Only half an hour from the university, the chewed-up field, bounded by its battered side-boards, stands in vivid contrast to the well-lit indoor Carrier Dome, with its nearly all-white crowd of lacrosse boosters, players, and coaching staff. It's even a far cry from Archbold Stadium, where he played for Syracuse. But it is in the Indian world, where lacrosse had its origins, where the Creator invented it for the Indians to amuse him.

Figure 5 • Bossy Bucktooth about to scoop a ground ball in a 1971 pickup game on the Onondaga reservation. Players are, left to right, Joe Johnson, Mitch Farmer, Omar Gibson, Freeman Gibson, Fab Shenandoah, Dave Waterman, Bossy Bucktooth, Kevin Bucktooth (his brother), "Big Man" Gibson.

Their car turns a sharp corner, and the front of one of the Christian churches on the reservation comes abruptly into view. They always seem so out of place to Bossy—an intrusion of foreign beliefs on Indian soil. Long ago, before the Protestants arrived, say the old-timers, it was the Catholics, but they lost out by complaining that the lacrosse games were competing with attendance at Mass. Bossy has heard of recent declines in church membership, as Indian people are returning to the Longhouse, the traditional Iroquois religion, where lacrosse is an integral part of the cycle of ceremonies. Just as important as the June trip to Washington are the upcoming annual spring games among the reservation clans, when the Hawk, Deer, and Eel clans will play the Wolf, Turtle, Snipe, and Beaver clans in ritual competition. No matter how uneven the teams—ten against three, forty versus fifty— they will play until the third goal is reached. And in the Indian game the distance between goals is adjusted according to the turnout of players. The goals might be 75 yards or even a quarter of a mile apart, without any sidelines to speak of. This is traditional.

Bossy smiles to himself as he realizes how annoying he finds the referees' constant whistle blowing whenever a loose ball goes "out of bounds" on the white man's field. Only yesterday he was sitting on Scanandoah's front porch with some elders who were reminiscing about past games. Old Man Scanandoah brought up one game between the Hobart and Onondaga teams some years earlier. The college players, accustomed to sidelines on a field, were caught unawares when the Onondaga began to play by Indian rules. Near the game's end the Hobart players lost track of the Indian ballcarrier, who simply disappeared into the woods that lined one side of the field, only to emerge at the other end of the trees and score the winning goal. As the elders enjoyed a good laugh, old Fred Logan, now so crippled with arthritis that he'd long since given up using his drawknife to shape hickory lacrosse sticks, sat back in his rocker. Logan's sticks were prized by players, Indian and white alike, and his talent was so well known that Syracuse players would even dare to come onto the reservation and trek up to his house on the hill to acquire a stick carved by the master craftsman. Bossy was holding two new sticks he'd bought for his sons in downtown Syracuse. Logan pointed with his chin at the sticks and said, "Think it's gonna be a bad winter. You're not gonna get very far on those white man's plastic snowshoes." Embarrassed, Bossy put the sticks on the floor behind him and gazed out into the yard at the dismembered cars scattered about, the children playing hide-and-seek among the rusting hulls.

As he heads up the steep hill to his driveway, Bossy continues to ponder the gulf that separates the white man's field lacrosse from the Iroquois *dehuntshigwa'es*.[1] The Indian game is deeply rooted in the religious beliefs of the Onondaga, or "people living on the hill," and matches continue to be played as they always have been, not only to strengthen the bodies and minds of the players but also to heal the sick. Bossy knows that he has successfully imbued this spiritual aspect of the game in his boys, for during the recent wake for Bossy's father, Drew presented his grandfather's wooden lacrosse stick to be buried with him, so that he could continue to play for the Creator in the afterlife.

Bossy puts the kids to bed, urging them to get a good night's sleep in preparation for tomorrow's practice. He very much hopes to include them in "the Washington bunch," but he has to be fair, and if they aren't playing up to par, he can't justify selecting them. As he returns to the living room, he notices his battered, handmade wooden stick resting in a corner, dented and scarred from years of rough combat. These traditional hand-carved sticks probably won't be around much longer. But they are an integral part of Indian lacrosse, and even though he starts reservation youngsters on plastic sticks because those are easier to teach with, he converts to wooden ones by the time the kids are twelve or thirteen. Compared with the modern plastic variety, the traditional Onondaga version, like all Iroquois sticks, has a certain character, and each stick seems to have its own personality. They are also much tougher in play—you don't want to get hit with one of them. If you see an opponent covering you with a wooden stick, chances are you'll pass the ball. Bossy chuckles to himself. Recently he had to play with a modern plastic stick that had a loose head, because

Drew took his traditional stick over to his cousin's and left it there. The cousin's dog chewed off most of one side of the unattended stick as well as part of its gut-wall.

Bossy joins Joni in their bedroom and tells her about that afternoon's game. After tossing and turning for a while, he gradually falls into deep sleep.

He is in some ancient village of the past. The houses are all small, dome-shaped and covered with bark. People are speaking Onondaga, but not the kind he can understand. They point at him and laugh. He looks down at the aluminum shaft he is holding in both hands and sees the plastic head lying on the ground. An old man shakes a turtle-shell rattle in his direction, but Bossy is not in the Longhouse and doesn't understand why. Some ceremony is about to take place. He hears a thumping sound, then another, and another. The man with the rattle starts to stumble, then loses his balance and falls to the ground. *Crash!*

Bossy scrambles upright and sees the early-morning sun shining on shattered glass and the hole in the new bedroom window that he installed only last week. A rubber ball rolls across the floor. Drew has gotten up early and is practicing his skills, using the house for a backboard. Drew wants badly to go to Washington.

Huron Country, 1637

A grand shout rang out, and in its wake yet another, even louder. They must have scored a goal again, thought the priest, as he turned fitfully on his rude cot, attempting in vain to complete his afternoon nap. Even though the playing field lay well outside the palisaded walls of Ihonatiria, one of the northernmost Huron Indian villages, the multitude of savage yells echoing through the surrounding woods easily penetrated the flimsy bark walls of his small hut (Figure 6). Father François Joseph Le Mercier, already a seasoned missionary, suddenly gave up all hope of further sleep, for he could tell from the approaching chatter that the game was done and the villagers were beginning to return. Now that the foolish affairs of the Devil were over for the moment, Le Mercier should rise and attend to his ministry in the work of the Lord. But he lay there to avoid the scene he had witnessed all too often. He could well envision the noisy entry through the narrow village gate—women excitedly displaying to friends the gorgets and porcelain collars they had won, players with bloodied noses and bruised limbs, some of them limping, perhaps even carried on litters, the winners among them banging their sticks victoriously together in the air as they encountered teammates. There was little compelling him to rise and revisit this hideous spectacle. He would wait and allow the villagers to settle down from their afternoon indulgences and busy themselves with early-evening chores.

Some had already entered the village. He could hear the laughter of young women as they passed his hut. Doubtless they had profited sinfully from wagering on the game. But how selfish to gamble for personal gain. Did they not understand "Blessed are the poor in spirit, for theirs is the Kingdom of Heaven"? Could they not comprehend that the eternal life awaiting them was worth more than all the gorgets and collars and fine moosehair-embroidered buckskin coats that the entire village would squander on this ridiculous sport? The players were approaching the gate now. He could always tell, because several would

Figure 6 • An early seventeenth-century palisaded Indian village under attack in New France.

run the heads of their crosses along the outside of the palisade as they walked along it, the wood bumping along the surface of the log uprights and making a frightful noise. The racket reminded him of the awful sounds made by simple peasants back in France, swinging wooden-ratchet noisemakers on Saints' Days in accordance with their superstition that the noise would drive away evil.

A young head in a fur cap poked into his doorway. It was Giles, one of the French boys from the mission. He carried a large dead hawk with an arrow still embedded in its body. The lanky fourteen-year-old had been practicing the archery skills he had learned from Huron boys. With his other hand he kept hoisting the trousers he had inherited from one of the traders; they were too large for his narrow hips, and the rope cincture was of little help. Giles explained how he had put a wounded rabbit out as bait to attract the bird. His description was interrupted by the abrupt entrance of one of his Indian friends, who grabbed the hawk, quickly plucked several tailfeathers from the carcass, tossed the bird back to Giles, and disappeared—nearly all in one motion, it seemed. Le Mercier frowned in consternation. "The feathers," Giles pointed to the few remaining ones. "They use the feathers, you know," and as he said this he went through the motions of throwing a ball with a racquet, then pointed to his hair. "Makes their sight better." Le Mercier understood. He had arisen and was taking down a fur cape from a hook over his cot. The late-afternoon chill was descending, and he had not yet started his fire. Yes, he knew full well that the savages tied these feathers in their hair before departing to the ball field. But what a peculiar notion, that wearing a hawk's feather in your hair gave you such keen eyesight that you could see the small wooden lacrosse ball in the grass from a distance, as though you were a hawk circling overhead and spotting a tiny field mouse in the weeds below. Such ignorance and superstition abounded in the village that at times his task seemed impossible. Was it not enough to have to live in this miserable insect-ridden hut, to have to cope with a people whose feathers, body paint, and bone necklaces stood in vivid contrast to his black robes of piety and humbleness? The priest crossed himself and opened his Bible. Giles took it as a sign that he should leave.

A week later, in the early evening of 21 May 1637, Le Mercier returned to his hut with an armload of firewood. The small village seemed particularly desolate, with Fathers Jean de Brébeuf, Pierre Pijart, and two of the hired Frenchmen away at Ossossane, busy constructing the new missionary center that the local chief had recently agreed to. After stoking the smoldering embers, he lit a splinter of cedar and transferred the rising flame to the large candle on his desk and prepared his journal for entries describing the events of the past week. Despite the strain on his eyesight, he carried out this task in relative isolation and secrecy, for the illiterate Indians were suspicious of note taking and feared writing as one more bit of cunning that the Frenchmen used against them. They simply could not comprehend how messages and instructions could be conveyed on pieces of paper. Some Huron considered the ability to send information on paper clear evidence that the "Black Robes" were powerful shamans.

As a Jesuit, Le Mercier had been trained to make intimate observations and to record them for posterity. Here in the wilderness of New France, his mission was not only to convert the savages around him but also to keep detailed accounts of his activities and of the manners, language, and customs of his native charges. This information would provide a better understanding of the people for missionaries who would follow and would facilitate their continuing efforts to save souls and bring civilization to Huronia.

One of Le Mercier's annual duties was to collate his notes into a report forwarded to his superior in Quebec. After collecting the journals of all the missionaries in districts under his supervision, the superior would create a summary narrative, called a *Relation*. This document was sent on to France, where the Jesuit provincial edited and published the text.

The *Relation* was always eagerly received by members of the court circles in France, as well as by the pious souls funding missions in the New World. These sponsors awaited news of how the missions were faring and a tally of the newly converted. Certainly Father Le Mercier's journal entry on this night would reassure them that their investment had not been in vain. The events of the week had strengthened his hand in the war for Huron souls.

Two days earlier, scarcely a week after the corn seed had been planted, a freak late-spring snowstorm from off the Great Water to the north had dumped half a foot of snow on the country of the Huron. The temperature had plummeted to below freezing, producing a thick crust on the fresh snow. The severity of the storm and the sudden weight of the snow caused the rear portion of Le Mercier's flimsy bark roof to collapse, forcing him to seek shelter for the night in the lodge of his neighbor Tsiouendaentaha, one of the few villagers favorably enough disposed toward the priest to take him in. The next day Giles and Petit-Pré, one of the hired men, helped Le Mercier to remove the snow from his hut and relash the roof to the bent-sapling frame with basswood-bark cord.

Astonishment and anger at the inclement weather ran rampant through all the villages, for only three days before the storm nearly every male citizen had taken down his lacrosse stick from its wooden hook in the family lodge for the first time this season and repaired outside the protective palisade to the field where village lacrosse games were customarily held. There the men had played feverishly all day long. Clan had played against clan until everyone was exhausted. In Ihonatiria, the Deer clan played the Wolf clan and defeated it, only to be upset by the Hawk clan; in a fiercely contested game in Arente, the Porcupine clan was victorious over its adversary, the Bear clan.

The early-spring flurry of lacrosse games was attributable to none other than the sorcerer Sondacouane, the missionaries' great nemesis and the very agent of Satan. With the crop safely planted, Sondacouane had ordered the games throughout the territory of the Attignawantan, or Bear tribe, to ensure the most favorable weather for germination of the seed. Believing in the efficacy of the game not only to cure illness but also to provide favorable weather, the Huron naturally heeded the instructions of the ever-scheming soothsayer.

So the snowstorm was a slap in the face of the miserable Sondacouane, who, for the moment at least, faced a loss of credibility among his people. Exposed as a charlatan, the sorcerer had busied himself with various herbal cures for those suffering minor ailments, moving quickly from village to village in the vain hope of escaping embarrassment. But Le Mercier feared that this setback to the people's faith in Sondacouane's prognostications would be short-lived.

As he recorded the incident in his journal, Le Mercier wondered at the superstitions held so tenaciously despite his tireless efforts to instruct the people in the ways of the Cross.

Were these ancient beliefs not a clear indication of the simplicity of the savage mind and the low state of Indian culture? Could the Indians really believe that by playing ball they might control the weather? Or that human effigies of straw hung above the doorways of their bark lodges would scare off the Devil? At every turn the damnable Sondacouane had demonstrated his hold on the people.

Le Mercier fingered the cheap wooden cross that hung around his neck. It was a poor substitute for the small silver crucifix he had been given by his parents so many years before, at his ordination. He had parted with the silver piece a week ago in hopes that it would work its spiritual powers on one of the village's young families. Recently he had focused most of his missionary attention on them, and they had so much admired the silver icon— rubbing their fingers over Jesus' slender body whenever it was within reach—that he had loaned them the crucifix. He hoped that it would not be taken as just another human effigy, like the straw men.

He thought back to another incident, in early March. While visiting in Ossossane, he had awakened one morning to discover the dead body of a young man in the snow near their lodge. The villagers were certain that the cause of death was theft, for the young man had previously been caught stealing from the Algonquins who wintered nearby. Sondacouane, they remembered, had issued a solemn warning against anyone absconding with fishing gear from the Algonquins or bait from their hooks. Any thief, he predicted, would succumb to the epidemic that was venting its fury against the Indians at the time, causing the poor priests to hasten baptism of the stricken before their souls departed.

Playing lacrosse to bring fine weather or to honor some especially gifted player now deceased, thought Le Mercier, was innocent enough. But the use of the game by the *arendiwane,* or Huron sorcerers, to cure the sick ran counter to every Christian teaching. Only through God and Christ could one be truly healed. Le Mercier recognized that he was not the first to see the obstacles to conveying this belief to the savages. From this very village his compatriot Father Jean de Brébeuf had only the year before published information on Huron healing practices in the *Relation.* Brébeuf, too, had complained that the Huron resorted to sorcerers for divination when someone was ill. Among their cures were feasts, dances, and games, prescribed according to the affliction. In particular, Brébeuf had identified the games most commonly employed in heathen medicine. Of these, lacrosse seemed the most powerful Huron cure and certainly the most elaborate:

> Of three kinds of games especially in use among these peoples—namely the games of lacrosse, dice and bowl, and straw—the first two are, they say, the most healing. Is this not worthy of compassion? If there is a poor sick man, fevered of body and almost dying, some miserable sorcerer will order for him a game of lacrosse as a cooling remedy. Or sometimes the sick man himself will have dreamed that he will die unless the whole countryside organized lacrosse matches to be played for his health. And no matter how little they may

believe him, you will see them in a beautiful field, village contending against village, as to who will play lacrosse the better, and betting against one another beaver robes and porcelain collars, so as to excite greater interest.[1]

Brébeuf's depiction was accurate, thought Le Mercier, and should inform the readers of the *Relations* back in France just how difficult the missionaries' task in Huronia was. Contemptuous as well that the sin of gambling should enter into a healing process, Brébeuf had complained that lacrosse games were part of the scare tactics used by sorcerers to maintain the people's faith: "Sometimes also, one of these sorcerers will say that the whole countryside is sick, and he prescribes a game of lacrosse to heal it. No more needs to be said; his pronouncement is published immediately everywhere, and all the chiefs of each village give orders that all young men do their duty in this respect. Otherwise some great misfortune would befall the whole territory."[2]

Since the publication, Le Mercier had encountered the particular *arendiwane* that Brébeuf must have had in mind. He knew his name and had this to add to his own journal: "Meanwhile, the Devil, playing his pranks elsewhere, and speaking through the mouth of the sorcerer *Tonnerananont,* was turning aside these people from applying to God. . . . This little hunchback had declared that the whole country was sick, and he had prescribed a remedy for its recovery, namely a game of lacrosse."[3] Despite the exertion of the young players in the game, noted Le Mercier, the smallpox and measles afflicting the Huron continued their devastating spread. Within three years European diseases would wipe out half the population, reducing the Huron to some nine thousand souls.

Ever since he had arrived in this country, Le Mercier had been trying to come to grips with the Huron mode of thought, to say nothing of mastering the subtleties of the language. Only with such tools could he carry out his mission. The Jesuits had not been the first Frenchmen to penetrate this wilderness, but they, together with the Franciscan Recollects, were the first to settle among the Indians long enough to describe their culture in writing. The few fur traders' agents preceding them had been either illiterate or too preoccupied with profits to record Huron activities. Samuel de Champlain, with fourteen French soldiers, had visited the people two decades earlier. The soldiers were probably the ones who dubbed them *hurens,* or wild boars, for their peculiar mode of dressing their hair. Whereas most Indians to the north allowed their shoulder-length tresses to fall freely, the males of the *ouendat,* as the Huron called themselves, were extremely fussy in arranging and cutting their locks. Gabriel Sagard, a lay brother of the Recollects who had stayed briefly among the Huron, described the custom in *Grand Voyage,* published in Paris five years earlier and currently circulating (from Quebec) among the Jesuits in Huronia. Le Mercier flipped through the pages of his copy and came upon the exact passage: "Huron men have two great rolls like moustaches above their ears, and some of them only one, which they quite often twist and cord with feathers and other trifles. The rest of their hair is kept short, or else cut in sections, or with a ruff like that outside the shaven crown of the head."[4]

Le Mercier had been warned that his work was cut out for him among these "boar heads," who had peculiar beliefs and such barbaric practices as torture. Now Son-dacouane's loss of face over the unexpected snowstorm had in fact been nearly forgotten in the excitement about the capture of a marauding enemy. While most of the men of the village were away on a trading mission, several younger warriors who had been left behind as guards had surprised an Iroquois raiding party and taken one of its members captive. The Iroquois had intended to capture some of the Huron women and children who were hoeing and weeding the cornfields some distance from the village.

• 15

The captive now suffered the customary tortures. The Iroquois stood for three days, naked and bound to the torture platform post, after his toenails were ripped out (Figure 7). Later his scalp was half removed, and molten pine pitch, prepared for canoe repairing, was dribbled on the open wound. Meanwhile, villagers prodded him with firebrands and touched red-hot tomahawks to his fingertips and testicles. Throughout the ordeal, the prisoner tried valiantly to appear courageous and unaffected, singing from time to time his death song. His failure to scream in pain or beg for mercy was typically blamed on the Jesuits, whom the Huron suspected of befriending the Iroquois.

Figure 7

The good father had been able to sneak to the platform to baptize the Iroquois captive the night before he expired. Being seen by the Huron would have brought no end of trouble, for the Huron saw little distinction between their torture and Christian depictions of the agonies of those condemned to hell. By baptizing Huron enemies before they died, the Jesuits prevented their torments from following the Iroquois beyond the grave. Now the village was filled with the hideous spectacle of small children running about with pieces of the disemboweled prisoner's body pierced on the ends of sticks.

Untying the rope cinch around his habit, Le Mercier prepared for bed. These gruesome practices were as incomprehensible to Father Le Mercier as the Huron perception of the universe. They believed that everything contained a spirit—animals as well as humans, stones and rocks as well as trees and plants. The most powerful of the spirits they called *oki*, and these—especially the sky spirit—controlled their daily lives. These beliefs found expression in the strangest customs: For example, if a deer was killed for its meat, the Huron carefully saved and cleaned its bones so as not to offend its spirit. They were especially careful to keep them safe from the dogs, for dogs were contaminating agents, useful only for sacrifice.

Le Mercier pulled aside the elkskin blanket that would cover him. Such creeds, he thought, also led to the Huron obsession with dreams, which they understood as the expression of the somehow unfulfilled desires of the human spirit. If not acted upon, these desires could lead to illness, even death. Since most Indians felt powerless to discern what their dreams dictated, their normal recourse was to confer with sorcerers about them. Only these men were trained to interpret dreams and to prescribe action that would calm the agitated spirit. Sorcerers could ward off an impending sickness, or they could cure it if the patient had already been stricken. This belief system, the very basis of the Huron concept of disease, explained the great influence that the sorcerers had over the people. And so the prescribed courses of "the great deceivers" were considered by the Jesuits to be the ultimate hoax.

Just last fall, when the corn had been harvested and the women and children were busy shucking ears and pounding the kernels into meal in tall wooden mortars or tying the cobs together by their husks to store for the winter, a "dream episode" took place in a lodge at the south end of the village. Aenons, a respected elder of the Beaver clan, but one whom Le Mercier could proudly point to as an exemplary Christian, suddenly became feverish and soon lapsed into a coma. Fearing that he was near death, his daughter summoned the relatives, who began death lamentations and the assembly of funeral gifts. For the wake the elder's body was placed in a flexed position on a special mat at the end of the lodge. Suddenly, he came fitfully out of his torpid state and, much to Le Mercier's chagrin, demanded in great agitation that an *arendiwane* be summoned. That Aenons, a convert and companion to Brébeuf, had in his greatest hour of need reverted to primitive religious practices was a great surprise and a severe disappointment to the missionary.

Le Mercier had watched helplessly as runners were dispatched to Karenhassa, the closest village to the south, where the hunchback Tonnerananont, whose physical deformity was taken as a sign of his powers, was ministering to a sick woman. By noon they had returned with the sorcerer and gone directly to the afflicted man. Outfitted as usual in his thick collarpiece of interwoven snakeskins and his long cape of crow and eagle feathers, Tonnerananont ordered the lodge cleared. Then he performed incantations over Aenons, all the while shaking a turtle-shell rattle. From time to time, he put his ear to the afflicted man's mouth to listen intently, as Aenons poured forth the vision he had experienced while unconscious.

Aenons had dreamed of his own funeral, as though he were witness to it. He heard crying and singing in his honor, the civil chief announcing his death and sending messengers to other villages. He saw the preparation of *sagamite*—the Huron staple made of corn gruel mixed with fish and clams—ripe squash and pumpkins, turtle meat, and venison for the funeral feast and the great exchange of gifts and donations to his widow and children. He observed how his body was wrapped and elevated to the scaffold. He experienced the rotting of his flesh and the drying and bleaching of his bones by the sun (Figure 8). He saw his family remove the bones, clean them, and carry them in a beaver robe for the Feast of the Dead. There they threw the bones into the large pit with the funeral offerings, covering them with bark and sand. All of this Aenons related to Tonnerananont, who, after more chanting and turtle-shell rattling, summoned the civil chief of the village to insist that the only means of saving the poor old man from his dream was for the village to sponsor a lacrosse game. They were to challenge some neighboring village immediately.

At the time, a tribal council was already in session in the Ihonatiria civil longhouse, where chiefs from Toanche, a village immediately to the west, had assembled. The chiefs of Ihonatiria had summoned them to complain that several young men from Toanche had been observed poaching on the established trade routes of Ihonatiria to the Nipissing Indians. They had done so without receiving permission, and now the Toanche representatives were attempting to resolve the dispute. Specifically, they were trying to decide on goods to be exacted if their young men continued to use the contested routes. Le Mercier had seen the arrival of each Toanche chief and his entourage at intervals throughout the morning. After the traditional exchange of greetings and gifts to the more important chiefs, the elders from each village had harangued late into the afternoon. They were on the verge of summarizing the arguments and agreeing in principle when Tonnerananont's request for the lacrosse game was announced.

Members of the Beaver clan had been well represented on both sides. Some, in fact, were closely related to Aenons through kinship and thus enthusiastic about organizing the villages to assist in his cure. The game was set for three days hence, despite its interruption of post-harvest activities in both communities. Though Aenons's grave condition did merit immediate attention, the three-day interval would provide the time needed for preparations. Before such a ritual game, players were required to observe a taboo against sexual intercourse, undergo fasting before assembling for the Feast of Departure, and consult with their sorcerers. There had to be ritual applications of body paint, tying of luck charms to lacrosse sticks, and performance of a ball game dance in each village. The citizens also needed time to assemble goods for wagers on the game.

Meanwhile, Tonnerananont had the elder stripped to the waist and began to paint cabalistic designs on the sick man's arms, face, and chest, with meanings known only to himself. He also instructed the villagers, especially those who owned miniature lacrosse sticks that they had gotten from dream interpretations or friendship rituals, to bring their charms and talismans to the game to assist the Ihonatiria team.

The evening before the game, the Toanche players assembled for final consultations with their sorcerer, then departed single file in war-party fashion along the high-ground trail east to Ihonatiria. Overgrown in summer, the trail had been cleared after the fall harvest for exactly such social and political intervillage visitations.

About sixty ball players, selected by clan ball captains on the basis of demonstrated agility, speed, stick-handling skills, and endurance, had been prepared for each side. Le Mercier had noticed the diligence with which the captains made their round of the village, recruiting as they went. Most of the younger warriors met the qualifications—particularly as a result of their experiences in hand-to-hand combat. The game was a violent one, with players closely matched against those of the opposite team.

Nearly every male in Huronia learned how to play lacrosse as a child. Young boys, by the time winter was over, had long since tired of the snow-snake game—seeing who could propel a slightly bent stick the greatest distance along an icy chute. They eagerly awaited spring, to toss carved-cedar lacrosse balls back and forth from one to another down the narrow alleyways or ''streets'' of the village, or to use the log palisade as a backboard. The angle of deflection depended on where the ball struck the vertical log, and usually several of them would scramble to catch it in mid-air. Le Mercier more than once had seen a ball career through his doorway from some ''poor shot''—or so the mischievous youngsters claimed. This was but one of their annoying pranks. Once they had secretly severed his rawhide door hinges, so that the skin door collapsed when he left the lodge.

As the number of boys practicing lacrosse increased each spring, the whizzing of balls down the alleys became a dangerous nuisance, and Le Mercier learned to keep a watchful eye whenever he left his hut. The constant banging of balls against the palisade wall was unbearably noisy and interfered with his naps. Ultimately their otherwise overindulgent parents gently encouraged the young players to move their pastime outside the fortified village walls to the lacrosse field, where they could improvise some goal boundaries with piles of rocks and practice to their hearts' content.

The lacrosse field at Ihonatiria lay just to the west, adjacent and parallel to a small creek, where players could refresh themselves during pauses and wash off the sweat, grime, and blood from injuries incurred during play. The creek was also the site of secret ceremonies prescribed by the sorcerer before games, in which players immersed themselves. Le Mercier had been able to learn little about these rituals. He had once tried to hide himself near the creek to catch a glimpse of what went on, but his presence was quickly detected and the group dispersed. His fascination with this aspect of Huron culture, he thought, was an indulgence perhaps bordering on sin. Possibly God had chased the players off as a warning to the missionary.

Proximity of field to village was essential: Should the Iroquois launch a surprise attack against children at play or during the course of a game, it would be relatively easy to escape to the palisaded village. But the field was also convenient for the preparations, feasts, and dances that accompanied a game. Such activities customarily took place within the village walls, in one of the greater longhouses—the civil or war house—or in the village square. The field was also an ideal campground for visiting teams, for despite their having relations at Ihonatiria through kinship and clan, the small village could not accommodate large numbers of guests. The community was already crowded, and the soil of the nearby cornfields was nearly exhausted.

The lacrosse field had been there as long as anyone could recall. Elders remembered being told of its creation within a year or two of the founding of Ihonatiria. Originally the playing area had been cultivated for corn by three families, who created the field the usual way—by slashing bushes and grass and clearing trees and stumps for burning in great piles. Each year they added new land to the plot, gradually enlarging it to about twelve acres—the area of the present lacrosse field. One family expanded its fields northward along the stream, abandoning the original plot because of poor soil; the second moved to another village because of a marriage; and most of the third family was slaughtered in an Iroquois raid. The contiguous abandoned land reverted to the village, which, with the approval of the civil chiefs, created a playing field on it.

With the same moose-antler hoes used to create mounds for corn seeds, they gradually leveled the hillocks, ridding the area of small stones, sticks, and other detritus that might injure a barefoot player. After that, only occasional weeding and an annual spring burning were needed to produce a beautiful, smooth, grassy surface. Villagers from neighboring Toanche and Karenhassa preferred to play at Ihonatiria because of the field's size and its superb surface. The field at Karenhassa was considerably narrower, with rocky outcroppings along one side that provided ideal vantage points for spectators but adversely compressed the action of the game. And players from Ihonatiria and Karenhassa complained that the Toanche field, in a hollow with slow drainage, too often mired the players in mud. Some years it was unusable until mid-June.

Figure 8

Figure 9

For this occasion the players and their sorcerer arrived at the Ihonatiria ball field early in the evening to set up camp and start cooking fires by the side of the stream. Ihonatiria had sent several women, expressly forbidden to speak to or touch the Toanche players, to deliver special food supplies. These instructions were made clear by Tonnerananont, who dictated the conditions of his cure for Aenons. Likewise, he had forbidden all but the village night guards to leave the palisaded compound from sundown until the time set for the game the next day. Shortly after dawn, the watchmen from the village sentry towers had reported several hundred citizens from Toanche arriving at intervals. Nearly every other person carried a beaverskin sack containing items for wager and gifts for exchange with their hosts. Le Mercier stood in amazement near the gate, watching the huge quantity of riches flood into the village.

As the visitors arrived, Tonnerananont held forth in the *endionrra ondaon*, or civil council house, where sixty designated players of Ihonatiria had been sequestered for the ritual fasting and proscription of sexual contact before the game. The sorcerer produced special ointments for the players to rub on their lacrosse sticks, as well as feathers that could be tied to them. He ordered the village "dream bowl," a large wooden bowl used in another game that was believed effective in curing disease, brought forth for his divinations. Tonnerananont retired to one corner of the long council house, shook his turtle-shell rattle over the bowl while he sang, and placed in it the six wild plum stones used in the bowl and dice game. These pits were painted black on one side and white on the other. The sorcerer agitated them back and forth in the bowl, then suddenly tossed them in the air, catching them again in the bowl. By the number that came up one color or the other, he claimed, he could determine the outcome of the lacrosse match as well as select the strongest players and plan the strategy of the game. If the stones revealed unfavorable odds, he would resort to other tricks for a successful match and the ensuing recovery of the sick man.

Father Le Mercier was awakened from his late-afternoon slumber by criers running through the village to announce the game dance in the central square that evening, reminding everyone that full participation was essential to a successful cure. Ordinarily such ceremonial dances were held in one of the two large longhouses, but they were simply too small to handle the expected crowd this time. People had begun to ready their costumes and apply body paint, so that they would look their finest for this important event. Lest he should appear supportive of the machinations of Tonnerananont, Le Mercier had refused to attend this pagan "service," but he could scarcely avoid hearing its noisy progress. He had seen many similar ceremonials and could easily imagine the course of the evening's proceedings. Naturally he was upset that those who had embraced Christianity, through the ceaseless efforts of the mission priests, would attend the event. Le Mercier had tried to dissuade Giles and the other boys from watching the rituals, but he was certain that his admonishments had been in vain.

He knew that mats would be laid out on the periphery of the square for the elderly and the children and that Aenons would be brought out on a litter and given a prominent place from which to observe the dance and thank its participants, who would all wear charms and trinkets—but almost certainly not the Christian medals he had so generously distributed among the converts.

There had been a light rain shower, but now the weather had cleared. The remaining villagers must be assembling behind those who were seated, for the general din increased until suddenly the ceremonial entourage of ball players and female dancers must have emerged from the council house, prompting sustained war whoops from the throng. Each player would be paired off with a woman, and the sixty couples would form a snakelike column led by Tonnerananont and his assistant. The chains upon chains of baubles, shells, and other trinkets strung around the sorcerer's neck would do little to disguise his misshapen form, Le Mercier remembered thinking. The dancers would enter the square and begin to circle the large central fire in a counterclockwise direction. The players would be wearing only breechclouts. They would have porcelain necklaces, feathers woven into their hair, and designs in body paint like those they wore on the warpath. The women dancers would be naked except for a short skirt, and their bodies would likely be painted in fanciful patterns, with no two exactly alike.

Le Mercier listened as the two sorcerers shook their turtle shells in consorted rhythms, regulating the steps of the dancers (Figure 9). Four seated men beat wooden waterdrums in time with the rattles. Made from sections of a cedar log and hollowed by charring and scraping, the drums were partially filled with water. Each had a piece of untanned deerskin stretched over its top and held in place by a wooden hoop. The high-pitched sound could be heard at a great distance.

The women would dance with arms outstretched, clenching their fists one upon the other. The players would hold closed fists straight up in the air. The dance steps would be united by the steady rhythm of the rattles and drums—dancers lifting and stamping from one foot to the other, in time, too, with the chanting of the sorcerers directing the native "music." (Le Mercier, who had had extensive instruction in music, considered the liturgical repertoire to be clearly on a more advanced level.) He could hear Tonnerananont emit a fragment of melody, using only three pitches to some nonsensical syllables—"He ho ho"—which were then repeated by the dancers. Total gibberish, thought Le Mercier, who was accustomed to the soaring beauty of Gregorian melodies sung in Latin. As the dancers circled the fire, the melodic fragments would change in pitch. After every four or five repetitions, Tonnerananont and his assistant would stop to shake their rattles in a tremolo as some sort of choreographic signal. The dancers would then change steps, the women bending slightly and turning in place and the players turning to face them. After this pirouette they would face forward again, repeating the affair from the start, moving again around the fire.

Le Mercier soon gave up all hope of sleep that evening. The dancing and general noise making continued nearly all night. He tried to read from his breviary, but his resentment at Tonnerananont's control of the village ruined his concentration. He turned instead to the tenth chapter of Sagard's *Grand Voyage,* in which the Recollect described Huron "dances, songs and other silly ceremonies." Sagard, too, was appalled at many of the sorcerers' instructions, particularly at the direction for participants to dance naked. In one instance, claimed Sagard, a man was made to urinate into the mouth of a sick woman, and she was forced to swallow the foul liquid. In another "wicked ceremony," the girls of the village were coerced to choose young male partners for fornication in the lodge of the afflicted. Sorcerers accompanied the disgusting cabal with singing and rattling. Sagard closed his chapter: "May God be pleased to put an end to such a damnable and wicked ceremony, and to all that are of the same sort, and may the French who foster them by their evil example open the eyes of their mind to see the strict account that they will one day render for it before God."[5]

Le Mercier lay on his wooden cot, dozing and rubbing his bearded chin, as the light of dawn crept through his smokehole. Mosquitoes began to pester him, and there was the usual scampering of mice intent on depleting his meager supply of corn. As he reached to bang on his desk with a stick to scare away a mouse chewing on his journal, his eyes wandered to a painting of Judgment Day above the desk. He remembered how the image had aroused fright and controversy among his neighbors at Ihonatiria when he first unveiled it. The sorcerers had insisted that the Jesuits meant to instigate Iroquois attacks on their villages. The reaction was typical of the sorcerers' deceptions and intrigues against the priests, on whom they blamed everything from summer drought to the diseases running their course through Huronia.

To the missionary, it seemed that the only way to convince the heathens of the efficacy of Christianity was by analogy with their own superstitious practices. The Father Superior had related to Le Mercier how, upon a visit to the village of Ekhiondaltsaan, he had been pressed into explaining the purpose of holy water. Many had visited the chapel at Quebec and wondered what was the use of the vase of water at its entrance. When the Father Superior explained it was as effective in driving away devils as their own straw effigies, the villagers conferred, then announced their wish to obtain some of the magic water.

Meanwhile, their sorcerers continued to interpret the dreams of those in need and prescribe methods for their recovery. The medicine men were the only ones to whom the ill would reveal vision details. Consequently Le Mercier questioned whether the details of the ceremony were not the concocted fantasies of the sorcerers. They had been known to require that visitors to the sick make faces, or eat a huge meal and vomit it up, or that they—despite a fondness for the *andataroni*, or bran biscuits, that accompanied nearly every meal—avoid farting for twenty-four hours, on pain of death.

As he now lay beneath his elkskin blanket, he remembered vividly the conclusion to Aenons's "cure" last fall: Outside the Jesuit's cabin, the village stirred as everyone prepared for the march to the lacrosse field. Le Mercier had already seen several women with tiny lacrosse sticks tied with rawhide thongs around their necks, like religious medals. These women had been instructed to sit closest to Aenons during the game. About nine o'clock the players emerged from the council house in single file, headed by Tonnerananont and carrying their lacrosse sticks. They marched to the stream for ceremony, thence to take positions on the field. They were naked save for breechclouts, but most had woven into their hair feathers from birds known for sharp eyesight, swiftness, and dodging. They had painted their bodies mostly in red, as they did for war. The players were followed by Tonnerananont's assistants bearing Aenons on a litter. Behind him came a throng of villagers dressed in finery and carrying beaverskin bags of booty for wager. Several old men were perched on the shoulders of the strongest youths and carried to the lacrosse field. Once Le Mercier had inquired about this mode of transportation and learned that these were men who had dreamed often or previously been cured through lacrosse matches. Their presence at the game would be especially helpful to the Ihonatiria team.

Le Mercier knew the stakes were high for this game. Even though the missionaries were opposed to such practices, they enjoyed exchanging stories about the great winnings and losses they encountered among gambling Indians. Losses could run well in excess of two hundred crowns; one village was reported to have lost thirty wampum collars, each containing a thousand beads, whose value in France would equal that of fifty thousand pearls. Desperate gamblers were said to have wagered the clothing on their backs, their hair, and even their little fingers, cutting them off stoically without sign of pain, dishonor, or shame. Le Mercier waited for the betting to be completed and the game to begin before venturing in the direction of the lacrosse field.

It was from idle curiosity and for simple amusement, Father Le Mercier confessed to himself, that he watched the match between the two villages. He did so from a distance and out of sight, for the natives knew he disapproved of any activity in which Tonnerananont was involved. Still, many aspects of the Indians' major sporting activity fascinated and puzzled him. The wooden sticks they played with were not unlike the tennis racquets he and other priests had used in spare moments at the French monastery, except that they had a much smaller striking surface of rawhide webbing. And the Indians didn't really strike the ball so much as catch and balance it on the racquet, to run with it or toss it in the general direction of another player. The ball itself would surely have pierced a tennis racquet, as it was carved from wood and generally hurled with great force.

The game began, thought the Jesuit, somewhat like tennis, with a toss-up of the ball. There the analogy broke down, for tennis was a game between two players, as indeed was every other European game he had ever witnessed. Imagine—forty or more semi-naked bodies running tirelessly from one end of a long field to the other, all in pursuit of a *single ball!* This seemed as senseless as the purpose to which Tonnerananont put the game. The priest was certainly not prepared to await its outcome, when the Huron who had gambled would gleefully divide the spoils. That was a sinful indulgence!

Preparing to retire to his hut, Le Mercier suddenly remembered the ailing child at the north end of the village and took a detour. Later, he would have time to complete his writing for the day, before the hubbub of villagers returning from the game disturbed his concentration. Once he had accomplished his covert mission to the hut of the dying boy, he would work alone on his journal entries while daylight still flooded his desk. He, like the other Jesuits, had important news for France—how he had ministered to eleven sick babies that week and how Father Pijart had converted the dying wife of the war chief on her sickbed. He found the bark hut with little trouble. The rest of the village was at the game, but from a distance he could see the young mother alone, pounding corn in a mortar outside the dwelling. As he approached, she seemed both pleased to see him and very anxious. The priest followed her inside. The child's condition had clearly deteriorated, and the father sat listlessly on the mat next to his son, slowly bathing his forehead with a piece of moss dipped into a bark bucket of water. The infant would certainly succumb to the plague soon, and there was little time for Le Mercier to perform his surreptitious baptism. It had to be done secretly, for the parents had often protested that they did *not* wish the child brought into the faith. They believed that in the land of heaven he would be a stranger, with only Frenchmen there to greet him. The priest went about his business undetected. Pretending to administer to the infant a small amount of sugar water, saying it would ease his sufferings, Le Mercier quickly spilled a little of the liquid on the baby's forehead while quietly mumbling the In nomine Patris, et Filii, et Spiritus Sancti.

• 25

Le Mercier shuddered despite the warmth of the fur blanket. His mission complete, the priest arose and turned to depart. Suddenly he detected a bright glitter in a corner near the entryway. The sun shone through the smokehole at such an angle that it struck some silver object tied partway up one of the saplings that made up the frame of the hut. He moved closer to see what it was. At once he recognized the silver crucifix and smiled benignly. There were other objects at its feet, but he could not quite make them out because of the smoke from the fire. They'd built a small altar! he thought—triumphantly at first. A miniature version of the one they were familiar with from the village chapel. But something was wrong, it seemed, something out of place. He moved even closer and squinted to see what they had created. On a bark tray beneath the crucifix he discerned a small pile of round objects. At first he took them for pinecones, but when he recognized the pile of newly made lacrosse balls, his face flushed in anger. Jesus guarding the balls of Satan? The Savior showering his blessings on these sinful objects? The enormity of the crime shook Le Mercier. But then as he gazed at the crucifix itself, horror overcame him. The savages had implanted a miniature lacrosse stick horizontally behind Christ's slumped head and resting on each upraised arm, giving the wounded, pierced, broken Son of God the appearance of a fatigued and dejected ball player. Blasphemy!

"Christ twice crucified!" the missionary shouted, as he dumped over the bark tray, spilled its contents, ripped the crucifix off the post, broke the tiny lacrosse stick in half, threw the pieces in the fire, and stormed out of the smoky hut into the glare of the sun and the distant roar of cheering voices.

"How the Bat Got Its Wings"

The story of Le Mercier's frustration in converting the souls of the Huron in New France is but one chapter in the long history of missionaries' efforts to stamp out "heathen" practices. That their concern should reach to the realm of sports is not surprising, for in many of the world's cultures, games are deeply rooted in religious beliefs contrary to Christian teachings. In his revulsion over the Huron family's "desecration" of the silver crucifix, Le Mercier failed to appreciate that the Indians were in fact honoring Christ: Using his image as an icon, they simply wished the power of this god to be magically transferred to their lacrosse equipment to bring them success in the game.

Many sports, like lacrosse, had their origins in myth, and participation in these sports was believed to be in accordance with the wishes of the gods. Accordingly, games were organized as part of religious holidays and institutions or timed to coincide with particular changes of season or the position of heavenly bodies. Their purpose was often to honor or petition some god or spirit—the lacrosse "altar" to Jesus in Ihonatiria. For example, in North America at Zuni pueblo, a warriors' dart competition was held at the winter solstice to change the weather. The contestants sprinkled sacred cornmeal around a large ball, then threw feather-shafted arrows at it. The first person to pierce the ball held it aloft and offered prayers to the gods to send rain.

Such ancient belief systems attributed severe losses or accidents during games to a failure to honor some god or goddess properly or even to having offended the deity. The Homeric verses tell us that

Apollo was directly responsible for success in athletics; if an archer missed his target, it was probably because he had not remembered to offer Apollo a sacrifice. A chariot racer did not drop his whip on his own; Apollo, somehow angered, knocked it from his hand.[1]

Although the Jesuits seem to have made no specific attempts to condemn or curtail the playing of Huron lacrosse, they were at least remotely suspicious that the game was somehow connected to alien religious beliefs. Their attitude seems to have been that the game itself was innocent enough, but that it was being diverted to immoral ends by the religious leaders of the people they had been sent to convert. Far from mere amusement, the game actually was rooted in ancient Indian legend. The Jesuits appear to have been aware that a lacrosse match was a highly ceremonialized religious expression—that the players were required to undergo ritual cleansing before and after the sport, that the game's outcome was believed to be predetermined by spirits, and that success or failure was attributable less to athletic prowess than to the relative power of the religious leaders who controlled players and games at every turn. These leaders were the ones who called the games, directed the preliminaries, consecrated the athletic gear, and prescribed the players' dress and strategy.

Whether they were called conjurers, jugglers, sorcerers, or medicine men by Europeans, such persons functioned somewhat like today's coaches, but with an arsenal of magical powers to control a game's outcome. Indeed, for some North American tribes, the game was more a duel of shamans than a contest between two teams. As anthropologists James Mooney and Frans Olbrechts described the Eastern Cherokee game, "The whole affair takes the aspect of a contest between the occult power of the two medicine men conjuring for the teams of players. . . . And the victory or defeat is laid at the door of the medicine man rather than that the players themselves are congratulated or scorned for it."[2]

Lacrosse is deeply rooted in the mythology and oral histories of the tribes that played the game. One of the best-documented legends is that of a mythical game between birds and land animals (see Appendix A, No. 1). Different versions of the story have been collected from nearly all the major southeastern tribes of North America—evidence that it was widely known. Stories, like material goods, customs, and practices, over time become shared by neighboring peoples, who usually change the details of a tale while retaining the essential story line. Whatever the Mohawk story of lacrosse's origin may once have been, they appear now to have adopted the Cherokee legend of the mythical animal game as their own.[3]

In Indian accounts of the game between the birds and the quadrupeds, the central issue is how the bat should be classified—that is, on which team he should play (see Appendix A). One Creek version elaborates on the problem. In discussing the makeup of each side, the birds agreed that all creatures with teeth would make up one team, those with feathers the other. As was customary, the day for the contest was selected, preparatory arrangements made, the field readied, and the lacrosse balls conjured (treated magically) by the medicine men. But when the bat approached the animals with teeth, they refused him, pointing out that, because he could fly, he belonged with the birds. The birds, however, rejected the bat because of his teeth. Claiming that he was too small for their team, they sent the bat back to the quadrupeds, who grudgingly accepted him. As the game developed, the birds pulled ahead because of their ability to catch the ball in the air. The sluggish crane was at first the best player, but eventually the bat showed his quick skill at darting and won the game for the animals: "They agreed that though he was so small he should always be classed with the animals having teeth."[4]

One Cherokee rendition of the story included an epilogue that was missing from other Cherokee versions. The tale does not make it clear which of the two teams issues the challenge, but compared to the birds, who say little, the animals seem boastful and eager to prove themselves. Preparations are made, and the teams go into training. At the customary ball game dance that precedes Cherokee games, two rodents attempt to join the animal team but are rejected. Turning to the birds, they are accepted but first fitted with wings and thus transformed into bats. After wagers are complete, the game begins, and because of their talent at catching the ball and dodging their opponents, the bats immediately "chalk up" ten points, beating the animals, who retire from the field in disgust. The bird team, having donated the wings permanently to the bats, becomes boastful and tries to humiliate the quadrupeds. The captain of the animals, the Bear, however, is resigned to defeat and promises to join the birds in their victory celebration. An epilogue to the tale, missing from Creek and other Cherokee versions, introduces the character Rabbit, a notorious trickster figure in Cherokee legends. Rabbit joins the animal team and plots revenge upon the birds by bringing women to the victory dance to disrupt it. The celebration is thus turned into a free-for-all, but the animals feel satisfied, having achieved their vengeance.[5]

This widely told story is allegorical in many of its details. In American Indian legends, animals behave like humans and vice versa, as they freely intermix. The descriptions of arrangements for the game, the preparations and dancing, and even the techniques of play—keeping the ball aloft as the safest means to victory—all describe the activities of human ball players. But using birds and animals as the principal contenders casts the story in the mythological past of "Once upon a time . . ." Clearly one intention of the story was to explain the anomalies of flying mammals, and in this sense the tale belongs to the large category of etiological legends, often used to instruct children on the vagaries of nature ("How the Leopard Got His Spots," et cetera).

Southeastern tribes were not alone in using lacrosse tales to explain certain peculiarities of animals. In the cycle of Ojibwe stories about Wenebozhoo, a Great Lakes trickster and culture hero, much like Rabbit for the Cherokee, is one tale explaining "How the Turkey Buzzard Got His Scabby Red Head" as a direct result of the rough play typical of lacrosse games (see Appendix A, No. 4). Wenebozhoo, having turned himself into a caribou, played dead and was slowly eaten away by animals and birds. When all that was left of him was his anus, the turkey buzzard began to feast on that. But Wenebozhoo tightened his sphincter muscle, trapping the bird's head in his anus. Later, playing lacrosse, he tripped, and the turkey buzzard slipped out and escaped, but not without damage to his head and neck, which is why this bird has always looked so awful and smelled so bad.[6]

Several Algonquian-speaking tribes had stories explaining the origins and purpose of lacrosse, revealed supernaturally to people in dreams or directly as gifts of the Great Spirit. One Ojibwe belief is that the way of playing the game once came to a boy in a dream, when he fell asleep in his canoe and drifted into the deep waters of Chequamegon Bay (near Bad River Reservation). In his dream, the boy saw a large open valley and a crowd of Indians approaching him. A younger member of the group invited him to join them at a feast. He entered a wigwam "where a medicine man was preparing 'medicine' for a great game." The lacrosse sticks were held over the smoking medicine to "doctor" them and ensure success in the game. After the players had formed into two teams and erected the goalposts, the medicine man gave the signal to start, and the ball was tossed in the air amid much shouting and beating of drums. In his dream, the boy scored a goal. When he awakened, he related the details of his experiences to his elders, who interpreted it as a dictate from the Thunderbirds. This is how the game of lacrosse began.[7]

The Menominee, close neighbors of the Ojibwe, credit Manabush, their mythical culture hero (the equivalent of Wenebozhoo), with the invention of lacrosse to avenge the death of his brother, Wolf, by the evil underground spirits. In the story, Manabush invited the Thunderers to come and play against the evil spirits, after which the game would belong to them. The Golden Eagle responded to their invitation and brought the ball to be played with.

"He was accompanied by all the other thunderers, his brothers and younger brothers. Then the [evil spirits] began to come out of the ground, the first two to appear being the head chiefs in the guise of bears—one a powerful silvery white bear, the other having a grey coat. These were followed by their brothers and younger brothers."[8]

Algonquian beliefs surrounding the afterworld further emphasize the sacred nature of the game. The Northern Lights (aurora borealis), for example, are usually interpreted as images of spirits in the village of departed souls. While the Ojibwe regard them as the spirits of the dead dancing up and down, the Abanaki say that this heavenly phenomenon is their ancestors playing lacrosse. Most Algonquian traditions tell of a four-day journey that the deceased must undertake to reach the village of the dead. The Potawatomi believe that the soul is guided by Chibia'bos, the younger brother of their trickster culture-hero Wi'ske. When he arrives at his destination, the deceased is informed by Chibia'bos that he can remain there always, that in the village of the dead there is no sickness or trouble and all are happy, and that the deceased "[can] play lacrosse forever."[9]

In addition to the animal and historical legends, lacrosse shows up in stories otherwise filled with magical occurrences and moral lessons. For example, about 1823 the Eastern Cherokee said that, in the distant past, they played lacrosse only during a full moon because the moon presided over the game as a tutelary spirit:

> In the time of Te-shy-ah-Natchee, two chiefs made a ball-play, at which all the red people attended, men, women, and children. The contest between the parties was very severe for a long time, when one of them got the advantage by the superior skill of a young man. His adversary on the other side, seeing no chance of success in fair play, attempted to cheat, when in throwing the ball, it stuck in the sky and turned into the appearance which the moon hath, to remind the Indians that cheating and dishonesty are crimes. When the moon becomes small and pale, it is because the ball has been handled by unfair play.[10]

The origins of lacrosse are sometimes woven into historical legend. A former chief of the Creek Nation, Ispahihtca, narrated a migration story explaining the early formation of his tribe and the beginnings of lacrosse. Divided into three groups—the Chickasaw, Kasihta, and Coweta—they began their migration eastward. En route the Coweta had problems getting around a briar patch and became separated from the group. When they rejoined the others, they got into a skirmish with the Kasihta, who cut switches and beat the

Coweta warriors severely. When the group eventually reached the ocean, however, they settled their differences for a time and joined forces, subjugating all the local inhabitants: "In course of time no people were left willing to resist them, and they longed for someone with whom to fight. Hereupon Coweta challenged Kasihta to a game of ball in order to revenge for having been beaten with switches by the latter. The custom of having ball contests originated at this time and in this manner and has continued to the present day." In another, much longer, version of the legend, the punishment the Kasihta originally inflict on the Coweta warriors is more intense: They force them to dance, push them into the fire, beat them on the calves with sticks, cut off their ears, and put strings of dog feces around their necks. Later on, they settle amicably, and in midsummer at harvest time they hold a big feast, spending a number of days dancing and taking part in rituals preceding a lacrosse match. The tale goes on to describe a typical southeastern lacrosse game.[11]

Historical legends of other tribes acknowledge lacrosse to have been a gift from some spirit to the Indians. But they typically credit themselves as the first recipients, as is the case with the Fox, living in ancient times, they believe, east of the Great Lakes: "It was there that the manitou [spirit] came among them and gave them the knowledge and skill of playing lacrosse. He came with a lacrosse stick in one hand and a ball covered with buckskin in the other. The ball was painted red. He gave the stick and ball to them and taught them how to play. He told them that the game would belong to them, even though other people should learn the game from them."[12]

Doubtless the seventeenth-century Huron also had tales in which lacrosse figured prominently. Whether Jesuits like Le Mercier were familiar with them is not known; the priests seem to have made no effort to collect and publish them. The language barrier was formidable, and some Indian legends were so old that they were recounted in archaic speech. If the stories had sacred connotations, they were probably not told in the presence of missionaries. What the Christian proselytizers *did* recognize and record, however, was the use of lacrosse by Indian medicine men in curing disease.

When Tonnerananont in 1637 dictated a lacrosse game to help the ailing Aenons, others like him must have been making similar prescriptions elsewhere in North America. From the period of the Jesuits in New France, information on Native American healing practices has increasingly shown the religious and curative functions of certain games. Many tribes—the Wisconsin Potawatomi, for instance—made a clear distinction between secular and sacred sports. Whereas the Potawatomi moccasin game was not considered religious, in Huron culture both lacrosse and the bowl and dice game

were categorized as sacred/curative entertainments. The Potawatomi, who believed that lacrosse had been given to them by a god,
played the game whenever someone wished to honor his guardian
spirits. To sponsor a game, one selected captains for the teams and
provided a feast. Players were invited through the customary gift of
tobacco, and when the day arrived and all had convened, food and
tobacco were spread on the ground and offered to the spirits. Just as
the Huron used lacrosse to *cure* sickness, the Potawatomi engaged in
the sport to *prevent* it: "It was believed that if a person did not
sponsor a game once or twice a year he might fall into ill favor with
his spirit, and even become sick."[13]

Like the Huron, the Menominee felt obligated to play these
games if they had dreamed of doing so, "at definite times and in a
prescribed manner, according to the directions received in the
dream." If a Menominee man dreamed of the Thunderers, for example, he had to sponsor a lacrosse game to receive the help promised
by these guardian spirits. Furthermore, his dream required that he
reveal its details before the match. The sponsor gave a feast that
always included plenty of wild rice—the staple after which the Menominee were named—and usually some large animal. Snapping turtle
was often served, for it was believed that the Thunderers liked this
delicacy and would always attend the feast if turtle was prepared. At
the game field a "gift pole" was erected, with a horizontal bar resting
on two upright posts (Figure 10). Calico goods were draped over the
bar as prizes for the winners. If an unmarried man received one, he
could give it to a female relative, who would let out a shrill ululation
or whooping sound believed to be heard by and to please the
Thunderers.[14]

In front of the gift pole the Menominee sponsor placed his
lacrosse war bundle on a mat and opened it to expose the contents
for the duration of the game. A Menominee, David Amab, in the
1920s told how his grandfather always wore a fur turban with an eagle
feather projecting from its back whenever he held a game. The grandfather's bundle cover was of soft white buckskin painted red in its
center. It contained a lacrosse ball painted half red and half blue
(representing the sky), a small cross painted black on one side and
white on the other, and a little tobacco dish. The exact meaning of
items in a war bundle would be kept secret, known only to the
bundle owner. If the event was a ceremonial game, sick people were
brought to it to be cured, and a special song was performed if they
were present. (To cure illness, the Menominee still play the game in
the spring, before the first thunder.)[15]

Some lacrosse games, like the early Olympics, were played in the
context of religious events. As Lewis Henry Morgan described the

• 34

Figure 10 • Spectators
in front of a Men-
ominee gift pole at a
lacrosse game in Kes-
hena on the Men-
ominee Reservation,
about 1916.

Iroquois League's "national games," of which lacrosse was one of the most important: "[They] were not only played at their religious festivals, at which they often formed a conspicuous part of the entertainment, but special days were frequently set apart for their celebration." Similarly, lacrosse, the favorite sport of the Winnebago, was generally played on ceremonial occasions, and the Mexican Kickapoo played it as a religious celebration four times annually, beginning with the Kickapoo new year's renewal ceremony.[16]

A special one-day ceremony in midwinter is performed by the Cayuga to honor the Thunders, who are mentioned in Longhouse prayers. Its purpose is to appeal to the "grandfathers" for continued service to man. The principal part of the day's activities is an "old-fashioned" game of lacrosse between the young men and the old men. The ritual number seven is emphasized throughout the game: The goal is seven paces wide, and seven points are needed to win, although it does not matter who the victors are. When the game is over, the players begin to sing the Thunder, or War Dance, song and dance, and go into the ceremonial longhouse.[17]

Lacrosse was also played as part of funeral and memorial ceremonies. Linguist Truman Michelson, who wrote extensively on the culture of the Fox, elucidated Fox practices on "what they do and how they pray, when there is a death." An adoption feast is sponsored to ensure that the deceased will not return. If it is not held within four years of a death, it is believed that the person's spirit will be transformed into an owl and condemned to life on earth: "And when an adoption-feast is given for these men . . . they would play ball. . . . They used lacrosse sticks. It is as if they were playing with [the deceased] for the last time, so it is said. This is how it is when they play ball."[18]

Holding a lacrosse game to memorialize some famous player is mentioned in the earliest reports and was still being practiced well into the twentieth century. Mitchell Wakau, a Menominee, held such a game annually in memory of his father, Ke'sigabeta (Living in the Sky), and when Wakau died his own son was supposed to continue the games: "In his youth Ke'sigabeta was one of the fastest runners on the reservation. When he played lacrosse his opponents set four men to watch him, because if he got the ball it was considered to be already at the goal." When he was near death, Wakau's father told his relatives that he would die at midnight, that they would see a cloud rising on the horizon. When it reached the top of the sky, that would be the moment he would pass on, when Ke'sigabeta believed he would go to live with the Thunders.[19]

The sacred nature of lacrosse explains the paramount role of medicine men in nearly all of its ritual aspects. Although they themselves did not play in the game, their services were considered essential to success, and they expected to be paid for those services. Since some medicine men had reputations for greater powers than others, lacrosse players sought out the best available. Thus anthropologist J. B. N. Hewitt noted Iroquois uneasiness over the issue: "Shamans were hired by individual players to exert their supernatural powers in their own behalf and for their side, and when a noted wizard openly espoused the cause of one of the parties the players of the other side felt to a certain extent disheartened."

The Cherokee, who customarily hired more than one conjurer per team, carefully selected medicine men to ensure victory through certain magical spells and paraphernalia, to weaken opponents, or to make their own team invincible. Roots of beggar's lice, which, being forked, resemble human figures, were one popular device used. The conjurers employed these "dolls" to bewitch the opponents, assigning them names of rival team members and putting them under the sacred ball game fire. This ritual was believed to render the named players ineffectual, causing them to become feeble, feverish, and short of breath, and thus making it necessary for them to retire early from the game. Just as they weakened rival players, the Indian ball game conjurers had the means to improve the performance of those on their own side. Choctaw doctors on the sidelines used mirrors during a game to reflect the rays of the sun onto their players to increase their strength.[20]

Cherokee conjurers were at one time politically powerful. They accompanied warriors, who counted on them to divine the enemy's strength and deliberate on strategy. Although their political power diminished when warfare ceased at the end of the eighteenth century, the conjurers were still held in high regard, and their curative powers continued to be sought by traditionalists well into the twentieth century. A Cherokee ball team almost always selected a conjurer from its own township. He could be employed by other towns but usually assumed a less important role, working in tandem with their principal medicine man or helping a certain player in that town—usually some relative—with individual ceremonies. A conjurer would never accept the assignment of working against his own town of origin or residence.

When hiring a conjurer for a lacrosse match, the team had to formalize his services by entering into a contractual agreement whereby he was paid in money and the various material items required for the numerous rituals and ceremonies that must be conducted in preparing for a game. Payment normally included cloth, such as a large bandanna, colored beads used in divining, and a small amount of "old tobacco." In addition, he might be given personal items like clothing or shoes. The Cherokee referred to these transactions, which obligated the conjurer to work for his team, as a "toe hold."[21]

Once the teams had secured their conjurers and were in training for the game, each medicine man was actively engaged for the duration of the game and a period beyond it. Mooney and Olbrechts, when working to decode the meaning of a manuscript belonging to a Cherokee conjurer named Swimmer, found this mechanism still operative in Cherokee society well into the twentieth century: "Even now [1929–31], when two settlements are training for the ball game, a contest which with the Cherokee is as much of a social as of a sportive nature, the medicine man is exercising his influence and his personality in such a way that the whole affair takes the aspect of a contest between the occult power of the two medicine men conjuring for the teams rather than that of a match between two rival teams of players."[22]

While the identities of Cherokee ball game conjurers were well known locally, such information was often kept secret among other tribes. In fact, even if the conjurers were known to members of the tribe, their operations were carefully guarded and certainly never revealed to outsiders. George White, a clergyman in mid-nineteenth-century Georgia, could easily pick out the conjurers during the game because these men, whom he took to be over a hundred years old, sat near the center of each sideline, holding in their hands "shells, bones of snakes, &c." for divination. They were clearly in no mood to divulge the nature of their activities: "When I spoke to one of them, he did not deign even to raise his head; the second time I spoke, he gave me a terrific look, and at the same time one of the Indian women came and said, 'Conagatee Unaka'—go away, white man."[23]

The identity of a Creek lacrosse doctor was always kept secret. During the game he was secluded "back in the woods making medicine as hard as he [could] for his own side." Medicine men were active during practice sessions, such as one between Kaplako Indians in July 1913. Because of the conjurers' powers, even the place of the lacrosse match was kept secret until the last minute. Agreed upon in advance by eight men, the location was not revealed until shortly before play because each side feared that their opponents would "bewitch" it. This was ostensibly the reason that anthropologist John Swanton was not told the location of a game he wished to see between the Talahasutci and Kiwahali Seminole in the summer of 1913.[24]

Further evidence of the sacred nature of the game is the attention given to its basic equipment, namely the sticks and the balls. In some instances their manufacture was entrusted to specialists within the tribe. Once made, they were often decorated or specially treated to enhance their efficacy. Special functions for such equipment outside of games show that it was regarded as having extraordinary powers. Some of these practices and beliefs have persisted well into the mid-twentieth century.

The making of a lacrosse ball was assigned to the member of a specific clan, or some medicine man directed others to assemble the component ingredients. The skin for the Cherokee ball's cover had to come from a squirrel killed without being shot. Boys were dispatched by the players to obtain the animal for the ball maker, who then had to undergo ritual purification before he dressed the squirrel skin to form the ball. The night before the game, the ball maker placed the ball on a deerskin belonging to the team's conjurer and then fasted until the game was over. During a series of Dakota (Sioux) matches in 1852, the losers of the first game won the second by substituting a special old ball said to have had magical properties. It had been made years before by an old "war-prophet" named Ehakeku, a member of Wabasha's band.[25]

Certain lacrosse balls held objects hidden inside their stuffing to provide secret power. Because of the ball's covering, the items were invisible to members of the opposing team, who were therefore oblivious to the ball's potency. Through sympathetic magic, the properties of the animals or birds whose parts were selected for inclusion in the ball's manufacture were transferred to the ball itself. This practice was especially widespread among tribes in the southeast. When Creek Indians played, each side had available a special "chief ball" that contained an inchworm and was substituted for the regular ball once a team had scored three goals. Inchworms were believed to be invisible to birds, and so, by analogy, the worm hidden inside the ball was supposed to make it difficult for the opponents to see the ball.[26]

Another substance put in a chief's ball was a bit of material from the nest of the corduroy, or tie, snake. One story tells of an old Creek medicine man in Oklahoma who, seeking snake nest matter from a cave, sent a man with some magical substance to quiet the snakes while he stole from the nest. The man failed out of fear to obtain the material needed, so another was sent with a special cane that had calming powers. He was to poke at the snakes with it and then retrieve bits of their nest for the medicine man. The tie snake was thought to move by jumps or flips "strong enough to carry off a horse," and that ability was believed to be transferred to the ball, presumably making it difficult for the opponents to retrieve. Lloyd Sequoyah, a noted Cherokee ball game conjurer, said that sometimes fleas were put in a ball "to make it jump around"; Moses Owl of Birdtown on the same reservation stuffed balls with human hair, inchworms, and certain herbs to make them lively.[27]

Although a Cherokee challenging team usually supplied the ball used in the game, each team brought its own ball to the special dances held in the two hometown communities before a game. At that time, each rival conjurer "doctored" his team's ball together with the players' sticks, whereupon the ball was kept most of the night in the netting of the sticks of one of the "center fighters" (those players who face off at midfield). Such doctoring of gear was reported among the Ojibwe of Wisconsin in the mid-1930s. Before a game between the Bad River and Red Cliff bands, medicine men from Odanah (Bad River Reservation) were seen "loading with Indian medicine" the sticks that belonged to the local team, which ultimately won.[28]

Presumably, the designs on lacrosse equipment had meanings whose significance was known only to the artist or owner. Menominee balls are said to have been symbolically painted in red and black—possibly a reflection of the tribal division into two parts. The German cartographer Johann G. Kohl, on Madeline Island in Lake Superior to observe Ojibwe annuity payments in 1855, was disappointed not to witness a game because the authorities had prohibited it, but he was nevertheless able to watch Indians back in the woods creating round balls from willow, with "crosses, stars, and circles . . . carved upon them."[29]

The Cherokee burned, painted, or engraved designs on the surface of their ballsticks, some of them with generally known meanings: Jagged lines represented lightning, and diamond cross-hatching stood for rattlesnakes. Both designs were intended to impart swiftness of striking to the racquet. Rattlesnakes as well were believed to have the power to charm their prey—rabbits, squirrels, partridges—directly into their mouths. Thus, by analogy, a rattlesnake design on a lacrosse stick might cause the ball to be charmed directly into its cup.[30]

In preparing their teams for action, medicine men paid special attention to the sticks that would be used in the game. Cherokee racquets in particular had to undergo a variety of treatments to make them powerful tools. Because rivers and streams were sacred to the Cherokee, before a game the team's conjurer had his players at the riverbank dip their sticks over the edge into the water to increase the potency of the racquets (Figure 11). During this ritual immersion, he recited a special formula, "This is to Doctor the Ball Sticks to be able to Pick up the Ball." In the text of the formula he referred to the flying Red Bat—an allusion to the figure in the Cherokee legend of

Figure 11 • Eastern Cherokee players immerse their sticks in the Oconaluftee (?) River before a game in the fall of 1946. Their ball game conjurer stands behind them and appears to be divining their success with the beads in his hands. The secondary feathers of the wild turkey tied to the hair of two players are meant to give them the bird's speed and long-windedness in the game.

the game between birds and animals. If a player was unable to attend the dance, he was allowed to send his two sticks with a teammate so that they, too, could be conjured at the riverside. The bat, in fact the crucial actor in the legendary drama, was so honored that pieces of this animal, especially the wing, were tied to various ceremonial accoutrements associated with the ball game—the rattle used by the

Figure 12 • Oklahoma Creek ballstick rack about 1938. Each player's two sticks, together with his game uniform, are hung here the night before the game to increase their power. To suspend them, one stick is threaded through the webbing of its companion stick.

singer for the ball game dance, for instance, or the poles where the sticks were hung for sanctification before the game. The base of the cup on a Cherokee lacrosse stick might have attached a small wrapped piece of bat wing, in addition to feather bits from other avian creatures known for their swiftness of flight and darting abilities—the hummingbird, the peewee, the chimney sweep.[31]

While only the medicine man could create the potions to put on equipment, the players themselves often applied them. On the advice of their medicine man, Creek players would paint "medicine" on the strings of their lacrosse sticks to attract the ball to them. When the players retrieved their sticks from the ball rack (Figure 12), each one took some of the potion the medicine man had prepared and poured a bit on his sticks. At the same time, the chief who led them poured some of the liquid on the balls.[32]

Another way in which the sticks received power required the rituals of music and dance. These expressions generally played an important role in Indian lacrosse, just as they did in other important activities, such as preparations for the warpath and victorious celebrations upon the warriors' return (the Victory, or Scalp, Dance). The ball-play dance on the night preceding a game, for instance, was a feature of nearly every southeastern tribe that played lacrosse. The Yuchi dance was performed "in honor of the sticks which are used in the game, and the supernatural power residing in them." While sticks are resting on a scaffold, usually in the west lodge of the ceremonial square ground, a line of women stands behind the scaffold facing a line of men (including the lacrosse players), all of them singing and stamping their feet. In an early report on the Choctaw,

Bossu observed of this dance that all the men and women "assemble in their best ornaments, they pass the whole day in singing and dancing; they even dance all the night to the sound of the drum and *chichikois* [rattle]."[33]

Most Cherokee ball game dances were held outdoors at each team's hidden encampment (Figure 13), but in *History of North Carolina* (1714) the Englishman John Lawson described an indoor version:

After the Dogs had fled the Room, the Company was summoned by the Beat of Drum; the Music being made of a dressed Deer's-Skin, tied hard upon an Earthen Porridge-Pot. Presently in came fine Men dressed up with Feathers, their Faces being covered with Vizards made of Gourds; round their Ancles an Knees wer hung Bells of several sorts; having Wooden Falchions in their Hands, (such as Stage-Feneers commonly use); in this Dress they danced about an Hour, showing many strange Gestures, and brandishing their Wooden Weapons as if they were going to fight each other.

Figure 13 • Eastern Cherokee ball-play dance, 1888. The women dance in place while they sing, accompanied by the seated drummer using a waterdrum made of some keg or barrel and a medicine man shaking a gourd rattle in time with the drumming.

• 42

When the players (dancers) left the room, thirty or more women replaced them and began a circle dance "representing the Shape of the Fire they danced about. . . . This Female-Gang held their Dance for about six Hours, being all of them of a white Lather, like a Running Horse, that has just come in from his Race."[34]

Other ritual uses of music for lacrosse games have included Choctaw flute melodies played by medicine men on the sidelines before, during, and after play. These songs were intended magically to increase the chance of winning as well as to counteract the evil spells of the opponents' conjurer. Lake Superior Ojibwe began their games with a singer at centerfield. For a 1948 game between the Bad River and Red Cliff bands, Frank Gishkok, age ninety-nine, opened the game with a drum (and presumably a song). Some tribes accompanied the march to the ball field with ceremonial drumbeats. Baxter York, an unofficial tribal historian of the Mississippi Choctaw, depicted the players and their entourage as they moved to the field: "The teams would march down the trail, one-by-one. . . . The drum would beat, and the people would hear them coming. The leader of the group would lead a chant, and the rest of the group would answer with a 'Yoo!' The other group that was their competition for the match would meet them about half way, and there would be much shouting back and forth. Sometimes there would be wrestling." This practice has been revived in a considerably abbreviated form. Before games in the 1970s, the two teams assembled near the tribal offices about two hundred yards from the (football) field used for play, then paraded single file to the field, with a drummer pounding a small commercial drum in a slow, steady rhythm (Figures 14a, b).[35]

While ceremonial music and dance could infuse the game with spiritual strength, the team conjurers were the ultimate source of power. They were believed to be in control of the movement of sticks and balls while play was going on. They achieved this control in one of two ways: through sympathetic attraction, causing their team to score, or through "witchery," magically preventing the opponent from getting the ball in the goal. The Creek conjurer not only created medicine to apply to the strings and handles of the sticks as well as to the players' bodies but during the game he also placed behind the goalposts a dish containing the hide of a bull turtle, to bring the ball "home." Supposedly the ball would be attracted to the dish like a turtle to water. The conjurer could also sit behind his team's goalpost and "bring home the ball" with the hidden inchworm, believed to be magically drawn toward him. At Creek ceremonial games today, one can still see a medicine man behind the goal, shaking his rattle throughout the action, presumably to attract the ball.[36]

Figure 14a • Will E. Morris, a Mississippi Choctaw drummer in "national costume" about 1908. The horsehair tailpiece hanging from his right hip is worn as an ornament in the game.

Figure 14b • Following tradition, Choctaw drummer leads players about 1978 to the football field where they play.

"Witching" the other team's goal to keep them from scoring was also common. If a pregnant Yuchi woman could somehow be induced to circle the goal of the opposite side, it would cause them to lose the game. The Ojibwe even recently had "magic" balls, which, when casually tossed up and down in the air near the opponent's goal, would prevent them from scoring. I first learned about this in 1990 from Franklin Basina, a Red Cliff resident. After showing me the 350-pound bear he had hung in his back yard to bleed, he told me over coffee how this "witching" was counteracted:

> We played at Northland College [circa 1950], on the football field, and that's where we seen them two old Odanah squaws guarding the Red Cliff pole, so we wouldn't score. That's when they were throwing in their *jiibik* [magic] balls up. One on each side, post was in the middle, and they were standing on each side on the back of it. And there was a water puddle in back of them. It must have rained there a couple of days, and one of the boys said, "I'll get rid of one of them old squaws. I'll see if I can knock that ball out of her, when she throws it." Knock it out, you know, just knock it in that water. So when that ball hit that water, that ball is no good. That kills their spirit. . . . Them two squaws, they killed that ball. That ball was no good, she had to throw it out. [But] she didn't throw it out. I imagine she took it back home and [had] the medicine man work over it [that is, restore its power].[37]

• 45

Medicine men were known to "wage war" against each other in order to control lacrosse sticks. Menominee members of the medicine lodge in charge of ball games always feared the sorcery powers of their opponents. Since a medicine man possessed the ability "to carry away the power of the sticks," it was the duty of the opposing conjurer to pursue his adversary and "bring back the sticks" (restore their power). If, however, he was not powerful enough or was somehow deceived, he ran the risk of being killed through his opponent's sorcery: "It usually happens that the pursuer compels the rival to restore the virtue or power of the sticks before the day [of the game] approaches."[38]

Other uses of lacrosse equipment outside the context of games further reveal the special nature of this sport. Famous or especially gifted players of many tribes are still buried with their sticks, in the belief that such equipment accompanies them to the afterworld, where lacrosse games are played perpetually. Freeman Bucktooth said that in 1989, when his father died at Onondaga, "My son handed him his wooden lacrosse stick [to be buried with him], and as my father is playing for the Creator right now, that's what we believe in."[39]

Grandparents of newborn boys made tiny lacrosse sticks to inspire their grandsons to take up the game. Peter Jones, an Indian convert to Christianity, illustrates in his *History of the Ojebway Indians* (1861) a miniature lacrosse stick of the Missisauga, eight and a quarter inches long, said to be a divining instrument "used by Conjurers to look into Futurity." Small effigies of lacrosse gear might be included as part of a Menominee war bundle that belonged to one who had dreamed the right to own it. Bundles were considered gifts from the Thunderbirds or the Morning Star, and although their contents varied considerably, a typical Thunderbird bundle might contain a miniature war club, lacrosse stick, or ball, and possibly all three.[40]

The spiritual aspects of the game extended beyond the equipment used to the location and orientation of the field itself. For religious and symbolic reasons, Cherokee fields were usually adjoining or at least near rivers or streams to facilitate the "going to water" ritual. Ojibwe lacrosse fields were laid out east to west, possibly to conform to the ritual orientation of the medicine lodge and ceremonial drums; the latter were oriented east to west, with a yellow stripe down the middle of the drumhead to represent the "path of the sun."[41]

Like the fields, the players themselves were doctored in a number of ways. All manner of specially brewed potions and decoctions were prepared to induce vomiting (cleansing); players were instructed to bathe in sacred waters at specified times; protective ointments and salves were applied to parts of their bodies; taboos against certain foods or sexual intercourse before games were observed; expectant fathers were isolated from the team and given special medicines; and among some tribes, conjurers ritually scratched their players with instruments sharp enough to draw blood. The general purpose of all these practices was to render players "pure" before they faced the action of the game, thus allowing them to perform at full strength and avoid injuries.

The use of emetics, or vomit-inducing liquids, by lacrosse players is widely reported. In addition to fasting and bathing before a game, Iroquois players drank an emetic decocted from the bark of red willow and spotted alder. The Yuchi town chief prepared a special emetic made from red root and button snakeroot boiled in water to render their juices. The potion was believed to be the gift of the Sun, whose symbol was used as decoration on the pots holding the liquid, and all males of the town drank from the pots, four at a time facing east and beginning at noon, when the sun was at its highest point in the sky. At Wetumka in 1913, a Creek medicine man (*yatika*) was preparing emetics while players sat on logs around the dance ground. The medicine was divided into two tubs, each treated differently. Facing east, "he did his work very deliberately, sitting motionless for a long time and afterwards taking some time in blowing into the medicine." When finished, the *yatika* directed players who chose to take the emetic to form two rows facing east. They drank from each tub to induce vomiting.[42]

Emetics were also prevalent in the Great Lakes area. Before setting up the goalposts, men from the Maṇe'gi division of the Winnebago took an emetic that, by causing them to vomit, cleansed them internally; they followed the emetic with a sweat bath to further purify and strengthen them. Whether the potion given to Ojibwe players at a game on the Bad River Reservation around 1936 was intended to induce vomiting is not known; it was described as "a beverage supposed to strengthen the players." They won the game.[43]

Other medicines were meant to be applied externally to a player's body. A liquid made "of the track of a wolf and the burrow of a crawfish" was rubbed on Creek players' shoulders. Recognized for the efficacy of his potions, Jackson Lewis, a Creek, was once requested by a Choctaw team to create special medicine for them to rub on their bodies before a match. The team won, preventing its opponents from scoring more than a single goal. Similar medicines were once used by Menominee lacrosse players, who attributed their skill at winning to them.[44]

To toughen their limbs, Cherokee players washed themselves with leaves of catgut, whose roots are strong and difficult to break. Or they bathed their limbs with a decoction of small rush (*Junus tenuis*) "to enable them to spring quickly to their feet if thrown to the ground, [for small rush,] they say, always recovers its erect position, no matter how often trampled down." Another potent ingredient was wood from a tree hit by lightning, considered by many tribes to have strong magical powers. A Cherokee medicine man burned splinters of wood from a lightning-struck tree, reducing them to charcoal, with which players painted themselves in order "to strike their opponents with all the force of a thunderbolt."[45]

While these practices were external to the player's body, a type of surgery was also employed to infuse him with power. The practice of scarification, or the ritual scratching of lacrosse players, seems to have been restricted to southeastern tribes, such as the Cherokee, Creek, and Yuchi. Scratching, an ancient curing technique in North America, was accomplished with a native surgical instrument used to draw blood to the surface of the skin. The practice was also used for the treatment of rheumatism, much as the bloodletting or "leeching" of folk surgery was used to cure disease, supposedly by releasing "bad blood." John Lawson, while sojourning among the Esaw, for example, heard his Indian host express a desire to cure the lameness of one of Lawson's fellow travelers: "He pulled out an Instrument, somewhat like a Comb, which was made of a split Reed, with fifteen Teeth of Rattle-Snakes, set at much the same distances as in a large Horn-Comb. With these he scratched the place where the Lameness chiefly lay till the Blood came, bathing it bothe before and after Incision, with warm Water spurted out of his Mouth." Later, among the "Tuskeruros" (Tuscarora), Lawson observed a doctor treating a "young Woman troubled with Fits." After scratching her with rattlesnake fangs, asserted Lawson, the doctor sucked out nearly a quart of blood.[46]

When performed on athletes, scratching was meant, among other things, to build running stamina and relieve fatigue. The intention of this painful ordeal for ball players seems to have been twofold: First, it was a demonstration of the bravery needed to face an adversary; but it also had a magical purpose, and for this reason a specialist was required to perform it ceremonially. Such sacred physical ordeals have their counterparts elsewhere in North American tribes, such as in the Sun Dance of the northern Plains, where a participant's flesh is pierced and torn as part of his vows to the sun spirit.

Scratching instruments used in connection with lacrosse varied in their construction, but all made use of natural pointed objects, such as teeth, quills, bones, and thorns, embedded in some handle, either singly or comblike to effect multiple subcutaneous incisions. Whatever the pointed object, it had significance, for the particular attributes of the plant or animal from which it came were believed transferred to the player. By the twentieth century, the Cherokee, in making the *kanuga* (scratcher), were using leg splinters of the wild turkey, known for its speed and long-windedness; nineteenth-century sources, however, report the use until about 1880 of rattlesnake teeth bound together to enable a doctored player to strike his opponent like a serpent. One *kanuga* described was made of a single fang from the upper jaw of a rattlesnake, embedded in a quill of a white duck's feather. The quill was split for insertion of the fang, then bound with white thread, with a band of red thread tied to its middle. Thus the instrument incorporated not only the attributes of snakes and birds but also the symbolic associations of color: "The feather symbolizes speed of flight, and a strand of red thread . . . lightning and its destructive speed and force."[47]

Yuchi conjurers in ceremonies at Sand Creek in July 1904 and 1905, before scratching, dipped the instrument in a pot of sacred plant juices as a form of inoculation that would purify the players' blood against illness (Figure 15). The Yuchi had a legend that told of the Sun's being taken to the rainbow and scratched. When his blood fell on Earth, it created the first Yuchi. During the Yuchi rite no one was allowed to lean against a post or tree or to fall asleep; if that happened, the person would be struck with a staff.[48]

Only certain Cherokee players submitted to scratching in the early nineteenth century, but from the century's last decade until about 1940 the ordeal was mandatory for all players. Team members could ask to be scratched individually or in a group. The Big Cove scratching took place immediately after a ball game practice, when the players' bodies were still moist with sweat. But most reports suggest that players endured the ritual on the day of the game, sometimes even just before advancing onto the field. While some preferred the operation early, so as to allow the incisions to heal before play, others preferred to take their wounds into the game so that their skin would feel deadened, and they would be better able to endure the blows from their opponents' lacrosse sticks.[49]

For many, scratching provided a degree of exhilaration that enhanced their generally "psyched-up" condition for play: "Many [Cherokee] say that the scratching gives them a feeling of lightness and alacrity for the game. One man said that, while in the game, he would feel a burning sensation all over his body when lying on the grass or when held too closely by an opponent. The only relief afforded would be to get up off the ground and break free from the grasp of his rival."[50]

Cherokee players underwent the ritual facing east, standing either on a naturally bleached rock or near the edge of a riverbank

Figure 15 • Early twentieth-century (?) Yuchi scratcher made from a turkey quill with six pins inserted. The scratcher has a leaf of the button snakeroot attached to it.

• 50

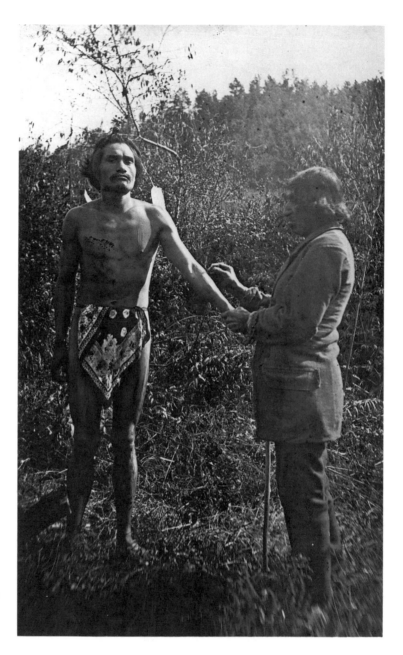

Figure 16 • Eastern Cherokee ball player Jim Johnson of Wolf-Town being scratched in 1888 by Standing Water, a ball game conjurer. Johnson wears a bandanna for a breech-clout. Scratches already made are visible on his chest.

(Figure 16). The proximity to water was important not only for religious reasons but also for hygiene, to rinse off the blood brought to the skin's surface. In former times, in fact, when many were scratched in one session, it was said that the stream they plunged into would run crimson from blood.[51]

Further evidence of the importance accorded this ritual is the special decoctions created to apply to wounds before or after washing them. Among the plant materials used were the "knive blade," whose leaves are chosen for their sticky quality, believed to help a player hold on to his lacrosse sticks or grab an opponent. Another important plant was the "great bulrush," which has a stalk that springs back to an upright position when bent; this property was believed to enable a player to jump back up to his feet after he was knocked down. The plant has a hollow stem, containing much air, and was also thought to improve the player's breathing.[52]

The complexity of native medical practices for an athletic event and the richness of Indian sports legends appear to have eluded the early missionaries. Le Mercier and his Jesuit colleagues in seventeenth-century Huronia—the first missionaries to draw European attention to an unusual North American sport—apparently savored nothing of the lore surrounding lacrosse and provided but a glimpse of the rituals connected to the game. That lacrosse somehow had sacred functions seems about all that was clear to them. As the New England colonies became established and the American frontier moved further west, it remained for later chroniclers to collect the lacrosse legends, describe in greater detail the many magical aspects of the game, and begin to probe the depth of its very spiritual nature. And even today, vestiges of the ancient, magical Indian world of lacrosse emerge, however subtly, with a quiet echo that reminds us of the past, when conjurers controlled the outcome of a game and medicine men prescribed it as a cure for illness.

Lacrosse as a healing mechanism emerged among the Mohawk in 1990, when the city of Oka, Quebec, announced a plan to expand the municipal golf course onto Mohawk burial grounds. An outcry arose from the Indian community, escalating rapidly into demonstrations and confrontations with the police and military. The protest traveled to the Akwesasne (St. Regis) Reserve, exacerbating an already divisive split in the community over the presence of gambling casinos. Before the drama had played out, cars had been burned and two Akwesasne residents had been shot to death by their own people. In an effort to "heal" the community and correct the breakdown of social values on the reservation, several lacrosse players in the spring of 1992 forwarded the idea of starting a lacrosse league that would integrate players from both factions. Despite some initial uneasiness, former enemies playing their traditional game together eventually restored the community to relative peace. Noted Mohawk Bruce Roundpoint: "I'd say it was a good idea starting this league. We've got guys on the same teams that were shooting at each other two years ago, and now they're playing lacrosse together."[53]

In the early 1980s, lacrosse coach Roy Simmons, Jr., of Syracuse

University, made the acquaintance of Eli Cornelius, a Canadian Oneida. Cornelius began attending Syracuse games, and Simmons, recognizing that this elder was experiencing a certain isolation and lack of appreciation from his own people, began to include him on trips to away games. Cornelius found a welcome audience among the Syracuse players: "He would sit on the bus with the kids and talk about Native American philosophy and magic potions that came up in the spring—anywhere from how to harvest cowslips early on when the snow melted—as he fixed their sticks." Although Simmons disavows any shamanistic powers that Cornelius might have had, a certain ambivalence is evident in the coach's reference to the Oneida as "my rabbit's foot." *And* Cornelius could improve the efficacy of a lacrosse stick. Said Simmons: "I really enjoyed his company, and on the sideline he would impart some wisdom from time to time in the heat of a game, and mostly stay out of the way. But he was always there for the kid who came off the field whose stick wasn't shooting well."

In 1983 Syracuse was battling archrival Johns Hopkins University for the NCAA lacrosse title. As usual, Cornelius was present on the Syracuse bench. Losing badly at halftime (11–5), Syracuse came from behind to win 17–16. In an article about Coach Simmons, the interviewer raises a provocative question: "Cornelius gave the players game pointers and served as confidant. But on this day perhaps he did a bit more. . . . Cornelius died not long after that game. Was the miraculous Syracuse victory his parting gift?"[54]

3 *Iroquois Country, 1794*

There was still anger throughout Seneca country over the grave offense committed by the Mohawk lacrosse player in the recent Grand River game. Rumors were also afloat—principally among the Allegany people under Seneca chief Cornplanter—concerning the role that Shagoyewatha (Red Jacket) might secretly have played in provoking the incident. Perhaps it had been a plot to embarrass Thayendanegea (Joseph Brant), the great Mohawk leader. Was it not Red Jacket, the persuasive Seneca orator, who had insisted that Mary Jemison's son be allowed to play, despite his reputation for a fiery temper—a blend of Irish blood and Seneca pride? And was it not Red Jacket himself who was now using his extraordinary powers of speech to whip the Seneca into a frenzy about going to war against the Mohawk to avenge this serious wrong?

Seneca opinion was fairly evenly divided about the next step to be taken. Those who had been on the playing field when it happened naturally sided with Red Jacket, for their honor was at stake, and, of course, those who had wagered felt they had been deprived of almost certain winnings, and their anger had not abated. Citizens of Buffalo Creek, where Red Jacket held sway, were the most adamant about revenge. Cooler heads, however, prevailed at Cattaraugus and Tonawanda. The Iroquois people, Mohawk and Seneca alike, had frankly tired of warfare. They had seen their lands cut from under them, their villages and cornfields slashed and scorched, their orchards decimated, as General John Sullivan's American troops rampaged their way through, driving the Iroquois ever westward or north to seek shelter with the British, as Brant and his people had done. Squabbling and fighting among themselves would only weaken their stance in upcoming treaty negotiations to protect what little of their lands they could hold on to. The matter required a council meeting to settle.

The incident occurred as follows: In a state of relative peace with the Americans, the

Seneca and the Mohawk, traditionally brothers at the council fire, had decided to mount a great game between the two nations as a gesture of their long friendship and their valiant struggle to protect their lands against further intrusions of European settlers. The British and the Americans had signed their peace treaty, and there was calm—at least for the moment, though at any time hostilities could break out again. Still, it had been some time since any large-scale lacrosse game had been played between the two nations, for until now they had been preoccupied with warfare, land cessions in treaties with the "Long Knives," and attempts to resupply their exhausted stockpile of weapons and ammunition.

The Seneca knew of the Mohawk plight in finding a new homeland but were aware that their bitterness against the Americans made the Mohawk adamant about staying in British territory. Thayendanegea had been negotiating for some time to secure a land base for his people in Upper Canada, but what the British had offered was unacceptable. Had the Mohawk settled on the north shore of Lake Ontario, as initially proposed by the British, they would have been far removed from their traditional brothers, and the Six Nations of the Iroquois Confederacy would have found themselves even further fragmented. The annual Grand Council would have been difficult to arrange, as travel for the isolated Mohawk would be awkward. The location would have hampered sending messages via runners, since there was no main trail leading from that part of Canada to the south and communication would have required navigating the rough waters of the Great Lake.

The Seneca were also nervous that American pressure on their lands might force them to remove to Canada as well. In any case, they did not wish to lose contact with the Mohawk. In fact, they had offered them lands of their own for resettlement, but the Mohawk declined. For that reason the Seneca had interceded on their behalf to attain for the Mohawk a new homeland on the Grand River, whose mouth emptied into the other Great Lake, west of Detkahskonsase (Niagara). Now, should the Seneca be forced to move or join forces with the Mohawk in combat, communication would be far easier. Their new proximity would enhance old friendships and family ties, for as with all the Iroquois— Cayuga, Oneida, and Onondaga as well—clan lines cut across national boundaries, and there had been intermarriage for centuries.

The challenge for the great lacrosse game had come from the Mohawk after meeting in council. As was customary, they sent two runners from Grand River to meet with sachems of the Seneca at Buffalo Creek, carrying with them the large lacrosse stick, painted red and festooned with feathers from birds of prey. The runners brought details of the challenge and, after presenting the usual two strings of white wampum and the invitation stick, retired for the night while the council met to consider the challenge.

The Seneca sachems were in general agreement that the game should take place. The young warriors of the nation had recouped the energy they had spent in the struggle over their lands and would be in good shape to play. Even though the event would take place in

the challengers' community, giving them the psychological advantage, the best Seneca
players would be selected to take on the Mohawk players, and there was a large pool to
choose from. The sachems were confident of early victory in the game, as years of fighting
and relocation had depleted the stock of Mohawk lacrosse players. Furthermore, many of
the finest and most renowned Mohawk athletes had recently returned from skirmishes to
the west and would be at a disadvantage physically, while the Seneca players were well rested
and ready for action on the field.

The Mohawk runners were called into council the next morning, as the coals of the
council fire were raked over and new flame brought to it. Discussions began in earnest concerning the timing of the game, the number of players that would be involved, and the
score that would be needed to win. It was agreed that a late summer game would be best, at
least a week before the final harvest, allowing the Seneca to return to their cornfields to lay
in their winter supplies. It was also decided that no more than a hundred players be available to each team—a condition insisted upon by the Mohawk, who knew that the Seneca
outnumbered them considerably. The two sides agreed they would play to twenty points.
Having arranged the details of the game, the runners departed, leaving the invitation stick
behind to be returned at the time of the contest.

No sooner had the Mohawk runners left than the Seneca began to spread word of the
game among their people. Runners were dispatched, first north to Tonawanda on the bor-
ders of the great swamp, then southwest to inform those living on Cattaraugus Creek,
thence eastward to the outermost villages in the Genesee Valley. Their mission was to enlist
the finest players from the nation and inform them of the time and the agreed-upon details
of play. Anyone wishing to be included on the Seneca team would touch the challenge
stick, thereby committing himself to be part of the contest.

Since this was an opportune time for the Seneca to display national pride, when the
time of the event drew near a general hubbub became audible in each village as families
began to assemble articles for their players to wager. Confident of victory in the game, they
spared little, picking out the finest silver gorgets, blankets, and even family heirlooms.
Many were engaged in making new tomahawks to bet with; mothers crafted new *ke:onshae'*
(cradleboards) with which to take their youngest to the event; stickmakers were busy repairing and restringing old sticks or making new ones for the game. Women began to estimate
how little cornmeal they could get by with for the two-to-three-day journey on foot, knowing they would be fed by the host community upon arrival and provided with return provisions. They also made new *kenka:'*, the traditional breechclout worn by Iroquois lacrosse
players and warriors. They cut recent purchases of blue broadcloth in two-yard lengths and
decorated the edges with fine beadwork. Players started to practice skills that had become
rusty through disuse. Each village had been given a quota that in total would not exceed the
one-hundred-player agreed-upon team size, so they began to hold small village games to

weed out ineffective players and identify newcomers who exhibited promising skills and potential. A match against the Mohawk would certainly perk the spirits of the youngest players, should they be chosen to take part in this important event.

Three days before their scheduled arrival at Grand River, players and families assembled and started out on their trails northward and westward, to meet at Buffalo Creek. There they would join others of the nation. That way the five hundred men, women, and children could arrive in the country of the Mohawk as a large, united group, rather than appearing one by one as stragglers. Attired in their finest, the Seneca would make a good initial impression on their opponents by demonstrating team cohesion and tribal loyalty.

In the interim, Red Jacket had taken advantage of his community's preoccupation with game preparations to make a discreet journey eastward to the Genesee Valley, under the pretext (should anyone ask) of securing lodges at Canandaigua for the forthcoming treaty negotiations with Timothy Pickering, who would represent the United States' interests. Only a few Seneca still lived by the lake, and accommodations would be needed for the large Buffalo Creek delegation that fall. But Red Jacket never got to Canandaigua, for his true destination was Gardeau, where Mary Jemison tended her small log cabin. Despite her white skin and European features, Mary was for all purposes a Seneca. Born at sea on a vessel from Ireland, she had been captured as a child during an Indian attack on her family's farm. She was raised by the Seneca and had later taken a Seneca man, who fathered her many sons. Some of the sons still lived with her, despite their maturity, and it was among them that Red Jacket intended to carry out his personal recruitment campaign for the lacrosse game—part of a delicate scheme that the Seneca orator had concocted. He had already surreptitiously set the stage at Grand River for the drama he hoped would unfold. But the key actor was yet to be tapped.

As Red Jacket made his way up the hill, Mary's cabin came into view, a wisp of smoke from the morning fire still rising from the crude chimney. At first there seemed to be no one on the premises, but off to one side he could see movement in the small garden. The woman was making her way slowly down the rows of squash plants, apparently weeding as she went. The Buffalo Creek orator approached and shouted a greeting. They had met only once before, but she recognized Red Jacket immediately by his famous attire—a gift from the British that had earned him the name now commonly used even by his own people. He looked down at the worn cuffs that were rapidly becoming threadbare. Still, it was his most prized possession, and, the spirits be thanked, at least they had not presented one to Joseph Brant, despite their close and continual dealings with him.

Mary dropped her pile of weeds in a trash heap and beckoned Red Jacket to enter the cabin. In a corner he spied right away a number of lacrosse sticks piled against each other, and knew he had come to the right place. As he began to talk with Mary, he walked over to the sticks and examined them one by one. They were of different lengths, and all showed signs of considerable wear. One had a crack in its crook, which had been repaired with tightly wound rawhide. Only the frame was left on a particularly battered stick. The outermost string holding the webbing on another had broken loose, and the net had begun to unravel. Mary apologized for the untidy corner but said she could not bear to part with her children's broken toys. The difference in stick lengths was a certain indication that the boys had grown up playing lacrosse together, probably starting very young, as revealed by the shorter, smaller sticks.

Their casual talk was interrupted by a commotion behind the cabin. Mary ran to the rear doorway and shouted angrily at two of her sons, who were on the ground, fighting violently. John, the older one, had Buffalo Tom pinned and was pummeling him on the head with a crude scraper made from a deer's shinbone. Given John's size and maturity, it was no match. Red Jacket helped Mary pull them apart. Tom's nose was bleeding and looked broken. The Irish temperament, thought Red Jacket, reminded of John's mixed ancestry by the strange color of his long tresses—a peculiar reddish-brown. The sons had been sent out to dehair a cowhide and cut the thin strips that would be twisted for lacrosse stick lacing, which Mary did in her spare time. They hadn't gotten very far, and the putrid hide, already begun to rot, still lay draped over the beaming post, with only a few patches of hair scraped off it.

Convinced that he had found his surrogate actor to play the lead role, Red Jacket took John aside and tried to calm him. Had the Mohawk runners gotten to Gardeau with the challenge stick? Did John even know about the impending contest? Red Jacket put his arm around the young man's shoulder and ushered him inside. Pointing to the pile of sticks, Red Jacket turned on the flattery. Looks as though Mary's boys have had years of experience in the game, he observed. He bet that John was a pretty powerful player, given his size. He was sure the contest directors would select him as one of the hundred on the team. They wanted the group to represent *all* the Seneca nation, and he guessed that there was no one from this area already chosen. The ranks were fast filling with the best-known players from west of the Genesee. Cattaraugus had already presented a list of forty candidates but was told it could have only half that number in the final selection. Red Jacket knew the game directors personally and would put in a good word for John.

Even though she was still angry over the ruckus and fighting between her sons, Mary began to sing John's praises as a talented athlete. Yes, he'd always been the best player among the boys, but, no, the runners had not yet reached her section of the valley along the river. Her pride overcame her annoyance with John, and she reminded him of the Grand River Seneca girl he had spent time with after the game the previous summer at Tonawanda. If he went with the team, he would have a chance to renew his acquaintance with her—*after* the game, of course.

And so it was that John Jemison took his place in the grand scheme that Red Jacket had hatched to embarrass—even humiliate—his archrival, the great Captain Brant of the Mohawk. He counted on John to show up at Buffalo Creek, with his lacrosse stick in hand.

Once assembled at Buffalo Creek, the entourage departed on the main trail north to Detkahskonsase, then crossed the river to continue on the Canadian side until they reached the village of Osweken, on the Grand River. Further along their route, at a Cayuga village about two miles from their destination, Seneca runners were sent ahead bearing the red-painted lacrosse stick. Their arrival at Brant's village would announce the proximity of the challenged team and allow the Mohawk to begin preparations for a communal feast.

That evening, Red Jacket interrupted Jemison's scrimmage with two teammates, took him aside into the woods, and asked to see his stick. Red Jacket examined the tip of the crook and pointed to the hooked protrusion beyond the groove securing the outermost string. He suggested a trick he had learned when he played years earlier: With a crooked knife, one could whittle the protrusion down more finely, so that it became sharper and more hooklike, thus a greater threat to the back of an opponent's webbing. But one had to be careful that the referees didn't notice this "refinement"; if they did, they would surely disqualify the stick and possibly ban the owner from playing in the game. They might even deduct a point or two from the Seneca's goals scored.

The runners soon returned to notify that all was in readiness, so the large group of Seneca gathered their belongings and began the final short journey to the playing field. There they would set up camp on the side closest to the river—the site designated by the Mohawk for their campgrounds. As the Seneca emerged from the forest trail, they saw that large numbers of Grand River residents had already gathered on the playing field to greet them. The Mohawk had hastily assembled a small team of their best players, who were now practicing ostentatiously in front of the two goalposts erected at one end of the field—a deliberate attempt by the Mohawk team to impress their visitors with fancy behind-the-back or over-the-head shots and quick maneuvers around goalkeepers.

The Seneca players, of course, pretended to ignore the scrimmage, moving with their families to set up camp and unload their fur bedding. Their sachems retired to the Mohawk council house to meet with Thayendanegea, or Joseph Brant, as he was known by the British, and the principal chiefs. After smoking the calumet, they would discuss matters of mutual concern but put off consideration of the next day's game until later in the evening, when individuals began to bet in earnest on the game's outcome.

The feast that evening provided an opportunity to renew old friendships between clan members from each nation, to catch up on the news, and to visit with distant Seneca relatives who had moved to Grand River a decade earlier. For many Seneca this was the first visit to the new Mohawk settlement. The residents proudly showed off their new bark houses and log cabins and pointed out their recently planted orchards and their large cornfields.

That evening a special war dance was put on by the Mohawk, and between songs, warriors spoke of their recent exploits at Detroit in the battle with the Miami against the Americans under Arthur St. Clair. General camaraderie prevailed, and there was much talk of the game that would begin the following morning. Several Mohawk players bragged that they expected they would win the twenty points by noon, so the Seneca might as well not even unpack!

Meanwhile, players from both sides were being attended by their medicine men, who had prepared special physics decocted from scrapings of red osier bark for them to drink and lotions for them to rub on their limbs. The players abstained from the feast and instead fasted until the beginning of play. No one got much sleep that night, given the crowd around the ball field and the bustle of players' families preparing the items to be wagered. Silver ornaments were polished to a bright shine, cloths were carefully folded, and bead-work was given a final tightening. The lacrosse sticks were each marked with the player's personal identification, then assembled in a special bark hut and watched over during the night by one of the medicine men. One of the Seneca lacrosse conjurers was opening the balls to be used, inserting small magical objects in them, and handing them to a woman who would sew them shut again.

At the same time, Mohawk women were busy preparing a supper for their guests, who they knew would be tired and hungry from their journey, having subsisted on cornmeal "snacks" for most of the trip. The large kettles were ready for hominy, beans, and squash; venison, supplemented with cow meat, was already being boiled with corn.

During the feast, Jemison spotted the Grand River girl he had met the summer before. He had forgotten how pretty she was; now in all her finery she seemed even more attractive than he had remembered. Their relationship at Tonawanda had developed rapidly and become quite serious. There were others on his team who had admired her, but Jemison was as aggressive in the pursuit of love as he was in pursuit of the ball on the lacrosse field, and so he had won out. Now, after supping and laughing over anecdotes from their early days together, she invited him to meet her family, who lived, she said, just a few minutes' walk from the village. When they had gotten out of view of the others, she put her arm around his waist, and they stopped and kissed. She motioned to a side path leading deeper into the forest, and for a moment John was tempted. But reality overcame his carnal desires, and he remembered the strict prohibitions of the medicine men against such activity until long after the game. Besides, there was no way for him to tell what part of the month she was experiencing. Much to the girl's disappointment, tradition prevailed.

The morning of the game was hazy from the late-summer fog, but by game time the sun had risen higher in the sky and the mist had burned off, only to be replaced by the smoke from early-morning cooking fires. Players were busy adjusting their breechclouts and engaging in footraces to warm up their leg muscles for the game. Lacrosse sticks were retrieved from the bark hut, and medicine men helped to tie small feathers to them for luck. Older warriors provided players with paint for their faces and arms, and women brought out the various ankle, wrist, and arm garters that would complete the athletes' game costumes.

Suddenly a gunshot rang out—the signal that all should move to the ball field and begin wagering articles on the outcome of the game. Four old men—two from each nation—served as guards for the items that were bet. Blankets were spread out for the articles to be placed on, and as each player selected an opponent from the opposite nation and they agreed together on what they would wager, they proceeded to the betting area. There the old men tied the two items together with a buckskin thong and placed them conspicuously on the blankets so that the winners could retrieve them easily following the game. The line leading to the betting blankets was nearly the length of the field, as players and members of their families placed their wagers. Soon a large collection of hatchets, silver brooches, tomahawks, knives, wampum, rifles, swords, furs, and beadwork had accumulated; the pile of goods grew so large that an additional blanket had to be laid out.

Ordinarily one of the Mohawk sachems would have been responsible for giving the opening oration and setting the first ball in motion at midfield. But since Brant had initiated the challenge and had achieved such great status as a warrior, the honor was accorded him. Brant had given up playing lacrosse when he became so involved with the affairs of the Mohawk nation. Being bilingual, he was in constant demand as a spokesman for his people. In fact, however, his rise in the warrior ranks could be attributed partly to his prowess on the lacrosse field as a youth. The Iroquois people kept a keen eye on the talent displayed by their young men during games and selected their warriors from the best of the lacrosse players. The energy, dexterity, speed, and durability that enabled one to score against the opposing team were the same attributes that prepared one for successful campaigns on the warpath in hand-to-hand combat against an enemy.

The Seneca players were arranged along the river side facing their Mohawk opponents at a distance of about fifty yards across the field. Thayendanegea made his way forward from the center of the Mohawk line. Dressed in his finest, he wore a heavy silver cross over his breast and a red kerchief tied around his neck; there were small feathers worked into his topknot of hair and thin red lines of war paint across his forehead. Brant marched proudly to centerfield and began the preliminary speech to the players, admonishing them against excessive force in the game and advising them to play by the rules. Turning alternately from one side to the other, he addressed the teams. Extending his right arm from beneath his blanket, he began with the Seneca:

> BROTHERS: You have accepted the challenge of the great Mohawk nation, who have sat with you on the same side of the council fire for centuries, to play against us in the game of our ancestors, as it pleases the Great Spirit to see his children forever united, though momentarily opposed. We owe our Seneca brothers gratitude that we should be able to play on

such fair grounds, for our new homeland on the banks of this great river has provided us with the perfect arena for all our sporting events. Such a challenge as we issued through council would have imposed great hardships on our Seneca brothers had they not interceded on our behalf to allow us to remove to Seneca country. Such a contest between our two great nations would have been difficult had we been resettled on the other great lake as the British had first intended. But the proximity of our two homelands should bind us even closer together and enable us to play these grand national games with greater frequency.

In the middle of his address Brant noticed that one of the several British medals draped around his neck was askew, having been hastily thrown on him by his cousin as he dressed that morning. Not becoming for a great chief, he thought, reaching up (hopefully unobserved) to align King George's face with the other adornments that he wore. Then he continued:

> BROTHERS: Now that the tomahawk has been put aside, we are aware that there are many fine warriors on your team whose energies tested in battle might now be brought to the playing field. We caution those among you not to take out your frustrations on your Mohawk brothers in play. We know full well that your lands have been taken from you, that General Sullivan laid waste your ancient villages and cornfields, and that even now the Americans eye with greed the land set aside for you by treaty. We, too, have had a long and heavy walk from our ancient homeland at the east end of the Great Longhouse of the Confederacy. But let us remember that we play lacrosse not to avenge our losses to the Americans but in friendly competition. You see before you the bountiful prizes that have been wagered one against the other. These should be your goal in the contest. Today we fight for silver armbands and blankets to take home, not for scalps and the plunder of war.

Jemison shifted his weight impatiently from one leg to the other. The butt of his stick pivoted on the ground, while his hands firmly grasped the crook end and moved it slightly in cadence with Brant's oration. His eyes were focused on his Mohawk opponent across the field, sizing him up. Even at this distance, he could tell he would need to call upon all his energy and skills on the field. The Mohawk was taller than he, with long, thin legs— probably a fast runner, thought Jemison. He could see that his left forearm was bandaged. Jemison would certainly take a swipe with his stick at that arm whenever he could. He looked down at the sharp end of his crosse. He had just carved it with a crooked knife, exposing fresh wood, and rubbed dirt on the point to make it the same color as the rest of the frame. He hoped the referees wouldn't get close enough to notice. He would need the "hook" against a fast runner.

Brant then turned to his own people, casting a quick glance downward to make sure that King George was in his proper place.

> KINDRED: As you see before you, our Seneca brothers have accepted the challenge of the proud Mohawk nation to engage in our ancestral sport, that it may please the Great Spirit. They have traveled from all parts of their homeland to join the best players of their villages in one team, to contest with our young players to see who is defter with their sticks, who

can throw the ball the farthest toward his home goal, who can knock the ball from his opponent's stick and still catch it on his own while in mid-air. Since our council received the Seneca acceptance of our challenge, you have been hard at work preparing for the contest, repairing broken strings on racquets left behind while you were on the warpath. Scarcely a day goes by when, walking through the village, I do not encounter dozens of you, one-on-one, practicing your throwing skills or engaging in footraces to build up stamina for the game. One cannot help but notice the fine new breechclouts provided by your womenfolk. Wear them proudly as Mohawk athletes, striving to win the contest with honor. NA HO!

Brant raised his arm to show the ball.

Immediately players arranged themselves on the field for the toss-up, ten of each side moving into positions guarding the goal, another ten halfway to the midfield, each standing by his opposing number, and the two captains joining Brant at the center. Brant separated them by extending his arms straight out with his forefingers pointing, positioning them at this distance. Then, without warning, he tossed the ball on the ground, simultaneously stepping back a few feet to get out of the way and giving the signal to start by yelling, "*Tahsatawhen!*"

The two centers dove with their sticks for the ball, which got caught between them. As they struggled to gain control of it, the ball was slowly lifted, then suddenly flew straight into the air. As it came down, the Mohawk center gave it a swift hit with the webbing of his stick, sending it in the general direction of the Mohawk home goal. Another Mohawk player scooped it off the ground and, balancing it on his stick, began to run with it. Partway downfield, he encountered four Seneca players coming at him in a diagonal line, so he dodged suddenly to his left, where another Mohawk player was ready for him. Running directly at his teammate, he dished the ball quickly into his stick but continued past him, with the four Seneca close behind. Since they hadn't seen the ball transfer, they continued to pursue him. The real Mohawk ballcarrier darted toward the middle of the field and, finding an opening in the goal defense, threw the ball between the two posts for the first score. Great cheers rang out from the host community, and the two centers returned to midfield for the next round of action. Brant's duties were over, since now after each goal the ball would be thrown on the ground by one of the sachems designated as a referee.

The game had progressed in a close contest for most of the morning, when "the incident" happened. The score stood at ten points for the Mohawk and eight for the Seneca. Two players, one of them Jemison, had been particularly aggressive against each other and were struggling for a ground ball. The Mohawk was about to scoop it up when Jemison abruptly shoved him aside, nearly throwing him off balance. Clearly infuriated, the Mohawk player lost his temper, grabbed his stick with both hands, and smashed it across Jemison's face, knocking him to the ground with the blow. This deliberate and vicious assault was witnessed by all. Several Seneca rushed to their injured teammate, who appeared to be unconscious and was bleeding severely from the nose and mouth. All action ceased. To a man, every Seneca player dropped his stick right where he stood on the field and retired to the sidelines. Hasty consultations went on with the Seneca sachems and conjurer, while the injured Jemison was being helped off the field by two of his teammates.

Before Brant could get across the field to soothe the feelings of the outraged Seneca, all members of the visiting nation who had made bets moved to the pile of wagered goods to get their stakes. Those guarding the wagers sensed what was happening and quickly untied the buckskin cords so the Seneca could retrieve their property. Women began to break camp, young Seneca boys ran onto the field to fetch the players' sticks, and sharp exchanges between Brant and Red Jacket concluded in little more than the Seneca orator's haughtily bringing one of his blanket-covered arms over the other, spitting in the direction of the Mohawk council house, turning on his heel, and joining the others, who by this time had already started up the forest trail to return home. The deliberate wounding of the Seneca player was taken as the greatest offense, an insult to the Seneca nation, particularly so in that the Mohawk had initiated the game. Indignant and angered by this atrocity, the Seneca departed for their own country in a grand huff.

• 63

As Red Jacket paced his log house, he thought through his strategy for the upcoming meeting with the sachems and war chiefs. So far his plans had worked out exactly as he had anticipated. The selection of the Jemison son to play in the game had been at Red Jacket's urging. Secretly he disliked "the White Woman," Jemison's mother, for frequently housing and entertaining Brant when he was in the area. But at Gardeau he had witnessed firsthand her son's reputed violence, which was exactly what Shagoyewatha wanted to bring onto the Mohawk lacrosse field. (Little could he anticipate that Jemison would later in life murder two of his brothers and then die himself at the hand of another.) Even before Red Jacket had devised his scheme, he had been aware that Jemison's temper was well known throughout the community. He would naturally be a likely target for an equally violent Mohawk on the playing field. Light-skinned and fair-haired, he would stand out as the only mixed-blood on the Seneca team; that alone would be cause for trouble in the game. Red Jacket, through his contacts at Grand River, had been able to determine discreetly which player on the Mohawk team would be the most easily provoked. In a sense, the two players served as proxies for Shagoyewatha and the detestable Thayendanegea. The incident and Red Jacket's machinations leading to it underlined the enmity between the two leaders.

Thirty-one years old but still living at home, John Jemison—as his mother had been quick to point out—was an accomplished lacrosse player, so it had not been difficult for Red Jacket to encourage him to try out for the team. And Red Jacket actually had had to do little to convince Cornplanter, himself fathered by a Dutchman, that Jemison, despite his mixed blood, would serve the Seneca proudly on the playing field. Nevertheless, others in the community were slightly apprehensive when they heard he had been selected to play, for they knew that his aggressive behavior in the game often led to fighting. Red Jacket had done what he could to dispel their concerns, however, and in the end Jemison made the final cut for the team.

Red Jacket chuckled to himself as he recalled what had led up to the incident in the game. On the journey to Grand River he had quietly advised Jemison on a certain "stick adjustment." Jemison had listened attentively when Red Jacket gave him explicit instructions on the technique. When dogging an opponent who had the ball, one of the surest means of making him drop it was to hook into the lacing on the back of his crosse with the protruding end of your crook and give it a sharp twist. This invariably caused the opponent to lose control of his stick or at least to tilt the plane of the webbing, dumping the ball on the ground. The sharpened end of Jemison's own stick had enhanced its "grabbing" ability and ensured that the maneuver would work.

Red Jacket had also indulged in further chicanery. Before the game managers had paired off the players, he had secretly bribed one of them to pit Jemison against the Mohawk player that he had determined was most prone to violence. He gave as a reason that the two were interested in the same Seneca girl from Grand River (neglecting to mention that Jemison was married) and that she would be attending the game, so each would play his best to demonstrate his affections for her. The game manager was happy to take the bribe, amused at the reason, and eager to witness the outcome. So easily had it been set up that Red Jacket applauded himself for his cunning.

Once the game began, things took their natural course. Jemison and his Mohawk opponent played vigorously against each other from the start. There was considerably more shoving, slashing, and body checking between these two than between other players on the field. The Mohawk was a strong player, and his teammates passed the ball to him frequently, as he was reputed to have the best shot against any goal defenders. But each time he seemed ready to run with the ball, Jemison managed to hook into his webbing and force him to drop it. The Mohawk's frustration at this constant interference progressed from annoyance to exasperation as the game went on. Several times Jemison twisted his stick with such force that the stick was knocked out of the Mohawk's hands and left dangling like a fish on a hook at the end of Jemison's sharpened crook. At one point, when it appeared as though the referees were approaching him to examine his game equipment, Jemison quickly "unhooked" his prize, let the Mohawk stick fall on the ground, and walked away, thus avoiding the officials. Another time that Jemison pulled the maneuver, he crashed into the backside of the Mohawk as well, ending up not only with the Mohawk stick attached to his but also with the opposing player sprawled facedown on the field. There were moments when it appeared that the referees were about to interfere and perhaps even suggest that Jemison be ejected from the game, but fortunately for Red Jacket, that never happened and the game continued. So the "incident" was perhaps inevitable.

The most damage done was really to Seneca sensitivity and pride. Jemison had a bloody nose for a while and a few scratches on his face, but they were minor injuries, the sort that one expected in a lacrosse game. The two players were really surrogates in the endless battle between Red Jacket and Brant, and Red Jacket had won this skirmish.

After his altercation with Brant following the game, Red Jacket stormed off the field and headed home, expressing his pretended indignation loudly and openly to anyone who would listen. On the journey back to Buffalo Creek his incessant angry remarks seemed to have their intended effect. He knew that his power of speech was great, that he could inflame warriors to action. In this case, he was certain that he had not only caused Brant considerable embarrassment but had also afforded himself the opportunity to carry things even further. Now the council was about to meet and would hear his demands to avenge the insult that the Mohawk had inflicted on the Seneca. He would propose nothing short of war to satisfy this injustice. This was brinkmanship at its best.

The forthcoming meeting would require his oratorical skills to be finely honed. Anything he could do to weaken the despicable Brant was worth a try. He was secretly jealous of the Mohawk's power, the fact that he was literate and could speak English and French, and that he was so highly regarded as a war chief. He was just as aware that Brant considered him a coward and openly expressed that opinion. Red Jacket had painful memories of a dinner hosted by Thomas Morris, the Philadelphia financier, who was speculating with the Dutch over Seneca lands. The dinner was attended by Brant, Red Jacket, and Cornplanter, the Allegany chief and half brother of Handsome Lake. At the time, fulminating for war, Red Jacket could scarcely have predicted that Handsome Lake, after a series of visions five years later, would emerge as the messenger of peace, establishing a new religious code and asking warriors to put aside their war clubs and to cease shaking hands together at dances. Red Jacket remembered his own embarrassment when Brant began telling amusing stories and deliberately brought up the one about "Cowkiller." Brant had delighted in spreading the rumor that Red Jacket was able to send Seneca warriors off to battle while he stayed at home and secretly butchered their cows for his own use. So when Brant told the story of an anonymous Seneca chief called Cowkiller, only the three Indians present knew to whom he referred. Cornplanter and the others all laughed at the tale, as did Red Jacket to cover his embarrassment, but it was the sort of public humiliation he expected from Brant. For his part, Red Jacket did all he could to frustrate Brant at every turn as well. And so the two had battled for years.

In the three weeks since the game at Grand River, Red Jacket had had plenty of opportunity to keep Seneca feelings against the Mohawk at a fever pitch. He anticipated that he would need community support to propose war against the Mohawk. For the moment, he had swayed even Cornplanter to his way of thinking. As a close friend of the Jemisons, Cornplanter was disturbed by the deliberate injury inflicted on Mary's son, so he was prone to side with Red Jacket on the issue of demanding some compensation from the Mohawk for the incident. But warfare? Red Jacket knew he would have to be at his eloquent best that afternoon before the council.

Once the council fire was burning and others had had their say on the matter, it was Red Jacket's turn to address the assembly. His eloquence in oratory had led his people to call him "He-keeps-them-awake," and so he would, as he launched into his tirade. Spreading his arms, be began:

> KINDRED: We must ask ourselves why the Mohawk wished us to come the distance to Grand River only to insult our players. Is it not that Thayendanegea, so full of ambition and used to having his way in all matters, was arrogantly trying to demean the great Seneca nation? Did we not come in peace to play a national game in a spirit of friendship and brotherhood, only to be handed this great insult? Does the great Captain Brant have so little control over his people that he allows them to run recklessly on the lacrosse field, injuring and maiming opponents at will? Is it not as though he were still attacking Americans that he would send a dog of a player onto the field to do injustice to one of our finest? Was he not accorded the privilege of addressing his players before the game and reminding them to play fairly, to keep physical combat at a minimum?

He paced back and forth before the council. Had it been a century later and had he been a white man, Red Jacket would have made a superb trial lawyer. The jury now awaited his next point, so he reached into his arsenal of incidents for the correct analogy:

> KINDRED: We must remind ourselves that we once went to war with the Erie people over a similar insult suffered while playing our ancestral sport, and that we finally won on the battlefield what we had lost in the game, driving those curs from our country forever. Should we not at least remind our Mohawk brothers that we are prepared to carry out such action again? That they are weakened from fighting Americans and that we would surely overpower them, that their great leader seems ever to care more for his friendship with the British than with the Confederacy, that we are aware of his intentions to bring the Anglican church to Grand River and weaken his people's belief in our traditional religious practices? Will we never see the white dog sacrificed at Grand River upon the new year, or our annual celebrations to honor the harvest of the Three Sisters, our corn, beans, and squash which were given us by the Great Spirit?
> KINDRED: We have no recourse but to demand satisfaction from the Mohawk for the affront of their lacrosse player. We must make our case known to them.

And so it was that Red Jacket persuaded the Seneca to send runners to the Mohawk to complain in the strongest terms about the incident in the game and to threaten war with them if the insult were not satisfied. Meanwhile, Brant, knowing his player had been in the wrong, had convened his council of chiefs and braced them for a strong Seneca reaction. Upon receiving the message from the Seneca council, the Mohawk sent the Seneca runners back with a proposal for a joint council of chiefs to settle all grievances over the matter.

While most leaders of the Seneca approved of this, having attended the voices of calm from Cornplanter and the older chiefs, Red Jacket continued to protest and was in fact meeting secretly with the younger warriors to inflame them to action, once again overstepping his bounds. The council of the two nations took place, despite his displeasure at the arrangement. A reconciliation was worked out, the peace pipe smoked, and all in attendance departed as friends and brothers in the great Iroquois Confederacy—all save Red Jacket, who retired from the council and was drunk for several days.

As late fall approached, however, Red Jacket had more important matters on his mind. The forthcoming meeting with Pickering at Canandaigua to draft the treaty recognizing Seneca land ownership was crucial to Indian interests. Red Jacket could not trust Cornplanter and the Allegany delegation to resist American pressure on the Seneca to negotiate with Morris over relinquishing title to Seneca lands. Pickering was going to be tricky, and Red Jacket knew he would have to draw on all his powers of intellect and oratory to keep him in line. As leader of the Buffalo Creek contingent in the talks, Shagoyewatha already had in mind how he would safeguard Seneca interests in drawing up the treaty.

• 67

It was while he was at Canandaigua that Red Jacket encountered Mary Jemison, who was there to represent her interests and protect her small property at Gardeau on the Genesee River. It was the first time he had seen her since "the incident," and she was eager to find out what measures, if any, were being taken to defend the honor of her son. The injury had not dampened John's enthusiasm for lacrosse, and he was even then at Squawky Hill playing in the late-fall games. Red Jacket was too proud to admit his lack of success in persuading the Seneca to go to war over the affair, so he simply denigrated the incident and promised Mary that he would be a spokesman for her property interests when it came time to work out the final terms of the treaty. Neither of them could have foretold that ten generations later, one of Mary's descendants would take up the lacrosse stick at Canandaigua to perpetuate the traditional game of the Iroquois (see Figure 70). For his part, Shagoyewatha, satisfied with its terms, signed the treaty while wearing a new scarlet coat, presented to him by the interpreter. The old red jacket had long since worn out, and the Americans wished to perpetuate the name that the British had bestowed upon the Seneca orator when they gave him the original garment.

As part of the reconciliation over the lacrosse incident, the Seneca and the Mohawk agreed to another game at the national level, which ultimately took place three summers later, in 1797. It was in the nature of a "rematch," as this time the Seneca were the challengers. But to soothe bad feelings that had lingered from the 1794 game, it was agreed to put the contest off for a while and to play once again at Grand River, as a gesture of goodwill on the part of the Mohawk, who again acted as hosts. Given the great attention to the rematch, the number of Seneca who attended doubled, betting was at its peak, with nearly $2,000 worth of goods piled high on the blankets as prizes, and more than five hundred players stood ready for action on each side. Team strength was increased accordingly, so that sixty were playing on a side at one time. Every twenty minutes they were relieved by another squad of substitutes, so that all had a chance to play. The game was hotly contested, but in the end, after three days of play, the Seneca scored the winning goal and collected their rewards, having humbled the once proud Mohawk.

This outcome was, of course, more than enough to avenge the foul committed in the earlier game. But the Seneca victory, sweet as it was, did little to put out the fire that continued to smolder in Red Jacket's breast, as he began to work out his plans for an ultimate assault on his archrival Brant's power and authority.

Once again Red Jacket had failed, but personal grudges between Iroquois leaders soon became irrelevant, as the relentless tide of white settlers, dishonest land speculators, and other frontier cheaters and swashbucklers inundated and destroyed the former homelands of the once great Iroquois Confederacy. Within two centuries the little land that was left for the Mohawk would be crisscrossed by power lines and freeways leading to Manhattan Island, while the Seneca would see their rivers plugged with dams and be forced to relocate. Any thought of a rematch to the 1797 game between the two nations soon disappeared.

4 The Bishop's Crook and Other Misnomers

How finely can we bring into focus the details of the 1794 Iroquois lacrosse game played by the Seneca against the Mohawk? What techniques did Jemison and his teammates use in passing or carrying the ball or retrieving it from the ground? How did the Mohawk ballcarrier maneuver around a phalanx of Seneca defenders to score? Unfortunately for the history of the sport, we have little published information about Iroquois lacrosse techniques from the last decade of the eighteenth century—no George Beers to tell us in 1869 what the Mohawk game looked like then, no Bob Scott in 1976 to describe in detail what the Indian game has evolved into today. Europeans and, later, Americans were clearly fascinated with this violent team sport, but, like Father Le Mercier, they failed to record much of anything about how it was played. True, in their reports they tell us where, when, and by whom Indian lacrosse was played, providing rough measurements of field size, the numbers that made up a team, and the time of day the reporter witnessed his first game. But beyond generalized descriptions of the impressive mass action and the resultant injuries, they say almost nothing about stick handling. Luckily some very old sticks have been preserved in collections, such as the Cayuga example at the University of Pennsylvania and Seneca sticks of the early nineteenth century obtained by Lewis Henry Morgan. They show a great uniformity in the Iroquois stick from one nation to the next at that time. Compared with Mohawk and Tuscarora wooden sticks still being made, it is clear that the general shape of the Iroquois stick has remained the same for almost two centuries. Is it possible that one of the sticks in Morgan's collection was on the field at Grand River in the 1794 game or the 1797 rematch?

In trying to reconstruct a history of Indian lacrosse, we are hampered by the nature of early European accounts. Attempting to inform their readers back home, they invariably related this strange "New World" game to various European stickball games with which they were familiar, but which employed unquestionably different techniques. We find lacrosse called a "game . . . managed with a Batoon and a Ball, [which] resembles our Trap-ball" or "a kynde of exercise . . . much like that which boyes call bandy [a form of field hockey] in English," or "nothing more than a game which was often played . . . in school-boy days, and which was called '*shinny.*'"[1]

The most frequent comparison was to tennis, widely known to Europeans after its invention by French clergy and nobility in the thirteenth century. One of the earliest explorers in North America, Peter Martyr, noted in his *De Orbe Novo* that the Indians "love games, especially tennis." Eighteenth-century chroniclers continued the tennis analogy. The explorer Jonathan Carver in his *Travels* (1781), in a subchapter describing Indian sports in the western Great Lakes area, wrote: "They amuse themselves at several sorts of games, but the principal and most esteemed among them is that of the ball, which is not unlike the European game of tennis." If not likened to tennis, lacrosse might be compared to some similar game, such as "battledore and shuttlecock"—a forerunner of badminton.[2]

Why Europeans found lacrosse similar to tennis, a one-on-one game confined to a small court, is not clear. As the most prominent team sport they encountered in America, lacrosse, unlike tennis, involved large numbers playing over wide areas. Possibly the common characteristic that a ball was tossed back and forth with netted racquets led to the comparison; conceivably, the techniques used in lacrosse when Europeans first arrived might have involved batting rather than throwing the ball. The sticks of that period could well have been racquets with taut surfaces rather than the pockets of later Indian sticks. Even recently, a Seneca elder described "the older" form of their stick as having webbing so taut that the player had to stop the ball in mid-air with his racquet, pick it up off the ground with the stick, toss it back in the air, and bat it to a teammate. Such a technique seems plausible with the densely woven webbing of a surviving Passamaquoddy stick from the 1870s (see Figure 21a).[3]

In any case, the tennis analogy persisted into the early twentieth century, when the association of lacrosse with tennis led to brief histories of the game being appended to standard tennis manuals. These poorly researched accounts do little justice to the Indian sport, often reinforcing earlier errors and misnomers and jumping to misinformed conclusions. Typical is William H. Maddren's five-page "history" of lacrosse, appended to J. Parmly Paret's *Lawn Tennis: Its Past, Present, and Future* (1904), in which he makes the following preposterous assertion: "So seriously was a defeat taken to heart that often a warrior would take his own life rather than face the derision of his people, and many would take a solemn oath before a [lacrosse] game to die by his own hand if not victorious." Such statements, totally without substantiation, are simply part of the lore of non-Indians, built on the fictions of earlier writers. Maddren's history, for instance, is clearly little more that a generalized rehash of lacrosse descriptions published by George Catlin, an artist on the frontier in the 1830s.[4]

Tennis, bandy, shinny—these were the English games to which lacrosse was compared, but it was the French who gave lacrosse its name, and there has been considerable speculation on why and when that happened. The earliest published use of the term *lacrosse* for the Indian sport appears in the reports of missionaries among the Huron in the 1630s, like Father Le Mercier, who lived in what is today southeastern Ontario, specifically the area near Thunder Bay. (The Reverend Jean de Brébeuf was the first [1636] to use the word in print.) Some sports scholars have traced the origins of the name to an early French folk football game called *la soule* (var. *choule*), which French colonists had brought to Quebec. In the fourteenth century *soule* was first played with curved sticks, and possibly colonists saw some resemblance between the Indian racquet and their own sticks. But some assert that the French named the game lacrosse because the long handle of the racquet, ending in a sort of hook, resembled a bishop's crosier, or crook. This erroneous assertion finds its way repeatedly into writings on the origin of lacrosse.[5]

To assign any ecclesiastical association to the lacrosse stick is pure folk etymology with little linguistic support. Before the exploration of America, most French curved game racquets, such as different kinds of shinny sticks, were called *crosses*. (The hockey stick and golf club, as well as the game of cricket in some parts of France, are even today called *crosse*.) In fact, more than a century before the Jesuits published the name, a game dating to the thirteenth century called "*la crosse*" and played with a ball and a curved stick was mentioned in Rabelais's *Gargantua* (1534). Thus the expression *jouer à la crosse* was in common use in France to describe playing *any* game with a curved stick and ball long before Frenchmen began to explore North America, discover the sports of its inhabitants, and report home on them.[6]

Alexander M. Weyand and Milton R. Roberts put forward a more interesting speculation in their *Lacrosse Story* (1965). The authors point out, correctly, that the French used "*lacrosse*" generically to describe any Indian stickball game. They suggest some relationship between a type of stick adopted by Indians in the Montreal area and the French perception of its resemblance to a snowshoe, for they began to call both by the same name, *raquette*. Since the earliest French settlers had used the term *lacrosse*, the authors conclude that "the long and large netted stick was of later development."[7] But the term *raquette* was also used in 1721 by Charlevoix to describe the Miami Indian Great Lakes variety of stick and more recently by French Creoles, who adopted the southeastern double-stick version of the game. Neither of those two types of sticks has much webbing—certainly not enough to justify any comparison with the intricate rawhide weaving on Indian snowshoes.

English and French terms try to describe what the basic equipment looked like but provide little information regarding stick handling, and native terminology only hints at it. The various Algonquian-language names for lacrosse, for instance, all derive from the verb stem (morpheme) that means "to hit with something"; that they are so widespread geographically suggests that the term and probably the stick and techniques for using it have existed for some time. In Ojibwe (Ontario, Wisconsin, Minnesota) it is *baaga'adowe* ("plays lacrosse"); in Potawatomi (Kansas, Wisconsin), *peki'twewin*; in Nipissing (forty miles north of Quebec), *pakatowan*; and in Fox (Iowa), *pa:kahatowe:wa*. All of these words begin with linguistically related Algonquian forms of the verb stem meaning "to hit." Iroquoian languages use a comparable term for lacrosse. In Onondaga it is *dehuntshigwa'es,* meaning "they (men) hit a rounded object." This word and variants of it in other Iroquoian tongues have been incorrectly translated in the past as "hitting with the hips," or "bump hips"—presumably, as one writer was told, a reference to the "boisterous character" of the game. This interpretation is another example of folk etymology, as is the incorrect translation of the Cayuga word for lacrosse as "beating the mush," which simply refers to the meal provided the winners by the losers (corn mush being an Iroquoian staple).[8]

Because nomenclature is of little help in explaining historical techniques of Indian lacrosse, our only recourse is to examine the sticks and balls used in games of the past that now survive in museums and private collections, or as family heirlooms. By adding what can be gleaned from historical accounts and a judicious assessment of historical photographs and illustrations, we can make educated guesses about the style of play prevalent when Europeans first encountered lacrosse in North America.

Ballistas and Cannonshot

Indian lacrosse balls were of two kinds—solid (mostly wooden) balls and lighter, resilient (usually stuffed-buckskin) balls. One generalization can be made: The hard, solid balls were not found among the southeastern tribes, who regularly used a small hide ball and whose relatively fragile sticks with minimal webbing could not have withstood the punishment of a wooden ball.

Linguistic evidence supports an early and close connection between the wooden ball and the manner in which it was made. Baraga's *Dictionary of the Otchipwe Language* gives the word *pikwak-wad*, "play-ball," as synonymous with "knob on a tree"—which is precisely what the Ojibwe used to make their balls. A knot of wood was charred and the burnt portion scraped away to shape the ball. Sometimes the ball was perforated, causing it to whistle when thrown. The Dakota, like the Ojibwe, used a rounded knot of wood or even *clay*, covered with hide and believed to have supernatural power.[1]

Decoration of the wooden ball included painting in one color or in two, one covering each half. If the ball was made of softer wood, designs might be etched on its exterior. Johann Kohl, on Madeline Island in 1855, watched Ojibwe carving sticks and balls in the woods: "The balls are made of white willow, and cut perfectly round with the hand: crosses, stars, and circles are carved upon them."[2]

Hide-covered balls were of two types—those sewn shut after being filled and the larger, more bag-shaped ball that closed with a sort of drawstring. The first kind came in several sizes, and a wide variety of material was used to stuff them. For example, Jonathan Carver in his *Travels* (1766–68) in the western Great Lakes area described them as slightly bigger than tennis balls, made of deerskin

Figure 17 • Choctaw
towa (lacrosse ball),
one and a half inches in
diameter, collected
from Robert Henry, a
leading ball player and
lacrosse conjurer,
around 1933, near Phil-
adelphia, Mississippi.
The ball is made of rags
covered with lattice-
work buckskin strips.

moistened "to render [them] supple." The lacrosse ball was "stuffed hard with the hair of the same creature, and sewn with its sinews." Some skin balls, such as those of the Choctaw (Figure 17), were made of interwoven strips of hide. Apparently the Mohawk at the end of the eighteenth century used similar balls. In his biography of Joseph Brant, William Stone described the Iroquois ball as "formed of net-work, woven of thongs of untanned deer-skin, strained to the tension of tight elasticity." Although the Huron had stopped playing lacrosse by the mid-nineteenth century, those of Lorette (near Quebec) around 1820 used a ball of worsted covered with buckskin.[3]

The softer, smaller balls were stuffed with "roe-skins," punk, fungus, bear sinews, tightly wound yarn, and woolen rags, with the stuffing always densely compacted. Usually the cover was moistened before being stuffed and then sewn shut with deer sinews or thread in the manner of a modern baseball. As it dried, the cover shrank, further compressing the filling. Although these skin balls are light-weight compared with the wooden ball, they could be very hard and quite capable of injuring a player.[4]

Some lacrosse balls made by specialists or medicine men were said to have special magical properties affecting their performance. Among the Mexican Kickapoo, the making of the ball was entrusted to a member of the Eagle clan. Using a new piece of buckskin eight inches in diameter, he folded the edges toward the center about half an inch, basted the seam with heavy thread, stuffed it with deer hair, and pulled the thread to close the opening. Following a game, the ball was disposed of by the captain of the winning team, who threw it far into the hills. If children found it, they could keep it and use it for play, but without lacrosse sticks and only after all adoption ceremonies were terminated and the summer houses occupied. Choctaw medicine men were hired to make a ball "that was sure to go straight," and each had his ball of a different color. Another type of Choctaw medicine ball was one described as having a long tail tied to it "that impedes their opponents in throwing it against the wind." Menominee made special balls according to dream instructions, such as inserting a sturgeon bone in the core.[5]

Lacrosse balls for use in certain ritual games continue to be surrounded with ceremony. For example, at the conclusion of the Oklahoma Creek Green Corn Ceremony, in preparation for the special lacrosse match marking the end of the summer ceremonial cycle, there is a special blessing ritual for the balls to be used in the game. After the players' final circling of the ceremonial fire, the medicine man leads the line of players away from the square while he holds two balls (about the size of golf balls) connected by a leather thong and dangling from a stick. The players form two lines behind him while

Figure 18 • Pair of
Mississippi Choctaw
lacrosse sticks
(pre-1934).

he leads a call-and-response chant. The balls have been filled with herbal medicines especially prepared by the town chief or medicine-maker. The man holding the balls makes a wailing sound for a brief period. Then his assistant, with eyes directed to the ground, lets out a long, rising wail, which is concluded with all players letting out a war whoop. This is followed in unison by "huh, huh, huh, huh" exclamations, as players bang their lacrosse sticks together and depart for the ball field.

Upon arriving at the field, the medicine man, still holding the stick from which the balls hang, leads his team counterclockwise around the goal for several minutes, while beginning another call-and-response chant. After a few moments they stop behind the goal, and the medicine man holds the balls aloft as the team moves in front of the goal to line up on the field in preparation for play.

There has always been an inseparable relationship between lacrosse balls and the construction of the sticks used to throw, catch, scoop, and carry them. The first to document Indian lacrosse sticks compared them to European material objects. For example, the English naturalist and social historian William Bartram about 1790 likened them to "a racquet or hurl, which is an implement of very curious construction, somewhat resembling a ladle or little hoop net." I. P. Evans offered a similar comparison in the early nineteenth century, calling Cherokee sticks "bats, resembling large ladles." Or, further confusing what they looked like, the chroniclers might incorporate an analogy to the human body in their description: The explorer Jonathan Carver in the late eighteenth century observed that at the end of the lacrosse stick common to that region was "fixed a kind of racket, resembling the palm of the hand."[6]

Early descriptions aside, all known examples of Indian lacrosse sticks fall into one of two categories: those with pockets completely enclosed by wood and those with unenclosed pockets. The enclosed variety were sticks used either in pairs or singly. These divisions conform as well to geographic areas that, for convenience of discussion, may be defined as the southeastern, Great Lakes (especially western), and Iroquois (St. Lawrence Lowlands) regions. Southeastern tribes—Cherokee, Creek, Yuchi, Seminole, Choctaw, and others—used paired sticks, one in each hand (Figure 18). The unenclosed single stick was used by Indians in the northeast on both sides of the Canadian/American border, principally the Iroquois, but also Algonquian tribes further east—the Passamaquoddy, for instance. This type of stick was adopted by non-Indian players in Montreal around the mid-nineteenth century and eventually evolved into the "officially" recognized stick popularly known to lacrosse players on high school and college campuses today.

Of the three stick types, the southeastern, made of hickory, is the shortest, averaging about two to two and a half feet long. Its length is appropriate to the technique used in ball handling. In the double-stick form of lacrosse, players carry the ball cupped between the pockets of each stick (Figure 19). The sticks are made in pairs, often with one pocket slightly smaller than the other, so that when a ball is cradled between them, the smaller pocket fits into the larger one, thus securing the ball. The difference in pocket size accounts for a slight difference in length; the stick with the smaller pocket is slightly shorter—perhaps as little as half a centimeter. If the pockets and sticks of a pair are identical in size and length, like those of the Eastern Cherokee, a ballcarrier may run with the two sticks simply clamped together and held in one hand. To control and guard the ball, the player keeps the stick as close to his body as possible. This most likely explains the relative shortness of these sticks, as opposed to the northern types, for which both hands control a single handle.

To prevent the ball's falling through the cup end of the stick, strands of lacing are inserted through holes in the cup to form the

• 77

Figure 19 • Ballcarrier crosses wrists to secure ball in a 1981 Mississippi Choctaw game.

pocket on each stick (see Appendix B). Today lacing is made from commercial leather, but formerly a variety of materials, both animal and vegetal, were selected. For example, twisted bark seems to have been used by the Eastern Cherokee for pocket lacing through the last half of the nineteenth century. Anthropologist James Mooney related an incident that occurred in 1863, in which a group of Cherokee Civil War volunteers became bored with guarding a bridge in Tennessee and decided to mount a lacrosse game. Lacking sticks, they made them on the spot: "Soon all hands were at work . . . shaping the hickory sticks, and twisting the bark for netting." The durability of such lacing material was so minimal that, as a rule, replacement strings were prepared before games in case they were needed.[7]

While a player could order a pair of southeastern sticks from a recognized maker, most males knew the craft, and many made their own, which accounts for the differences in stick lengths. Some variation is attributable to the traditional Indian practice of using parts of the body to measure things. Just as woodlands Indians placed the finger holes in flutes at the point where the player's fingers naturally fell or used the span between the thumb and little finger to determine rib distance in canoe measurements, Moses Owl of Birdtown on the Eastern Cherokee Reservation in North Carolina stated that the ideal length for lacrosse sticks was the distance from the player's fingertips to the ground when his arms were at his sides. The length of the stick and the shape of the cup also depended to some degree on the position one played or on personal preference.[8]

Like all lacrosse sticks, those of the southeast usually were decorated in some manner. Much depended on the taste of the owner, who might etch or burn some design on the stick's surface. Eastern Cherokee sticks typically have serrated notches burned along the tops of their cups; they were sometimes burnished in the fire to improve their potency. Creek sticks often had red yarn wrapped to form a bulge below the cup at the throat. Today among young Creek it is fashionable to decorate the handles of their sticks by wrapping them with black electrical tape; silver duct tape is another popular ornament.[9]

The lacrosse stick itself came to be used as a symbol applied to other material items of southeastern Indian culture and as a substitute for ritual props. When the Mississippi Choctaw revived a "national costume" in the 1960s, many of the decorations were designs cut out and appliquéd on shirts and dresses. One such design was a Saint Andrew's cross, interpreted recently as deriving from the lacrosse game: After a game, players hung their sticks on the wall crossed in the Saint Andrew's manner to say, "May our paths cross

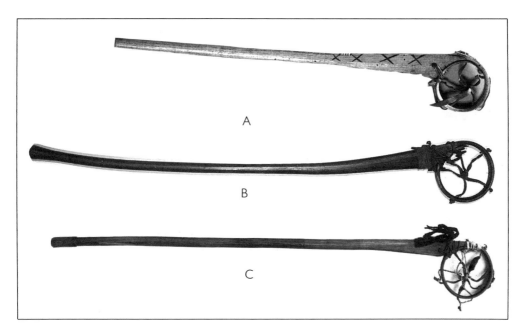

A

B

C

again and again."[10] In today's Creek Buffalo Dance, the leader ordinarily carries a cane, carved to terminate in a buffalo hoof; lacking such a cane, he may carry lacrosse sticks as ritual props to represent the front legs of the animal.

Like the southeastern tribes, the groups living in the woodlands that surrounded the western Great Lakes used a stick with an enclosed pocket (Figures 20a, b, c). These tribes included the Ojibwe, Menominee, Potawatomi, Saulteaux, Miami, Sauk and Fox, Winnebago, and eastern bands of Dakota (Sioux). Although the Dakota lived principally on the prairies and plains rather than in the woodlands at the time of contact, they had occupied territories farther east but had been forced west by the Ojibwe during the fur trade. From centuries of contact with their woodland neighbors—warfare, intermarriage, communal dances and games in periods of peace—the eastern bands of the Dakota shared many woodland cultural and ceremonial traits. The apparent absence of lacrosse among the western Dakota suggests that the eastern Sioux, such as the Santee, learned the game from the Ojibwe.

The major distinctions between southeastern and Great Lakes sticks lie in the number of sticks used per player, their size, and the pocket construction. Like the Iroquois, players from these tribes used only one stick. Slightly longer than southeastern sticks, Great Lakes examples show a remarkable degree of uniformity in size and

Figure 20a • (Probably) Minnesota Ojibwe lacrosse stick, 21.5 inches long, collected by aristocrat explorer Giacomo Constantino Beltrami, in 1823. This beautiful specimen, in pristine condition, is perhaps the oldest surviving American Indian lacrosse stick.

Figure 20b • Fox (Mesquakie) lacrosse stick, 25.5 inches long, from Tama, Iowa.

Figure 20c • Lacrosse stick from the Menominee Reservation, collected by anthropologist Alanson Skinner, probably about 1916.

shape over a large geographic area and time span, averaging three feet in length.[11] That there were some longer sticks may be attributed to the practice by some makers of leaving the stick long so that the player could cut it to his own desired length. The few craftsmen still actively making the Great Lakes stick—mostly to sell to tourists— follow the same design and proportions.

Unlike the oval or tear-shaped pockets of the southeastern stick, the Great Lakes pocket is round, about four or five inches in diameter. The cup is formed by thinning the unfinished wooden blank at one end, steaming it and bending it around inside the shaft to form a circle (see Appendix B). Butting against the shaft, it is secured by binding or lashing it with rawhide. The lacing, like that of pockets in the south, is inserted through holes drilled through the cup, producing a pocket roughly two and a half to three inches deep. Because the wooden balls used with this stick were about four inches in diameter, the pocket was made to encompass them without much extra room. Resting on the webbing, a ball might have only a third of its diameter protruding from the pocket. With proper cradling, it was fairly secure for running; snugly fit into the cavity of the pocket, it could be thrown with considerable accuracy and force. Great Lakes sticks were known for their hurling capacity, particularly when both hands were used in an overhead shot. And the distance was matched by accuracy. In 1970 I saw a sixty-year-old Ojibwe former player who was long out of practice hit a targeted tree at thirty yards.

Like their southeastern counterparts, many Great Lakes sticks were decorated. Menominee and Ojibwe sometimes cut deep, serrated grooves along the inner side of the handle—a design pattern also found on their ceremonial drumsticks and war rattles. Wilbur Blackdeer, a Winnebago stickmaker, applies occasional splotchy burn marks to the handles in no particular order—"just for decoration," he says. Franklin Basina, a Red Cliff Ojibwe, insists, however, that most ordinary sticks that he was familiar with were not decorated because they were often broken in games and discarded: "Some guys would [decorate their sticks] . . . like they're going to a big powwow or something, where you dance and all of that, it's all decorated, but in the regular game they're just plain . . . they wouldn't decorate them for show." And, just as the Great Lakes stick might have decoration applied to it, the stick image itself was used as a design element on other material objects of the region. A thirty-one-inch Menominee canoe paddle, for instance, has etched on it two lacrosse sticks facing each other just where the paddle blade begins beyond the handle; the other side is carved with floral patterns typical of woodlands art.[12]

The largest of the three types of lacrosse sticks is the Iroquois, the progenitor of all modern forms of "regulation" lacrosse sticks, both wooden and plastic. Like the Great Lakes variety, it is a single stick, distinguished from the former in that the pocket is not fully enclosed in wood. The shaft of the stick is bent to form a crook at its end, and the webbing begins with an outside string or strand of rawhide that joins the body of the handle—in nineteenth-century examples as far as halfway down its length or more. The webbing is considerably more densely laced and more elaborate than that of the other two types—certainly more taut. It fills in the entire triangular area formed by the crook and the outside string (later guard-strings or gut-wall) (Figure 21b).

The greatest distinction among Iroquois sticks is in the tautness of their webbing, a key factor in stick handling. Changes in the webbing over time reflect changes in the game and techniques. The earlier known sticks had much more loosely woven webbing, although examples to the east of the Iroquois have been described as very taut (see Figure 21a).

The key change over time in the Iroquois stick is the gradual evolution of a true pocket. Three Cayuga examples show the changes in stick style over three generations of the same family and provide a survey of this development over at least a century. They were collected by anthropologist Frank Speck in the 1930s from Alexander T. General (Deskaheh in his language), a chief of the League of Iroquois. The oldest stick of the three belonged to his grandfather, who died in 1845, although I take the stick to be considerably older (see Figure 1).

This type of stick was in use until about 1860. It has no guard-strings, indicating that juggling skills were vital to retaining possession of the ball. Other Iroquois sticks of the same period, such as Seneca sticks collected about 1825 by Morgan, are similar and have their outermost string anchored in a groove incised around the end of the crook. The outermost string is tied around the groove and brought down to another groove on the handle, much in the manner of stringing a bow. The webbing is woven into a flat surface, with the outermost string on the same plane as the others. Balancing or cradling a ball on the slightly taut surface must have been a feat: The only "wall" was the side of the bent portion that rose a bit above the

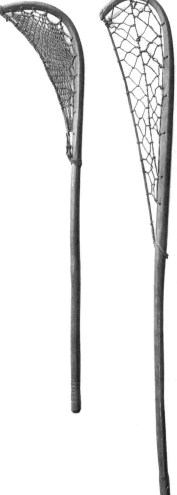

Figure 21a • Left: Passamaquoddy lacrosse stick (pre-1872) from Pleasant Point, Maine.

Figure 21b • Right: Mohawk lacrosse stick from St. Regis (Akwesasne) Reserve (pre-1875).

plane of the webbing, nearly perpendicular to the plane but scarcely useful in keeping the ball on the stick.

The stick that belonged to Alexander General's father, Isaac, represents a transitional form from the period that the Cayuga call "the middle game" (between 1860 and 1890). A large, four-foot-ten-inch stick of native manufacture, it nevertheless meets the standards for lacrosse sticks issued in the *Official Handbook* (1888). Although the webbing is flat, as in the older tradition, this Cayuga crosse was the first type to have guard-strings. Three of them at the outer edge of the webbing form at least the beginnings of a pocket, although there is still no sag near the throat. Not as dished as the modern stick, it could still serve to scoop a ground ball.

Deskaheh's own 1932 "modern" type of stick also met handbook regulations. Smaller than his father's, it measures three feet five inches and has a six-and-a-half-inch crook. The webbing meets the shaft twenty-five inches from the butt end, providing the player nearly ten inches more handle room than was available on his father's stick. Its wall is a sloped triangle in section, and the crosse is shovel-like in form. The thin and flattened crook facilitated its scooping capacity.

The newest feature on this stick is a real pocket. It retains the three guard-strings of the transitional stick and uses lengthwise runners of oil-tanned commercial leather, crossed by and interwoven with rawhide. The stick's pocket has been pressed and molded, probably by the owner's fist, as is customarily done with wooden and plastic sticks today. The guard-strings and sloped wall provide well-blended sides to the pocket.

The addition of guard-strings and subsequent development of a pocket are unquestionably the result of increasing non-Indian participation in lacrosse. Guard-strings had been required by the official handbook as early as 1880; since they covered the very tip of the crook, they were deliberately added to prevent a player from catching the webbing of an opponent's stick with the (formerly) protruding end of the crook—an action permitted in Indian lacrosse. The first guard-strings were left free, not interwoven with the edge of the webbing. Once they were tied in with the webbing, providing a snug pocket, what we know as the (wooden) stick of today was complete.[13]

6 Fort Michilimackinac, 1763

"*Ahaaw!*" he yelled, "*zhigwa!*" as he charged Maji-giizhig (Bad Sky). Cradling the ball back and forth, he dodged left, then right, heading straight for Bad Sky, who had planted his feet firmly to await the attack. Makoons (Little Bear) raced toward him. Within a few feet of each other, simultaneously and abruptly, each man changed the position of his right hand on the stick. Little Bear brought his to join the left hand at the base of the handle, while Bad Sky moved his to butt against the cup end, at the same time extending the stick horizontally at arm's length and shoulder height, bracing himself for the blow. "*Whack!*" Makoons slammed his stick vertically against the crossbar provided him by Bad Sky. With the collision of sticks, the ball catapulted straight past Maji-giizhig's head and careened toward the two saplings thirty paces behind him. The force of the impact sent the perforated wooden ball whistling through the air at high speed. But Makoons's aim was still off, and the ball sailed past the left sapling about three paces short of its mark.

They had been practicing this maneuver for half an hour already, thought Makoons, as he waited for one of the young Ozaagii boys to retrieve the ball and return it. Maybe it was the Ozaagii stick he had borrowed to work out with. Sticks of those people seemed heavier and slightly longer than his own Ojibwe stick, which unfortunately still hung from the framework of his birch-bark *wiigiwaam* in his home village on the island of *mooning-wanekaaning* (the place of the yellow-shafted flickers), some two weeks west by canoe. But he still had two days to correct his aim, and he had already begun making a stick for himself according to Ojibwe dimensions, a craft he had learned from his grandfather. In fact he was working on five additional sticks for others of his tribe who, like Makoons, had arrived at the fort unaware of the secret plan of the Ojibwe. By tomorrow afternoon he and Maji-giizhig should be able to practice the maneuver using a stick he was more comfortable with. If it was still too green to withstand the blow without breaking, he had been promised the use of a well-seasoned stick that would soon be arriving in a canoe from Big Turtle Island. While trading there, he had befriended Aanakwad (Cloud), a noted warrior, who had first informed Makoons of the forthcoming game. Cloud was to bring the balls the players would use after they had been properly doctored by the medicine men. In addition to his own lacrosse stick, Aanakwad was to borrow his brother's.

These practice sessions were held at a comfortable distance from the fort, lest English patrols come upon them and instigate some alarm. The saplings had been implanted in the ground about four paces apart to serve as a target area, and Makoons's intention was to fire the ball between them. Catapulting the ball in this manner was not really a scoring technique; rather it was used to rid yourself of the ball and get it quickly downfield if you were being pressured by opponents and a teammate was close enough to hold his stick out rigidly in front of you. When Makoons and his people played *baaga'adowe,* they needed even greater precision to hit the single goalpost and score a point for their side. But for these practices, the saplings had been positioned merely to represent the width of the fort's land gate opening, and Makoons knew that he would have only one chance to fire the ball through it in the heat of the game. He was proud to have been selected by the chiefs to play such a vital role; his fame as a great ball player must have been communicated to the Ojibwe and Ozaagii chiefs almost upon his arrival at the fort.

After several more tries with Maji-giizhig and three successful launches of the ball in a row, Makoons was satisfied that he had corrected his aim enough to quit for today. Following the path through the woods back to camp, he stopped briefly to pick up a few broken sections of dead birch branches for firewood and noticed a patch of ripe strawberries that he would remember to tell his wife about. As he neared the camp clearing, Little Bear could see two columns of smoke rising above the trees and knew that hot food awaited him. Soon the large bark *wiigiwaam* came into view, and the small children of the Odaawaa family who had taken them in were noisily splashing around in the adjacent creek. Although Makoons and his wife, Boodoonh (Polywog), shared sleeping quarters with the Odaawaa, out of courtesy he had cut poles to raise a second tripod where Boodoonh could cook their own meals. A large copper kettle he had recently traded two marten skins for with the English hung over the small fire, and he could see the handle ends of six lacrosse sticks protruding from the steaming pot. By now Boodoonh must have finished burning the lacing holes into the flat ends of the sticks with her red-hot awls and was now boiling them to make the thin ends pliable enough to bend. They would be curled around into the crotches of the sticks to form the round cup, and rawhide would be lashed to hold them in place while the sticks dried.

Little Bear had been fortunate to find a white ash large enough for sticks. Most of the ash trees in the surrounding area were young saplings, too small in diameter to make a proper lacrosse stick. After felling the tree with his ax, he had cut a thick section to the proper length, which he determined by measuring with his outstretched arm plus the additional width of one hand. From the width of the tree he knew that he could get six sticks from the log. Back in camp, he cut out the rough form of each stick with more ax work and further reduced each piece with his large crooked knife. Seated cross-legged with the handle end of a stick butted against his stomach and pulling the curved blade toward him, Makoons peeled off strip after strip of ash, and the lacrosse stick began to take shape. He put the shavings to one side in a pile to dry for kindling. The task was not that hard, but it did take time. White ash was ideal for carving sticks; a strong wood with straight grain, it served the Ojibwe well for many of their utensils. It was always used to reinforce the edges of birch-bark pails and wild rice winnowing trays, as well as strengthening canoe gunwales.

The king's birthday was fast approaching, so there was some haste to complete these sticks for use in the game. Makoons knew there would be little or no time to add decorative features, such as teethlike notches carved into the interior side of the handle. The English would certainly never know that the sticks had been recently created with a purpose in mind; they would probably assume that every Indian, as a matter of course, kept a lacrosse stick handy at all times or packed it into his canoe when traveling. In any case, all the sticks would be doctored by the medicine men before the game, making them powerful weapons in the hands of the Ozaagii and Ojibwe players; should the Indian plan succeed, these quickly made sticks that Makoons now worked on would become treasured trophies for those who had played with them—passed down to future generations as family heirlooms.

Makoons pulled a stick from the kettle and gingerly began to force a bend in its end to test the pliability. Not yet, he concluded, perhaps another hour or so of soaking in boiling water; he and his wife would have to cook over the Odaawaa fire or share the other family's meal, which would probably be offered them in any case. The Odaawaa family had been more than generous in taking in Boodoonh and Makoons since the couple's arrival by canoe the previous week. The family's grandmother had recently moved south to stay with relatives at Cross Village, so there was extra sleeping room. Already a whitefish gruel was keeping warm over the Odaawaa cooking fire, and Boodoonh had earlier retrieved her *makak,* or birch-bark storage pail, where she kept a good supply of *manoomin* (wild rice): The three handfuls of rice that she had thrown in would almost double the size of the stew—their contribution to the meal. The Odaawaa considered *manoomin* a treat hard to come by, for the plant was not native to the area as was corn, their principal food, which they cultivated in large amounts at Cross Village to trade at the fort. Omanoominii or Wiin-ibiigoo from the western side of the great sea had regularly brought wild rice to trade with the French when they had commanded the fort. The Odaawaa remembered seeing pile upon pile of fawnskins packed with rice being unloaded from canoes onto the shore and carried through the water gate of the fort. But since the English had seized control from the French, trade had been drastically reduced, for the English were stingy with gifts to the Indians and refused to sell them gunpowder.

Returning the stick to the boiling kettle, Makoons joined the others around their cooking fire. As his wife bent forward to hand him the large maple ladle, her slender wrist came out from beneath the shawl to expose her recently completed shell bracelet. The shiny bone-white beads stood out against the background of her dark skin. She had been working on the bracelet in spare moments and was now proud to show it off. Makoons dipped the ladle into the kettle for some of the fish gruel. While eating, he inquired of his Odaawaa host about materials to repair his canoe. The Odaawaa tongue was fairly close to Ojibwe, so communication between the two families was not that difficult. A combination of brief spoken phrases and sign language sufficed most of the time, and each was in fact getting pleasure from learning words in the other's tongue. Conversing with the Ozaagii, however, was more difficult, and the Ojibwe relied on interpreters for most of their dealings with them—particularly the crucial preparations for the big game—to make certain that plans were coordinated down to the last detail.

Makoons had built up his hatred of the English only recently. Their arrival at La Pointe earlier in the year had abruptly changed the lifestyle of his people on *mooningwanekaaning*. Even before the English soldiers took over the fort on the island, the French had enlisted the help of Makoons and his island companions to travel almost weekly in their canoes to the mainland southeast of the island and assist in filling in the many excavations the French had made searching for copper. Not wishing the valuable coral-colored chunks of ore to fall into their conquerors' hands, the French were working at a feverish pace to disguise the mines' locations and paid the Ojibwe handsomely for their help.

The English takeover of the island had been swift and unceremonious. Makoons re-called how the new English commandant had almost immediately summoned their great chief White Bird and his *oshkaabewis* (aide) to the fort, demanded that the Indians change their trading pattern, and dictated a new set of price lists for skins at a rate less than half what the French had been paying. White Bird had protested greatly but in vain. Within a week the great chief had been replaced by the English with a younger Ojibwe, more to their liking. He was a foreigner from *baawiting* whom the English had brought with them. His large medal showing the face of the English king, which he wore around his neck in his haughty dealings with the local villagers, soon came to be a detested sight. Makoons was still resentful over the sudden fall from power of the kindly and wise White Bird. There was a score to settle with the English.

By this time, the boiling water had made the flat ends of the sticks pliable enough to curve without breaking. One by one, he removed each stick and forced the bend to coil under. Ordinarily a stick at this point in its construction would simply be put aside for a week or so to dry and hold its shape. But the upcoming game required speeding this pro-cess, so Makoons had put up a small rack near the fire from which to hang the sticks to has-ten the drying. Despite the green wood and wet rawhide, he calculated that the heat of the fire and a full day's exposure to the hot sun would make the sticks ready for finishing.

Surely not the most desirable way to make a durable lacrosse stick, thought Makoons, but these sticks would be needed only for a single game and would probably survive the rough play. Even if one or two of them were to break in the course of the game, it would only serve to amuse the English, viewed by them as an indication of the inferiority of Indian products. It might even cause them to increase their wagers during the game, bringing more of them outside the fort to marvel at the ferocity of Indian play. It was all part of the total scheme.

That evening, four leading players from each team, including Makoons and Bad Sky, the Ojibwe and Ozaagii chiefs, and interpreters, retired to a large *wiigiwaam* to plan strategies for the attack. One tall Ozaagii chief who had traded at the fort for years rolled up one of the floor mats. Removing his fur turban and putting it to one side, he flattened out an area of loose dirt and with a sharp stick began making a rough sketch of the fort's southern flank, showing clearly where the land gate was located. Bad Sky reached into his bandolier bag and brought out small pegs that he had whittled that afternoon to stick in the ground representing the players and their positions. Ordinarily these teams would have played on a field as much as a mile in length, but stables and gardens to the southeast of the fort would restrict the size of the playing area immediately outside the land gate, while hills to the southwest would prevent extending the field very far in that direction. Therefore they decided to set one of the goalposts near the base of a hill and run the length of the field in a northeasterly direction toward the shore, diagonal to the southeast corner of the fort. They would then extend it to insert the other goal beyond the platform where the English punished their soldiers or kept captives in stocks.

The Ozaagii chief, who had been mapping out on the ground while kneeling, sat upright, resting his buttocks on his heels. He reached under his sash to produce a red pipe bowl, elaborately covered with bright lead inlays. He signaled to a friend to produce the stem and fetch tobacco. The layout he had sketched seemed advantageous for several reasons: It would locate midfield just opposite the southeastern bastion and induce spectators to congregate in that vicinity, bringing them even farther from the land gate opening (Figure 22). The English would surely focus their attention on centerfield, where much of the game's most violent action would take place and where the toss-up of the ball occurred after each point scored. Being in that area would then distract the soldiers so they would not pay much attention to the fort's entrance. It might have the further advantage of luring greater numbers that far out of the fort, perhaps even around to its east side so they could gain a better vantage point from which to witness the play, especially whenever the Ojibwe were about to score or if the ball "accidentally" landed in the water.

Bad Sky was handed the lit pipe stem first and took several puffs of the aromatic smoke. The women of both tribes were to play key roles also. The plan was for most of them to be lined up along the south picket wall, where they would watch the game in the

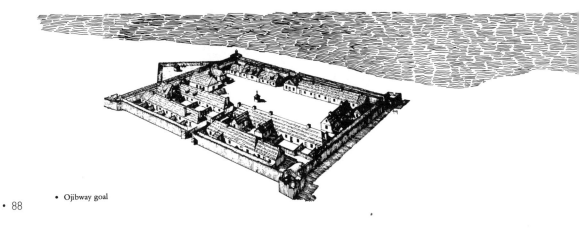

• Ojibway goal

• Centerfield

Sauk goal

Figure 22 • Bird's-eye view of Fort Michilimackinac in 1763, showing the layout of the Indian ball field.

shade. The shade would also help obscure any unusual protrusions or lumps under their blankets and shawls, where the tomahawks, knives, and war clubs would be hidden. To seem as natural as possible, some would carry babies wrapped tightly in *dikinaagan* on their backs. They would be clustered in groups to allow the English to intermingle with them, receive friendly nods, and generally become more involved in the game as they heard Indian women shout words of encouragement to players from both teams. Those women that were not carrying arms were to conceal valuable items under their shawls—beads, foxskins, trade cloth. From time to time, as a goal was scored, a woman would select a friend from the other tribe and ostentatiously make a wager with her on the sidelines, agreeing on something of equal value, the items to be held by a neutral party until the game's conclusion. The hope was that such public wagering would encourage more of the English to bet among themselves, thus involving them even more deeply in the game.

The pipe had made its round to Makoons. One woman, it was planned, would approach an English soldier through an interpreter and jokingly offer to bet him her baby. The women who carried most of the concealed arms, however, would be positioned on either side of the land gate opening. A few of them, pretending that they were being crowded out of viewing the action and that they did not wish to block the land gate opening, would back up slightly into the fort, presumably unobserved—or at least giving no cause for alarm. The remainder would actually be within the fort, casually going about their affairs or examining recently arrived trade goods.

Before this evening planning session, the two previous days had been spent in active trading by the many Odaawaa, Ozaagii, Odagaamii, Ojibwe, and Boodewaadamii who were encamped in the woods near the fort or in *wiigiwaamaak* strung along the shores of the great sea. Although they wanted to obtain as many of the small tomahawks and knives as possible from the traders, they had other reasons for their frequent visits. Since many had never been to Fort Michilimackinac before, it was important that they familiarize themselves with its interior layout, try to come up with an accurate head count of the troops garrisoned there, and distinguish between the English and the several hundred Canadian settlers who lived there and would be spared from harm. The prices of items, the stock available, and the English dress of the traders helped them determine that there were four traders and their clerks.

• 89

Arriving at an accurate assessment of the military strength of the post was another matter, however. English patrols were almost always out on reconnaissance, and reinforcements sometimes arrived unnoticed in the dead of night at the water gate, so the exact military population was never known to the Indians. Still, by pooling their observations over the past week, they guessed that between twenty and thirty-five soldiers were stationed there—certainly no more than forty. With the forty players on each team who would lead the fighting and a hundred or so women spectators, each concealing at least one weapon and usually two, they were certain to gain an early upper hand in the surprise encounter and then be quickly joined by reinforcements. Those English not immediately killed would be taken prisoner, and the Canadians, who hated the English as much as the Indians did, could definitely be counted on merely to stand by and watch the slaughter.

The trading visits had another purpose too. The Indians could view in advance the stock of items each trader had, knowing that these would be available free of charge as they plundered the supplies after the attack. The expensive silver gorgets, the large brass kettles, silver crosses in a number of shapes and sizes with designs etched on them—there was really no need for the Indians to offer their valuable skins for treasures now. They could have them at no cost after the fort was captured. Instead, they concentrated their trading on small tomahawks and knives that would be useful in the fight.

But soon the traders became unsettled at the run on these particular items and bothered by the atypical lack of Indian interest in the more expensive stock, which was going unsold. Realizing the risk, Indian families began to pool their resources of furs and purchase at least a few of these items to allay the traders' suspicions, lest their concerns be conveyed to the military. Already, it was feared, Wawatam might have tipped off an English trader he had befriended, for it was noticed that he and his wife were quickly striking camp, taking down their lodge and packing their canoe. Wawatam was a weakling, an outcast and a loner, given to sentimental musings directed toward anyone who would listen. Lacking the customary Indian backbone and unwilling to share with others—he and his wife, it was said, secretly hoarded provisions—Wawatam naturally fell in with the stingy English when they took command of the fort. So his departure was regarded with mixed feelings. Had he gotten wind of the plan and conveyed it to the trader? In any case, his absence would make the trading excursions easier to bring off.

Makoons himself had earlier attended one of these trading exchanges. A formation of about six other Ojibwe men en route to the fort suddenly appeared at the Odaawaa camp and inquired whether Makoons wished to join their trading party. As Little Bear and Polywog had only just been taken in by the Odaawaa, Makoons knew they would have need of an additional cooking kettle, so he retrieved a few marten and small beaverskins from his canoe with which to trade and followed the group as they left the clearing single file and took the narrow path that led through the woods.

The trading party was led by a tall Ojibwe named Weniway, who had told Makoons that he knew a recently arrived English trader at the fort whose exchange rates were more favorable to the Indians than those of the other traders. Weniway was originally of "the people of the falls" band of Ojibwe, who were living on Big Turtle Island to take advantage of the great fishery at *baawiting,* where they speared whitefish in great numbers each fall to smoke-dry for winter rations. It turned out that he was also a fine lacrosse player and would be on the team with Makoons. Because of his considerable height, they would use him at centerfield, for with his long reach he could easily snap up the ball in mid-air at toss-up and gain initial control for the Ojibwe. Weniway was imposing, accustomed as he was to appearing at ball games and ceremonial occasions with his upper torso painted completely black with a mixture of bear grease and charcoal and large white-clay circles painted around his eyes. With such an impressive appearance, he was fairly easy to spot in the midst of a crowd of players on a ball field, and he made a good target for an Ojibwe player to pass the ball to.

As the group neared the fort, they encountered several other trading parties of various tribes and numbers both entering and exiting the land gate. The fort was guarded by a cannon mounted in the turrets over each bastion, where several English soldiers could watch the Indians' comings and goings. Weniway continued to lead them single file directly to a house where the English trader and his clerks stored their goods and kept samples on display for Indians to choose from. As the Ojibwe entered, they found two Boodewaadamii in an argument with the trader over extending them credit, the trader insisting that they had not settled their bills from the previous season and refusing to give them more goods on account with nothing in return. They continued to prevail upon him to advance them at least a little "English milk," which the Ojibwe knew meant the deadly *ishkodewaaboo* (firewater). The trader steadfastly declined, knowing that the two Boodewaadamii had already drunk a goodly amount. More rum would only complicate his efforts to get rid of these two pests so he could begin trading with Weniway's party.

The clerks escorted the two unruly Boodewaadamii to the door, threatening to call the English soldiers if they did not depart immediately. Meanwhile, Weniway and his group seated themselves in a circle on the floor, and his pipe-bearer produced a red stone pipe bowl and a long, spiral-carved stem to which he attached the bowl. Filling it with *apaakozigan,* he lit the Indian tobacco and the pipe was passed around the room, as each in turn silently took a few puffs and handed it to the next until it finally reached the trader and his clerks, who smoked as well.

The Indians had deposited their furs along one wall and now began to examine the variety of trade goods, fingering the knives for sharpness, testing the balance of the small tomahawks, trying on silver armbands, all under the watchful eyes of the clerks. Makoons noticed a handsome silver breast gorget that, when he turned it toward the light from the window, revealed the figure of a crane etched into its center. Being of the Crane clan, Little Bear took special care to return the gorget to exactly where he had found it. The trader offered it to him for three beaverskins, but Makoons declined and asked instead after a copper kettle smaller than the one on display. The Englishman sent a clerk upstairs to get one, while he and Little Bear haggled over the price, settling at last on two marten furs.

After years of doing business with the French, Makoons and his people had become accustomed to a different style of trading. The French had always preceded each session with the customary gifts; whether of great value or not, a gift was always given, following Indian custom, and assumed to be a part of any dealings. The cursed English, however, having fought the French and Indians over Canada, which they had now controlled for three years, were quite another matter when it came to trade. The Indians contrasted the general haughtiness of the English with the more easygoing French, whose king had become their Great Father and they willingly his children. One had only to compare the French with the English lifestyle, mode of dress, and personal habits to realize that the Indians would be more comfortable in the company of Canada's former rulers. The French didn't mind if their faces became greasy and their hands grimy from hard work, and the loose-fitting shirts tied with a cord around their waists were quite similar to the buckskins the Indians wore. The English, on the other hand, seemed obsessed with the finery of their clothes and the fastidious cleansing of their skin. And they were stingy. Rarely did they offer gifts, and since the Indians had used up most of their French gunpowder supplies in fighting them, the English refused to sell "the savages" more of the precious stuff, thus rendering many Indian firearms completely useless.

As the trader put the two marten skins aside in return for the kettle, he inquired of the group why so many of the cheaper items, like knives and small tomahawks, were selling so briskly. Makoons took the opportunity to inform him of the forthcoming lacrosse match between his people and the Ozaagii. With Weniway interpreting, Makoons let the trader know that it was customary at such games for Indians to place wagers on the outcome, and that the value of what was bet was insignificant, only that it matched the worth of the item bet against it. The trader should attend the game, he urged, to see for himself how so many Indian women would be betting items from the trader's very own stock. Little Bear stressed the importance of this particular game, because it was to be a rematch, requested by the Ozaagii, who had been badly beaten by the Ojibwe the previous summer in a game on Big Turtle Island. The wagers were likely to be especially high because the Ozaagii wished to recoup their losses.

As Makoons continued, he realized the importance of enticing as many English as possible to leave the protection of the fort to watch the game firsthand. Here was a good chance to attract the attention of the trader and his two clerks and try to pique their curiosity about this unique sport. Makoons stressed the agility and speed of the Ojibwe players and urged the trader to bet on the game; he would have an opportunity to make big winnings. He should follow the example of the fort's commandant, who had already announced his intentions of betting on the Ojibwe team. There was no way the Ojibwe could lose, pointed out Little Bear, with such stalwart players as his friend Weniway here, whose great height made him a particularly fine player at centerfield. Weniway went through a few ball-tossing motions with an imaginary lacrosse stick, prompting the English to break out in laughter. Yes, said the trader, as he turned a page in his account book and seemingly scanned his inventory. Perhaps they just might come out to see the match and think seriously about betting on the Ojibwe. He had heard much about the game in his travels, but he had never seen it actually played.

The trader finished adding some figures and put down his quill pen. Yes, he had guessed there must be practices going on because a number of Indians trading with him lately had brought their lacrosse racquets and balls with them, which he was able to examine. Little did he suspect, thought Makoons, that the daily scrimmages outside the fort were all part of the general strategy. The trader reached under the counter, pulled out an inexpensive knife, and handed it to Makoons, telling the interpreter to have Little Bear wager it upon himself for good luck in the game. The trader would attend, he assured them, if he was able beforehand to get caught up with his letter writing and bring his much-neglected diary up to date.

As the English noticed Indians with lacrosse sticks, their curiosity about the forthcoming match was heightened. To give them a taste of what they could expect to see, one Ozaagii trading party only yesterday had brought two young boys along, with their sticks and a ball. While their fathers were busy inside a trader's house, the two were purposely left to practice passing and catching in an open area just outside the trader's house in the fort's central square. Their antics and the novelty of their play had quickly attracted a number of onlookers, who were amazed at the boys' ability to catch a ball using a racquet with such a small pocket, particularly as the boys were constantly in motion. One boy with the ball in his stick whirled it around and around overhead, as though it were some toy or noisemaker, while the other chopped frantically, trying to catch the stick with his own as it came around. Brief shouts of delight and occasional applause could be heard as one of the boys caught the ball and spun all the way around on his heels, only to release it immediately to his playmate. Laughter broke out when one of them, cradling the ball back and forth in his stick, enticed the other to chase him around the arms depot in circles, trying to knock the ball loose but missing each time.

Their business finished, Weniway and the others left the trader's house, but not before the interpreter had jokingly inquired of the trader if he would bet him his personal services on the game. Should the Ojibwe lose, Weniway would be obliged to do the trader's chores for three days, but should they win, as expected, the trader would have to move into Weni-way's smoky *wiigiwaam,* put up with the flies and mosquitoes, haul his water, gut the deer he would shoot, and sleep on a rush mat on the ground—in short, experience a lifestyle unbecoming to an English gentleman. The trader declined the invitation but wished Weni-way good luck in the game.

The chiefs and interpreters began to insert the small pegs in the ground to represent the players' positions as the game began. Two goaltenders from each team would be stationed in front of the respective goalposts. Ten men on each side would play at midfield, spread out in two lines across the field. The remaining players would be clustered at centerfield, which meant that thirty Ojibwe and thirty Ozaagii players would be pushing and shoving in a large mass, awaiting the toss-up of the first ball by the elder selected as referee. This was many more men than would ordinarily play centerfield, but it was vital to keep the English-men's attention directed away from the land gate. Many of them could be counted on to move along the southern wall of the fort to watch the most intense action, where body blows would be the most frequent and the most scrambling after ground balls would occur. The rough-and-tumble of the play would deliberately be made to occur in that general area; the rest of the field in both directions would be kept free for a single player to break away with the ball downfield and score.

The day chosen for the game had been timed to coincide with the English celebrations of the king's birthday. The garrison would be in a relaxed mood, with most soldiers relieved of their duties for two days and thus free to be entertained by the Indian game. The defense of the fort would be minimal. Indians who lived near the fort remembered that, when the French possessed it, they too had celebrated their king's birthday, inviting the Indians inside for special feasts. But gradually their great French father had grown old and weak; having tired of fighting the English over Canada, he now lay asleep in his home across the great sea to the east, which explained to the Indians why the English had taken advantage of the situation and seized Canada from him. The Indians believed that their French father would soon awake and reclaim his former territories. In the meantime, they were doing what they could to destroy the English on their own. Inspired by the messages of the great prophet, Chief Pontiac, who had successfully rearmed a number of Indian people, tribes had put aside minor territorial disputes and former animosities to join in one concentrated effort to defeat the English. The recapture of Fort Michilimackinac would give them a strategic as well as a psychological advantage. Because it served as the pivotal depot for the English as they pushed ever further to control the rivers and woodlands beyond the western great seas, almost all goods needed to resupply their traders and military in the interior came through the fort. Whoever controlled it could effectively cut off the support system of the region; once the fort was theirs, the Indians might even be in a position to strike at the next important depot, Detroit. By then, the French king might have awakened from his long sleep.

As the chiefs and players inserted the last of the pegs, they began deliberations on the strategy of play. At the suggestion of chief Minavavana it was agreed that the game should begin shortly after the midday meal of the English, when they would be at their greatest leisure, sluggish and stuffed with food. The players, by contrast, would have fasted for a full day and would be lean and hungry for action. Ready for combat both on and off the field, having received the blessings and prayers of their medicine men, they would be in the proper psychological condition to carry out their plans with suddenness and brutality. Imagining the carnage, Minavavana, whose bitterness toward the English was intense, nearly salivated in delight. *"Gaawiin onizhishinzinoon, zhaaganaash!"* (No good, English!), he would shout as each detail was settled.

The chiefs calculated how long it would take for the maximum number of English to exit the fort to watch the game; they also took into account how long the foreigners' attention could be occupied before they might begin to tire of the spectacle and return to the fort. It was decided that an hour of play would be about right and that the score would be kept close throughout to sustain interest in the game. The English would be informed in advance that the Indians would play to four goals. Although the players would be instructed to perform at all times as though they were giving their all, every step of the game was carefully calculated and agreed upon.

The Ojibwe would guard the southwestern goal. After an initial mad fracas and pileup in centerfield at toss-up, Weniway would be allowed to catch the ball and fire it downfield toward the Ozaagii goal. The ball would be worked back and forth from side to side, totally controlled by the Ojibwe, who would score early with a fast breakaway by one of their forward players down the left side of the field. At a point about opposite the English pillory platform, he would run directly for the Ozaagii home goal and, dodging their goaltenders, run right at the post, smashing the ball—still in its pocket—against the post as he passed it and thereby scoring. Goaltenders simply had to fake a defense but allow their opponent through. This way the scoring could be better timed and controlled according to plan.

One aspect of lacrosse essential for the English to see early in the game was the large number of inaccurate shots. Particularly if a player ran with the ball and an opponent was pressing hard from behind, rather than risk having the ball knocked out of the stick, the player would get rid of it—preferably to a teammate. If none of his teammates were free, then he would at least fire the ball downfield toward the goaltenders, in hopes that a teammate would spot the ground ball and be able to beat his opponents to scoop it up. The Ojibwe in fact had rules against "hogging" the ball: If someone was carrying it and an opponent was dogging him directly from behind, he could yell *"Apagidoon!"* (Throw it!) three times in a row, and if the ballcarrier had not released the ball by then, his pursuer was free to crack him over the head with his stick. This rule kept a game from getting stalled by anyone who simply wished to run around the field exhibiting his personal skills.

Even before the first goal was scored, it was planned that the ball would be fired at least once so as to hit the picket wall of pine and bounce back out onto the field. This was to happen near the far southeastern end of the fort, as far away from the land gate entrance as possible. That way, by the time Makoons made his specially aimed shot, the English would be so accustomed to seeing a free ball flying astray that they would pay it no particular heed. Also, it was decided that at least one "inaccurate" ball should be bounced off the wall to the left of the land gate, so that if and when Makoons succeeded in aiming at the entrance and the ball went careening through the gate opening, the English would assume that this was just part of the usual action. Probably they would not be alarmed to see several players, in hot pursuit of the ball, run right into the fort to retrieve it. By then, of course, their fate would have been settled.

The chiefs continued to map out the course of action for the game, point by point. Majikiwis (Elder Brother) forwarded additional strategy. After their first goal, the Ojibwe would be allowed to score again. The Ozaagii would score twice in a row to tie the game at 2–2; then the Ojibwe would score, making it 3–2. The Ozaagii would score quickly once again, tying it at 3–3. This would be the signal for all to prepare for the attack. Crowd interest in the game would be at its peak, and few English would wish to retire to the fort until the match was decided and the winners had collected their dues. For the final match point the ball was to be allowed to roam all over the field; playing was to increase in intensity, the Ozaagii would come close to scoring, which would be the sign for the Ojibwe goaltenders to recover the ball and pass it to Makoons. Bad Sky would already have positioned himself about twenty paces outside the land gate to wait for Makoons to dodge his way through a number of Ozaagii midfielders. Then Little Bear would finally make the now often rehearsed ballista with Bad Sky's stick to send the ball careening through the entrance to the fort. What followed would live on in the oral history of these tribes for generations.

The meeting broke up, and the chiefs dispatched the eight players present as runners, to take tobacco and make the rounds of their camps, recruiting players for their teams and quietly spreading the news of the planned attack. Special care should be taken that the Odaawaa not be informed of the plan, as they would surely demand to take part in the post-game plunder. Makoons was unconcerned about his Odaawaa host; he already had some inkling of the forthcoming events, but his *wiigiwaam* was so isolated that his contacts with his fellow Odaawaa were infrequent if at all. Meanwhile, trading parties to the fort were encouraged to be very visible in making wagers on the game among themselves, to continue eliciting greater English interest.

A week earlier, having learned of the impending birthday celebration in honor of the English king, a delegation of chiefs had been dispatched to approach the commandant of the fort, proposing that their athletes put on a grand lacrosse game between two nations for the entertainment of the fort's inhabitants as the Indians' contribution to the general festivities. Most of the English had never witnessed anything on the scale of a lacrosse match, although they had almost all seen an occasional moccasin game or a bowl and dice game. The commandant, before giving his approval, assumed that the Indians had in mind either an exhibition of the game of ball and racquet, such as he had seen their children playing, or the scrimmages with only a few players that the Ojibwe had engaged in among themselves the week before. He was astonished when it was explained that two *teams* of forty men each would pursue a *single ball* over a lengthy field, attempting to score points by hitting a goal-post! Like most Europeans in the New World, the English conceived of sport almost exclusively in terms of individual contests, such as boxing, horse racing, fencing, golf, or tennis. Such a novelty as the lacrosse game was certainly worthy of support, and the commandant enthusiastically embraced the chiefs' proposal, granting them permission to measure out their field, as they had suggested.

The evening before the game, the two teams and a few substitute players for each side gathered in their respective camps. Because the game would evolve into an actual battle, there were certain precautionary measures to be taken and ritual purification to undergo. Ordinarily a war dance would have been held in each camp. Knowing, however, that the high-pitched sounds of the drums beating would certainly be heard at the fort, they necessarily omitted these ceremonies for fear that it would cause alarm among the military. Still, there were obligations they could take care of. The players all began a fast, taking no food or drink except an occasional sip of water. The lacrosse sticks and balls were assembled, together with the weapons of warfare—the scalping knives, war clubs, and tomahawks—and the medicine men began to rub vermilion onto each item. Red, the color of battle, was also applied to lacrosse sticks that would be used in important games. None of the players were to have sex with their women, and all of them were to purge their bodies of impurities by entering their small *madoodiswanan,* or sweat huts, where they sat naked two at a time, sprinkling water on the red-hot rocks to produce a stifling steambath, which they endured for a good hour. When the evening rituals were complete, each man departed for his home encampment, knowing that he would get no sleep that night, as he would be rehearsing the plans over and over.

Makoons made his way along the beach until he could see the fire of the Odaawaa camp in the distance. They had invited their Odaawaa friends to be spectators at the game, and Little Bear had given several pelts to their Odaawaa hostess to hide under her shawl until she felt like betting them. He had also secretly brought a doctored tomahawk and a long, sharp knife for Boodoonh to hold under her blanket. She would be stationed directly at the land gate opening, ready to divest herself of these arms as the players rushed past her. While the Odaawaa couple retired to sleep, Makoons and his wife stoked the fire and prepared to remain awake for the duration of the night. They discussed the events of the past few weeks and pondered who would be chosen to name their child, expected in a few months. They talked about the game the next day and reflected upon the implications of a successful attack on the English. Makoons all the while was etching the figure of his clan, the Crane, on one side of his stick with a sharp awl. Because of the special role assigned him, the priests had tied a kingfisher feather to the stick's webbing. The kingfisher had great vision and could fly rapidly in a straight line; the feather would ensure that his aim was well directed when he struck Bad Sky's upraised stick.

As dawn approached, the mosquitoes began to swarm around them. Makoons took an old pail from the beach and shoveled some embers from their fire into its bottom. He filled the pail with cedar chips from the spot where they chopped wood, and it immediately began to produce a thick but aromatic smoke. There was a slight breeze, so he moved the smoldering pail upwind from where he and Boodoonh sat on a log. The smoke enveloped them and soon did its job of ridding the area of the pesky insects.

Boodoonh expressed to Little Bear her concern about the aftermath of the battle with the English. She admitted a certain homesickness, particularly now that she was pregnant. Although word of the successful raid would reach *mooningwanekaaning* within a few weeks, surely her parents would be anxiously awaiting their return. Makoons assured her that he had no intention of joining other war parties heading for Detroit and that he, too, was somewhat impatient to start the long journey back. Furthermore, after looting the fort, they should return with an impressive array of gifts for their relations.

As morning came, Little Bear readied himself for the game. Bad Sky had provided him with some bear grease, and Boodoonh removed charcoal from the ashes of their fire and mixed the two together to form a black paste for decorative designs on his body. His Odaawaa friend loaned Makoons a small trade mirror so that he could put on his own face paint. Using a partially burnt twig, Little Bear carefully drew a line down the middle of his forehead and continued down the length of his nose. Turning to the bear grease, he began

his facial design by filling in one half with black, while Boodoonh applied a small dot of vermilion to each of his cheeks.

Makoons let his wife wrap one of his pigtails while he wrapped the other. From behind
she tied two crane feathers into the rear of his hair. It had been agreed in advance that the
Ozaagii would shave their heads, except for a small tuft on top. Any feathers attached to
this hair would be dyed red. Since the game had been so thoroughly planned as to the role
of each player, it was vital that he be able to spot teammates from a distance. The tufted
heads would certainly be the one aspect of dress most quickly recognized—any player without one could be taken to be an Ojibwe.

It was already late morning, and the sky was overcast; although the weather was still
hot, it seemed that rain might threaten, so there was no time to be lost departing for the
fort in order to get the game started. Gathering up the two remaining new sticks to take in
case an Ojibwe broke one during play, Makoons and the entourage, with their concealed
weapons and goods to wager on the game, started down the path toward the playing field.

As they neared the fort, they came upon several Indians about to insert one cedar goalpost in a freshly dug hole. Stripped of branches and bark, the shiny yellow wooden post had
a strip of bright-red stroud trade cloth tied around its very top—the banner of war.

Many of the Ozaagii players were already practicing at the other end of the field, passing the ball around and using their home goal for shooting. There were plenty of small boys
behind the goalpost to retrieve errant balls for them. Several English soldiers watched the
preparations, reclining along the pine wall and enjoying a smoke. En route from transport-
ing furs from other distant outposts, groups of Canadian *voyageurs* had gathered near the
beach and were lounging on the grass, using their large overturned canoes as backrests and
waiting for the game to start. In midfield Indian women from one tribe had begun to place
wagers with those from the opposite side. Two men, one from each of the two opposing
teams, were designated stakeholders and were busy tying the bets together—a length of
trade cloth to a blanket, two foxskins to a new copper kettle, a *dikinaagan* to beaded knee-
bands. As the number of bets increased and more and more people excitedly made their
wagers in the middle of the field, the goods formed an impressive mound. Some women
reported that English soldiers seemed to be betting among themselves; they had seen them
take coins out of their pockets and count them in what looked like negotiations.

Makoons spotted Weniway from a distance—he was hard to miss with his tall black
torso and white-circled eyes. Bald Ozaagii were affixing the red feathers to their heads, while
more inhabitants were emerging from the fort. It was nearly game time, and so far the rain
had held off.

The referee gave the signal for the field to be cleared, and the two stakeholders began to
move the pile of bets to a place reserved for them against the garrison wall. All eighty players

now assembled at centerfield, as a chief from the Ojibwe bearing a pipe and one from the Ozaagii came from the sidelines to join the players, give them last-minute instructions, remind them to play fairly, and wish them luck. There, out of earshot of any English or their interpreters, the chiefs were also able to quickly rehearse all final plans for the performance of the game and the subsequent attack on the fort. Minavavana scowled in the direction of the soldiers and muttered, *"Gaawiin onizhishinzinoon, zhaaganaash!"* By now several English officers had joined the spectators, although they seemed unwilling to venture far from the land gate. Makoons spotted Boodoonh with her back to the fence, slowly inching her way closer to the opening, holding her blanket wrapped tightly around her.

The referee stood in the middle of the shoving and jostling mass of players and suddenly, without warning, tossed the ball straight into the air. Immediately twenty sticks were raised aloft amid yells and war whoops. The clashing of wood against wood obscured the fact that Weniway, as intended, had been given plenty of room to get the ball, and none of the others seriously attempted to interfere with his catching it as it descended.

The game went according to plan. By the time the score stood tied at 2–2, the Indians counted at least eighteen soldiers and officers among the spectators, along with perhaps another twenty civilian inhabitants of the fort. This number had not diminished by the time the crucial 3–3 tie was reached—the signal for all to prepare for the attack. The referee called a brief pause in the game, so thirsty players could get water at their respective sidelines and last-minute bets could be placed by Englishmen eager to up the ante, for the next goal would determine the winner. The pause was also a strategic move on the Indians' part. It provided them the opportunity to determine the exact location of each soldier who was outside the fort and who soon would become a hapless victim of their intrigues. It was also the signal for the "water-toss," carefully planned to entice the curious English spectators even further east of the land gate to watch the "crazy savages" swimming after the ball.

Meanwhile, women known to conceal weapons had entered the fort or stationed themselves as close as possible to each group of military, and by now Boodoonh and a few others had quietly backed themselves into the fort alongside the two gates. The players knew that they had to keep up the pretense of the game, but psychologically they were preparing themselves for battle. Some were already bloodied from being hit with sticks or bruised from falls; several had had to be replaced during the previous inning, one with a broken arm, others limping off the field. With the last toss-up the game was reaching a feverish climax, for the final score would be made against the English, not against an Indian lacrosse team.

As the ball fell into the pushing mass at centerfield, an Ozaagii forward quickly grabbed it and dropped it almost instantly. Another Ozaagii scooped up the ground ball with a twist of the wrist and passed it behind him to the safety of their midfielders, who controlled it for a good minute of play until too many Ojibwe were threatening. But an Ojibwe forward decided it was time to distract the soldiers with a ball landing in the waters of the great lake. He managed to intercept the flying ball in mid-air, stumbled forward a few steps, pretended to trip and, in an effort to rid himself of the ball, gave it one huge, arcing toss in the direction of the water.

Immediately, all players near that end of the field ran screaming toward the shore. The ball, painted bright red, could be seen bobbing in the waves about ten yards offshore. Dashing into the surf, about ten players began to wade toward it, pushing opponents underwater as they went. Three men, two Ojibwe and one Ozaagii, were within reach of the ball with their sticks, swimming frantically to retrieve it. The Ozaagii arrived first, splashed his stick down over the ball and was about to turn and throw it shoreward, when his opponents each grabbed his head and shoulders and pushed him under, as planned. With the ball still cupped in his stick, he swam a few strokes underwater, suddenly emerging several yards away from his opponents. Turning toward teammates on the shore, he gave the ball a mighty toss and disappeared from sight once again.

The Ozaagii forward who clamped his stick on the beached ball quickly gained the protection of several teammates. In a phalanx they deftly maneuvered their way through the mass of Ojibwe swarming to protect their goal. Suddenly the Ozaagii ballcarrier headed straight for the goalpost, but one of the Ojibwe tripped him, knocking the ball out of his stick. One of the Ojibwe forward players immediately scooped the ball up, looking desperately upfield to spot Makoons, but he couldn't find him. So as Weniway came into view near the sideline, the forward passed a high arcing throw to him.

The tall player snatched it from mid-air with ease and began heading across the field toward the Ozaagii sideline, when he abruptly turned. Having kept Makoons's position in view throughout, he fired a quick toss across the field, and the ball landed at Makoons's feet as he scooped it. Bad Sky was already in place facing centerfield, but with one eye still on Makoons, who was charging in his direction. Suddenly he wheeled around and braced his stick outright in front of him. *"Smack!"* Makoons crossed the two racquets, just as they had rehearsed so often. The ball sailed perfectly into the land gate entrance, deflected off the open right gate, and bounced off an adjacent house even farther into the fort's interior, coming to rest near the centrally located arms depot.

Immediately players of both teams who were closest to the land gate began to run after the ball, right into the fort. Spectators at the gate moved quickly out of their way to avoid being trampled. Meanwhile, mayhem broke out on the field, as players rushed toward their women along the fence, dropping their sticks and grabbing the outstretched implements of warfare that emerged from the folds of blankets and shawls. The sudden actions caught the English completely off guard. A few who had been resting seated against the palisaded wall had no time to get up. Totally defenseless, some began to run toward the gate but were cut off. Already several soldiers had been stabbed or clubbed with tomahawks. Some, not yet dead, were being scalped, held between the legs of Indian players. At the far end of the field, one distracted British soldier, unaware of what was going on, watched two players running in his direction. The one in front appeared to have the ball, cradling his racket back and forth in front of him. But the implement was in fact a war club, its sharp metal spike having been removed to disguise it. It resembled a lacrosse stick with a ball in its pocket. In an instant the hard maple knot of the war club's end came crashing down on the soldier's skull.

One by one the military were incapacitated. The commandant's reward for having bet on the Ojibwe was to be stripped of his clothing and led off to the woods by a rope to face whatever fate the Indians had in store for him. Those not immediately killed were taken as prisoners and their hands bound behind them. Makoons joined the throng rushing into the fort, grabbing the knife handle Boodoonh held out to him and following other players, who were by now chasing unarmed soldiers through the interior of the fort to dispatch them before they could get at their firearms. Coming around one house, he could see the Canadians at the windows, passively watching the slaughter of their former enemies. One hapless soldier, noticing an open door at one house, ran frantically for shelter, only to have the Canadian occupant slam it in his face. The tomahawk behind him landed in his head with so much force that he fell forward, breaking down the door under the weight of his lifeless body. Makoons ran into an English soldier being chased by Ozaagii and plunged his knife into his belly, emitting a fierce war cry as he accomplished his act of revenge for White Bird.

The shrieking and noise rang throughout the fort. Groups of Indians were already searching houses to make certain they had killed or captured everyone in the entire garrison. One group broke into a trader's house and were plundering his goods, throwing articles out the broken windows to the women, who fought among themselves for them. Several had found the rum supply and were slaking their thirst in great gulps. They brought some goblets from one house and, standing around the arms depot, filled them with rum, raising them on high in a mocking English-style toast to the English. Canadians as well were participating in the plunder and could be seen dragging packs of hides into their houses to secure them. English blood covered nearly every lacrosse player's hands by now; many were dipping into the torn stomachs of the dead and smearing the blood over their torsos.

Makoons and Bad Sky joined two others in search of English traders and clerks who had been missing at the game. They entered the home of one Canadian, who stated emphatically that he harbored no Englishmen, but he let the Indians search his premises to satisfy themselves. They ascended to the second floor and discovered a locked door leading to an attic. Demanding a thorough inspection of the premises, they had the Canadian open the door with his key. The room upstairs was empty except for a large pile of birch-bark pails used in collecting maple sap for sugar in the spring. Little could Makoons have known that the very object of his search, the English trader, hunched breathless and quivering in terror behind the pile of sap buckets, where he had scrambled to escape detection. Nor were Indians elsewhere within the fort aware that one English boy had hidden himself inside a chimney or that the German trader crouched beneath some corn. Disappointed that no English were in the house, Makoons kicked at a few of the pails and descended quickly with his colleagues.

Outside, Boodoonh and the Odaawaa couple were waiting for him, their arms loaded with goods and trophies taken from the English. The Odaawaa host was already wearing a British officer's jacket and brandishing his sword in the air. Boodoonh had had her fill of the slaughter and wanted to return to camp before it began to rain.

They were about to leave the continuing conflict, but players from both teams surrounded Makoons, praising him for his brilliant performance in piercing the fort's security with a lacrosse ball. Suddenly he remembered a task as yet unfulfilled and asked leave of Boodoonh for a moment. Fearing that he was about to join those drinking rum, she begged him not to partake of the firewater. As he made his way to the house where he had traded his marten skins, he saw Ozaagii coming out the door with the two clerks, bound with ropes. Makoons entered the store and headed for a far corner of the trader's shelves, which by now had been almost completely stripped of goods. But mostly hidden from view by a torn blanket, a small piece of silver shone through, and Makoons grabbed the breast-gorget with his clan emblem engraved on it. Throwing it around his neck, he emerged wearing it triumphantly over his blood- and sweat-smeared chest. A generation hence, he thought proudly, his as-yet-unborn son would wear this in the war dances and recount the bravery of his father, Little Bear, the great Ojibwe lacrosse player.

7 *A Stake in the Game*

The Ojibwe and the Sauk succeeded in their ruse to capture Fort Michilimackinac by enticing the British garrison into watching an unfamiliar sport. The possibility of betting on the game also lured the soldiers in. Their curiosity and proclivity to wager on athletic contests combined to distract them from safeguarding the fort and led to their demise.

But what about the native lacrosse fans and their own investment in the outcome of games? Aside from Makoons's covert intentions, when he encouraged the trader Alexander Henry to follow the commandant's example by betting on the Ojibwe, he was simply following Indian tradition, for gambling was an integral part of native North American games. In fact, the decline and disappearance of many of the traditional American Indian gaming activities began in large part because of the objections of missionaries and government officials about the gambling involved. Such officials judged the practice to be not only sinful but also impoverishing and thus an impediment to their efforts to "civilize" Indians and bring them into the mainstream of American society. In many places, betting on games was prohibited outright, and it brought predictable consequences. The government's 1920 prohibition of gambling on Ojibwe moccasin games on the Nett Lake Reservation in northern Minnesota marked the beginning of the decline not only of the game but also of the rich repertoire of moccasin game songs that once existed. Today, on the few occasions when the Ojibwe game is still played, as teams try to guess under which of four moccasins a marked object has been hidden, it is accompanied by drumming, but the songs meant to go with it have mostly been forgotten.

Wherever lacrosse was played, it was a community-based event.

It attracted a larger audience than, say, a moccasin game, which might be confined to the interior of a wigwam or the shade of a tree with only a handful of spectators. With many team players in the open on a large playing area, more spectators would be attracted, and more could be accommodated. Because a lacrosse game was a major event, usually arranged well in advance, news of the appointed day spread and the intervening time permitted the excitement to mount. George Copway noted of a Lake Superior Ojibwe game in 1836 that at game time "every kind of business was suspended, not only by the Indian, but by the whites of all classes." On reservations, where one village played another, the event was attended not just by people of those two communities but also by those from other parts of the reservation. When two *nations* played each other, such as the rematch between the Seneca and the Mohawk in the summer of 1797, the audiences numbered even higher: "On one side of the green the Senecas had collected in a sort of irregular encampment—men, women, and children—to the number of more than a thousand. On the other side the Mohawks were actively assembling in yet greater numbers." One game played by the Creek and the Choctaw to settle a territorial dispute is said to have been attended by about ten thousand spectators. Only in its decline did lacrosse lose its Indian audiences. When the game was revived by the Mississippi Choctaw in the late 1960s, between one thousand and two thousand spectators might have been in the stands, but the bulk of them were curious whites. The native population mostly stayed away, partly because they were intimidated by the large non-Indian audience but also because they objected to the constant banter of the announcer, who made many "instructive comments" for the benefit of the visitors.[1]

In its heyday, lacrosse was as much a social as a sporting occasion for Indian communities. It enabled people who did not see each other frequently to renew friendships as well as to identify with a larger group. Much in the way that large summer powwows today strengthen Indian identity and pride, lacrosse matches provided the opportunity to express social alliances, at the kinship, village, reservation, and national levels.

For such a social event, at least in the nineteenth century, spectators customarily dressed in their finest clothes. At an Eastern Cherokee game in 1848, people began to gather about 10:00 A.M., "all dressed in their holiday attire, so that feathers, shawl turbans, scarlet belts, and gaudy hunting shirts were quite abundant."[2] Forty years later on the same reservation, "Sunday best" continued as the rule, though by then the Cherokee wore the Anglo clothing of the period. Today's audiences, like most sports fans, are generally dressed informally.

Before the Cherokee game began, team supporters freely mingled with players and provided words of support to them (Figure 23). Once preliminary betting had concluded and players took positions for the opening toss-up, spectators retired to the sidelines for the game. Before the days of bleachers, they either stood along the sidelines or took advantage of hills, mounds, or outcroppings along each side of the field to provide a better view. Many lacrosse fields were laid out in small valleys, so they were surrounded by naturally elevated land. Cherokee spectators at Qualla Town in 1848 took positions in groups ranging from five to fifty on the Great Smoky Mountains hillsides under trees overlooking the playing field.[3]

Once a game was in progress, there were definite restrictions on the interference of fans in its action. In some places, a circle was drawn around the field to limit the proximity of spectators to players.[4] Where no side boundaries were indicated and players simply followed the ball wherever it landed, fans might find themselves integrated into the play. If a ball happened to fall among them, they could be overrun by the players, who had little regard for anyone in their way. Because of this, spectators occasionally exposed themselves to serious injury, as is evident in Basil Hall's experience during a Creek game in 1828:

> The ball pitched within a yard or two of the spot where I was standing. In the next instant a dozen or twenty Indians whizzed past me, as if they had been projected from cannons. I sprung to the nearest tree, as I had been instructed [by the Indian Agent], and putting my hands and legs round, embraced it with all my might. A poor boy, however, close to me, had not time to imitate

• 105

Figure 23 • Eastern Cherokee women in their finest, some with babies strapped to their backs, mingle sociably on the field before an 1888 game. The long skirts, sun hats, and kerchiefs reflect the adoption of nineteenth-century Euro-American dress.

my example, and being overwhelmed by the multitude, was rolled over and over half a dozen times, in spite of his screams, which were lost in the clatter of sticks, and the yells and shouts of the combatants. . . . I felt rather awkward, I must confess, as they rushed past me, and very nearly scraped me off; but I held fast, and escaped with a good daubing of rosin from the pine-tree.[5]

The fan attempting to walk onto the field or become otherwise involved in the game could expect severe admonishment, as Nicholas Perrot wrote of eighteenth-century Huron games: "If . . . anyone who does not belong in the game . . . hits the ball, thus giving any advantage to either side, one of the players on the other side will upbraid the outsider, asking him if the game is any affair of his and why he meddles in it."[6] Penalties were imposed in some places. The direct interference of a Mississippi Choctaw fan in the play could cost his team one or more of the goals already scored.[7]

Female supporters during Indian lacrosse games often took an active role. Eyewitness accounts agree that women sometimes offered refreshments to players—usually water or coffee. In Creek games today women with water buckets and a dipper freely wander the field offering thirsty players a drink. One source indicates that Choctaw women had small switches as well with which to beat their husbands if they thought they were not giving their all. This assertion, though probably erroneous, continues to be accepted and repeated unchallenged in the literature on lacrosse.[8] Such whippings, if they occurred at all, more likely took place on the sidelines and *not* on the field, despite certain details in an 1844 lithograph by George Catlin, the source of this confusion (see Chapter 10). Recently Mississippi Choctaw consultants have described a seemingly related practice. According to Jackson Isaac, "Sometimes the women would get an ax and chop down little [two-inch-by-eighteen-inch] trees and pile them up close to the goal by the center. Then, when [players] started a fight, that's when [the women] started throwing those sticks. Just get those clubs and throw at you; just hit anybody and get into the fight."[9] But Isaac's account implies that sticks were thrown from the sidelines, not that the women were free to roam about the field whipping players, as Catlin would have us believe.

As do fans of any sport, Indian lacrosse spectators occasionally shouted support to their teams. Bystanders at a Yuchi game in the early twentieth century, according to Frank Speck, added to the general confusion by yelling encouragement and shouting directions to the players, such as *kyē* (here) or *gyä* (hurry up). Creek fans today usually line the fields with cars and pickup trucks and honk their horns when their team scores and at the game's conclusion, when the winners emerge onto the field through the goalposts. These supporters also yell for their sides, *pazo'zah* (east) or *akalat'ka* (west). But for the most part Indian fans, by Euro-American standards, have typically shown considerable composure and restraint. An anonymous reporter in the *Literary Digest* of 1928 characterized those on the sidelines of a Cherokee game as follows:

> Through all of [the game] the crowd remains silent—unless there are white spectators. The Indian enjoys watching the game immensely. That can be seen by the intent way in which his eyes follow every move. But rarely does he utter a sound. There are no bursts of cheering, no frantic "Attaboys!" . . . Even when the game ends there is no cheering. The victorious team struts off with something of an air of triumph, perhaps, but they don't make any noise about it.[10]

This is not to say that the *players* were so composed. When Alexander Henry characterized Ojibwe lacrosse as "necessarily attended with much violence and noise . . . all eager, all struggling, all shouting, all in the unrestrained pursuit of a rude athletic exercise," he referred to the behavior of players, not spectators. Indeed, George Copway heard Ojibwe players shouting, "Ha! ha! yah!" and *"A-ni-gook"* to each other in the heat of action.[11]

Cherokee spectator behavior at lacrosse games is consistent with the restrained nature of Indian social gatherings, filled as they are with nonverbal communication such as nods, glances, and silent smiles. Unlike rowdy American athletic events, the Cherokee lacrosse match, as Raymond Fogelson characterizes it, exhibits "instead, a low-keyed bubbling undercurrent of talk, and light laughter." But crowds are still responsive to the occasional humorous incidents that erupt during the game.[12]

As would be expected, once victory is declared, a winning Indian lacrosse team and its supporters display obvious pleasure. But postgame cordiality between native victors and losers contrasts with the customary boisterous behavior of non-Indian audiences, and Indian responses to a lacrosse win are generally subdued, as the *Literary Digest* observed. But while Indian enthusiasm may have been subdued and internalized, before the game began nearly everyone bet on its outcome.

Universally in native North America of the past, much leisure time was devoted to games, and nearly all of them were wagered on by players and spectators alike. The earliest Europeans in North America made particular note of the high amounts wagered but stressed the dispassion of the losers. The Jesuit François du Peron in a letter of 1639 listed the principal Huron amusements: "Their recreations are the games of straw, of dish, and of [la] crosse, in which they will lose, to the value of two or three hundred écus." Pierre de Charlevoix in his publication of 1761 elaborated further on Huron betting, saying they would continue raising the stakes "till they have stript themselves stark naked and lost all their moveables in their cabbins; some have even been known to stake their liberty for a certain time."[13]

Wagering human services was not limited to the Huron. At one time, Choctaw men are known to have wagered their wives and ultimately themselves for limited periods of service. The practice of putting humans up for stakes continued well into the late nineteenth century. Ojibwe playing the moccasin game wagered blankets, shirts, and hunting traps, as well as their children. Recalled Dan White (born in 1905) of the Leech Lake Reservation: "When these people played those games, well, they lost everything they had and they even . . . lost their wives and some of their children, at times . . . I don't know why that they put in their wives as betting there, whether they loved the game that much, but I suppose that after the person started losing, why he tries to see if the luck would change." The Cherokee, who were once slaveowners, were known to bet their servants as well as captive Chickasaw and European children on lacrosse games. Similar patterns of wagering on the game are reported for the Dakota, Iroquois, and others.[14]

The nature of Indian gambling on sporting events is different from that of Euro-Americans and is perhaps best reflected in the composure shown by Indian bet-losers—something that never failed to impress non-Indians.[15] Because lacrosse provided an arena of enormous betting activity, it offers clues to the nature of Indian attitudes toward gambling in general. To begin with, there is little doubt that stakes on a game's outcome made it a serious affair; the higher the bets, the harder and more valiantly the teams would compete. The Jesuits noticed this in Huronia of the 1630s.[16] As rematches were scheduled to recoup losses, the betting became more desperate and the stakes higher. *The American State Papers, Indian Affairs* of May 1792 reported that the Cherokee chief Eskaqua kept the governor of Tennessee waiting for two days to conduct business while he indulged in chicanery to make up his losses of the first day:

> The gambling the day before had so excited the chiefs that they had staked their clothes on the second game, reserving only their flaps [breechclouts]. Eskaqua recovered his losses. The governor comments, "His getting drunk on Monday night was supposed to be a maneuver to get some of the best players on the other side in the

same situation, which he effected. He did not play himself, and none of his players drank to excess.''[17]

That the nature of the stakes encouraged players to put forth their best efforts was recently commented on by a former Choctaw player: "It probably would have been important as a team to win the whole thing [all the wagers] . . . I think I would have tried harder if some-one was betting that much on me. In a lot of cases, they even put up a woman, too. And sometimes a man would think he was that good and he would put his kids up, too. And he had something to play for. I think he would have tried his best. If I had my wife and kids standing out there as my stakes, I would have played like hell.''[18]

Clearly, the *act* of betting was more important to Indian specta-tors than the monetary value of items won, for it made them active participants in the contest. An anonymous French memoir, "Rela-tion de la Louisiane," discussed the relative value of bets once placed on Choctaw games: "They wager a new gun against an old one which is not worth anything, as readily as if it were good, and they give as a reason that if they are going to win they will win as well against a bad article as against a good one, and that they would rather bet against something than not bet at all.''[19]

The belief that the acquisition of possessions increased one's monetary wealth was foreign to Indian people. In fact, only late in historical times did cash exchanges take place at lacrosse matches, a development cited by many Indian people as contributing to the decline of the traditional lacrosse game. In 1823 Pushmataha, a famous Choctaw leader, warrior, and lacrosse player, was discovered to be lacking a horse when he attended a council of chiefs and government officials. One agent decided to give Pushmataha a horse, but only on the condition that he not sell it or exchange it for liquor. When he revisited the agency on foot, it was discovered that he had lost the horse betting on a lacrosse game: "'But did you not promise Mr. Pitchlynn,' said the agent, 'that you would not sell his horse?' 'I did so, in the presence of yourself and many others,' replied the chief, 'but I did not promise that I would not risk the horse on a game of ball.'''[20]

Of equal consternation to Europeans was the fact that wagering on games, a natural part of Indian life, was totally accepted by their spiritual leaders. In Lewis Henry Morgan's *League of the Ho-dé-no-sau-nee or Iroquois* (1851) he complained that "as this practice was never reprobated by their religious teachers, but, on the contrary, rather encouraged, it frequently led to the most reckless indulgence.''[21] In fact, ritual betting was common among many tribes. In the tradi-tional Winnebago four-day wake or Feast of the Dead, on the final night men might play games for wagers—moccasin games, dice and bowl, or lacrosse games. Eastern Cherokee lacrosse conjurers recited a magical formula just before the game to ensure that bettors for the opposing side would lose: "As for the other admirers of the ball play, the Bear has just come and fastened him upon them, that they may never be happy. They have lost all strength. He has let the stakes slip from his grasp, and there shall be nothing left for their share."[22]

Blanchard's analysis of the role of betting at former Choctaw *toli* (lacrosse) games explains why it was so perplexing to non-Indians. Although bets were made between individuals, the Choctaw attached little importance to personal material gain or loss. The sum total of wagers on each side amounted to a *collective* bet placed on each team. There was none of the whites' customary speculation, point spread, or odds; the winners simply took all. No matter how high the stakes, the matter of winning or losing was relatively unimportant. Even today, without the gambling of the past, Indian people are relatively unconcerned with who wins or loses. What was once the collective *bet* has become the collective sense of community support, as Onondaga Oren Lyons makes explicit in reminiscences about growing up in a lacrosse family:

> I used to sit by lamplight and watch [my father] fix his pads and his stick—with care, great care, and I could see the great satisfaction it gave him. And I would be allowed to fuss with his things, and then run around with his pads on, and watch him get ready for a game. And then I would go with him to the game. . . . And there would be a winner and a loser, but that didn't seem to be so much a point of the game as the celebration, the sense of community, the being together with pride.[23]

By contrast, the element of white greed was one major factor in the decline of lacrosse among the Mississippi Choctaw at the turn of the century, when increasing numbers of local non-Indians attending the games began using them, like cockfights, as an opportunity for gambling. These games were increasingly marked by heavy drinking, unruliness among spectators, and violence on the field. As Blanchard noted, "Death and injury were not new to Choctaw *toli* in Mississippi, but the preoccupation with the maximization of one's investment in the game's outcome was."[24]

The distinction should be noted between "bets" won by players and "prizes" awarded to them—a practice seemingly confined to tribes of the western Great Lakes. Among the Menominee, for instance, when a lacrosse game was held as a dream obligation, the sponsor awarded goods as prizes to the players of both sides. The frame for hanging and displaying the goods to be offered was placed about midfield on the eastern side of the field (see Figure 10). During breaks after each goal had been scored, players participated in ritual smoking while the sponsor awarded prizes for that period of play. (It is not clear whether these awards were presented to the scoring team or to individuals based on performance.)

Indian betting on lacrosse matches was incorporated in myths and celebrated in song. One Cherokee song performed by women during the ball game dance the night before a game expresses their anticipation of a particularly desirable stake. Freely translated, the text begins, "What a fine horse I shall win! I shall win a pacer! I shall be riding a pacer! I'm going to win a pretty one!"[25] The Cherokee told a legend about a Seneca war chief whose people in the distant past were said to have visited the Cherokee. During their stay, the hosts were approached by a messenger from a tribe to their east, challenging the Cherokee to a lacrosse game:

> They came on the appointed day and the next morning began to make the bets with the Cherokee. The Seneca were still there. The strangers bet two very heavy and costly robes, besides other things. They began to play, and the Cherokee lost the game. Then the Seneca said, "We will try this time." Both sides bet heavily again, and the game began, but after a little running the Seneca carried the ball to their goal and made a point. Before long they made all the points and won the game. Then the bets were doubled, and the Seneca won again.[26]

In ancient, mythical time, "very heavy and costly [fur] robes" would have been regarded as highly valuable. In the 1850s, before Ojibwe lacrosse matches on Madeline Island began, the value of wares and goods that were bet was claimed to reach $1,000 or more. In a Georgia Cherokee game of 1825, bets were estimated to total $3,500; it was said that "at such times the Indians went wild, putting up against a bet anything and everything in their possession: horses, cattle, hogs, guns, copper kettles, and clothing." Before an 1834 match between the Hickory Log and Coosawattee Cherokee communities, their respective chiefs bet $1,000 each on the game.[27]

The sum total of bets usually reflected the nature and purpose of the match and the number of spectators. When the Eastern Cherokee played a "big match," one could expect to see veteran players and extensive betting; a "small game," on the other hand, generally involved younger, less-experienced players, and betting was not as heavy. Since the majority of lacrosse games were played by one community against another, the amounts wagered were comparatively modest. But if two or three towns joined forces against others, the stakes were considerably greater.

Not only goods and money but also land and the rights to its use were wagered. National disputes over territory were often settled by lacrosse games. Cherokee oral tradition includes the claim that the Cherokee won a huge tract of land in present-day Georgia by beating the Creeks in a ball game. Similarly, in the early 1790s an argument between Creeks and Choctaws over rights to a large beaver pond in what is now Noxubee County, Mississippi, was supposed to be settled by a lacrosse game, although the outcome was contested and bloody fighting erupted.[28]

Because rematches were usually scheduled to recoup losses, the items available for wager often determined the duration of a series of games. George Tyosh of the Lac Court Oreilles Reservation remembered games played in the spring over a number of days, lasting "as long as they had something to bet. When they ran out of money, they would bet beadwork or clothes."[29] An incremental, back-and-forth sequence to games and wagers was reported by the editor of the *Dakota Friend*, who intended to underscore the impoverishing effect of gambling on the local Indian population.

In July 1852 Little Six's band had negotiated a game in Oak Grove against a team representing the combined bands of chiefs Good Road, Sky Man, and Grey Iron. The game began the day after they arrived. The property bet on the game totaled $1,600. Little Six's team won, and two more games were played with fewer items wagered. After Little Six's players had won a total of $2,600, they quit until the following day. On the second day the losers became winners, challenging Little Six's team to another game: "They adjourned to the lodges to despatch a barrel of pork, two kegs of lard and ten sacks of corn (which SKY-MAN's farmer had just arrived with from the Agency,) and made up the stake for to-morrow." The next day at 10:00 A.M., blankets, coats, tomahawks, pipes, and other items valued at $300 to $400 "were tied up [matched as bets], and the ball started [tossed up]." After Little Six's team lost, the bets were renewed:

> But while a new stake was being made up, a dispute arose between the parties concerning some of the property which had been won from SIX's band, but which they kept back. They broke up in a row, as they usually do. GREY IRON's band leaving the ground first, ostensibly for the reason above named, but *really* because Six's band had just been reinforced by the arrival of a company from LITTLE CROW's band. Thus ended the ball play of three days continuance, during which time not less than $4,600 worth of property had been bet. How can Dakotas be otherwise than poor?[30]

Although the items may have differed, whatever was wagered was agreed to be of equal value. Players as well as spectators participated in the betting, and whereas a fan might simply pick out some friend from an opposing community to bet against, the player usually bet against the opponent selected for him from the other team. Among the Dakota, the population of a village staging a game would be equally divided in number. A player offered a blanket or some article of clothing, placing it on the ground, whereupon his opponent laid down something of equal value. The two items would be put aside, and the next two would deposit their stakes, and so on until the betting was completed.[31]

Items wagered were customarily guarded for the duration of the game by men appointed as stakeholders—usually trusted tribal elders. During the Mohawk and Seneca game of 1797, as Stone describes it: "By the side of the stakes were seated a group of the aged Chiefs— 'grave and reverend signors,' whose beards had been silvered by the frosts of many winters, and whose visages gave evidence of the toils of war and the chase."[32] The Ojibwe practice was for each team to choose a captain before the game, who in turn appointed a stakeholder. At some Cherokee games all bets were thrown into one pile and guarded by stakeholders from each side, who inserted sharp sticks into the ground "to register the bets." Items wagered at the Cherokee midfield were wrapped into bundles, carried off to the sidelines, and put into one pile. The above-described procedures applied to material goods; cash bets were usually entrusted to a neutral party.[33]

Apparently the Cherokee at one time housed wagers rather than leaving them in the open. One mid-nineteenth-century observer noticed "several rude tents, containing numerous articles, mostly of Indian manufacture, which were the stakes." Choctaw left articles on a specially constructed scaffold directly opposite the center of the field on one side and under the charge of a single stakeholder. Items bet against each other were tied together and deposited on the scaffold. To collect the bets, four or five men on horseback rode around through the crowds in advance of the game: "Whatever is bet is put with what is bet against it. If handkerchiefs, they are knotted together and thrown over the [mounted] stakeholder's shoulder; if money, the sums are put together in his pocketbook. His memory is remarkable, and he never fails to turn over the stakes correctly."[34]

The participation of spectators through wagering became ritualized by the Eastern Cherokee. Before betting at midfield, each team lined up at the goals with fans from their town behind them. At a signal, marching abreast and carrying all the items to be wagered (Figure 24), the team led its supporters a third of the way toward centerfield, then stopped. At another signal, the opposing team did

Figure 24 • Eastern Cherokee players carrying goods to be wagered prepare to line up for the march to centerfield (about 1908). Their "driver," holding the long switch at far right, leads the yelling as they march downfield to meet their opponents.

the same, and so on until they reached the center, where a noisy confusion of spectators and players intermingled while the bets were agreed upon.[35]

Once a lacrosse game was over and all bets were claimed, dispassion for the most part characterized the mood of both parties. Rematches were common and served to vent ill feelings as much as to recoup losses. The relaxed and friendly atmosphere following the games clearly perplexed Europeans. In the early historic period Perrot noted this trait among the Huron, stressing that spectators—particularly those who had not participated in the game through betting—could not interfere in the action without consequence: "They take what they have wagered and their winnings, and there is no dispute on either side when it comes to a question of payment, no matter what game they play." Huron men and women might lose everything they possessed, including their clothes, but they departed the grounds cheerfully, naked and singing.[36]

The great wins and losses that typified many games were accepted quietly or stoically, for the economic effect of games on a community was, over a period of time, minimal. A village that had bet heavily on its team and lost might have to cope with temporary shortages of food, clothing, and livestock, but regaining property through rematches allowed the people to recover over time. No single team was able to dominate the scene for a long duration or accumulate great wealth at the expense of other communities. Because wins and losses balanced out over time, there was little severe impact, such as is suggested in Pond's report of the Dakota bands' rematches.[37]

There were exceptions, however, to the general dispassion following Indian contests of any sort. In fact, as a precaution against violence after lacrosse matches, Oklahoma Choctaw deliberately left weapons behind. Often gamblers at Indian games became desperate, wagering to the extreme. Several examples of Huron incidents over gambling losses have been reported, including one in which a man who lost all he owned bet his hair, which he also lost—the winner cut it off; another gambled his little finger and had it chopped off upon losing, without showing signs of pain. Some became despondent. A Choctaw chunkey player in 1771, having lost all his possessions, returned home, borrowed a gun, and shot himself. The Jesuits reported that the son of a Huron chief, having lost a beaver robe and a porcelain collar in a game of straws, became so depressed and fearful of facing his relatives that he hanged himself from a tree.[38]

Several after-game incidents show anything but a peaceful resolution. At least one Jesuit in Huronia reported back to France that "gambling never leads to anything good; in fact, the Savages themselves remark that it is almost the sole cause of assaults and murders." Even when fallout was nonviolent, considerable quibbling about bets often erupted on the heels of contentious contests. Mystic Lake Sioux were suspicious of the role medicine men might have played in wins: "Another unfortunate result of gaming was quarrels over the stakes. The defeated side often asserted that the other had won too much or unfairly, or had overdosed with charms, and demanded return games instantly."[39]

In the case of lacrosse, tensions could interrupt and even cancel a game. The aforementioned Creek and Choctaw lacrosse match to settle rights over a beaver pond in Mississippi eventually ended in great bloodshed, with more than five hundred killed before the fighting stopped. Jim Gardner, a Mississippi Choctaw, recently gave the following handed-down account of a particularly contentious game in the late 1800s. As one side was about to win, "the rainmaker [a shaman] representing the team faced with imminent defeat pulled the last trick from his repertoire and caused it to rain with such suddenness and ferocity that the game had to be called, thereby saving his team from a demoralizing and expensive loss. Immediately, however, both parties broke for the scaffold where the wagered items were being held. . . . Riotous fighting broke out as everyone got into the act and tried to salvage what he thought was legally his. Several hours of bloody rioting ensued."[40]

Gambling and associated violence were definite factors in the decline of Indian lacrosse beginning in the late nineteenth century.

Even earlier, missionaries showed displeasure at the wagering that accompanied games. A Cherokee lacrosse match at New Echota in August 1825 prompted one American Board missionary to pronounce it "a scene of national iniquity." Members of the clergy were also unhappy that the value of the bets was being wasted sinfully, where it should rightfully, in their opinion, be going to the mission.[41]

There is little question that government officials began to interrupt the traditional flow of Indian lacrosse activity, and probably the gambling involved was their greatest concern. When the Lake Superior Ojibwe gathered to receive their annuities in 1855, it was an obvious opportunity for intratribal athletics but also for traders to collect money due them for goods given Indians "on account" during the year. With so much cash flowing into Indian hands, the government may have been trying to protect the traders' interests by forbidding that lacrosse be played, for it was certain to attract gambling.[42]

H. S. Halbert, writing in the 1890s, complained that in the previous decade lacrosse games had become "the greatest obstacle in the way of the educational and religious progress" of the Mississippi Choctaw: "To put it mildly, the ball play is the most demoralizing institution in Mississippi. It is, in a great measure, now-a-days manipulated or controlled by a white swashbuckler element, and gambling, whisky drinking, fighting, and not infrequently bloodshed have become the regular concomitants of the play."[43] His characterization of the degeneration of games into drunken brawls is confirmed today by Choctaw who remember that period. Simpson Tubby, a native leader and clergyman, spoke of games during his youth: "I shall never forget those brutal ball games of my childhood days. The Indians always had whiskey on such occasions, and sometimes a number of them would get drunk, and the Indians, women and children, would scatter in every direction. With battle axe, war hatchet or knife, these drunken demons would pursue their best friend, and while yet a child, I have run from 5 to 10 miles through the darkness to escape from them." The intrusion of whites at the games marked a rapid degeneration in the nature of traditional Choctaw ball game betting: "On one occasion, a local Anglo was selling peanuts during a stickball game at the Pearl River community and got into an argument with another white compatriot over a wager. Eventually there was gunplay, and an innocent Choctaw bystander was fatally shot."[44]

Halbert's concerns were answered in 1898 when the State of Mississippi outlawed gambling at all Indian lacrosse games, cockfights, and duels. As a result, the popularity of the game waned rapidly. As the clergy had hoped, the church became the new focal point of tribal social life. Meanwhile, American sports—particularly baseball—began to fill the void left by lacrosse.[45]

Restrictions on gambling and violence by the Eastern Cherokee were undertaken even earlier. In 1848 a plan was adopted to make the Cherokee more "civilized" by eliminating many of their "amusements." The one exception was "the manly game of ball," although it, too, felt the pressure of government intervention, specifically regarding the violence of play and the nature of gambling, which was greatly reduced in scope: "They are not allowed to wager their property on the game, as of old, unless it be some trifle in the way of a woollen belt or cotton handkerchief."[46]

Gambling on Indian lacrosse games tapered off in most communities where the sport was still alive. When stakes became increasingly high, problems with fraud and bribery emerged, in some cases leading to incidents in which "many expert players are prevailed upon to play falsely ["throw" the game]."[47] By 1900 the pervasive poverty on reservations precluded most Indian people from wagering any large financial stake on sports. The removal of this traditional mechanism for spectator involvement is one clear reason for the declining popularity of lacrosse and its ultimate disappearance from many North American tribes. Where the game still thrives, as among the Eastern Cherokee, teams can still win cash awards put up by the chamber of commerce or the Cherokee Fair committee for events designed to attract tourists. (Losers are also rewarded for their participation, but not as handsomely as winners.) The open betting among spectators of the past no longer exists, although culturally conservative Cherokee may do so quietly among themselves, as Fogelson indicates: "After a game in 1958 [I] asked Mollie Sequoyah how she enjoyed the battle, and she responded with a sly wink displaying a new handkerchief she had just won."[48]

8 "The Overhead Flourish" and "The Pounce"

As with equipment in all sports, a distinct correlation exists between the type of stick and ball used in Indian lacrosse and techniques of play. Those accustomed to today's field lacrosse, when first witnessing a southeastern game, for instance, are immediately struck by the seeming lack of strategy, teamwork, accuracy in passing, and the slow progress of the ball. It is safe to say that in this game the ball is on the ground more than it is in the air. Given the construction of the sticks and their function as extensions of the player's arms, all aspects of ball control—scooping, passing, carrying—differ greatly from those in the northern versions of lacrosse.

The size of the southeastern ball—usually no larger than a golf ball—and its manufacture from soft skin make it difficult to spot, particularly when the field has grass of any length. These factors also allow considerable deception in ball handling. Because players and referees easily lose track of the ball, a player who gains control of it in secret might pretend he does not have it until he is open enough to run and score. The ball is invisible when held between the two sticks, and thus a player can act as a decoy, removing pressure from a teammate who actually does have the ball.

Typically, five or six players form a tight circle somewhere near where they *think* the ball has landed, with lots of noisy clicking of sticks and everyone poking around, pushing others out of the way, even laying them out. The whole mass in fact resembles more a rugby scrum than a field lacrosse game, with those on the inside fumbling around with their sticks, trying to keep opponents away from the ball, and those on the outside shoving and flailing with their sticks, attempting to break open some room to get inside the throng where the ball lies (Figure 25). Even when grass is not an impediment to

Figure 25 • Pileup of young Eastern Cherokee as they fight for a ground ball. Player at far left restrains his opponent from joining the fray.

finding the ball, the general scrambling produces such a ruckus that the ball stays grounded for some time.

Basil Hall, watching his first Creek game in 1828, was obviously impressed by the "glorious clatter of sticks mingled with the cries of the savages" and described how one might break away from the pack and try to score:

> At length an Indian, more expert than the others, continued to nip the ball between the ends of his two sticks, and, having managed to fork it out, ran off with it like a deer, with his arms raised over his head, pursued by the whole party engaged in the first struggle. The unfortunate youth was, of course, intercepted in his progress twenty different times by his antagonists, who shot like hawks across his flight from all parts of the field, to knock the prize out of his grasp, or to trip him up—in short, by any means to prevent his throwing it through [the goal].[1]

The technique used in throwing the ball can scarcely be considered passing, as the ball most often is simply thrown downfield in hopes that a teammate will find and retrieve it. Other times the ball is released just to get rid of it in the right direction. As the player runs forward, he takes aim, bringing the sticks over his (usually right) shoulder. Leaning with his left foot, he turns sideways and, using the full upper torso, throws the ball over and out by separating the sticks and following through with his right leg. The action is not unlike that of a baseball pitcher, pulling both hands back before a throw. To wind up, however, the lacrosse player may take a few preliminary steps in the direction of the throw. The man who has retrieved the ball but is hemmed in in the "scrum" turns outward from the circle, bringing the sticks overhead while simultaneously leaping to get the ball over opponents' heads. Sometimes a player may grab him from behind by the waist and try to pull him over (Figure 26). If he can retain the ball, he may right himself sufficiently to fire off a shot from a kneeling position.

The centers' stick techniques at toss-up are slightly different. Usually the centers hold the two sticks together over the right shoulder, like batters waiting for a pitch. Or they might have the sticks outstretched together behind them and to one side, ready to lean into the ball as it falls. While the ball is in mid-air, some jump with both sticks together, trying to bat it out of the cluster. Sometimes they try to snatch the ball during its descent; some talented (usually taller) centers can do it.

Scooping a ground ball is not always easy. To do so, the player must come down on the ball while trying to bring both sticks together to capture it (Figures 27a, b). Often the player misses and must try a second time. In scooping a ball, the player may jump into the air, descending with both sticks in a "pounce," not unlike a coyote descending on a field mouse.

There is little passing in today's southeastern game. Describing Mississippi Choctaw passes, Kendall Blanchard notes that they *are* attempted, but not as successfully as in field lacrosse: "The movement of the ball through the air is generally characterized by misdirection, confusion, and scrambles for control." Earlier accounts, however, suggest that the ability to catch the ball in mid-air with two sticks was common. The Irish trader James Adair, writing of Chickasaw (possibly Cherokee or Choctaw) games, asserted that the players could throw the ball a hundred yards and that it was in the air most of the time. He stressed, however, that players were not allowed to use their hands—clearly an old rule governing the game. The painter George Catlin cited similar playing techniques of the Choctaw in the 1830s: "By leaping into the air, they catch the ball between the two nettings and throw it, without being allowed to strike it, or catch it in their hands." The southeastern legend of the game won by the birds over the land animals suggests allegorically that keeping the ball airborne enabled a team to win and was therefore a valuable technique.[2]

Scoring in the southeastern game is more a combination of luck and individual skill than of preplanned strategy. Because accuracy is

Figure 26 • Young
Oklahoma Choctaw
players at the Smith-
sonian Institution's Fes-
tival of American
Folklife in 1976. The
ballcarrier has the ball
"put away" between
his two sticks, while his
opponent tackles him
from behind.

Figure 27a • Action in an Oklahoma Creek game about 1938. Player in white appears to have just lost the ball (his sticks are up), as an opponent has grabbed him from behind. Heavyset player facing him, flailing sticks apart in the air, is also about to attack the ballcarrier to knock the ball loose.

• 123

Figure 27b • The ball, having been lost, is on the ground, with heavyset player and player in white, who has just dropped it, each trying to scoop it—not an easy feat. Player with white kerchief around head also goes for the ground ball. Man wearing necktie and hat with white feather is a referee.

not a hallmark of throwing, there are many more attempts made than goals scored. Furthermore, opponents sensing an imminent shot at the goal, like soccer players in a penalty kick, may form a sort of human wall in front of the goal, raising and crossing their sticks to block the shot.

Individualism rather than team play and strategy characterizes the southeastern game. Players become noted for their particular skills (or lack of them) and gain appropriate nicknames. Mississippi Choctaw refer to them by their speed—*palki* (a fast player), *sala'ha wašoha* (a slow player). Or they might call someone *siti* (snake), *căna'să* (moccasin snake), or *opa niškin* (owl or owl eyes), clearly referring to writhing, escaping, and striking skills, or keen eyesight. The absence of strategy in the Eastern Cherokee game has been noted by Fogelson. Passing to a teammate occurred usually only out of necessity, and the only "play" he saw was in a game where "the center fighter, a notably large and powerful man, held two members of the rival team while his teammates all managed to tie up their particular opponents. This situation left one Wolftown player free to score the requisite number of goals [to win]."[3]

The principal means of "tying up" one's opponent is to grab him from behind around the waist, invariably leading both players to drop their sticks and indulge in a wrestling match. This observation was made in the early nineteenth century: "Sometimes eight or ten or more couples, are engaged in personal conflicts, each individual striving in the most vigorous and adroit manner to gain the mastery. A stranger will shudder to see the violent manner in which they throw each other to the ground." If the ball is not quickly found in a cluster of players, such wrestling may result in a mass pileup (see Figure 25). Watching Cherokee players in 1848, Charles Lanman aptly described it as "presenting, as they struggle for the ball, the appearance of a dozen gladiators, striving to overcome a monster serpent." Fogelson, who once took part in an Eastern Cherokee practice, commented on how exhausting this style of play could be: "The toll of energy [striving to free oneself or keep an opponent from getting free] spent in these exertions with one's opponent is tremendous. Add to this constant tugging and pulling, the fact that the player must periodically sprint long distances at top speed, and one can readily comprehend the degree of stamina required of successful ball players."[4]

When not wrestling or poking around for the ball in a cluster of bodies, players may stand around resting, watching the action from a distance, with sticks held together or arms dropped at each side. Occasionally the Eastern Cherokee practice "double teaming," where two players gang up on an opponent. This maneuver has its risks, since it leaves one player unguarded and free to score if he gains the ball.[5]

Although lacrosse is still very much alive in the south, it has almost disappeared from the Great Lakes area; for the most part, the game was given up about two generations ago. Most elders recall the game from their youth, and some, such as Wilbur Blackdeer, a Wisconsin Winnebago, have attempted to revive the game with their children, but have had only limited success. In this region of North America, baseball appears to have supplanted lacrosse as the summertime game of choice.

Controlling the ball with a single stick while running demanded a different technique from that used in the southeast. Walter James Hoffman's report on Menominee stick cradling in the late nineteenth century provides a good general description: "When the ball is caught, the runner carries the stick almost horizontally before him, moving it rapidly from side to side, and at the same time turning the stick so as to keep the ball always in front and retained by the pocket. This constant swinging and twisting movement tends to prevent players of the opposite side from knocking the ball out or dislodging it by hitting the stick."[6]

Great Lakes ball handling could be done with both hands or only one hand on the stick. Saulteaux players around 1804 had "a peculiar way of working their hands and arms while running, [so] the ball never dropped out of their hurdle." The Ottawa cradling technique of that period was similar: To keep the ball from falling out, the ballcarrier twisted the stick rapidly back and forth; but the use of both hands was said to diminish his speed. Frank Mayer's sketches of Dakota players in 1851 show the use of both hands in carrying and throwing the ball (Figures 28a, b). Franklin Basina, however, discounts the use of both hands by Lake Superior Ojibwe, saying the player "waves it with the ball in it. One hand, he's running towards the goal," and I have seen a demonstration of the "overhead flour-

• 125

Figures 28a, b • Mayer's drawings of Dakota players at Traverse des Sioux during a large gathering for treaty making show them (a) cradling the ball while running and (b) preparing to launch a long overhead throw.

• 126

Figure 29 • Oil painting by Charles Deas (about 1850?) of Dakota lacrosse game. Player on the left attempts to scoop a ground ball, while player on the right tries to block his stick. Note the variety of designs in body paint, the feather tail-piece, and the moc-casins worn by some of the players.

ish" involving the swinging of the stick in a full circle above the head with one hand only. Wilbur Blackdeer, a former Winnebago player and stickmaker, recalls players who could swing their stick overhead around and around in the air without losing the ball.[7]

Scooping a ground ball was generally accomplished with one hand as well (Figure 29). The technique involves slamming the racket down upon the ball and, with a sudden twist of the wrist, turning the stick over and catching the ball on the webbing, all in one motion. In discussing recovery of a ground ball, Basina contrasts the advantages of long and short sticks, saying that, while longer ones were better for passing, the shorter ones were ideal for scooping.

Pocket size affected throwing accuracy. Historical reports indicate that certain Great Lakes players had exceptional passing and throwing skills. Among Lake Superior Ojibwe about 1850 were "great ball-players, who can send the ball so high that it is out of sight, [and thereby] attain the same renown among the Indians as celebrated runners, hunters, or warriors." Elders on the Lac Court Oreilles Reservation in Wisconsin in the early 1940s suggested that the ball was often thrown in a high arc (Figure 30). Said one, "The higher the ball would go, the faster the boys ran." Copway seems to have described the same Ojibwe technique, indicating players' ability to catch a falling ball in mid-air and "with such dexterity . . . strike the ball that it is sent out of sight. Another strikes it on its descent, and for ten minutes at a time the play is so adroitly managed that the ball does not touch the ground."[8]

The arcing throw was sometimes used in passing, particularly from out of bounds, according to Basina: "You gotta throw it high enough, too, you know, you have to throw it just high enough so this guy can't reach it, that's a guy with his stick over him, just like an arch." Catching a passed ball also required skill, and certain players were noted for it ("like you catch a hardball"), particularly those using long sticks, such as members of the Bear family on his reservation: "Everybody made their own sticks to their liking . . . some guys may like the big stick, like big, long one . . . It's Bears boys, Billy Bear, Simon Bear, and all them . . . they were the guys that catch [the ball] in flight, just like a catcher, an outfielder would do, throw that stick out and that goddam ball would be right in there."

Because of its construction, there was no real distinction made between a Great Lakes right- or left-hand stick, as there was among the southeastern and Iroquoian tribes. The soft webbing of tanned deerhide or even heavy string easily fell to one or the other side of the stick, depending upon how it was held, so that one could catch or cradle a ball in either side: "You ain't got time when you're running [to] take a look at that goddam stick, know which way the pocket is. You can catch that going either way, and it's still flexible. You see, that's the catching glove, or any kind of glove, the more softer it is, the better off it is. [If] it's stiff, well you ain't got no [play]."[9]

Running skills were also stressed in the Great Lakes game. Wrote Jonathan Carver in the eighteenth century: "They run with amazing velocity in pursuit of each other, and when one is on the point of hurling it to a great distance, an antagonist overtakes him, and by a sudden stroke dashes down the ball." More recently (1968) Fred Jones of Mille Lacs Lake, Minnesota, described himself as a poor player because of his inability to elude opponents, but he mentioned a relative of his, John Percy, who, although bowlegged from many years as a rodeo horseback rider, was nevertheless a good lacrosse player because of his speed: "He's all over, he's wearing a big ten-gallon hat and his cowboy shoes. I told John, I says, you can't run, I says, not as bull-legged as you are. You go out there and show us. And, by God, he did too. That guy could really run, so bull-legged. He got that ball, you know, he'd be where it was at, that was always good. There's nobody could catch him."[10]

That some sort of zone defense may have been the Great Lakes practice in the past is implied in an early report on Huron games: "Each party endeavors to toss the ball to their side; some run to the ball, and the rest keep at a little distance on both sides to assist on all quarters." On the other hand, a type of phalanx defense of the ballcarrier has also been described, suggesting that zones were abandoned when a player was trying to score. His teammates would surround him to keep opponents at bay: "He never fails, however, from being dispossessed of the ball unless he throws it towards his home [goal] which is sometimes difficult." Clearly, then, Great Lakes play falls somewhere between the southeastern game and today's field lacrosse: if a player could not pass to a teammate, he threw in the general direction of the goal.[11]

One special technique seems to be exclusively a Great Lakes practice, namely the catapult of the ball—the ballista that Makoons and Bad Sky used in the Trojan horse capture of Fort Michilimackinac. Basina told how it was done: "Like if a guy is chasing

Figure 30 • Menominee players in a game about 1910 await the descent of a high, arcing ball, possibly tossed backward over the head by the player whose stick is in motion (the blur in the photograph).

him, the guy with the ball, and if you got a fast runner on your side, and he keeps ahead of the guy that's carrying the ball, if he sees that the guy's chasing him, gaining on him, then he goes in front of him like that, and that guy comes and hits it with his stick, and the ball goes out in front, flies away.'' That this tactic was old and widespread is made evident by Colonel Landmann's writing on Ottawa lacrosse in 1799. Apparently, holding out the stick horizontally was a signal to the carrier to get rid of the ball. Certainly the nature of Great Lakes stick construction was what enabled this ''cannon-shot'' to be performed. It would have been difficult to accomplish the maneuver with either the southeastern or the Iroquoian stick.[12]

Ironically, the techniques used in the Iroquois game that has developed into what we call lacrosse today are the least well documented. The changes evident in the construction of the Iroquoian stick obviously parallel changes in ball handling (Figure 31), but the details of exactly how they do are missing from published descriptions of their game. The Iroquois are consistently reported as prefer-

• 129

Figure 31 • Two Onondaga players about 1910. From left: Howard Hill (?), unidentified woman and child, John Isaacs. Note gut-wall on sticks, triangular and rounded crooks, flattened considerably from the earlier stick to improve scooping capacity. Also note the short handle, less than a third the length of the stick. Isaacs's stick is right-handed, the other is left-handed. The commercially manufactured rubber ball approximates regulation ball of the early 1990s in size.

ring the *old* style of play to more contemporary ways, for it allowed players to showcase more individual skills. Probably matches against Canadian teams in the last half of the nineteenth century encouraged an increased emphasis on team play.[13]

Lewis Henry Morgan is one of the few sources on techniques used in the historical Iroquoian game. His fieldwork was carried out from 1825 to 1845, mostly among the Seneca, but what he described can be accepted as the general style of other Iroquoian peoples of that period as well.

There is a suggestion in Morgan's writing that the Iroquoian game was as sluggish as the southeastern game, moving in fits and starts, for he told of the ball's being "imprisoned" in one part of the field or another. Morgan seems to refer to a ball that had been passed and caught or else intercepted by another's stick; a struggle ensued, after which the ball could be either thrown on the ground or passed again. The implication seems to be that the players fought over the ball while it was still in (or on) someone's stick until it was knocked out; then it could fall to the ground or be batted or thrown through the air. The ball was carried with the stick held out in front of the player, the plane of its "network" as parallel to the ground as possible, for at that time there were no guard-strings to prevent the ball's slipping off if the stick was tilted.[14]

Maintaining control of the ball with sticks of the sort that Morgan collected had to have been a balancing feat. The stick had no pocket, and so the slightest jarring would cause the player to lose the ball. Thus it seems safe to conclude that before the introduction of guard-strings the game was more a running than a passing game. These early lacrosse sticks also differ from later ones in that in cross-section the curve of the crook is the same rounded shaft as the handle, though somewhat thinner. This construction would have made modern techniques of scooping the ball difficult, if not impossible. To my knowledge it is nowhere recorded how an Iroquois player picked up a ground ball with this type of stick.

Lacrosse players I have queried on the matter seem puzzled to learn that *any* sticks lacked guard-strings. Linley Logan, a Seneca player, suggested that, to discern what techniques would have been used, one might have to let lacrosse players attempt to play with sticks lacking a gut-wall and watch how they handle the ball. That it *is* possible to balance a ball on taut webbing in a game Logan made clear to me when he recalled practicing lacrosse as a youth. Whenever he and his friends lacked lacrosse sticks, they used old tennis rackets instead.[15]

Morgan provided two other details of Iroquois game play—one on stick handling under pressure, the other on a sort of team strategy. The first statement suggests ridding oneself of the ball by throwing backward over the head: "When the line of the runner [carrying the ball] was crossed, by an adversary coming in before him upon a diagonal line, and he found it impossible, by artifice or stratagem, to elude him, he turned about, and threw the ball over the heads of both of them, towards his gate; or, perchance, towards a player of his own party, if there were adverse players between him and the gate [goal]." The other passage describes a means of preventing the ball-carrier from scoring: "Some of the players detached themselves from the group contending around the ball, and took a position from which to intercept a runner upon a diagonal line, if it should chance that one of the adverse party got possession of the ball."[16]

By reviewing George Beers's 1869 book on how *non*-Indian lacrosse should be played, one can in fact glean something about the Mohawk game of the mid-nineteenth century. Many of the techniques that Beers forwards are derived from the Indian style of play *or* are suggested as alternatives (i.e., improvements) to Iroquois lacrosse.[17] Beyond Beers, one can also look to newspaper accounts of nineteenth-century games between Iroquois and Canadian teams to learn something of the differences in the two styles of play. For example, a Dominion Day match in 1874 between the Brampton Excelsiors and the Six Nations Reserve, marked by much betting and fighting, was ultimately won by Brampton. A report on the action suggests that the Indians had not yet developed an adequate defense against Canadian dodging skills:

> The Indians made some excellent catches and "played into each other's hands well", but were outclassed in running by the Excelsiors whose dodging also appeared to puzzle their opponents. According to McClelland the Indians played in all their warpaint and feathers and nothing else but a breech-cloth. They were strong and agile and their chief and captain "White Eagle", was a magnificent runner and "could jump over a man's head without the slightest effort."[18]

Once Iroquois players began to compete regularly with Canadian teams around the Montreal area in the mid-nineteenth century, their techniques of play undoubtedly changed accordingly. For information on that style of game, however, one needs to consult the standard non-Indian manuals on lacrosse published beginning in the last half of that century.

Fort Gibson, Indian Territory, 1834

The peculiar request was brought by Snapping Turtle, who had come directly from the Indian Agency. It seemed that a famous white medicine man was visiting Fort Gibson. His exceptional powers lay in making likenesses of people on paper, working very quickly with sticks, some that looked like they had small animal tails on their ends and others that left thin marks on the paper wherever pressed. The white man dipped the tails into a number of small bowls, each containing some medicine of a different color, although it wasn't certain what leaves and roots he had made it from. That was probably the medicine man's secret. Snapping Turtle had been shown many of the magical drawings that the man carried with him, and he was able to recognize some of them when told whom they were meant to represent. Even if he didn't recognize the likenesses, he could tell whether they were Creek or Cherokee people. In any case, the medicine man had already produced one of Snapping Turtle, which impressed him, and had shown him one of Chief Mo-sho-la-tub-bee. It must have been made earlier, because the chief had since perished from the white man's red-mark disease. Or perhaps he had appeared to the medicine man in a dream.

Even though the great game would not be played for a week, Snapping Turtle had been requested to invite Thirsts-for-Stone to appear at the agency wearing his full ball-play uniform and to bring his sticks. The medicine man, it seemed, was intent on making images of only the finest chiefs, warriors, and sportsmen, and Thirsts-for-Stone's reputation as an outstanding lacrosse player was well known to the lieutenants at the agency.

Thirsts-for-Stone paced his cabin, stopped to pick up a dirty kettle from the floor, and quietly handed it to his woman with a look that said, "This really needs cleaning." The talented Choctaw athlete was at first hesitant and apprehensive. Once the medicine man had his head on a piece of paper, there was no telling what he might do with it. If he were a sorcerer, could he not carry away the head and work evil charms on it? Thirsts-for-Stone had already gone into training for the game, reducing his diet to cold foods and removing rabbit from the menu. And he had begun sleeping on the opposite side of the room from his woman. Wasn't it possible that the white man might counter all these preparations and somehow cause Thirsts-for-Stone's team to lose?

A mangy-looking dog sheepishly tried to slink through the door, but the Choctaw ball player noticed it, grabbed a small pot, and threw it at the dog, which ran yelping from the cabin with its tail between its legs. Turning to Snapping Turtle, Thirsts-for-Stone had more questions. And what of his lacrosse sticks? If the medicine man captured them on paper, could he not render them useless in the forthcoming game? But Snapping Turtle appealed to his vanity. His flattery about Thirsts-for-Stone's lacrosse prowess and the curious request itself were at least intriguing enough for Thirsts-for-Stone to have his woman retrieve the items needed for his appearance at the agency later that day. The game equipment was carefully kept in the rear of the small log cabin that served as their home, and even though they were in mourning at the time over the red-mark death of their infant son, it was always prudent to honor requests from the agency.

So it was that Laughing Bird took down from a shelf those pieces of costume that her man would also don several days later for the game and began to examine each item carefully for wear and tear to determine what immediate repairs would suffice for the agency visit. The tailpiece caught her attention, for some of the horsehair had become matted and tangled during a previous game. She began to comb gently through it, taking care not to pull too hard where it was attached to the rod that held it aloft when it was worn. Thirsts-for-Stone took similar pains with the horsehair necklace that he would tie around his neck, straightening out several intertwined strands of different colors and seeing that they would hang properly together, grouped by color. As usual, to stay cool in the hot, dusty climate of their new homeland, he was wearing only his breechclout and moccasins. He removed his footwear as he prepared to paint the lower part of his legs.

Several small leather pouches contained the various powders that Thirsts-for-Stone needed to mix with water and smear on himself in the ornamental designs that great ball players chose to cover a good part of their body. There was powdered charcoal for black, red vermilion traded for at the agency, and a deep yellow made from a certain rock found in a nearby creekbed and easily pulverized to obtain a paste. Working quickly, he covered his feet and calves in a solid red, used more red for zigzags on his forearms and across his face, then rinsed his fingers in the bucket and began to work with the yellow. Hands and wrists were colored solid, then parallel lines were put on the face and around the thighs at intervals. Finally, he dipped his forefinger into the charcoal to outline the various designs he had already made.

Thirsts-for-Stone was admired for the great care with which he prepared his body for the combat of play. Each design had a meaning, each circle a purpose—the whole effect was one that would honor the spirits of the game and maintain his elevated status as a great ball player. Meanwhile, his woman was looking for her bead collection to replace several that had apparently been lost from the belt in the violent tussle of former games.

Fully painted but without his tailpiece, Thirsts-for-Stone went to the rear of the cabin to get his two lacrosse sticks. Looking up at the peg from which they usually hung, he suddenly saw that one was missing. It had been broken the week before in a scrimmage, and he had forgotten to get to the stickmaker for another pair. There was still time, since the sketching session would not take place until just before supper. So, still in war paint but putting his moccasins back on, Thirsts-for-Stone started out on foot in the direction of Wildcat's cabin, about twenty minutes from his.

• 135

Wildcat was one of the few Choctaw stickmakers who had survived the long, tragic trip on foot some two years earlier. The relocation of his people to Indian Territory had been dictated by the terms of the treaty made at Dancing Rabbit Creek. Although the government had promised that they would be transported by horse, wagon, and steamboat, in fact most had been forced to make the long, arduous journey on foot because the authorities suddenly explained that there was no money to send them any other way. Thirsts-for-Stone and his woman, pregnant with their son at the time, had somehow managed to make it; many others had not been so lucky. His prowess and stamina from years of running on the playing field had paid off in this tragic twist of fate experienced by the Choctaw people.

Because the great game later that week had been planned several months in advance, nearly all the stickmakers had been kept busy filling orders. But Wildcat was one of the best; back in the old country he had made sticks for Thirsts-for-Stone's father. Thirsts-for-Stone needed a completely new pair of sticks, for it was useless simply to replace the broken one. Choctaw sticks were always made in pairs, with one pocket slightly smaller than the other, so that when the ball was "put away," it would be snugly secure and difficult for an opponent to dislodge. Sticks were in effect extensions of a player's arms, and their spoon-shaped cups functioned like his hands.

As Thirsts-for-Stone neared Wildcat's yard, he spotted a teammate just leaving the compound with a fresh pair of hickory ballsticks and called to him. When his friend laughed and pointed at him, Thirsts-for-Stone suddenly remembered that he was in full combat paint; the other player must have wondered if he had misunderstood the designated day for the game. Inside the compound, several players were checking through Wildcat's inventory, looking for a pair of sticks that would suit their preferences as to length, balance, and cupping capacity. They had practice balls with them and tested one pair of sticks after another, holding the stick with the smaller cup in the left hand and crossing it over the right-hand stick upside down, so that the wrists were locked together, the smaller cup fitting firmly into the larger. Some were swinging the sticks overhead to feel their weight and control; others were taking turns firing balls at an imaginary goal.

While Wildcat bartered with a player over a pair of sticks, his two sons worked busily on new sticks that were laid out in various stages of completion on a table against the cabin. Many of the sticks were clearly recently made, and the wood was probably not dry enough to withstand actual play. Using old ax blades as wedges, one son had just split a four-foot hickory log lengthwise into two halves and was testing the grain in each to see which half would withstand further splitting better. The other boy had just finished thinning the middle section of a peeled V-shaped blank that would form the cup when the end was bent back over onto the shaft and secured with rawhide wrappings. Behind the cabin, Thirsts-for-Stone could see Wildcat's woman and daughters hand-drilling holes that would be threaded with the deerhide lacing. One was using flint rock to smooth the handles and round off the edges of the cups.

As Thirsts-for-Stone approached, Wildcat, too, seemed astonished to find a player dressed for action several days before the event. But Thirsts-for-Stone told him of the white medicine man at the agency, and the stickmaker, who always bet on this great player's team, went indoors and came out with a particularly elegant pair of Choctaw lacrosse sticks that he had completed a month earlier. Thirsts-for-Stone examined them carefully, ran his finger over the rim of one cup, and tugged on the lacing to test its strength. He cupped the sticks together and tested their balance, swinging them together overhead, then flailing like a windmill with one in each hand. They were fine sticks, as he had expected they would be.

When Thirsts-for-Stone further explained the purpose of the agency's request, Wildcat again disappeared briefly and returned with some red yarn tassels, which he began to tie on the sticks below the cups to provide added importance. They agreed upon a price for the sticks—if they held up well in the game, they would be worth at least two new knives and perhaps even a copper kettle. Thirsts-for-Stone went home to get his tailpiece and then left on his horse for his appointment at the agency.

When he arrived at Fort Gibson, the area around the agency was churning with activity. Large numbers of Choctaw people were encamped outside the fort, and, although he was dressed for a ball game, Thirsts-for-Stone seemed not to attract any particular attention. Small boys were racing in nearly every direction, and the famous ball player was nearly trampled by several of them suddenly coming around a tent. Others were testing their wrestling skills—talents that would enhance their performance later in life on the ball field. He could hear the thunder of hoofs nearby and realized that horse races were also in progress, and the beating of drums in the distance informed him of dancing somewhere in the encampment. The pattern of the percussion suggested perhaps a rehearsal of the Eagle Dance, which had been promised to the medicine man as part of the entertainment provided by the commandant for visiting dignitaries.

Thirsts-for-Stone entrusted his horse to a young man and, spotting Snapping Turtle near the entrance to the fort, went to join him. Snapping Turtle was one of the few who had learned the language of the white man, and he could act as interpreter in most proceedings at the agency. When their mission was announced, they were escorted by a young soldier to the agent's house, where the white medicine man worked with his small sticks. The man had been waiting for the ball player and seemed both astonished and delighted at his appearance. Thirsts-for-Stone had expected to see the man in the customary jacket and vest of an important white man, but over his ruffled white blouse he had on a new buckskin jacket, clearly of Indian manufacture—possibly Cherokee, Thirsts-for-Stone thought, but how odd. He sat at a table with a notebook in hand, and after Thirsts-for-Stone took a chair, he began quickly to sketch aspects of the young ball player, turning pages as soon as he finished with them. Then he took out a larger paper and removed an animal-tail stick from an assortment protruding from a cup. He dipped it into one and then another of the eight small bowls that held colored medicines. Each time, however, he dipped the tail in a cup of clear water before using it again. He doesn't wish the medicines to contaminate each other, thought Thirsts-for-Stone. They would probably lose their power if they did.

The ball player, naturally curious to see what was being put on paper, kept trying to get a closer look, but each time he was admonished to sit still and look straight ahead (Figure 32a). He had inadvertently left his ballsticks on the table, and after a few preliminary sketches, the medicine man picked them up and placed them in Thirsts-for-Stone's hands— upside down. The athlete instinctively corrected the position. Then, through Snapping Turtle, the interpreter, the man asked that the ball player stand in a posture as though he were in a game. Snapping Turtle helped him remove the cloth turban he was wearing and assisted in inserting the tailpiece and adjusting it to flow elegantly from his beaded belt.

Thirsts-for-Stone had not worn the tailpiece into the agency, knowing that it would have been crushed or bent when he seated himself in a chair of the style customarily used by white people. Now he could wear it proudly and look the warrior-player that he was. Since he'd been requested to pretend he was in a ball game, Thirsts-for-Stone began to swing the sticks overhead, then bent over to scoop an imaginary ball off the floor, and then . . . He was told to stop, that he was supposed to remain "frozen" while the white man worked. The term "frozen" made him nervous, but he complied with the man's desire.

Meanwhile the agent had come to watch the medicine man at work. Each time he made a request, Snapping Turtle conveyed the medicine man's wishes. Translating into Choctaw, Snapping Turtle informed the athlete how he should pose: "Now turn your head slightly to the side." "Ballsticks up a little higher." "No, take the wrists apart so we can see each stick." "Head back a bit." "Now put your right foot slightly behind the left, with only the toe touching." "Good." It all seemed so artificial, so unnatural to the athlete, who was beginning to develop a cramp in his left calf (Figure 32b).

All of this procedure took less than an hour. Then the adjutant announced that supper was being served. The medicine man arose and showed the ball player one of the sketches

Figure 32a

Figure 32b

he had made. It was slightly disturbing to Thirsts-for-Stone, as it showed only a bodiless head with the right ear and eye missing, but it did manage to duplicate his facial designs. The white man shook his hand, and promised that he would attend the game and bet heavily on Thirsts-for-Stone's team.

The day of the grand game arrived. Thirsts-for-Stone had traveled the distance with his family and friends to set up camp in the woods near their end of the playing field. He had already met with the opposing team captain to work out details of the game, decide the number of players and goals to be scored, and select the elders to act as referees and trustworthy men as stakeholders. Since their removal from their original homelands to the east and with their population so reduced, the Choctaw people had considerably relaxed the restrictions on who might play for each side, and the games consequently had become more seasonal amusements, without regard to clan affiliation, marital status, and the other matters that formerly had controlled the selection of teams. Nowadays, since the Choctaw had considerable free time, their games tended to pit entire districts of the nation against each other rather than villages or clans. Consequently the games drew huge crowds, and the amount of goods and valuables wagered had grown considerably in just the two years since the last group of refugees arrived in Indian Territory.

As promised, the medicine man made his appearance at the event. He was seen with two soldiers from the fort, riding around the encampments on their horses, while spectators from throughout the area continued to arrive in streams and set up lodgings. The two goals with their crossbars had been put up and the betting line drawn between them, as swarms of women, children, and even players themselves positioned themselves opposite each other to bet one article against another. The wagered items would be put in charge of the stakeholders overnight. The medicine man on his horse seemed to be making notes to himself, keenly eyeing everything going on around him. As evening fell, each team retired to its respective seclusion under the watchful eyes of the spiritual leaders who would give them final instructions. At intervals throughout the night, the ritually required ball game dance was performed, with rows of specially selected women singing to the accompaniment of rattles and drums as they danced in place, raising and lowering their heels (Figure 33).

Figure 33

Despite the full night of dancing and abstinence from food and drink, Thirsts-for-Stone and his teammates were in a mood of exhilaration on the morning of the game. At a signal from the four referees, each team proceeded to its goalposts and began to circle them counterclockwise. Because of the many players for this particular event, there was an unusually large mass circling, nearly five abreast at each end of the field. Upon another shout from centerfield, all players raised their sticks in the air, pointing them toward the top of the goalpost, and began to bang them together noisily, all the while letting out the most ferocious war whoops. Now the medicine man on horseback was slowly circling the field, stopping occasionally to enter something in his notes.

Following their "huddle," each team lined up across the field and began to march toward centerfield, where they faced their opponents. After a harangue from one of the elders about playing the game fairly, players took their positions together with their opposite numbers and spread themselves fairly evenly over the field, with concentrations near the goals and at midfield, for the first toss-up. The referee holding the small buckskin-covered ball began to chant a prayer. Then suddenly a gun was fired from the sidelines as a signal for him to toss the ball in the air—and mayhem commenced. Thirsts-for-Stone had been following the progress of the white medicine man, wondering exactly what he was up to, but now he needed to focus his attention on the game.

One of the tallest of his team, Thirsts-for-Stone usually took part in the midfield action at the toss-up. His height gave him an advantage in trying to catch the ball between his sticks upon its descent, but in this case the ball eluded both him and the opposing centerman and fell somewhere between them. Immediately a pileup of players began pushing and shoving with their sticks, poking around on the ground in an attempt to locate the small ball—a difficult task in the short, dry grass which, at this time of year, was almost the color of the ball cover itself. Suddenly, a teammate raised his sticks over the heads of the others in a gesture of success and let fly the ball, which he had somehow managed to find and clamp between his sticks. The ball landed downfield but was on the ground only a moment before another player on Thirsts-for-Stone's team found it and secured it, only to discover himself surrounded by members of the opposite team. He tried to break away from the pack, but the player next to him brought his sticks down hard on the carrier's, thereby dislodging the ball. He immediately picked it up—and found himself facing three opponents.

Extending his arms and sticks to his left, he turned to run. Because of the numbers pursuing him, he was quickly ready to throw and brought his sticks up and over his head in a feint of doing so, which distracted them and caused them to look momentarily in that direction. This fake allowed him enough time to get in the clear, so he decided to hang on to the ball. Breaking out of the pack, yelping and hollering, he ran, leaping over injured and prone players, progressing rapidly downfield, all the while swinging his sticks overhead from one shoulder to the other, dodging one opponent after another. A nearby player crossed his

Figure 34

path flailing wildly with each stick in the air, hoping to strike the carrier's sticks. But he was too late. The ballcarrier, sensing the danger, managed to get off a shot in the general direction of his goal just as his opponent came down hard with one stick (Figure 34).

By now the white medicine man was on the other side of the field near the goalposts. He had been joined by another, and they were in animated conversation. Thirsts-for-Stone was close enough that he thought he recognized the man in the tall hat as the Frenchman he had seen at the agency. But he should not become distracted from the game, he thought. Suddenly Thirsts-for-Stone found himself near enough where the ball had landed to capture it. But he no sooner had the ball than six pursuers were upon him, forcing him to rid himself of it. With his wrists securely crossed, he ran forward, took aim, and brought the sticks over his right shoulder. Leading with his left foot, Thirsts-for-Stone turned sideways and, using his full upper torso, threw the ball over and out by separating the sticks and following through with his right leg. Just beyond him, one of his teammates was in a fistfight with a member of the opposite team, the two of them having dropped their sticks to settle the matter.

Most players had little idea of where the ball had landed. Given the general congestion on the field and the mass confusion of so many players running in opposite directions, it was some time before a player actually clamped down on the ball and began to run with it. But, no, he was only faking—acting as a decoy for a fellow teammate who was several yards off to his side and pretending not to have the ball, while it lay securely between his sticks resting on the ground, a pose he kept until the others were sufficiently distracted to turn their attention away. This left him in the clear to begin a mad dash at the goal and score the first point, prompting his side of the huge crowd to let out an uproar of war whoops and yells. In the brief interim following the goal, Thirsts-for-Stone looked for the medicine man, but he had disappeared. He gave a sigh of relief, thinking perhaps the white man had gotten bored and departed.

After a short respite, the players took up their original positions, and Thirsts-for-Stone returned to midfield to await the gunshot that would signal the next toss-up. As he gazed past his opponent, out of the corner of his eye he caught a glimpse of the white medicine man standing on the left side of the field, holding the reins of his grazing horse. The man again had his notebook out and seemed to be making sketches of the game. This was fairly unsettling to Thirsts-for-Stone. Why was the man working his magic down here at the field? There was something devious, something furtive about the situation, but before Thirsts-for-Stone could dwell on it, the gun was fired. With his two sticks outstretched behind him, he successfully leapt higher in the air and caught the ball this time. But no sooner had Thirsts-for-Stone himself landed on his feet than an opponent behind him threw his arms around the champion in a tight bear hug, effectively tying him up and preventing his passing the ball to a teammate. The opponent leaned back with full effort, trying to pull Thirsts-for-Stone over on top of him and cause him to lose the ball. But he managed to give it a short toss toward a teammate, who scooped it up, jumping in the air and descending on it with both sticks. He quickly broke away from his pursuers and, as if to taunt the closest one, began to stab his sticks (carrying the ball) in his face while taking steps backward and letting out yelps at him.

And so the game progressed for several hours without letup. The field was littered with broken sticks, which had to be removed after each point was scored. Players who had looked so handsome at the start now had most of their brilliant war paint smeared and streaked into indiscernible patterns over their bodies. The rough play had taken its toll on tailpieces, manes, and beaded belts as well, although each player tried to rearrange his costume as best as possible between goals scored. Still, so much wrestling, tripping, stick smashing, and general melee left a fairly battered set of players on the field. Undaunted, however, they continued this grand spectacle until the other team finally reached the required number of goals to win with a spectacular final goal—the player ran nearly the length of the field to score.

Thirsts-for-Stone's teammates were already throwing angry glances in his direction;

some even completely snubbed him. They all knew about his visit to the agency and the white medicine man's tinkering with his image. Maybe those bowls of colored medicine that Snapping Turtle had mentioned so casually were much more powerful than they had suspected. Word had spread quickly about bodiless heads and detached arms and legs that filled the pages of the white man's book. The game had been unusually rough, and more limbs had been broken in the scuffle than was common. Had the medicine man been responsible for this as well? Had he pulled all his magic together because of what happened to the horse? Thirsts-for-Stone strode dejectedly off the field to find his woman. Inside himself, he was fuming and in a near panic. Anxiously, he now sought out Snapping Turtle. It was vital to retrieve the sketches made at the agency before further damage could be done. Meanwhile, the winners collected their bets from the stakeholders, then went off good-naturedly to take a few pulls from whiskey jugs brought for postgame celebration. And justly so, for they had valiantly won this "little war."

• 143

Such was Choctaw lacrosse in Indian Territory in the year 1834. But one incident during the game deserves mention. As he had promised, the white medicine man had appeared on the sidelines of Thirsts-for-Stone's team and watched the action intently from astride his horse, although for some peculiar reason not in the customary fashion. For a period of time the man had reversed himself and, like an Indian "contrary," was seated backward on the animal's bare rump, occasionally leaning forward to rest on his elbows. Was he trying to mimic a "contrary," to show off his powers? The game appeared to have fascinated him as much as his ridiculous perch had amused the Choctaw, as their eyes followed the actions of his horse, who casually was allowed to move about while grazing. In such a vigorous contest the action of the game occasionally spilled over into the crowd, and most Indian spectators learned from long experience to be able to move quickly and avoid being stampeded by the players. Partway through the game, a long-tossed ball had landed on the ground near the sideline where the white medicine man's horse was munching what little grass there was this time of year. As a player retrieved the ball and was about to throw it in the direction of his goal, he was suddenly run over by an opponent, who brought his sticks down hard on the ballcarrier, causing the ball to fly with great speed directly toward the horse. It struck him squarely in the buttocks. This unexpected slap on the rump caused the startled animal to bolt upright, dumping his tiresome load undecorously on the ground as George Catlin's hat fell flying. The uproar from both sides of the field at this ridiculous sight equaled any noisy hubbub following the winning of a closely contested lacrosse match and was the talk of the Choctaw nation for several weeks, rivaling even the final score of the game. Thirsts-for-Stone, however, did not find it so amusing.

10 "The Indian Gallery"

At his best, in his "studio" portraits, [George] Catlin deserves to rank among the better portrait painters of his time. . . . Catlin's field sketching style, however, was impressionistic. It was developed to meet the needs of his working conditions—a bold, rapid technique for pictorial reporting. . . . In his haste to make his field record as complete as his limited time permitted Catlin could not wait to fully exploit the artistic possibilities of each subject. To speed his work he adopted some shortcutting conventions—his own system of pictorial shorthand.

—John C. Ewers, "George Catlin," *p. 505*

What can works of art tell us about American Indian sports? Before photography, artistic renderings like Catlin's constitute our only visual sources, but how reliable are they?[1] The camera was the first tool for capturing images with any accuracy, so in the case of lacrosse it was half a century after Catlin before we could find out accurately what the game really looked like; how its players were dressed, held their sticks, were arranged on the field; and what techniques were used in passing, scooping a ground ball, and body checking.

Precisely because Catlin's lacrosse paintings are so vibrant and his action scenes so intensely exciting, they have been reproduced often and are widely known. What they depict from more than a century and a half ago is so vastly different from what is played by non-Indians today on school campuses that they have caught the imagination of players and buffs alike and in many ways have become stereotypical impressions of the former Indian game.

Pictorial representations, however imperfect or misleading, are still our earliest visual sources on lacrosse. Catlin's sketches and paintings fill gaps in our knowledge about Indian forms of the game.

Before then, one had to rely exclusively on eyewitness or secondhand verbal accounts, which were sketchy and subjective, few and far between. From the seventeenth-century Jesuits, we have little beyond the Indian use of the game and the European name for the sport. Catlin's art at least brings lacrosse alive visually for the first time in history. Few, if any, artifacts of the game from that period survive—sticks, balls, and uniforms long since lost or surrendered to the elements—and the landscape of the playing fields is altered beyond recognition, overgrown or converted to farmland. Catlin in the 1830s at least provided a glimpse of the lacrosse practices of two tribes. Cautiously evaluated, he has much to tell us.

Such consideration must be based on contemporaneous written descriptions, including Catlin's own, and take into account our general knowledge of the game derived from later and more objective observers. For example, James Mooney's 1890 report on the Eastern Cherokee form of lacrosse is useful in corroborating some aspects of the Choctaw practices represented in Catlin's artistic works. Because most southeastern tribes played essentially the same game, despite their removal to Indian Territory in the 1830s, we can work back in time half a century from Mooney and find that many of the details Catlin depicts for the Choctaw seem not only plausible but even probable—the use of two sticks, for instance, the row of female singers in a preliminary ball game dance, wrestling matches between opposing players—all suggest a continuity of tradition. But an examination of his artistic methods and motivations should give us pause in accepting his illustrations at face value. Ultimately we must conclude that Catlin's lacrosse paintings are a rich mix of fact and fantasy. In creating them he was led as much by his preconceptions of Indian life as by what he actually witnessed. His lacrosse paintings were constructed to match his idea of what this wild, massive combat sport *should* look like on canvas. Clearly, he was carried away by what he saw. As Catlin would write of his attitude during this period of his life, "I have become so much of an Indian of late that my pencil has lost all appetite for subjects that savor of tameness."[2] Lacrosse offered him the perfect opportunity to depict wildness.

As a youth George Catlin had collected arrowheads and other Indian artifacts in the rural setting of his family's farm on the Susquehanna River in New York. Although he expressed an early interest in art, he went on to become a lawyer, but after practicing with his older brother for two years in Pennsylvania, he abandoned this career and decided to become a painter. A meeting with the Seneca Red Jacket near Buffalo revived Catlin's earlier interest in "the noble Savage" and led the thirty-year-old artist to paint his first Indian portrait in 1826—an unfinished likeness of the aging chief. A chance encounter with a delegation of Winnebago visiting Washington in 1828 produced nine additional Indian portraits. In 1830 Catlin departed for the frontier to immerse himself more fully in the creation of his ultimate goal, the "Indian Gallery." In 1832 Catlin left St. Louis on the steamer *Yellowstone* for a two-thousand-mile journey up the Missouri River with the expressed interest of recording "the history and customs of [Indian] people, preserved by pictorial illustrations, [the] themes worthy of the life-time of one man." Catlin's determination was clear: "Nothing short of the loss of my life, shall prevent me from visiting their country, and of becoming their historian."[3]

Catlin pursued his task at a feverish pace. Although a few other artists were painting at about the same time and in the same areas beyond the Mississippi—the Swiss Karl Bodmer, for instance, on the Upper Missouri—none came close to producing as many pictures or such a great variety as Catlin did in documenting the frontier West. Catlin followed his Missouri River voyage with later field trips to the southern Plains and the Upper Mississippi. Almost from the start he exhibited the products of his travels. A Pittsburgh showing in 1833 was moved to Cincinnati, and the next year the artist returned to the frontier. It was in 1834 that Catlin visited Fort Gibson and witnessed the grand Choctaw lacrosse game that provided a worthy subject for several paintings and sketches. In 1837 his Indian Gallery opened in New York. It drew so many viewers that it had to be moved from Clinton Hall to Stuyvesant Institute on Broadway to accommodate the vast crowd of the curious, avidly awaiting their first glimpse of the frontier. By any standards Catlin's output was prodigious: when he took his collection abroad to open in London two years later, he had finished around five hundred paintings, three-fifths of them portraits and the remainder landscapes and scenes of everyday Indian life.

Catlin's two-volume publication, *Letters and Notes on the Manners, Customs, and Condition of the North American Indians,* is a classic—regularly reprinted since its first appearance in 1841. Part adventure story, part ethnologies of the tribes he visited, Catlin's text was illustrated with vastly simplified line drawings of many of his paintings. *Letters and Notes* contains his description of Choctaw lacrosse, several illustrations of the game he purportedly witnessed, and portraits of several "well-known players," including Dakota (Sioux)—the last sketched during his travels on the Upper Mississippi.

How accurately depicted are these lacrosse games and players, and how much of Catlin's written account can we accept? Although he left behind few clues as to his artistic methods, given the brief time span in which he worked and his enormous output, we can assume that many details in his paintings *had* to have been added later from memory, probably with the aid of artifacts, including lacrosse sticks he had collected. Concluding that many details and props in Catlin's portraits probably were not done at the time of the sitting, art historian William Truettner points out: "[Catlin's] schedule was so demanding at times that he was obliged to rough in half a dozen portraits per day. . . . Many of the weapons held in the hands of male sitters, one suspects, were calculated additions of a later date." Where memory failed him, he no doubt invented lacrosse details to conform to his notion of what the game should resemble. Some scenes, critics conclude, may have been painted in only minutes. This painting technique contrasts greatly with the fastidiousness of, say, a Karl Bodmer.[4]

It is generally accepted that Catlin developed an artistic shorthand enabling him to convey quickly the general impression of some Indian scene or event, enough to allow him to complete his work back in the studio. In some instances the completion took place months or even years later. Historians have been able to reconstruct some of his methods from cleaning a number of paintings: "He commonly painted the backgrounds of his landscapes and scenes first. Then he drew his figures *over* the background. In some pictures the figures are so thinly painted that the backgrounds under them show through. Catlin quickly roughed in the figures in brown outline. If he had time he filled in the outlines. . . . Sometimes he never bothered to develop any part of the painting but the head. At other times he added or refined details after his return to civilization."[5]

Because Catlin had a wide range of experiences on which to draw, he could delve into his memory to supply him with objects, costumes, and poses. In at least one case he changed his subject's clothing and posture: In his Indian Gallery portrait of the Blackfoot Iron Hand, the warrior is seated, wearing a decorated quill shirt; but in the Duke of Portland's album Iron Hand appears standing, in a painted buffalo robe.

Occasionally it is possible to check Catlin's accuracy with museum specimens surviving from the period in which he painted. Such is the case with Indian musical instruments. Like most Euro-Americans, Catlin found Indian music itself unattractive. His assessment is evident in such published remarks as "My ears have been almost continually ringing since I came here, with the din of yelping and the beating of drums." Nonetheless, in his depiction of Indian drums, flutes, and rattles, Catlin is at his ethnographic best, despite his avowal that they were "rude and exceedingly defective." The three known Siouan wind instruments, for example, are shown side by side in a sketch, in proper proportions and with accurate other details of their construction: The single-tone *ši'yotaŋka,* which he calls "mystery whistle," the six-hole courting flute, and what he says is a war whistle, made from the humerus bone of an eagle—these all match museum specimens perfectly.

There are some paintings, however, whose ethnographic accuracy is extremely suspect. They suggest that Catlin occasionally allowed his imagination to run its course, for he had his own agenda to fulfill in providing eastern viewers of his Indian Gallery with pictures of curious, sometimes bizarre customs from the wilderness, portraying the Indians as a race apart, the way *he* conceived of them. One troublesome illustration is Catlin's sketch of "the snow-shoe dance," whose authenticity remains doubtful. He infers that it is Ojibwe (Chippewa) but illustrates the dancers wearing both the long, pointed Siouan style of shoe and the stubbier bear-paw Ojibwe variety. (He shows each type in detail in separate plates.) In his commentary Catlin limits his information on the dance to the following: "The *snow-shoe dance* . . . is exceedingly picturesque, being danced with the snow shoes under the feet, at the falling of the first snow in the beginning of winter; when they sing a song of thanksgiving to the Great Spirit for sending them a return of snow, when they can run on their snow shoes in their valued hunts, and easily take game for their food."[6]

No other reference to such a dance is found in the literature on the Ojibwe. Catlin does not specifically say that he ever saw it performed. Why the Ojibwe (and/or Sioux) would have dragged their snowshoes to Fort Snelling (or, for that matter, their winter leggings, which they are shown wearing in midsummer when he presumably painted them) remains unanswered. Possibly such items were under construction at the time, enough so for him to sketch them, and conceivably one could shuffle along in time to drumbeats while wearing snowshoes, but probably not in such proximity as Catlin has painted the dance. Also questionable in Catlin's illustration is the eagle-feather war banner stuck in the ground inside the circle of dancers. It seems to be simply another prop, in this case an out-of-place one, since it had nothing to do with hunting, which was supposedly the purpose of this dance of thanksgiving. The pair of snowshoes hoisted aloft as though affixed to an offering pole may be another contrivance.

Snowshoes seem to have been one Indian invention that appealed to Catlin and may have inspired his imagination as to their use. Another painting whose authenticity was questioned, even by Catlin's contemporary Rudolph Kurz, is the illustration of Indians chasing buffalo on snowshoes in midwinter. Kurz, like Catlin, painted on the Upper Missouri, though slightly later. He claimed that Catlin distorted his narrative for effect, and he felt that many of the drawings in *Letters and Notes* were "in bad taste and to a high degree inexact." The winter buffalo hunt is a case in point, because Catlin had never been on the Great Plains in the winter, when Indians would wear snowshoes. Furthermore, there is also the anomaly in the painting that the hunters are shown with minimal clothing, wearing, in fact, their summer war dress.[7] But the addition of such lively scenes to his "Wild West Show," whether based on fact or fantasy, was certain to enliven the otherwise preponderant sameness of portrait after portrait to the unsuspecting public and convey the "wildness" of his subjects.

The text of Catlin's *Letters and Notes* was meant to excite the reader as much as his illustrations. Thus it, too, is replete with exaggerated accounts as well as blatant fictions. Sexual licentiousness, for example, was certainly another "uncivilized" trait of Indians. Clearly a bit of a wag, Catlin on occasion would titillate his reader by approaching some subject having sexual overtones and then lapsing into language faked to look like an Indian tongue, as though he were writing "naughty" words in Latin. He did this in recording the antics of a sort of clown character in the Mandan Okippe ceremony, whose costume, purports the author, included an eight-foot phallus terminating in a red ball, with which he pretended to threaten women bystanders. Catlin tells how the character carried out his "obscene" gesture, not in English but by reverting to pseudo-Mandan and heightening the reader's excitement and frustration with exclamation marks.

Because Catlin's individual portraits of lacrosse players—"Nature's most beautiful models" in his opinion—are among his most noble and manly, it should be stressed that the artist often exaggerated the social status of his subjects, whether high or lowly, in details of costuming and bodily adornment. Catlin always selected the most prominent Indians—chiefs, warriors, the best athletes—for his portraits. Not surprisingly, they possessed and were accustomed on important occasions to wear the most elaborate costumes and to carry the most decorative and expensively ornamented items. And that is how he painted them. Whether the extremely elaborate dress and body paint shown in his portraits of the leading Choctaw and Dakotan lacrosse players were worn as well by the average player is not known. Catlin ignored the everyday Indian, choosing only the most elegant and exotic, who matched his preconception of what Indians should look like.

Were the extraordinary adornments worn by Thirsts-for-Stone—the beaded belt, the woven mane around the neck, the rigidly erect and lengthy horsetail, the elaborate designs painted on his body—reserved for only the finest players as a mark of distinction? Did everyone dress this way for the game, as the hundreds of figures on the field in his paintings suggest, or was this costume available only for special preparatory ceremonials or worn in special games played for religious purposes and involving fewer numbers? Did Choctaw players dress this way for practice? We know that much of the finery that Indian warriors donned for the Victory Dance back in the home village was *not* what they had worn into battle, when they would be stripped for action and unencumbered by such elegant accoutrements. In the case of lacrosse, Catlin's narrative gives us no clues to these questions. And how is it that such dress could survive even a few minutes of the rough-and-tumble of the game? Despite the fury of the action and Catlin's written description of the brutality of the contest, not one tailpiece has been broken, bent, knocked askew, or otherwise damaged or disarranged. Indeed, all the players resemble miniature Thirsts-for-Stones, as elegant and intact as he was when Catlin painted his out-of-combat portrait.

In a study of another painter on the frontier, Seth Eastman, John McDermott assesses Catlin's work: "Though he was at times an excellent painter, he was always a showman, but the haste of his travels did not allow him leisure for close observation of daily life. His purpose was to develop a 'wild West show.' What he sought was the broadly representative and the spectacular . . . all excellent selections for a travelling exhibition, for they highlighted the distant world they presented." McDermott, of course, had the point of view that what *Eastman* painted was accurate, and that Catlin ignored everyday Indian life, selecting always the sensational over the commonplace "reality" that is depicted on Eastman's canvasses:

> The sight of a dismounted hunter being rushed by a wounded buffalo was more exciting [to Catlin] than a glimpse of an Indian shooting a fish with a toy-sized bow; a proud Indian warrior dressed in his finest costume had more show appeal than a very ordinary looking fellow slouching around in leggins which appeared about to fall off. One turns to Catlin for a sense of the wildness of the West, not for the daily round of Indian life. . . . Catlin provided a thrill of excitement, but his very large gallery of views of a world now long ago and far away failed to preserve the common reality of their lives.[8]

We must conclude that the "true" or accurate portrayal lay somewhere between the works of the two artists; ultimately, there is no way of telling which of the two "got it right."

With these precautions in mind, what can we learn from Catlin about lacrosse practices west of the Mississippi in the 1830s? Consistent with the avowal in his narrative, George Catlin must have had an abiding fascination for the game. Lacrosse was the subject of eight of the nearly five hundred paintings of his Indian Gallery. Four are portraits of distinguished Choctaw and Dakotan players, the remainder are depictions of either games in progress or preparatory events, such as the Choctaw ball-play dance. It should be remembered that most Europeans had never witnessed *team* sports before arriving in the New World. That fact is one thing that inspired Catlin to make the most of his lacrosse paintings: The games were the closest events to actual hand-to-hand combat among "warlike savages" that he was able to experience. Certainly the spectacle of large numbers of athletes scrambling for possession of a single ball in a sport with few apparent regulations to control the ferocity of their battle must have been astonishing to those whose exposure to athletics had been limited to tennis, boxing, wrestling, foot-racing—all one-on-one competitions with clearly defined rules of play. This knowledge undoubtedly was what prompted Catlin to admonish his readers that "this wonderful game . . . can never be appreciated by those who are not happy [lucky] enough to see it."

Catlin's population estimate of some fifteen thousand Choctaw recently resettled in Indian Territory is fairly accurate. Newly arrived and as yet not totally converted to sedentary agriculture as the previously removed Cherokee and Creek, the Choctaw certainly had a great amount of free time available to indulge in their traditional dances and games. Such comparative lack of acculturation made them prime candidates for Catlin, who was similarly attracted to the Osage, a group who still hunted, dressed in skins, shaved their heads, and dangled strings of wampum from their slit earlobes.[9] Catlin is also correct in noting that lacrosse was the favorite sport of all southeastern tribes and that they played the same, or at least similar, forms of it.

The first assertion in Catlin's narrative that bears questioning concerns team size. He claims that commonly from six hundred to a thousand players were on the field during the game—an impression clearly conveyed in his Choctaw action paintings. But Catlin's figures are staggering compared to contemporaneous reports on the game; they are obviously designed to fascinate an audience accustomed to more "civilized" sport. What Catlin claimed to have witnessed and sketched was announced at the Indian Agency to have been "a great [ball] play." Whenever the term "great game" surfaces in the historical literature on lacrosse it usually signifies some sort of special event, generally involving a larger-than-usual number of players.

Whether the Choctaw event that Catlin saw was staged for him as an important visitor is not known. Surely, among fifteen thousand Choctaw there would have been more than one thousand capable players, for nearly every male of the tribe grew up playing lacrosse. And a crowd of several thousand onlookers would have been feasible, given the popularity of the sport and the amount of leisure time available to these removed peoples. But practical problems come to mind: Were there five hundred or even three hundred per side on a field only 250 yards in length? Aside from the general congestion—aptly shown in Catlin's paintings—because all the players appear to be dressed nearly identically, how could one locate a teammate to whom the ball might be passed?[10] Or was the game simply a free-for-all in which one hoped to make a dash with the ball through the throng to reach the goal? Such mass confusion as Catlin depicts would certainly preclude any kind of team coordination in scoring, although that was certainly a characteristic of the southeastern game.

In his narrative Catlin noted that the "confused mass rushing together around [the ball]" raised considerable dust, making it difficult to locate a ground ball for as long as fifteen minutes, by which time it might well be at some other part of the field. Such a situation is well illustrated in his action paintings, which make it appear as though several different games were in progress simultaneously on the same field.

If Catlin's team size is exaggerated, so must be his commentary on scoring. With so many players on the field, so many lapses attributed to ground balls, and so little distinction between teams by uniform, one would presume that the game would proceed at a snail's pace. Yet Catlin would have us believe that whichever side first scored 100 points was the winner! This is a preposterously high figure—probably designed to match the "preposterous" expectations of his readers—and, like his numbers per team, the highest ever recorded. Furthermore, it does not jibe with contemporaneous accounts. And how could six hundred entangled players rearrange themselves on the field, either by finding their designated opponents (as is customary in most southeastern games) or, at the very least, by evening up the number of opposing players in various parts of the field—all within the one-minute pause between a score and the next face-off (toss-up), as Catlin avers?

Although these aspects of Catlin's work may be challenged, there is still much that is acceptable and informative: the encampment of opposing teams and families half a mile apart at either end of the prairie where the game would be played; the measurement of the field and erection of goalposts; the old men (probably conjurers) selected as judges; the enormous amount of betting on the game and

Figure 35a

safeguarding of stakes by those specially appointed to the task; the type of sticks used and the rule against touching the ball with the hands; the "arrangement" of the match by using runners; the ball-play dance the night preceding the game; the start of the contest the following morning; and the manner of face-off, signaled by a gunshot. These practices are remarkably similar to those of the game Mooney described for the North Carolina Cherokee half a century later. Catlin thus helps to confirm the fact that all southeastern tribes played pretty much the same form of lacrosse and that the style of playing and ceremonialism surrounding it were culturally intact traditions, slow to change despite their tragic removal to Indian Territory.

Some details in Catlin's 1834 Choctaw paintings bear a striking resemblance to Mooney's Eastern Cherokee photographs taken during an 1888 game. For example, Catlin tells us that a no-holds-barred philosophy virtually prevailed in keeping an opponent from the ball and that, as a result, individual fights would often break out: "These obstructions [to prevent someone from gaining the ball] often meet

Figure 35b

desperate individual resistance, which terminates in a violent scuffle, and sometimes in fisticuffs; when their stricks [*sic*] are dropped, and the parties are unmolested, whilst they are settling it between themselves."[11] Mooney was apparently so intrigued by the many wrestling matches on the field that he used up considerable film documenting them. A detail from one of Catlin's paintings shows a "lacrosse wrestle" nearly identical to one photographed by Mooney, half a century later and a thousand miles to the east (Figures 35a, b).

The Cherokee had specially designated "stickmen"; should players' wrestling continue for too long with no clear winner in sight, these game officials had a long hickory switch with which to beat the contenders back into the game. That the Choctaw had some similar mechanism is probable, and one curious detail in a Catlin painting (that I take to be his way of drawing attention to it, however erroneously) shows a Choctaw woman holding a handful of sticks or a tree branch, apparently beating on the back of a player who is either about to stop an opponent in his tracks by clutching him from behind with his arms or has just released him (Figure 36a). (Possibly the woman has lashed him to make him let go.) This sort of clutching maneuver—or "obstruction," as Catlin called it—was indeed permissible in the southeastern version of lacrosse, as Mooney's Cherokee photograph of 1888 shows (Figure 36b). But whether *women* were the ones to break up the clutch is highly questionable, though it has led more than one recent writer to accept Catlin's assertion that during the game women would beat their husbands with switches to encourage them to play harder.[12]

Catlin created several versions of *Ball Play of the Choctaw—Ball Up* that are nearly the same except for sideline props—in one case a row of tepees added to the far sideline; in another, Catlin himself on his horse Charley, watching the game from one end of the field with another white man. The detail of the woman with a switch appears only in his *Portfolio* rendition of the scene (Plate 23), published in London in 1844, ten years after Catlin was at Fort Gibson. The detail is missing from oil paintings of the scene done a decade earlier, as well as from the sketch appearing in *Letters and Notes,* in which he explicitly remarks that "no one is allowed to interfere in any way with the contentious individuals." In the text accompanying the *Portfolio,* however, Catlin goes to some length to describe the practice of a Choctaw woman going into the woods to get materials for the "whip," hoisting her skirts to run onto the field, "yelling and screaming" as she runs, trying to overtake her husband to remind him of all the goods they have wagered on the game. In so doing, writes the author, "she lashes him over the naked shoulders, and often to the degree that the blood will be seen trickling down over his back, drawn in the *affectionate* hints thus given by his wife . . . for the manly protection of their mutual interest, by desperately playing to save their property at stake."[13]

At the end of the nineteenth century, George Starr noticed Choctaw women running around offering coffee to the players but also carrying a quirt to whip those who they judged were not playing hard enough. But surely such refreshments and rebukes took place on the sidelines, not on the field. Given the ceremonial nature of lacrosse games, as a rule women were not allowed on the field, lest they come in contact with the sticks (a taboo). Also, that a woman could keep track of her husband in a throng of six hundred to give him a beating seems problematic. Halbert, writing of Choctaw games some fifty years after Catlin, is adamant about the regulations governing spectators and the penalties imposed should they become involved in the action: "During the play, no outsider is expected to interfere in the play in any manner whatever. Should he do this, the party to which the offender belongs is expected to forfeit one round [score] or otherwise make some reparation."[14]

Figure 36a

Figure 36b

It seems likely that Catlin's detail of the female flogger represents a conflation of actual practices that the artist did indeed witness but then adjusted to his own view of Indian life. We should take into account that Catlin's *Portfolio* was intended principally for his aristocratic English patrons at the time, who surely would have been more than amused at the notion of a woman beating her husband! After all, the *Portfolio*'s title page makes special note that the artist made his illustrations among "the Wildest and Most Remote Tribes of Savages in North America." How exotic and unthinkable it was to "civilized" society to have women encroaching on an athletic field to inflict punishment on male athletes by beating them with switches! If Catlin wanted the game to appear to be wild, the later addition of this minidrama to earlier canvasses would make it ever the more so. Other anomalies in the lithograph are the dress worn by the woman with the switch, which is clearly northern Plains, not Choctaw, in style, and the fact that the four referees are seated in the middle of the field, where they would surely be overrun by the players. Furthermore, they are shown wearing northern Plains feather warbonnets.

Catlin, probably unconsciously, took liberties with his paintings in this manner. As much as he admired Indians, he was guided by his preconceptions of them as an exotic, albeit inferior, race. His "adjustments" of reality were intended to intensify the distinctions he felt between whites and Indians. Another case is his sketch of a Dakota wild rice harvest, showing women gathering this aquatic grass seed from canoes that they had purchased from the Ojibwe. One of the craft also contains two male hunters shooting at ducks. While it is true that ducks fed on ripening wild rice at harvest time and that men in canoes ventured into the rice beds to hunt them, there is no way that the small Ojibwe ricing canoe could have accommodated hunters and gatherers simultaneously. In this instance Catlin has simply conflated two activities that took place during the same season.[15] "Wild" rice alone was totally unknown to his audience at that time. What an exotic food for a "wild" people! And shooting ducks from a birch-bark canoe was a curious sport, although it did show the contributions of Euro-American technology—shotguns having replaced the bow and arrow for the purpose. What a wonderful chance to convey all of this in one illustration!

In his lacrosse paintings Catlin is at his best in depicting the violent group action of the game, as well as individual skirmishes. Clearly overawed at what he witnessed, and grateful to find Indians as violent as they were supposed to be, he was prompted to extol: "I pronounce such a scene, with its hundreds of Nature's most beautiful models, denuded, and painted of various colours, running and leaping into the air, in all the most extravagant and varied forms, in the desperate struggles for the ball, a school for the painter or sculptor, equal to any of those which ever inspired the hand of the artist in the Olympian games or the Roman forum." Such sincere feelings are behind the liberties he took in painting, for, as Catlin himself confesses, "it is impossible for pen and ink alone, or brushes . . . to give more than a *caricature* [however exaggerated] of such a scene!"[16]

Beyond Catlin's paintings, how much can we trust his accompanying narrative on lacrosse in *Letters and Notes*? Fortunately, the Choctaw game has been fairly well documented over time, so that earlier as well as contemporaneous and later descriptions are available for comparison. Except for Catlin, accounts over a period of two centuries giving the size of a Choctaw team and the number of points played to win are vastly smaller. Reports of the combined number of athletes on a Choctaw lacrosse field during play range from sixty to two hundred, compared with Catlin's figure of one thousand. Goals needed to win? From ten to sixteen, say these writers, versus Catlin's assertion of one hundred!

Still, there is much in Catlin's narrative that is confirmed by other observers, and some of the Choctaw practices described have continued well into this century. Take, for instance, his report on the "ball-play dance" repeated intermittently throughout the night before the game. Some similar ritual was noted seventy years earlier by Bossu, who wrote, "Men and women gather in their finest costumes and pass the day singing and dancing; indeed they dance all night to the sound of the drum and rattle."[17] Halbert's manuscript from the end of the nineteenth century shows the practice still intact, although the ceremonial singing of the women took place at the goalposts and not midfield, as Catlin shows it. But since, for good reason, each team held separate ceremonies, at a distance and probably concealed from each other, it is doubtful they would have coordinated the ritual into the one large combined dance as suggested by Catlin's painting of it (see Figure 33). Once again, he may simply have conflated two separate events and presented them simultaneously. Nonetheless, Halbert's narrative fits so well with Catlin's painting that one wonders if he was using it for his description.[18]

With a judicious approach to sports iconography, there is much to learn about American Indian lacrosse from painters, like Catlin, newspaper illustrators later in the century, and photographers, like Mooney. Mostly what the records show are changes in dress and equipment over the years. Documentation of other aspects of the game, such as playing techniques, would have to await the arrival of motion picture and video coverage to provide similar information.

Breechclouts and Bare Feet

One cannot argue with Catlin's depiction of lacrosse dress that, as a rule, players were barefoot and wore breechclouts (loincloths), since similar attire was almost universal among North American players until the latter part of the nineteenth century. Also, the considerable body paint in various designs and the feathers worn in the hair, as Catlin shows, are confirmed by photographs taken later in the century. Still, Catlin took liberties in depicting his "noble athletes." For example, Thirsts-for-Stone's portrait is believable in most details except for the tailpiece, whose elegance seems vastly exaggerated for effect.

That Choctaw players *did* wear the tail of some animal as a rear ornament is attested to by the earliest sources. Bossu, for example, wrote that players' bodies were "painted with various colors, having a tiger's [wildcat's?] tail fastened behind and feathers on their heads and arms which move as they run, and have a very odd effect." In a game between Toucksey and Sugarloaf counties of the Choctaw Nation, "[the player's] only ornament was a coon tail stuck up straight along the spine, or a horse tail falling on the breech clout behind. This was attached to the belt, a leather strap or revolver belt."[1] Attaching a tail to hang down from some belt became part of lacrosse dress when the Choctaw revived the game in this century (Figures 37a, b, c). Earlier, undated specimens from the Mississippi Choctaw suggest similar practices (Figures 37b, c); while one tailpiece is mounted and somewhat arched, it is by no means as elaborate and long as Thirsts-for-Stone's tailpiece. What Catlin has depicted may possibly have been inspired by the unnaturally erect tails of European show horses. Artistically, its elegant length balances the two unusually long southeastern ballsticks that the Choctaw athlete holds before him; it also blends well with the "mane" around his neck and the player's generally swept-back hair. In short, Catlin seems to have created more a showpiece stallion than a typically dressed Choctaw lacrosse player.

If Catlin's portrait of a Choctaw player has these dubious features, how should we assess his paintings of the "two most distinguished" Dakota players, Ah-no-je-nahge (He Who Stands on Both Sides) (Figure 38a) and We-chush-ta-doo-ta (The Red Man)? The artist claims that he witnessed several "very spirited plays [games]," that the subjects in each case came directly to his studio "in the dress in which they had just struggled," and that he painted their portraits "in the attitude of the play."

How many games Catlin actually saw is questionable, given his short stay at Fort Snelling and the fact that in the background of a portrait of one of the Dakota players he depicts the double-post goal of southeastern tribes rather than the customary Great Lakes single-post goal, which suggests that he simply borrowed what he had seen among the Choctaw for a prop. He does record that late in the morning on the Fourth of July, 1835, the players appeared "with no other dress on them than the flap, and attached to a girdle or ornamental sash, a tail, extending nearly to the ground, made of the choicest arrangement of quills and feathers, or of the hair of white horses' tails." These details are adequately portrayed, but the Great Lakes stick held by the players seems too thin (cf. Figure 3 and Figure 20). This game could only have been a brief demonstration match between the Dakota and the Ojibwe encamped there, for the Indians soon retired to the agent's office to give dance performances and haggle over the gifts they had been promised for their "theatricals." Nevertheless, Catlin's Dakota lacrosse dress seems consistent with Frank Mayer's sketches sixteen years later (Figure 38b) and Edward D. Neill's description, "painted in divers colors, with no article of apparel, with feathers in their heads, bells around their wrists, and fox and wolf tails dangling behind."[2]

Ball players of both tribes wear ornamental headgear. That of We-chush-ta-doo-ta seems to fit other descriptions, but Ah-no-je-nahge has on a roach—an ornamental headdress made from the tail of a deer with horsehair or porcupine guardhairs added. The roach was usually worn as part of a dance costume, as it continues to be today, but whether or not roaches were worn during lacrosse play is moot. There are a few action photographs of games that show a roach headdress. But participants in "Indian Fairs" or pageants in this century frequently served multiple roles as dancers, handgame gamblers, and lacrosse demonstrators, so they often wore the same ceremonial garb for a number of activities and may have been photo-

Figure 37a • A young Mississippi Choctaw wearing contemporary (horsehair?) tailpiece suspended from wide leather strap belt.

Figure 37b • Late nineteenth-century (?) Choctaw animal tail attached to calico breechclout, collected near Philadelphia, Mississippi.

Figure 37c • Early twentieth-century (?) Choctaw rear ornament of wood and horsehair, collected near Philadelphia, Mississippi.

• 164

Figure 38a • Catlin's
1835 oil painting of the
Dakota Ah-no-je-
nahge, titled *He Who
Stands on Both Sides*, *a
distinguished ball player*.

graphed in just such dress, holding a lacrosse stick. Catlin's Dakota
players were en route from a brief game to a dance demonstration, so
which costume they wore—game or dance—is debatable. When
Great Lakes players got ready for a game, according to my information, they usually discarded such finery in "stripping for action."

The dress of Catlin's Dakota lacrosse players should be compared to that painted by Seth Eastman. Unlike Catlin, whose visit to
the Upper Missouri and the Upper Mississippi was relatively brief,
Eastman was stationed at Fort Snelling for seven years, beginning in
1841, and he had ample opportunity to witness and paint both men's
lacrosse and women's shinny games. A landscapist with formal art
training, Eastman was just as attracted to Indian life as Catlin was.

How does the attire of Eastman's Dakota ball players compare
with that of the players in the two portraits by Catlin? What is

Figure 38b • Frank Mayer's 2 July 1851 drawing of Makah mon Oton mahnee (The Sounding Earth That Walked), a Dakota lacrosse player at Traverse des Sioux during treaty negotiations.

striking about Eastman's *Ball Play on the Prairie* and his *Ball Play on the Ice* is that the combatants are dressed in normal, everyday clothes—loose fringed-buckskin shirts. Aside from an occasional feather in the hair, also standard attire of the period, none of Eastman's players have any of the distinguishing animal tailpieces, body paint, or other elegant features that Catlin shows. Eastman's players on the frozen river in the 1840s are likewise dressed in conventional winter garb, some wearing the hooded capotes—Indian creations fashioned from Hudson's Bay trade blankets. On the other hand, Mayer's sketches of players at Traverse des Sioux in 1851 show them wearing some sort of headpiece (roach?), with animal tails or skins hanging from their waists. These athletes, from a large crowd of thousands gathered for treaty making, and their lacrosse games appear to have been part of everyday activities to occupy leisure time rather than any sort of special display for non-Indian dignitaries.[3] Do these discrepancies suggest that different bands of the Dakota wore different styles of lacrosse dress?

The considerable differences among these artistic renderings in regard to Dakota game dress are noteworthy. Were Eastman's mundanely clad figures supposed to represent informal, "pickup" village amusements, while Catlin's subjects were elaborately painted and adorned for "exhibition" games, and Mayer's fell somewhere in between? We may never know for certain.

At least until the nineteenth century, nearly every source on lacrosse states clearly that players wore only the breechclout, for an obvious reason: Anything other than this bare essential was a hindrance to speed and agility in the game. When Canadian Victorians took up the sport, although they disdained the immodesty of Indian lacrosse dress, at least they recognized its advantages. As George Beers wrote: "Though we would not advocate the nudity of the original players, we think the less and lighter the dress the better."[4] The near-naked condition of Indian players also deprived one's opponent from something to grab onto to impede progress, much in the way that Greek athletes purposely kept their hair short, in order to avoid a liability in wrestling and pankration. In fact, Cherokee players took the additional step of rubbing themselves with an eel skin, slippery elm, or sassafras to make themselves slimy and thus difficult to hang on to. They even made their clout strap deliberately weak so that it would break if an opponent grabbed it in a scuffle.[5] When they turned to wearing cutoff dungarees in the twentieth century, they removed the rear pockets to deprive opponents of another "handle" (see Figure 25). Aside from decorative body paint and feathers in the hair, the loincloth was the only article of game dress. For the same practical reasons, the Creek lacrosse costume was as minimal as that worn on the warpath: "The players on both sides paint and decorate themselves, in the same manner as when they are going to war. Thus decorated, and stripped of all such clothing as would encumber them, they set out for the appointed field."[6] The Iroquoian *gä-kä* (loincloth) is fairly representative of most tribes: a strip of deerskin or broadcloth about nine inches wide and two yards long, ornamented at each end with beadwork or quillwork. The cloth was held in place by a belt of deerskin.[7]

There is little evidence to support the assertion that, before contact with Europeans, Indian men ever went without loincloths, either casually in public or for sports, for they had their own standards of modesty. Such claims of nakedness simply support the general concept of colonists that contact with Europeans had a "civilizing" effect on native peoples throughout the world. This false notion is reflected, for example, in John Lawson's comment that among Carolina Indians, "Betwixt their Legs comes a Piece of Cloth, that is tucked in by a Belt, both before and behind. This is to hide their Nakedness, of which Decency they are very strict Observers, although never practiced before the Christians came among them."[8] There is, however, one illustration showing nude Indian lacrosse players—a drawing in 1853 by Henry Kirke Brown (1814–86), the so-called Father of American Sculpture. The sketch shows two naked Indians with long hair, one holding the other in the traditional southeastern armlock from behind in an apparent attempt to prevent his reaching a ground ball (Figure 39). Brown, an early student of anatomy, was heavily influenced by classical sculpture, having traveled to Europe and copied models of Adonis and David and then returning to his studio in Brooklyn. To our knowledge, he never ventured west, but he did create another "fictional" Indian work— his *Indian and Panther* (1846), showing the subject defending himself and a child against the attack of a mountain lion. Critical assessments of Brown's work by contemporaries noted, "His studies have been mainly among the purest and best remains of the antique, assiduously compared with living nature."[9]

In Brown's lacrosse illustration he has clearly combined classical Greek sculptural elements with details of the Indian game, which, I suspect, he drew from Catlin's paintings and writings. The nude, muscular bodies are a far cry from the typically lanky Choctaw of the period. The bird wings surmounting the head of the racquet carrier suggest more a Mercury or a Hermes of antiquity than any Indian use of feathers in the hair. The armlock appears in Catlin's Choctaw paintings, but while the ballstick appears to be somewhat southeastern in construction, its cup is too round, the netting too densely woven (a tennis racquet?), and there is only one stick shown instead

• 168

Figure 39 • Untitled drawing of nude lacrosse players in a clutch by Henry Kirke Brown about 1850.

of the customary two. The ball is also too large. In short, Brown, having never seen a game, used his imagination, classical ideals, and Catlin's information to create a misleading fiction concerning Indian game dress.

While the loincloth was a universal Indian sports uniform, reports vary as to whether or not men played barefoot as a rule. Moccasins are said to have been worn in games between the Whites and the Tcilokis of the Creek, but a photo from around 1900 shows Creek players barefoot. Mexican Kickapoo in the early 1950s, in addition to breechclouts and leggins, wore moccasins with specially reinforced soles, but that was principally a response to the hard, rocky Sonoran soil and brambles. Catlin's Dakota and Choctaw players are shown barefoot, as are those in the earliest Cherokee photographs (1888), but Charles Deas depicts Dakota in the same game, some wearing moccasins, others barefoot (see Figure 29). (Apparently weather was not a factor influencing footwear and other coverings: Ojibwe players at International Falls on the Canadian border were said to play nearly naked on the frozen Rainy River, and a ritual Cayuga game held for someone sick at midwinter would be played by barefooted men also stripped to the waist.[10]

The apparent lack of any significant distinction in dress between

players on opposing teams in illustrations of lacrosse by Catlin, Eastman, and others raises the question of team uniforms.[11] In today's
competitive sports, the fact that players are distinguishable by the
colors and emblems of jerseys and helmets gives visible assistance to
strategy and team coordination. But the former absence of any such
means of distinguishing sides suggests that this consideration was less
important or even absent. The scoring of a goal was left to chance,
for an individual to break free of the pack and demonstrate his personal skills of speed and agility. Eventually, however, by the end of
the nineteenth century, some Indian lacrosse clubs were wearing
team jerseys, just as non-Indian athletes did for lacrosse and other
sports. This later adoption of a Euro-American custom reflects major
changes in the game itself as well as the fact that Indians were now
competing against white teams.

Some Indian peoples did in fact distinguish opposing teams in
some fashion, whether through color of body paint or breechclout or
various articles, like feathers, that made up part of the lacrosse
player's uniform. Whether practical or symbolic purposes were at the
root of this practice is not always clear. Because it was common for
many traditional games to be played clan against clan, town against
town, there were already distinguishing marks or articles of clothing
that identified them on any important occasion. When Mexican
Kickapoo lacrosse players dressed for lacrosse games, for example, as a
matter of course they colored themselves with white ashes or black
charcoal to signify their membership in one or the other tribal division, a custom still adhered to in 1955: "In the game the paint [white
ashes and charcoal carbon] is applied to the face, chest, arm and
legs—all exposed parts of the body that are not covered by the loin
cloth, leggings and moccasins."[12]

Designs made with body paint, whether symbolic or "lucky,"
were principally for ornamental reasons. This practice as part of
lacrosse dress gradually died out, probably about the same time that
facial designs became no longer fashionable in everyday wear. One
reason for abandoning face painting was the ridicule from the white
community, who began to refer derogatorily to such decor as "war
paint," calling those who wore it "bucks" or "braves." At the time
of European contact, body painting was fairly universal for Indian
athletes; by the twentieth century only vestiges of it remained, probably merely as a symbol of native pride.

Tails and feathers were worn for their symbolic attributes and
were meant to impart to the player the particular skills attributed to
the creature from which they were taken. Creek players wore "a tiger
tail" over the breechclout in the rear because of that animal's
reputed strength and courage; if the player's father belonged to the

Panther clan, that provided him an additional reason for wearing it. Other items worn by the Creek included bison tails and eagle and sparrow-hawk feathers, all desirable because they belonged to "masterful animals." Cherokee players might wear a deer or fox tail because of the swiftness of these creatures, or the tail of a flying squirrel because of its grabbing ability.[13]

Feathers were also a traditional part of Indian lacrosse dress. American Indians generally wore feathers for ornamental purposes, and usually a special significance was assigned to the type of feather displayed. Fogelson compiled a list of "Feathers or Animal Tails used by [Cherokee] Ball Players." Among creatures whose attributes were believed to be transferred to a player wearing its feather, wing, or other body part were the chimney sweep for its swiftness and agility; the rattlesnake, whose rattles were sometimes tied to the hair, for its striking power; the sandpiper for its endurance and capacity for quick acceleration; the pewee for its darting skills; the raven or screech hawk for its sharp vision—all of them desirable skills for a lacrosse player.[14]

Probably the best-documented history of change in lacrosse dress over time is that of the Eastern Cherokee. Early sources fairly consistently agree that the breechclout and hair feathers were the only articles worn, although there is some indication that Cherokee players, like those of other southeastern tribes, once wore deer or fox tails. Cherokee consultants remembered the wearing of tailpieces in the ball-play dance as recently as around 1914, though they may have been included only in the ceremonial costumes worn before play and taken off for the actual games.[15] That feathers, on the other hand, were worn both in the dances and during play is apparent not only in the literature but also in Mooney's photographs.

The principal change in Cherokee lacrosse dress was the abandonment of the breechclout in favor of trunks modeled after the shorts worn by whites. That this change was gradual is evident in Mooney's 1888 photographs, which show a few players still adhering to the older breechclouts of patterned cloth. By that time, most players—particularly younger ones—have on white muslin shorts with designs such as stars, crosses, and circles sewn on them. A star indicates a first-rate player; a cross, one that is talented but not yet "a star."[16] Also apparent is the use of emblems to designate team affiliation; for example, a player from Big Cove has "BC" initialed on the back of his shorts. Although Mooney's photographs are in black and white, we know from the field sketches of the Dutch ethnologist Frans Olbrechts in the 1920s and from surviving museum specimens that the designs were mostly in red and blue (Figure 40). Photographs from around 1916 show young Cherokee players having aban-

Figure 40 • Eastern
Cherokee muslin
trunks with red cloth
decorations and bone
button, collected by
James Mooney, proba-
bly about 1888.

• 171

doned the muslin shorts and wearing used dungaree cutoffs. Such shortened blue jeans and even bathing suits are worn today not only by Cherokee but also by other southeastern players. If they play barefoot and wear long pants, the trousers are likely to be rolled up and tucked tightly around the calf.

The discarding of traditional, even pre-contact lacrosse dress and replacing of it with clothing and athletic-team gear of the dominant culture was gradual. For Iroquois players, by the early 1890s body painting was already a thing of the past. Creek consultants in the 1910s barely remembered the brilliant designs that had formerly been applied for good luck. An eyewitness to a Creek game in July 1913, Swanton was able to describe the transitional attitude toward dress reflected in costume: Some wore white store-bought clothes; others had on only the traditional breechclout; a few had red paint on their faces; and at least one wore a tiger tail "strapped straight up along his back." Some traditional items, such as eagle feathers, became scarce, as wild animals and birds faced extinction. But because these creatures continued to possess their symbolic value, their feathers and other accoutrements began to be imported. For example, by the 1890s eagles had already vanished from the Eastern Cherokee reservation. When the ball game conjurer Lloyd Sequoyah visited Oklahoma Cherokee in 1958, he bought twenty golden eagle feathers in an Anandarko craft shop to bring home, ostensibly to make them available to players.[17]

Before photography, we relied on the pictorial representations of Catlin and Eastman for information about Indian lacrosse dress. While their artistic renderings improve upon or confirm verbal descriptions, there is still no way to assess the degree of subjectivity in their works. When photography became a tool for documenting the game, visual data became considerably more reliable. Unfortunately, however, early photographs are not necessarily any more informative, since they lack adequate documentation. Often it is impossible to tell from many old and undocumented photographs when they were taken, who the subjects are, whether a game shown in progress was particularly important or just a minor pickup event, or even whether the photographer's manipulations of his subjects, such as assembling the players to stage the action or otherwise pose for the camera, affected the document. Once lacrosse began to be photographed, however, one aspect of the sport, game dress, becomes more clear. We can see that, increasingly, by the end of the nineteenth century players wore store-bought clothing somehow altered to make a sports uniform, adapted athletic dress from other sports, or simply played in normal, everyday dress. By the twentieth century a wide variety of lacrosse dress had in many places replaced the older, traditional styles. Some players were even remembered for the novelty of their costumes: Fred Jones, a Mille Lacs Ojibwe, recalled how his bowlegged friend John Percy used to play lacrosse wearing a large ten-gallon hat and cowboy boots. What the Manitoba Bungi (Plains Ojibwe) wore playing lacrosse on horseback before 1930 is anybody's guess.[18]

When Canadians first took up lacrosse, a number of changes occurred that affected game dress of both races. As lacrosse became popular in the Montreal area, it began to receive attention from photographers and lithographers; consequently, our record of changes in Iroquoian lacrosse dress is more complete than records elsewhere on the continent. The tradition of team photographs for sports of the dominant culture was soon adopted by Indians (Figure 41). Like college athletic photographs of the period, the Indians are posed, one row standing behind a seated group, with one or two players resting on one elbow on the ground in front.

Photography makes evident the cultural exchanges between Indians and Euro-Americans that affected lacrosse dress. Even though the traditional Iroquoian game was played barefoot, in the 1860s most Canadians were wearing moccasins for lacrosse. Later, Montrealers exchanged the Indian footwear for light boots, which provided better footing, and photographs indicate that Indian teams followed suit. Whatever they wore for reservation games, Iroquois in demonstration games before non-Indian audiences donned some article of dress to express their Indian identity. In 1867, when the Six Nations Reserve was invited to Troy, New York, to give an exhibition match before a crowd gathered for a baseball tournament, its players wore brightly colored tights and a variety of feathered headdresses.

At some time, Indians began to wear for lacrosse the kind of

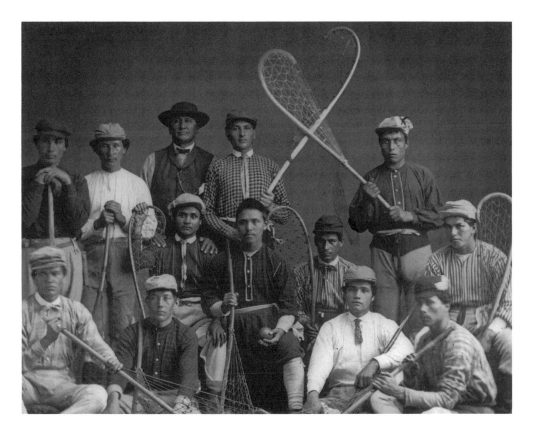

game jerseys used by other Anglo-American sports (mostly football). A team photograph of twelve Caughnawaga Indians who accompanied the Montreal Lacrosse Club to England for demonstration matches in 1876 shows all of them wearing horizontally striped jerseys. All have on long underwear and leather booties. Two players wear light-colored kerchiefs knotted around the neck. The team captain (?), identified as "Sawatis Aientonni Baptiste Canadien— Chief 'Big John'" is seated in the middle. Apparently as an expression of the Indian identity of his team, he has donned a feathered headdress of the Iroquoian variety, with the feathers gathered vertically.

Two early-twentieth-century team photos from the Onondaga Reservation show that jerseys continued to be worn. In a photograph from about 1902 the shirts have a large white "O" sewn on their fronts to identify the team's origin (Figure 42). Players wear white shorts or white pants and tennis shoes. The same reservation's team was photographed about three years later, also with football jerseys. Players are in white (cloth?) shorts and wear what seem to be

Figure 41 • Photograph of the Caughnawaga lacrosse club, 1867.

Figure 42 • Onondaga team photograph. Front row, from left: Joshua Scanandoah, Ike Lyons, Emmett Lyons, Adam Jones. Seated: (unknown), (unknown), Eli Scanandoah, Mose Logan (manager), Sidney Isaac. Standing: (unknown), Adam Thomas, (unknown), (unknown), Jesse Lyons, (unknown), Bill Beckman, (unknown).

tennis shoes. An unidentified player seated in the middle wears a feathered headdress, this time a splayed-feather Plains bonnet.

Such lacrosse dress emulated for the most part what Anglos of the period wore and attests to continuing matches between them. Still, for ceremonial lacrosse of the Longhouse on the reservation, Iroquoian players then and even today revert to Indian dress of former times. When the Six Nations Cayuga hold their game at midwinter ceremonies for someone who is sick, it is still played by men who are barefoot and stripped to the waist.[19]

Wherever ceremonial lacrosse is played today, one can expect to find vestiges of the older game dress. This is especially true of the Oklahoma Creek, who wear their most traditional costume in lacrosse matches during their summer ceremonial cycle for the Green Corn Ceremony. At one time, breechclouts of small animal hides and bare feet marked their traditional game uniform. In the second half of the nineteenth century, red wool cloth decorated with velvet ribbonwork in abstract geometric patterns replaced the skins. These new clouts were oblong in shape, but in the 1940s a tapered V-shaped clout began to make its appearance, and players today wear breechclouts right over underwear or swim trunks.

Today, the Creek continue to wear traditional dress, but they also wear informal everyday clothes. Teenage stickball players in particular tend to wear T-shirts, football jerseys, sneakers, jeans, or swim shorts with white tube socks. Still, one or two may have a knotted red scarf around the neck, recalling the original warfare connotations of the game.

Modern lacrosse wear has also made its way into the Great Lakes version of the game. Franklin Basina mentioned that Ojibwe who had formerly worn moccasins for games switched to tennis shoes once they became available, but he noted that the rest of game dress was fairly informal. Asked about a painting of two former players from his reservation that showed them wearing beaded vests and roaches while fighting over a ground ball, he insisted, "Well, that's what it is, for show. . . . You can't do that in a game." Basina discounted the wearing of a roach as a headpiece when playing, but he indicated that for games between northern Wisconsin Ojibwe reservations a sort of colored sweatband was used as a team identifier as well as for practical purposes, to keep perspiration out of the eyes.[20]

Indian lacrosse players wore no type of protective gear until it was available as standard sports equipment in the twentieth century. Assertions such as Canadian sports chronicler William Bull's that "players donned heavy furs and skins as protection against the blows of their opponents' sticks" are totally fanciful. According to hearsay, admits Bull, "the blows were not all received in the actual course of the game, since, if the braves showed any slackness in play, it was afterwards the privilege of the squaws to give them a thorough beating." This claim suggests Catlin and others as the source of the confusion. In fact, it was not until Canadians began playing lacrosse that any sort of padding, face masks, or the like made their appearance on a lacrosse field. Even the early Montreal teams were dressed not unlike their Mohawk counterparts. It was when George Beers began drawing up the "rules" of the game that the subject of protective gear was first broached. In his *Lacrosse* (1869), Beers drew attention to the fact that Indians never threw a hard ball at a goal when playing each other. By contrast, writes Beers, Canadians prefer shoes over moccasins and score from short distances, which should justify the goalie's use of "leg-guards" such as cricket players wore to protect their shins. Beers also forwarded the suggestion that perhaps gloves padded on top should be worn.[21] Ultimately, Indian goalies began to wear such protective gear (Figure 43), just as today Indian players have adopted the helmets, shoulder pads, gloves, jerseys, and even plastic sticks of their non-Indian counterparts.

Euro-American conventions in regard to sports gear and uni-

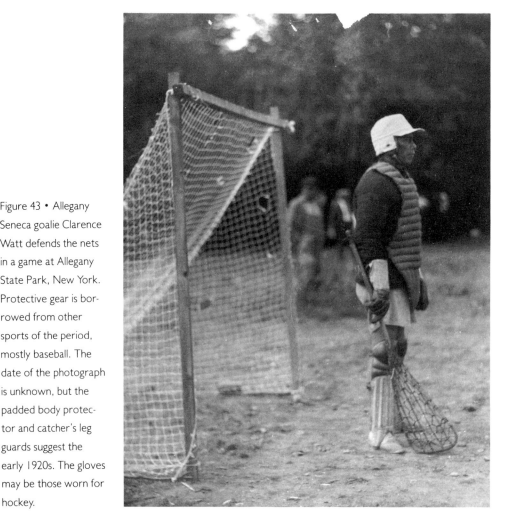

Figure 43 • Allegany Seneca goalie Clarence Watt defends the nets in a game at Allegany State Park, New York. Protective gear is borrowed from other sports of the period, mostly baseball. The date of the photograph is unknown, but the padded body protector and catcher's leg guards suggest the early 1920s. The gloves may be those worn for hockey.

forms continued to be copied by Indian teams. The practice of displaying community association with capital letter abbreviations sewn on shorts (B[ig] C[ove]) or jerseys (O[nondaga]) was taken up by Indian players, but there the designation of a player's identity stopped. Providing a lacrosse player's name for fans to pick him out on the field was an idea totally created by the Euro-American lacrosse community. In the minutes books of the Montreal Amateur Athletic Association for 14 July 1909 is noted that the committee should "carry out the idea of numbering the players and to have a programme issued with a printed slip showing the nos. of the players."[22] To improve spectator ability to identify individual players from the stands, following a rule change regarding uniforms in 1930, it was required that each player have a six-inch number on the back of his jersey. But such vanity is foreign to the traditional Indian world of lacrosse.

The discussion of lacrosse dress has shown a gradual acceptance of non-Indian articles of clothing or sportswear for the game. Some have improvised uniforms—the Eastern Cherokee cutoff dungarees with rear pockets removed, for instance. Others have emulated the developments in team dress of the non-Indian world, such as the adoption of striped jerseys by Iroquois teams in the early twentieth century. Because game dress is often a crucial factor in distinguishing between teams on the field, the whole topic of teams—their selection, player eligibility, coaches, training—needs addressing.

No matter what they wear while playing, Indian teams continue to be organized by civil or religious leaders, who are responsible for team selection and pregame arrangements. Distinctions between everyday, informal lacrosse and more serious, sacred games usually determine a team's makeup. For games purely recreational in nature there is no restriction on who might play. But for ritual games, such as those within the context of, say, Iroquois Longhouse religious rites, there have always been rigid prescriptions on how the games will be played and who can participate.

The one figure whose involvement in team selection has disappeared is the war leader, who formerly in many places determined player eligibility. Among the Creek, whose nation was organized from ancient times at the town level, lacrosse games were arranged by the Big Warriors of the towns involved. Their duties included the announcements of council declarations of war, punishment of those who broke council laws or failed to attend the annual busk (harvest ceremony), and the organization of lacrosse games in consultation with Big Warriors from other towns. Together they decided whether men who had married into the town were eligible and whether men who were originally from the town but had married outside and now lived elsewhere could play. One Big Warrior might propose playing with sons-in-law, to which another could object. They took great care throughout the negotiations to see that neither side had undue advantage. In the end they either settled on the terms for team makeup or called off the game.[23]

More commonly, games were arranged by civil officials at the village, intratribal, and national levels. When the Seneca and the Mohawk played in 1794, decisions were made by their respective councils. The Choctaw entrusted team selection to the local leader, called the *miko*, who resolved questions of community affiliation, particularly if both teams claimed the same player. The *miko* was also responsible for settling problems of illegal recruitment or unfair train-ing practices. His decision was always final, and he had the power to exclude players from the game altogether.[24]

Such leaders directed intercommunity matches, with one or more villages or bands of the same tribe united to contend against a similar number. The earliest sources on Indian lacrosse noted this kind of game organization; not only was the concept of team sports generally unfamiliar to Europeans of the time but community com-petition was equally novel. Father Le Mercier's fellow missionary, the Jesuit Paul Le Jeune, wrote in 1636 of games with one Huron village pitted against another, and Bossu in 1759 mentioned the taunt-ing that accompanied a Choctaw challenge, when "they invite the men of the neighboring villages to play and tease them by shouting insulting remarks at them." Carver drew attention to the intratribal nature of Great Lakes lacrosse in 1766–68: "The game is generally played by large companies, that sometimes consist of more than three hundred; and it is not uncommon for different bands to play against each other." The only larger level of competition—the "great" national game—was sometimes played to settle territorial disputes and avoid open warfare.[25]

At the community level, however, team size was much smaller. Among Great Lakes tribes, once a game was decided upon, two captains were chosen to select teams. If the game was ceremonial in nature and sponsored as a ritual obligation, the man receiving the dream in which the game was ordered to be played became responsi-ble for all arrangements. A Potawatomi dream recipient chose two captains. As each player arrived at the ball field, he put his stick in a pile; one of the two captains was then blindfolded to select the two teams by drawing from the assembled lacrosse sticks and dividing them into two piles. The sticks had personal marks of identification, so that each player could easily locate and retrieve his stick, then join others from his team. (The Ojibwe stick in Figure 20a, for example, has four small, scarcely visible incisions on the underside of the han-dle, which I take to be the owner's identification marks.) Usually five members, but sometimes as many as nine, made up each Potawatomi side. The Menominee in the early twentieth century had a similar mechanism. Their leaders collected sticks from the players, shuffled them together, then spread them out in two equal parallel rows (Figure 44). Believing their selection to have been spiritually deter-mined, the men joined the side on which the Thunderers (spirits) had determined that their sticks would fall. Sometimes, to expedite religious obligations, the same Menominee teams could play for two different sponsors consecutively on the same day or combine teams into one large game, with twice the usual number playing.[26]

Figure 44 • Menominee teams face each other before a game at Keshena on the reservation about 1916.

Ritual games of some tribes called for a specified team size, the number of players being determined for symbolic reasons. In the Cayuga Thunder Rite, seven men played on each side—one team made up of older men from one division of the tribe, the other of younger men from the opposite division. The seven players in each case represented the seven Thunder gods, and the game was conceived of as being played by fathers against sons. (Cayuga games for curing the sick were sometimes played with even fewer per side.)[27]

Clan systems and kinship played an important role in the social organization of tribes and affected alliances in games, warfare, and other important matters. In late May, for instance, the Onondaga still divide players by clan according to affiliation with the Mudhouse or the Longhouse. Because the game is religious in nature, the number on each team may be different, but it is immaterial; they simply play to three goals.[28] Other tribes, like the Winnebago, had a twofold division, with teams organized accordingly for village games. The divisions consisted of a number of clans; the WañgEre'gi (Those Who Are Above) included the Thunderbird, War People, Eagle, and Pigeon clans, while the Bear, Wolf, Water Spirit, Deer, Elk, and Buffalo clans belonged to the Mane'gi division (Those Who Are on Earth). This clan system was observed while on the warpath, at the chief feast, and in ceremonial lacrosse games.[29]

The competition offered by lacrosse games strengthened group identity, whether at the clan or the tribal level. It bonded relationships between kin units, as players directed their combined efforts against the opposing team. At the same time, lacrosse served to ward off local infighting and factionalism. Potential hostility between different clan groups of the Iroquois Eagle Dance Society was defused through the friendly competition offered by ceremonial lacrosse and clan joking.[30]

While most intravillage games ended peacefully, the identity factor sometimes allowed old interfamily squabbles to resurface and even gave rise to feuds. A historic photograph shows Creek players circling their goalposts before a game (Figure 45). On the back of the photograph Archie Sam, a Creek visiting the archives where he found it in 1967, penciled these words to clarify what the photograph represented: "Grudge battle fought against clans or families until stopped by government."

Lacrosse at the community level continues as a common recreational activity among Indian people. In historical sources one can read about a Cherokee game (probably in the 1820s) between the towns of Chicamunga and Chatooga in what is now Walker County, Georgia, with fifty men on each side "headed by their chiefs," or about an 1834 game between Hickory Log and Coosawattee near the present site of Jasper. Around 1880 the Rainy Lake Ojibwe (Ontario) and the Nett Lake Ojibwe frequently played wintertime games. The two bands, closely related through marriage, played on the ice of Rainy Lake near International Falls on the Canadian border. The summer tourist pageants of the 1920s on the Red Cliff Reservation

Figure 45 • Oklahoma Creek players circling goalposts in the 1930s as part of psychological preparation for a "grudge match."

featured lacrosse games between four or five teams representing various Wisconsin Ojibwe reservations. Each reservation was encamped in its own small "village." They played round-robin exhibition tournaments for tourists, with teams drawing the name of their opponents from a hat and two out of three games determining the final champions.[31]

Two or more communities sometimes joined forces for larger games within a given tribe, such as when three Dakota bands began a three-day series against Six's band in 1852. According to one report, 250 men and boys took part in the action. In the summer of 1836, several Ojibwe bands from the interior were encamped on Madeline Island in Lake Superior, probably on trading missions. Players from Sandy Lake, Lac Court Oreilles, and Lac du Flambeau challenged the Lake Superior bands to a game. Altogether, about 250 players assembled for the event.[32]

Problems could arise in putting together the teams of several communities. When two or three Cherokee towns joined forces in the 1830s, betting could be expected to increase considerably, so the boundaries of the competing towns were always clearly defined in pregame consultations. Game negotiators took care to prevent cheating through misidentification of a player's place of origin. Precautions were also taken against bribery—always a problem when the stakes were so high.

The pairing-off of Creek towns in joint play was complicated. The Creek at one time identified their towns as Red or White, and their citizens carried beads of those colors for identification. Red towns carried out warfare, White towns maintained peace. Lacrosse games appear to have been the only occasions upon which the two divisions had much contact; otherwise they avoided each other. There was little intermarriage between them, and those of opposite colors were never invited to each other's busk ceremonies. White towns were traditionally expected to oppose Red towns in games. Town alliances changed, however, once the Creek were removed to Indian Territory. But the Red versus White pattern persisted. When anthropologist Mary Haas conducted fieldwork among the Creek in 1938–39, however, she found that the ancient Red-White division no longer had any terminology to describe it. Still, towns were distinguished as *anhíssi* (my friend) or *aŋkipá-ya* (my enemy, or opponent), and games were organized accordingly.[33]

Choctaw lacrosse games of the past were often characterized by an opposition of kin groups, a trait that survived until the 1970s, particularly among the more conservative communities. Showing a high degree of group loyalty, such communities were the ones least likely to forfeit games by not showing up because of bad weather, for instance. They also invested a higher interest in lacrosse league events than the less traditional communities did: "So strong is this commitment [to the community] that many Choctaws openly admit that the obligation they have to their respective teams is more binding than that which they feel towards their jobs. One can be late to work or simply fail to report without violating any familial responsibility. Such is not the case with a ball game."[34]

How many players took part in a typical Indian lacrosse game? The question can be answered only by separating accurate eyewitness accounts from hearsay. And, in oral history repeated over time, "great games" have tended to become exaggerated in their details. Also, the *full* report of a game must be considered. Hasty readers of William Stone's published account of the 1797 Seneca-Mohawk rematch often stop in astonishment when they see: "The combatants numbered about six hundred upon a side, young and middle-aged men—nimble of foot, athletic and muscular." This number has often been cited without consideration of a later paragraph, which qualified the earlier statement by noting that only sixty per side played at once. They were rotated every fifteen or twenty minutes until all had had a chance to be in the game.[35]

One explanation for the large numbers cited as on the field is that such games may have been staged to impress visitors perceived by Indians as important personages. Catlin had such a game arranged for him in 1835 at Fort Snelling. Through the services of Major Lawrence Talliaferro, the Indian agent stationed there, the artist used the same strategy that induced Thirsts-for-Stone to pose for him a year earlier:

> To aid my views in procuring sketches of manners and customs, [the agent] represented to them that I was a great *medicine man*, who had visited, and witnessed the sports of, a vast many Indians of different tribes, and had come to see whether the Sioux and Chippeways were equal in a ball-play, &c. to their neighbors; and that if they would come in on the *next* day (fourth of July), and give us a ball-play, and some of their dances, in their best style, he would have the *big gun* fired twenty-one times (the customary salute for that day), which they easily construed into a high complement to themselves.

Beyond the enticement of a twenty-one-gun salute (which would have happened anyway), Catlin added the promise of barrels of flour, pork, and tobacco to the Indians. Their exhibition match lasted just two hours, whereupon they departed to the agent's house to demonstrate various dances.[36]

For an important display before some visiting dignitary, every player would have wanted to "get in on the act." Still, the large numbers participating in such exhibition games continue to be accepted by many writing on lacrosse as the general rule rather than the exception. One seventeenth-century game was purportedly played by more than two thousand Miami "warriors." But this game was clearly staged, possibly even as a show of force to the new French Indian agent. Furthermore, the account of the event merely specifies that two thousand Miamis with lacrosse racquets showed up, not that this number actually played.[37]

When "exhibition" games are compared with intratribal matches initiated by Indians from the same tribe in the course of their usual activities, the number of players diminishes vastly. For example, a Cherokee game witnessed by the Duke of Orléans (later King Louis Philippe of France) in 1797 at Tellico was said to have been played by six hundred—ten times the largest number of players ever reported for a Cherokee game. There is no question that the event was special. The duke had guaranteed six gallons of brandy to the winners, and the visiting French were escorted to the ball field to the accompaniment of the garrison's drums. By contrast, Mooney's report on the Cherokee game in 1890 cited only nine to twelve per side, and twenty-two players were the most that any of his consultants had heard of.[38]

Whatever the size of the team, organizers of nearly all Indian lacrosse games were careful to see that numbers and skills were evenly matched. Creek and Cherokee teams compared numbers by having teams meet at centerfield and lay down their sticks at the opponents' feet (Figure 46). Officials would then wander back and forth between and behind them to assess individual players' size, weight, height, and other factors; they would make adjustments by moving individuals from their original positions in the line to other places, facing opponents more their size.[39]

Mohawk researchers investigating their lacrosse traditions consider a decline in the number playing the game to reflect social changes as well as evolving game tactics. Where once there might have been a hundred per team, the numbers playing gradually lessened, partly because of population reductions, wars with Europeans, and intratribal division into separate settlements and reservations. According to the Mohawk, the mass game began to fade, as did field strategy. Formerly, if a goal were in danger, the Mohawk tended to put all defenders in front of the goal to block a score, much as soccer teams form a human wall when facing a free kick. With fewer players, the Mohawk began to train one or two to specialize in blocking shots. This, they say, was the birth of the "goaltender."[40]

The Cherokee have experienced similar reductions in team size and increasingly emphasized position skills. Whereas formerly there

Figure 46 • Eastern Cherokee players of two teams in 1888 select opponents.

were two center fighters per team, within the past seventy-five years the number has been reduced to one. Usually the biggest and strongest on the team, this "shortstop" or "center knocker," as he is sometimes now called, also serves as team captain. By the 1940s teams from each town played just three games a summer with twenty members organized by the captain but only twelve on the field.[41]

In one exceptional kind of Indian lacrosse—when men played against women—sides may not have been equal. The Dakota, for example, allowed women a five-to-one ratio over their male counterparts. Although it was more customary after an all-male lacrosse game for women to put on a game of shinny with the double-ball and single-pointed sticks, females and males are known to have opposed each other in lacrosse or even to have played on the same team. In mixed matches other adjustments might be made. When Shawnee men and women played lacrosse in Indian Territory, the women used their hands while the men played with sticks. Also, the goals were moved closer together.[42]

Early sources indicate that women learned the game in girlhood. Perrot commented on the makeup of Huron teams: "Men and women, young boys, and girls all play on one side or the other, and make bets according to their means." Thomas McKenney on his tour to the lakes at Sault Ste. Marie in July 1826 watched (probably Ojibwe) Indian children at mixed play. While their parents sat around smoking, "the little naked Indian boys, and hardly better clad girls, were meanwhile sporting over the green, playing ball—*baggat-iway* [lacrosse]."[43]

Little has been published on Indian women's lacrosse, but the sport has been mentioned among others played by several tribes. As early as 1765, Timberlake called attention to Cherokee women's playing the game. The mother of Will West Long, James Mooney's consultant, recalled playing it, like the Shawnee, with the hands instead of sticks. Such games of the Oklahoma Creek were photographed in the 1920s.

Intramural games involving both sexes were mostly for recreation; as Hoffman noted for the Dakota, "a mixed game of this kind [is] very amusing." Nevertheless, Paul Buffalo at Leech Lake Reservation in Minnesota acknowledged in 1968 that Ojibwe men and women used to play serious lacrosse together in his community, and he characterized it as a rough game.[44]

Team selection was preceded by a simple, informal challenge from one team or community to another. Many neighboring towns played each other on a regular basis, so rematches were frequent—often arranged at the end of a game after a challenge from the defeated team. A winning Cherokee team refusing challenges several times was ultimately obliged to issue a challenge to the loser to allow a chance to regain lost prestige. Cherokee rematches always took place on the field of the challenged winners, who controlled the terms of play. Games of new rivalry, however, were played on some neutral field midway between the two communities. (According to Lloyd Sequoyah, a Cherokee ball game conjurer, it was once the custom to "wipe the slate clean" by beginning each season with a fresh start, ignoring former wins and losses.)[45]

When a game was decided upon, whether to satisfy the wishes of a town or clan chief, to commemorate a famous player who had died, or simply because the players desired one, a council was called to define the terms of the challenge. They sent runners to deliver the terms, carrying "message sticks" as tokens for this purpose. When one Winnebago tribal division challenged the other, it tied tobacco to the invitation sticks. Choctaw challenge sticks were once used to keep track of game schedules: the chief of the challenged village threw one stick away each day; when he came to the last, he knew the game would take place the next day.[46]

Before Cherokee runners were sent, the team manager and con-jurer, or "ole cunjer-man," as the Cherokee still call him in their thick North Carolina English, carefully observed three or four ball game practices to determine their chances of winning. These scrim-mages might pit married men of the community against single men or players from different parts of the town against each other, all teams being matched on the basis of weight, size, and skill. Once the conjurer divined that the team might win, a spokesman was selected to bring a formal challenge to the other town and enter negotiations. The man chosen was required to be a persuasive speaker and know all the intricacies of lacrosse. Still, he was *not* to be an active player, lest his conference become a sort of bragging that would leave him vul-nerable to the spells of the opposing conjurer.[47]

The working out of details had to be satisfactory to both parties or the game would be called off. This is why the Seneca went into council meeting after they received Brant's challenge in 1794. The matters to be settled included agreement on the eligibility and num-ber of players, the size and location of the field, and the date of the contest. Also to be decided was whether the game would be a "big match" involving older, more experienced lacrosse veterans—a "high stakes game" in which much wagering could be anticipated—or sim-ply a "small game," with more amateur players and less betting.

In preparing for a game, individual players practiced their skills in pairs or in small groups. Most had learned the game as children, playing improvised forms of "sandlot" lacrosse in neighborhood pickup games as part of their general socialization.

One of the few specific training practices mentioned in the published literature was an Ojibwe means of strengthening leg mus-cles. Players wore a thin bag containing lead buckshot around their ankles "while at their ordinary avocations." When they removed the bags, they claimed to feel "light-footed." Lacrosse players, especially in the southeast, had to follow restrictions concerning their relations with women, what they ate and drank, and how much they could sleep. Once a Choctaw *toli* match was announced, players, like Thirsts-for-Stone, could not eat pork or grease and had to abstain from sex before the game. Beginning two days before the contest, they fasted, taking only minimal food and drink, and their sleep was reduced.[48]

Players in training, like the Ojibwe at Fort Michilimackinac, took sweat baths and drank certain liquids to purge their bodies. When Winnebago decided on the size of the field and the number of points for winning, they drank liquids to make them vomit and entered sweat lodges to gain strength and rid their bodies of impuri-ties. Before Iroquois games, players were subjected to "stringent fasting, bathing, and emetics." The vomit-inducing drinks were made of decoctions of the bark of spotted alder and red willow.[49]

As noted earlier, ritual scratching as part of game preparation had both physical and religious intention. In the nineteenth century, the Mississippi Choctaw scratched their children to improve circulation as part of a general effort toward industriousness and stamina. Worried that children might succumb to *itakobi* (laziness), parents also forced them to swim in cold weather, lift heavy weights, and play lacrosse.[50] The Creek still perform ritual scratching for ceremonial ball games during the Green Corn Ceremony. At the edge of the stompground square, the chief "makes medicine" by blowing through a bamboo shoot into a pail of water while chanting softly to himself. After the women have helped themselves to this medicine liquid, the players are scratched four times each on the back of their calves, upper arms, and forearms. They bathe the wounds with the medicine water before donning their stomp dance rattles for the Feather Dance. (This is called "touching medicine.") The scratching supposedly enables the medicine to penetrate muscles and release its powers.

As part of the mental readiness for games, Indian lacrosse players were lectured by their leaders or captains to be psychologically prepared for action and to play well. Before eighteenth-century Huron games, in the afternoon "the captain of each team harangue[d] his players and announce[d] the hour fixed for beginning the game." Before a 1913 Creek game, players had reached the field by 8:00 A.M. Each side then went off to hold council, and after a speech by their leaders, they left to dress for the game. Players listened carefully to the exhortations and took them seriously.[51]

The typical speech reminded players of local pride and former victories—obviously intended to "fire them up." At the end of the eighteenth century, one old chief in the Eastern Cherokee town of Cowe began his talk after all were seated during the indoors ball-play dance. He spoke of games won by Cowe in the past, "in commendation of the manly exercise of the ball-play, recounting the many and brilliant victories which the town of Cowe had gained over the other towns in the nation, not forgetting or neglecting to recite his own exploits" and those of other elders present.[52] Such inspirational talks were similar to battle preparations in warfare, where former warriors related their accomplishments on the warpath, usually in the context of some departure ceremony.

The Creek custom of circling the goalposts just before a game, still practiced in the 1980s, has its parallel in their final circling of the ceremonial fire each year, carrying lacrosse sticks and equipment while leaders give out high-pitched wails to serve as a farewell to the fire and to honor the balls used in the game. When they arrive dressed for the game at the playing field, they repeat this performance at the goal to protect it and keep the players in a high mental state (see Figure 45). (Victors circle their goalposts after a game, perhaps symbolically to suggest that the goal is still "safe"—that is, that it has survived being "attacked" or scored upon.)

Care was taken to bless, secure, and protect the equipment against evil spells before a game. Each Menominee captain selected an influential medicine man to ensure the safety of sticks deposited at the ballground the day before the game. His presence at the ballground was unnecessary because he had the power "to influence the sticks at any distance."[53] In the 1980s Creek players still tied their sticks, breechclouts, and belts in a bundle for hanging on a special arbor overnight before the game (see Figure 12). They retrieved the items the next morning, yelling and whooping.

On the day of the game, teams coordinated their arrivals at the field to occur simultaneously. Because of the distance of the agreed-upon field from the residence of the players, the journey often progressed in stages, with only part of the distance traveled the first day. This movement in stages was repeated ritually in the Cherokee game once players were actually on the field. Basil Hall described the arrival of Creek players at the field in 1828. Following a loud cry from the woods, one team suddenly emerged, "advancing to the ball play ground in a most tumultous manner, shrieking, yelling, hallooing, brandishing their sticks, performing somersets [sic], and exhibiting all conceivable antics." They circled their goal in customary Creek fashion, then went to centerfield to await the emergence of their opponents—"squatted down in a thick cluster till their antagonists made their appearance." Once the other team arrived, "the two groups remained eyeing one another for a long time, occasionally uttering yells of defiance."[54]

Like the Eastern Cherokee, the Oklahoma Creek today also advance in a line to midfield to meet opponents—a practice continued into the 1980s. After players circle their goals, the medicine man stands behind the goalposts, holding the two balls aloft on a short stick while the team divides into two columns behind him. A long wailing is punctuated by war whoops and concluded with all players noisily banging their lacrosse sticks overhead in the air, much like the final huddle before a football or soccer match. They then spread out across the field in front of the goal and behind the medicine man. He begins chanting rapidly in a monotone as he leads the line to centerfield, where the other team, similarly advanced, awaits.

The origin of this practice is obscure, but there seems to be a striking similarity between the forward moving of the lines in stages to the mode of warfare that the Europeans brought to North America. Whether Indian people were emulating the continually advancing lines of riflemen is not known for certain, but the warlike nature of lacrosse and the infusion of war symbolism in many of its rituals suggests the possibility of this adaptation.

Once the teams were on the field, referees commenced play.

12 *Cherokee Reservation, 1888*

We were already about two weeks into practice when this white man Mooney came by and wanted to make a picture of our team with his camera. He usually stays with the Yellow Hill conjurer, but since we weren't going to play Yellow Hill, there didn't seem any danger in letting him take some snapshots. So we lined up, like you see us here (Figure 47). Actually, we hadn't been scrimmaging long, and some of the players hadn't gotten to practice yet. So it wasn't really all the Wolf-Town players that were going to play Big Cove Saturday after next that got in the picture.

I didn't see this picture until about twenty-five years later, when Mooney returned to Cherokee Reservation and asked us to help identify the players. I think we all look pretty serious in the picture, maybe even a little angry. That's 'cause this game is risky, and in case this picture got to Big Cove before the game, we wanted to look pretty mean, like we meant business. Also, we usually save the feathers for the ceremonial ball game dance and the game. But since this was gonna be our first official team picture and we wanted to look good, we managed to dig up a few feathers to stick in our hair.

Anyway, that's me, Twister, in the middle of the back row, fourth from the left. I was twenty-two at the time and captain of the Wolf-Town team. That was partly because I played center fighter, even though I was light. Usually they have someone heavier, but I had a pretty long reach to grab the ball at the toss-up in centerfield, which is one reason I was put in at that position. Plus I was the tallest—you can see that. Way down, standing on my right are the Crow brothers, Eldredge and Joe. The Crow family has always had some of the best players for Wolf-Town, and these two guys were no exception. They played close together since they were about eight or nine, so they knew how to work the ball. They could make fast breaks, so we used them as the home stick players in front of our goal at the toss-up—just in case the ball got thrown in their direction right away. Sometimes, though,

Figure 47

they were put in as lower fielders, on the river side of the field, but they were just as good upper fielders. They were usually paired in any case.

The short guy between me and Joe is Duck, or Kuwa'na in Cherokee. He was one of our older players but a real good shortstop. One way you can tell the older players in pictures is their uniforms. Both Duck and Jim Johnson, on my left, have on the old-fashioned loincloth, like my father and his friends always used to wear for games. The rest of us have on the more modern uniforms, those knee-length shorts. These were getting pretty popular among younger players, and we were usually allowed to have our girlfriends or mothers sew designs on them, like red or blue crosses, or stars and stripes and such. If you were really good, you could have stars on your shorts. Everyone liked something a little different. I was captain, so my mother made the designs on my shorts look pretty flashy, sort of like lightning bolts. Shorts were a lot easier to keep on during rough play, especially if you had a belt. Maybe we were getting too modest, like the white man, but you could be embarrassed if you still wore the old loincloth. A guy from the other team could tear off that loose cord pretty easy if you were grappling with him. Break it without much trouble if you were wrestling with him. I heard about one guy who was running with the ball and got caught from behind. His opponent grabbed his uniform when he was just about to score. Even though his loincloth was torn off, he kept on running completely naked through his home sticks to score the point. He was pretty embarrassed, so he just threw the ball back over his head without turning around and kept going all the way back to his house and never came back to the game.

The guy next to Johnson is Sawanuka, and kneeling next to him is Lewis Hornbuckle. They were both good home stick players, like the Crow brothers. In front of them is Joe Standing Deer—Ahawi-Kata'ga they called him. He was one of the fastest runners on the reservation, and guys from other teams, well, if they learned they'd be matched with him, they almost always went straight to their doctor to do special ceremonies just so they could keep up with him.

The oldest teammate in the picture is Peter Crow, kneeling in front of me. His Cherokee name is Kagu-Ayeltiski, which in English means Crow-Mocker. That's someone who can make a crow call pretty good, good enough to fool the birds into answering him, anyway. Pete's the uncle of Joe and Eldredge. Even though he looks a little paunchy in the picture, the guy had great stamina. His weight was enough to crush an opponent. Once he got running, there was no stopping him, and he knocked over just about anybody that got in his way.

A couple of our regular players didn't make the picture. They'd been kicked off the team for breaking one of the training rules. The weekend before, Jim Welsh was out drinking with his girlfriend, and a couple of the guys caught them fooling around in the bushes. This was really stupid of Jim because we suspected this had been going on and we'd warned him. See, you can't have anything to do with girls until you're freed up by the old conjure-man after the game. It's because of their bleeding. You never know when that's going on, but an unclean woman can ruin a player and hurt the whole team. That's why they hide the ballsticks away from women the night before a game, because if they even touch one, it's gotta be thrown away. The medicine men are real serious about these rules. Another player kicked off the team—too bad, 'cause he was a great shortstop—was Pete Otter-Lifter, whose wife got pregnant about a month earlier. You're automatically dropped from the team if that happens 'cause, in making a baby, you lose a lot of energy and become sluggish. All your strength has gotten used up and you're no good to the team.

Another guy we missed for that game was Joe Doublehead. He managed to stay away from the girls, though they were always pestering him because of his good looks. But Joe was real fond of eating, and the food rules for training were just too much for him, I guess. Most of us got used to going without salt and eating only cold food before a game. When it came to mealtimes, though, Joe found the *gaktûn'-ta* rules too hard to stick to. The story we got was he was over staying with relatives in Bird-Town who didn't know he was preparing for a ball game against Big Cove, so naturally they treated him to the rabbit stew on the stove and *atûnka*, our favorite greens. Since none of his teammates were around to see, he took big helpings of those forbidden foods. You're not supposed to have *anything* to do with rabbits, especially not eat them; otherwise, it will affect your playing. Everyone knows the rabbit is timid. When you hunt him, he gets spooked real easy and he loses his wits, running crazy all over the place. If you eat rabbit during training, you're gonna be the same way in the game, so they toss you off the team.

Joe might have gotten away with it, but his cousin snitched on him. Those greens are no good for you either. Like frog-bones—another tasty meal players have to give up. You can break *atûnka* stalks real easy. If you eat those greens, you sure might break an arm or leg early on in the game. That's why players in training aren't supposed to handle little babies either, or for that matter, *any* young animal, 'cause their bones are brittle and weak.

Anyway, we'd started out practice with about twenty players—twice as many as we needed for the Big Cove game. The conjure-man still had to go through the final team selection. He usually does that with his beads close to game time, down by the river's edge. Extra players who made it that far could at least be used for the medicine bucket carrier and switchmen, which you always have to provide, even if they weren't fit for action. The medicine carrier is kind of a water boy, and there's a special drink he carries around on the field in a bucket. It's made from pine needles, crab apples, and water, and you drink it from the bucket with a plant stem like a straw. You can see him in the background of this snapshot (Figure 48). He's wearing a hat and holding the bucket. He's probably just noticed those two guys wrestling, so he's getting ready to head in their direction. They're going at it pretty hard. They'll sure appreciate a drink once they're done fighting. The switchmen act as ballstick pickers, so when you throw your sticks down to get into a scrape with your opponent, he picks 'em up and hangs on to 'em 'til you're done wrestling, so you won't role over on 'em and break 'em.

The way this game against Big Cove got started was that we beat them real bad late fall the year before, holding them to just two goals. They wanted a rematch right away, but winter came early and the ground froze up. When it's that cold, you don't want to run around playing ball in your bare feet and stripped to the waist, so we agreed to put the match off until the next year. They sent their business guy over from Big Cove two weeks before Mooney took our team picture, and we agreed on when we'd play. Once that happens, things get real busy 'cause there are lots of people you need to help the team. Someone has to take charge of arrangements for the ball game dance, and we had to find a singer with a drum and a *talala* (woodpecker) who could "whoop" good and a medicine man who knew the songs for the dance. He's the one that shakes the rattle when we circle the fire. We also had to find women who'd agree to sing and cook for us and dance.

But the first person we needed right away was an old conjure-man who knew all the ceremonies we had to have done before playing. If you didn't have him, you wouldn't even consider a challenge from another town. When I was captain there were about four ball game elders in Wolf-Town, so we started going down the list. Old Man Swimmer had been our conjurer the year before, but he was "tied up," 'cause a team from Bird-Town had

• 193

Figure 48

already hired him for another game, and a ball game specialist is too busy to work for more than one team at a time. We finally settled on old John Panther, even though he walks kinda funny—I hear he was born that way, like with one leg longer. But sometimes that means he's pretty powerful, and you don't want to mess with him. Anyway, we went up to his shack, and he was sitting in a rocker with an old straw hat with holes in it and stroking his long gray beard. We asked him right away, but he reminded us we still owed him from a game the summer before. So we had to pay him off first before he'd even consider it. That didn't take too long, 'cause the players could put some groceries together in a hurry from their family gardens, and most of their mothers had some extra pieces of cloth or bandannas they were willing to donate. John Panther wanted Standing Water to be his assistant 'cause he was a specialist at scratching and knew those sayings that went with the turkey-bone *kanuga*. He could also act as manager and help in the final selections of the team.

After everyone heard that Big Cove had challenged us, we had a meeting and lots of players showed up, more than we needed. That's usually what happens, and it's up to the conjure-man to find out which ones are the best. You don't know for sure whether you're in till the last minute when you get to the ball field to dress for the game. They keep it a secret who's gonna play to make sure the other team doesn't know exactly who it is and get their conjure-man to work against certain players.

See, the conjure-man has to work with his beads to figure out who's gonna play well and what players should stay out of the game 'cause they'll get hurt. They do it a little different in each town, but it works about the same way. I hear in Yellow Hill they make all the men that want to play stand in the river while the conjure-man takes his beads and prays over them and presses them into the riverbank mud. If the beads jump out of the mud into the conjure-man's hands when a player comes out of the water, well, that means the player is okay for the team. Usually, though, they use the beads another way. Even though every-one gets out on the field to scrimmage together and toughen up the team as a whole and fix anyone's ball picking and ball carrying if they've gotten rusty, the conjure-man weeds out the weak ones from the way the beads move. You aren't really supposed to watch how it works, but sometimes he does it when you've been taken to water, so you can't help but see what he and the manager are up to on the riverbank.

Those two guys usually find some secret place by the river the Friday afternoon before the game. The conjure-man spreads out his handkerchief and rolls two beads like dice for each player. The manager has the list, and when he reads off each name, the conjure-man rolls the beads. The red one stands for your team and the black one is the enemy team you'll be playing. He watches real close to see how they move. If the red bead rolls fast, it's a good sign and the player definitely makes the team, but if one red bead moves slow, they should keep him out of the game completely or else make him a stick picker. If the black bead rolls slow, that's real dangerous, 'cause it means your rivals have lots of power. There are other things he does with the black bead, like pushing it into the ground and saying magic words. He says something like "*Ske!* Big Cove is crawling along the crooked trail and are beaten. The hearts of our enemy are crawling with germs," or something like that. It's like the ones the medicine men use when you're sick and they're doctoring you, but they use real old, funny-sounding Cherokee, and it's hard to understand what they're saying most of the time.

Sometimes, if they're picking the team earlier than the day before, they use those sharp pegs that stand for the enemy players. The team gets into a circle around the conjure-man, and he shoves one of the wooden pegs in the ground and points at one of the players. That man is supposed to hold up his ballsticks, one in each hand, jump over the peg, and yell loud. If the conjure-man likes the way he hollers, then he's allowed to play in the game.

Almost as soon as Cherokees start a practice for a game, 'specially a rematch, they try to find out who's gonna be playing on the other side. They spy on the other team when they scrimmage, so they have a pretty good idea of who'll be playing what position. The conjure-man needs all that information so he can start working against the enemy team right away. There's lots of things you have to watch out for, too, 'cause their conjure-man's working just as hard for his team against you, and they have spies too. Like you have to be real careful about spitting anywhere someone might see it, 'cause your spit can be scooped up and taken to the other conjure-man to work magic with it. What I hear they do with it is supposed to make you weak. They mix the spit up with earthworms and wild parsnip, which is poison, and then some splinters from a tree that's been hit by lightning. They dig a hole right by that tree and put the whole mess in the hole with yellow pebbles and bury it, then build a fire on top of it. If it's your spit they got, you start getting overheated all of a sudden every practice and may even have to drop out. If you feel any weakness coming on, you know someone's working charms against you, and you tell your conjure-man. He can start doing things to block off that magic power that's hurting you and save you in time.

I heard my grandfather say in the old days they could do even more powerful things, even kill someone off before the game ever began. The conjure-man would get up before sunrise every morning for seven days before the game and dig a little make-believe grave about six inches deep. On the bottom, with a stick, he'd scratch out the ball player, make his picture in the dirt, with his head pointing west. Then he'd punch a hole where his heart'd be and drop in black beads wrapped with spiderwebs and do magic sayings, speak magic words to weaken him or kill him. If the conjure-man had his players with him, he gave each one of 'em a splinter of wood from a tree hit by lightning. Then he started a fire in the little grave. Each player'd give his splinter the name and clan of the guy he'd be matched against in the game, and one after another they put those splinters on the fire for the conjure-man to watch what happened to it. While a splinter was burning he'd say prayers in old Cherokee and look real close to see how the splinter was burning. If the splinter rolled around and curled up, that meant that the enemy player it was named for was going to be pretty active in the game—probably tough to handle. But if the splinter just burned without curling, it meant he wasn't gonna be much trouble on the field. My grandfather said if the splinter broke while on fire, it was a sure sign the player'd break an arm or leg in the game. All of this was pretty powerful stuff, and if the splinters kept moving less and less while they were added, it showed the enemy team was getting weaker all the time. To keep up the pressure, they put a white stone on all the burning enemy splinters to make them real uncomfortable. You know the ceremony'd worked if some of the players from the other town had accidents before the game or lost their nerve and didn't show up.

The afternoon Mooney took our team picture, those who hadn't been scratched yet met with Standing Water. Scratching isn't absolutely necessary, but you kinda get looked down on by the other players if you don't go through with it at least once before the game. Some of the older teammates asked Standing Water to do it again when we got closer to the game. It really hurts a lot when the old man plunges those sharp teeth into your shoulder and drags that *kanuga* down your arm, but you know what's coming 'cause you've done it before. The first time, though, is tough on the youngest players. They try not to wince, but you can't help notice them flinching and gritting their teeth and keeping their eyes shut real tight. They really make a run for the river to cool off their scars and cool off their bodies from all the cuts. Some players like to show off their scratches and scrape them with sticks to make the blood run more. That way everyone in Wolf-Town will know they're already pretty brave getting ready for the big game. My dad told me that Cherokee warriors used to do this when they were getting set to go out on the warpath. It showed they had real courage and it'd help them come out alive when they got to fighting the enemy.

I was next in line for scratching when Mooney took this picture of old Standing Water working on Jim Johnson (see Figure 16). Jim comes from a pretty strict family, so he was wearing a loincloth the old way. You can see he's got it on in the team picture, too. It's a big bandanna, but you can use any kind of cloth just so it's big enough to cover your privates in front and hang down some over your butt. I guess he liked that one 'cause of the flashy patterns and colors. You can see the marks where Standing Water has scratched up and down above his left chest. Those turkey-bone scratchers are real sharp and the cuts start to swell up right away. Standing Water's a little lame and you can see his cane hanging from his right arm. Here he's finished with Jim's upper arm and is starting from the elbow to come down to his wrist. Jim's been scratched a lot, so he looks pretty calm. Actually, Mooney was more nervous than Jim. He said he could hear the *kanuga* cutting through Jim's flesh. It was pretty cold that time of year and Jim shivered a little, 'cause of the wind, not the gashes.

About a week before we played Big Cove we had to start getting up early every morning to meet the conjure-man at the river before eating. Cherokees call this "going to water," and it's an important part of our lives. See, the water in rivers and streams in our country is real powerful. It can help you out if there's any kind of sickness in your family, or if someone's trying to witch you, or if you need to get clean after someone close to you dies. My grandfather used to tell me that the old Cherokee warriors always went to water, too, before starting out on the warpath— so they'd win in the fight and come back home alive. I guess the water also protects you in taking on the enemy town in a ball game too.

We'd gone to water as soon as Big Cove sent their guys over to challenge us to the rematch and we had a toehold on John Panther. You have to do this to find out whether or not to accept a challenge. There's no point getting into a game if you know in advance you're gonna lose, and the conjurer is the only one that can find that out, with his beads. So before we accepted Big Cove, all the guys that wanted to play went with the old man down to Soco Creek, not too far from Wolf-Town. He found a place up from the mill where the creek bends, but with no trails coming to it and lots of brush, so no one ever visits that spot. It was safe to go to water there 'cause no one could see what we were doing, 'specially any spies from Big Cove—they're too far away. The conjure-man keeps changing the secret spots along the creeks to be sure he's safe when he goes to work.

Anyway, after John Panther took us through the brush to the bend in Soco Creek, he got us all to line up and stand real quiet while he sat down behind us. We had to change places a couple of times 'cause there were lots of players and not a lot of room between the bushes and the creek. The conjure-man's gotta be facing upstream, looking east, when he rolls the beads. The one in his left hand is the enemy team, and the one in his right hand is the home team. While he's muttering something you can hardly hear, he sticks his arms out and starts the beads rolling in each hand. He kinda lets them roll around a while, then the beads seem to know what theyre supposed to do, 'cause one of them always starts moving around pretty fast, and that's the winning team. Since this time the bead in the old man's right hand was pretty active, we would beat Big Cove. He gave us the okay.

These ball games are serious business, and you gotta be real careful about whether you challenge someone or accept another town's challenge. Plus you better be sure you got a good toehold on a conjure-man before you start going around bragging you're gonna beat so-and-so. My dad told me about one time Raven's-Town players were really set on playing Wolf-Town, 'cause his team had lost a few games in a row and Raven's-Town thought they must be pretty weak so they could beat 'em easy. They were too much in a hurry to get the game going and sent their representatives over to make the challenge without even trying to get a conjure-man. I guess they figured they could do it later. After my dad's team accepted, the Raven's-Town team started looking around for a conjure-man, but word had already gotten out that they hadn't bothered with doing things right. They had a hard time finding a conjure-man who'd work for them. See, there are some things you just don't do before you get a medicine man to back you up, and arranging a ball game is one of 'em.

Anyway, Raven's-Town finally got Ed Old Tassel to conjure for them, but they had to pay him plenty and even then he wasn't too happy about the prospects. But he set about it anyway, trying to figure out their chances of winning, so he tried lighting the two cotton snakes to see which would burn up first. When that didn't look too good for Raven's-Town, he put a deer tongue on a stick and roasted it over the fire, to see what direction the meat cracked, but that didn't work out so good either. He told the team that the most they could expect to score was five goals out of the twelve you need to win. They didn't want to take back the challenge and look like dumb cowards, so they asked the conjure-man to take them to water and try once more. So he took them to Raven's Fork Creek and told them to line up and be quiet while he said his prayers and rolled the seeds in his hands—see, in the old days they used colored seeds instead of the beads we have now.

Everyone was looking upstream like they're supposed to, when all of a sudden this huge snapping turtle came floating down the river. When he spotted the people, he got spooked and tried to dive, but it was too shallow. He tried to climb up the steep bank across from them but kept losing his balance and flipping over and trying again. This really scared the shit out of the players, and they took off in all directions, leaving Old Tassel still sitting there with his seeds. See, the Wolf-Town conjure-man knew they'd made the challenge before they had any real protection. So he'd used some magic to get that snapping turtle to swim downstream. He knew it would spook them, 'cause that water's supposed to stay calm without anything floating by when the conjure-man's busy. Anyway, my dad said it worked. Wolf-Town beat the pants off Raven's-Town, and everyone knew why. Raven's-Town was pretty careful after that about challenging other towns and didn't even ask for a rematch.

You go to water a lot when you're getting ready for a game, usually starting seven days ahead. That number seven is sacred, so lots of things, like songs or dances, have to be done seven times over. Once you get down to the riverbank, the conjure-man already has some medicine brewed up that's been cooked up with some special kinds of plants to help make you strong for the game. The first thing you do, even though you haven't had breakfast yet, is drink from his bucket and then puke it out into the river. You watch your puke, too. If it sinks to the bottom, that's a bad sign and means you aren't gonna play well in the game, so the conjure-man needs to treat you special to make you stronger. But if the puke floats downstream, which it usually does, well, then, that's okay and means you'll help your team win.

My white friends from over near County Corner don't understand this puking business and think it's silly. The only time most of them puke is when they're drunk on moonshine, and it's not something they like particularly, so they can't figure out why us Cherokees would do it on purpose. I've tried to explain it to them that you gotta clean out your body real good when you're getting set for anything as rough as a ball game. You gotta be in top shape. That means practicing a lot and staying away from certain foods. But you also gotta be cleaned out. See, your body is just like a tube that air can go through. But that tube can get plugged up with germs or pus or spit and you get sick, or that tube can get twisted somehow and needs straightening out, which puking does. It also helps build up your wind.

'Specially on the morning of the game, going to water takes a long time. The conjure-man has extra prayers to say and he has to treat each of the players one at a time. It was always hard to understand what he was saying most of the time since it's in old Cherokee, and most of us at that time were trying to speak English whenever we could—you could really get in trouble at school for speaking Cherokee! But my dad told me pretty much what that old man's chanting meant. When the conjure-man faces the river for the team he calls it "Long Man," what we call water in ceremonies. He says he's come to the side of Long Man's body and reminds him how powerful the river can get, like raging and foaming when it's running in the spring with snow melt-off. He asks the river for its strength, like in tossing floating logs around like twigs and smashing them against the rocks. He wants to be able to do that to the other team. Then he starts praying to the birds who won the game in our story about them playing against the animals. And he gives them all the color red, which stands for our team. Like the red bead he conjures with is us, and the black bead is the enemy team. He prays to the Red Bat so he'll be able to dodge fast in any direction to get away from his opponent, and he prays to the Red Hawk for sharp eyes, so he can keep his eye on the ball all the time in the game. He also prays to the Red Rattlesnake so he can scare his opponents.

Then he picks out one of the players and takes him aside. He asks him the name of the guy on the other team he'll probably be matched up against, also what clan he is. By this time you've got a pretty good idea of who it is, so you whisper his name to the conjure-man so he can start cursing him by name. Then he starts praying to the black spirits who can cause your opponent trouble or even hurt him, like making him break an arm or leg in the game. In the old days, my grandfather said, he heard the conjure-man had prayers that could actually kill a guy during the game.

Anyway, the conjure-man asks the Black Fog to surround the enemy team so they can't see. He asks the Black Rattlesnake to wrap his slimy body in a stranglehold around the opponent and the Black Spider to wrap his black thread around your opponent's soul and drag it out of him and take it to a black coffin and bury it.

This is all pretty strong stuff, but I've seen it done this way lots of times. When he's telling the Black Spider to bury that enemy player, the conjure-man bends over and jabs his finger in the dirt, just like he was knifing someone in the heart. Then he drops the black bead in the hole and covers it up by stamping hard with his heel. That black bead has been doctored beforehand with spiderwebs wrapped around it. That's supposed to make the other team's eyes all blurry. When he buries the bead you're supposed to dip your ballsticks in the river, then pull them out and touch the spoon ends to your lips, like you're kissing them. Then you cup your hand to get some river water and wash your head and chest, then cup up a little more to take a sip from.

After everyone has done all this, the conjure-man usually tells the team how things are shaping up. If he made any mistakes, or something weird happened, like the snapping turtle thing, it meant that the other conjure-man was working hard against him and the ceremony is no good. That's why sometimes they have to do these things all over again.

When we were practicing for the Big Cove game that last week, we went to water every night after practice. After that you're free to go home for supper. Some of the players, like me, lived a good ways from the practice field at West Fork Creek, so we usually stayed with teammates living closer. This meant eating supper with their families. I stayed at Joe Standing Deer's, 'cause his older brothers had both married and moved out, so there was always a spare bed. His aunt did the cooking that time because Joe's ma was gonna have a baby, and you're not supposed to touch any food made by someone who's knocked up. Also, about four days before the game, Joe's sister all of a sudden moved out of the house, but no one said why. I think she was about to start bleeding. They wouldn't let her use the paths to the practice field or the trail to where they have the ball game dance either.

A couple of days before the Saturday game we were in good enough shape to skip practice and rest up for the all-night ball game dance on Friday. Usually that ceremony doesn't start until after dark when the fires are going, but Mooney wanted some pictures of the doings, so we agreed to start it early while it was still light out. Some of the older players weren't too happy about this picture-taking business, 'cause a lot of this is kept secret and the conjure-man was real nervous about Big Cove spies finding out and watching. Mooney promised there was no way he could get his pictures ready until long after the game. Plus he said he would bet heavily on the Wolf-Town team, and he gave John Panther some money to calm him down. So we set up and posed for him after we let the singers and seven women dancers and the *talala* and whooper know to be there early.

We used the same ball game dance-ground in a hollow next to Wright's Creek that we'd used the year before, 'cause we were pretty sure by that time we were going to win. Someone thought Big Cove might have guessed where our dance-ground was, so we posted guards for several days and nights to make sure none of their spies could sprinkle medicine out on the grounds. That stuff could make you weak for the game the next day.

The dance always starts with the *talala,* a guy who can really let out a loud, high whoop. They say that the most powerful yellers can be heard in the enemy town and make their players nervous. Before they start dancing, your players always get into two lines for the *talala* to run back and forth between them. He's hollering six short whoops and then one long scary-sounding one, which we all answer with our own whoops. You always line up pointing in the direction of the town you're going to play, so it's almost like the lines of players are the goalposts with the *talala* running through them to score.

Then the dancing part begins around fires started a while back. After the fires have been going a while, the conjure-man sprinkles some old medicine tobacco on some of the hot ashes. While it's smoking, he rakes it off to one side. Any witches or bad spirits around will catch a whiff of this smoke. It's supposed to kill 'em or at least keep 'em from ruining the doings.

You dance seven times during the night, sometimes right up to sunrise. Anyway, once you're all in the circle, like in Mooney's snapshot (Figure 49a), the old man starts up the dance. He's outside the circle, but he moves right along with you. While you're moving in rhythm he sings a little "Hey, ya" and then you all answer, "Hey, ya." Then maybe he'll go into a little "He ya ha," and you do the same. It's not all that hard singing with the group. You just gotta listen to that dance leader and sing what he sings, but if you don't have a good lead singer, then you might as well forget about it. At certain times in the song the whooper lets out his yell. Then all the players point their sticks to the ground, like you see here, and pretend they're picking up a ball like they would in a game (Figure 49b).

There are a whole bunch of these songs. As soon as you finish one the leader starts up another, so they're all sort of strung together. Sometimes the dance leader makes up insults about the enemy team before he starts up another song. We keep up that way for about

Figure 49a

Figure 49b

twenty minutes. Then it's time to go to water, where the conjure-man is waiting for you, and let the women dancers take over. We leave our sticks behind, hung on the special ball-stick rack so that they can get doctored during the women's dance. That happens seven times during the night, so the sticks keep getting more and more powerful (see Figure 13).

It takes us about an hour each time to go to water, and that's when the women dance. They have a drummer sing for them. He's gotta be real good and have another one ready to back him up if his voice starts to give out. Sometimes you get drummers from another town if they're good, but you wouldn't have one from the town you're playing against. There are usually three or four really good drummers on the reservation, and they get a good workout during the fall ball game season. Usually you gotta pay them with a shirt or pair of shoes or something like that. A long time ago, I guess they used drums made out of clay with water in them and a deerskin head on it. Later on they started using nail kegs with groundhog skins for heads. I guess the pottery drums must have broke pretty easy, which is why they shifted over when the white man brought in those wooden kegs.

You don't get any sleep that night, 'cause those dances gotta be done seven times. The only difference is that the last time the women dance around their fire, they throw in pine-knots to make it really blaze up and smoke a lot. The players stand next to it so their bodies can be cleaned by the pine smoke, just like they use pine smoke to clean up a house where there's been a body lying for a wake. Some of the women pick out burning pineknots and throw 'em over the ballstick rack like they're scoring goals. When they're done the conjure-man takes them to water too, 'cause they've gotta be as clean as the players. While they're at the river the manager pulls burning branches out of the fire and uses them like switches on the backs and legs of the ball players. That leaves charcoal marks on their bodies to show they've gotten some of the fire's power.

The whole time from the beginning of the ball game dance to the start of the game is pretty tense and dangerous, 'cause you've been building up so much power. Plus you can't have anything to eat and you get no sleep, so by the time you get to the ball field you're pretty fired up for the game. The conjure-man and the manager make sure you don't do certain things. Like the women dancers can't eat anything till after the game, just like the players. And even though you're real tired from all the ceremonies, you're not supposed to lie down. If you're going to lean on anything, it's gotta be a teammate, not a tree or a rock or anything like that. And you're not supposed to fool around with your sticks, like picking up a rock and throwing it just for the heck of it, 'cause you'll just be wasting the power that's been put in your sticks for the game.

When it's daylight the conjure-man figures out how long it will take to get to the ball field. He breaks the march up into four parts, where you stop and rest each time. If the game's in your hometown, of course, it doesn't take long, so maybe he'll put off starting for an hour or so. If you're the challenging team, you generally take all morning to get there. But you gotta be careful that the enemy team has no idea what path you're taking. Otherwise they'll send their spies out to sprinkle magic rabbit soup on the trails, so if you step on it you'll tire out easy when you're playing. Sometimes they pour that soup between your goalposts during the game when no one's looking. That makes it hard to score.

When I was little once I helped John Panther make up a bunch of that soup. He had me go around and collect the things that get all boiled up together, like plants that bring bad luck and sawbriar roots. Then I had to find him a dead rabbit and a mouse. He threw the mouse into the fire till it was nearly burned to a crisp, and then he pulled it out by the tail and dropped it in his medicine pot. He cut the bladder out of the rabbit and squeezed its piss into the pot, and threw in the plants and started boiling up the whole mess. The hardest thing for me to get, though, was some spit from a bleeding woman. The only thing I could think of was to bother my older sister. I could tell she was having her monthly, 'cause she was so crabby and crying a lot. Anyway, I kinda egged her into a spitting contest. I spit on her when she was napping and woke her, and she chased me around till she had me pinned to the floor. Then she let a long drool down onto my face. When I broke loose, I scraped the spit into my hand and ran to old man Panther's house before it could dry up. I didn't know at the time what he needed all those funny things for, but he gave me ten cents for my work.

The resting places are always at secret spots by the river so the conjure-man can take you to water again. Before you start out on the path again, you form two lines and the *talala* goes through his motions. He yells four or seven times—I forget—and then all the players whoop together and take off again to the second and third resting place. There you finally get your first bite of food in about twenty hours. It's just cold cornbread and water and you get just a little bit, but it tastes great.

The last resting place is called "the stripping-off place." That's where the guys that will play are finally told so by the conjure-man. They strip down to their playing uniforms, and the others are given jobs as medicine bucket carriers and ballstick pickers. They look around for some long hickory branches they can cut, then strip off the leaves for the two ballstick pickers. These guys point out the ball when the players can't see it. They also use those sticks to whip players who look like they're playing lazy.

You usually get to the last resting place by about early afternoon. Then you hide in a secret spot by the river to go to water one last time before playing. That's when the conjure-man gives all his last-minute predictions to each player. He tells him how he'll make out in the game, how many times he can expect to score, and how long he'll last on the field. The conjure-man says a real long prayer at this last stopping place. Even if you don't understand most of it, you recognize the names of all the birds and animals that he mentions will be your helpers or opponents. They all come from the ball game story everyone has heard over and over again since they were little. Then the conjure-man gives final coaching instructions, telling each player what position he'll start at. He uses a sharp stick to draw certain plays on the ground. He's learned from the beads what plays will work the best against the enemy team. He marks off a little ball field in the dirt and sticks little pegs standing for each player into the ground. This shows the players where to be on the field after the first goal's scored. He also marks four or seven players with charcoal from a tree hit by lightning. This gives them extra power in the game. After all this is done, the *talala* gives out seven sharp yells—or maybe four. All the players answer him with war whoops, and the whole group takes off for the ball field.

Whenever we played Big Cove, it was usually on the mound just below Rattlesnake Peak. We used to follow West Fork Creek up over the mountains, then cross down past Ca-lal-su-la's land to the river for the last resting place. Then it's just a short way through Sah-an-ta-kah's land, and you're on the mound. Those guys from Big Cove have about twice as far to come, but then they can come downstream along the river the whole way—not so much climbing for them.

When you get there, the whole field is packed with people from both towns, milling around. It's real crazy, 'cause the betting is still going on. See, nearly everyone wants to bet something on their home team, and you can do that right up until game time. There's a lot of money and clothes at stake in a ball game and that makes you play all the harder. My grandfather said they used to bet teams of horses and even land, but nowadays it's mostly money and almost anything else worth something, like watches or jewelry or guns. The women mostly bet clothes, handkerchiefs, cloth—things like that. Even the players can bet, getting right down there in the middle of the field to make a wager yourself, or maybe if you're too busy you get a friend or relative to do it. For that game with Big Cove I had my mother and sister bring down all the family things to bet. It took me some time to find them in the crowd, also the guy from Big Cove I'd arranged to bet against. I had to be sure that what he was betting was worth what I was putting up. You always bet equal this way.

While this was going on, it was a pretty confused scene on the field. Everyone wanted to see how high the stakes were getting. Mooney was there taking a bunch of pictures that he showed us later. Here you see one of the Big Cove players in front of his pile of goods he's arranging on the ground. And that's him a little later after more stakes have been added (Figure 50). That's probably his girlfriend or a sister maybe, about to add a hand-kerchief to it. (You can see Mooney's shadow on his leg in the picture.) Once all his stakes are there, he takes off to join the team.

• 205

Once your pile of stakes is set, you get someone with a blanket to wrap them all up in it and carry them off to the sidelines. There's a place where all the bets are guarded by peo-ple from each town, so no one makes off with anything during the game. If the bets are high, you can expect a pretty fierce battle in the game.

After the goods are off the field, you're matched up with your opponent. Each team goes back to its end of the field to make last-minute checks, fix up gear and uniforms, get feathers tied in your hair, and pieces of bat wing stuck in the web of your sticks. About half an hour before game time, the whole team lines up in a row in front of its goal, facing the enemy at the other end. The people from your town are right behind you, carrying all the things that have been bet on your side. That's when all the final bets are made and people are sure the bets are even. Here you can see some of the Big Cove players and townspeople waiting to move toward centerfield (Figure 51). You can see some of the guys using their sticks to carry the shirts and bandannas and blankets and things that they're gonna bet.

After all the goods have been carted off the field and stashed in piles, then they start matching up the players. Since you already pretty much know who your opponent's gonna be, you find him and lay down one of your ballsticks on the ground with the spoon end pointing at him. That means you challenge him to play against you. Almost always he's gonna accept that challenge by putting down *his* stick, pointing at you. Since the center fighters and the shortstops are pretty special at what they do, they're usually challenged by guys playing the same positions. It's a little less certain with fielders and goal players—'cause some guys can play both. Players usually try to match up with guys they're related to by blood or clan. That way, if you break his rib or collarbone or something serious like that, there won't be a lot of his people out to get even with you. That's how they pretty much keep the lid on things and keep it from getting out of control.

Figure 50

Figure 52

Figure 51

Once you're all matched up, the team gets in a line facing the two home sticks making up its goal. The other team lines up right in front of you with the center fighters in the middle of the two lines. Then one of the officials, like the guy here stepping over the sticks (Figure 52), walks between the lines to make sure each player has an opponent pretty much his size. When everything's okay, he calls for the toss-up.

The game starts when two old men, usually guys that played a lot when they were younger, give little speeches at midfield, telling all the players to play hard but play fair (Figure 53). Then the two center fighters get ready for the attack. You never know when that one old man's gonna toss the ball straight up in the air right between you, but when he does, the battle begins. The sticks start flying as those center fighters are all over each other to catch that ball when it comes down.

But let me tell you about the game against Big Cove. It was almost thirty years ago, but Mooney's snapshots brought much of it back. I still play the game, mostly with the old-timers, but we talk about that time we played Big Cove a lot. I guess at the time it was a real important game, 'cause it meant we'd beaten them three years in a row, which was quite a winning streak—the best on the reservation in years. So many of the details came back to me right away when I saw Mooney's pictures. It was one of Wolf-Town's best teams in years, and everyone on the reservation said so. We were practically unbeatable that fall and only dropped one game, to Raven's-Town. Anyway, we scored fast and early after the first toss-up, a good sign that old John Panther knew what he was doing. The Big Cove center fighter was strong and much heavier than me, but I had a longer reach, and I picked that ball out of the air before he could get to it. There, you can see us going up for the ball (Figure 54).

Yeh, here's the one I remember. My pass went to Crow, but when he tried to throw he missed 'cause his Big Cove opponent shoved him while the ball was in mid-air. The ball hit the ground and was rolling pretty fast, but Eldredge could run faster and scoop up a moving ball and get rid of it downfield in a hurry when he had to, which you see he's just done here (Figure 55). You can see another teammate, his brother Joe, who's got that Big Cove upper fielder around the belly so he can't get in the way of his brother's pass. I think Mooney got a little too close to the action on that picture.

Anyway, Crow's pass was to Joe Standing Deer, who was right next to the left stick of the home team goal. He cut across right through it to score. I can still see it. In all, that first goal probably took only about three minutes, and that got us really excited. We scored two more goals before Big Cove got their first score, a long shot from their shortstop right down the middle of the field. I guess their home stick players were able to block our two men down there just in time to leave the goal open.

Compared to the games my white buddies play, this Cherokee ball game is a lot rougher. Almost anything goes except you can't handle the ball with your hands. I remember in this game one time my opponent got the ball cupped between his sticks, and I just ran at him and jammed my sticks between his arms to pry the ball loose. It worked, and the ball went flying. There's lots of ways to tie up your opponent if your team is running with the ball and you wanna keep him out of the action. I used to like to put an armlock on my opponent. That keeps him from getting his sticks free. Once you've got him, you kinda spin him around in that position so he can't run away toward the action. Right before Joe Standing Deer made that first point, I tied up my Big Cove man by grabbing one leg and holding him balanced on the other, so he just had to watch Joe and there was nothing he could do to stop him. Sometimes you can even get that guy in a bear hug from behind, so he's not going anywhere.

It's rough and some players are bound to get hurt in a game. In that game against Big Cove, Duck got hit pretty hard early on and had to leave the field or be helped off. It turned out he didn't have any broken bones, but it sure looked like it at the time. Once in that game I got the wind knocked out of me pretty bad, probably from a jab in the gut with the butt ends of someone's sticks. I remember having a cramp afterward for a couple of days. Since you're running around so much, you get overheated too, so they usually have a short break after a score. Then you can get over to your sideline for a few minutes and catch your breath before the next toss-up—look for the medicine bucket carrier to get a sip from that bucket before starting play again. Joe Standing Deer was so hot from that run that he grabbed the bucket and dumped all of it over his head.

Once the game gets going and you've been building up steam against your opponent, you look for the right time to wrestle him to the ground. Wrestling is about the best way you can show him up, so even if it takes you out of the action, almost everyone wants to have at least one good tussle with his opponent. Sometimes you can throw your sticks any-where on the ground, and the stick picker will get them for you. Just before Duck got hurt, I remember he threw his sticks so fast that they went way off to the side, and the picker didn't know where to look for them. When Duck got free, the stick picker just shook his head and put his hands in the air, so Duck had to run around all over the place looking for his sticks, which were in two different places.

You're allowed almost anything when you wrestle. You can pin your opponent, pull his head back, twist his arm behind his back, whatever you want. Sometimes it gets to be a real pileup, with one of the guys underneath you probably digging for the ball with his sticks. His teammates wrestle their opponents to get them away from him. The officials let you wrestle like this for a while, but if there's a stalemate or you're just not letting the other guy up, well, that wrestle switcher will come over with his hickory stick and start smacking you to let go. Otherwise the game would come to a halt. They need you out there with your sticks to keep the ball moving.

Everybody turns out for these games, 'cause Saturdays you don't have to work, and on

Figure 53

Figure 54

Figure 55

Sunday you can recover. Everybody from our town was there for that game, I remember. My girlfriend brought a lot of her friends with her to bet on our team, and she showed me the pile of things they got after the game was over. Lots of people bet on that game. There weren't any other games on the reservation that day, so you could expect visitors would come from all over. Lots of white people living nearby like the game, so they come down too.

The game against Big Cove lasted about three hours in all. It got pretty tense when the score was seven to four, but then we put some pressure on and pulled ahead to ten. We were about to make it eleven when Lewis Hornbuckle tried to pass to one of the Crow brothers at the home sticks. A Big Cove upper fielder slammed across his sticks right when he let fly, and the ball landed way over near the sideline, and one of their fielders scooped it up and ran the whole field to score. No one was guarding him, and he got a head start on the rest of us. When the score was ten to five we got word that John Panther was in the crowd at the sidelines, so we knew we had them licked. The last two goals—Peter Crow got one and Lewis the other—gave us the game, and the Wolf-Town crowd went wild—three years in a row!

People went to collect on their bets, and both teams went down to the river to meet their conjure-man. Since we won, we had to go to water one last time with John Panther. Even though the losers act all polite and friendly, they're plenty angry underneath, particularly when they've asked for a rematch. You can bet they've got their conjure-man still working some bad stuff on you, so you go to water as protection against his curses. It doesn't take all that long. After Panther did his chants, we all dove into the water and splashed around, washing the dirt and sweat off our bodies. Because it was fall, the river was getting cold, but you always had some bruises and cuts from the game and needed to wash off the blood, so the cold bath was pretty welcome. Also, they got a couple of leaf doctors down there that put stuff on your wounds and help clean you up. Then you put on your everyday clothes and get back to the field to claim your own stakes. The womenfolk of the town bring down a lot of food, so you get your first chance to fill up in more than a day.

Guys from both teams try to behave nice and proper to each other—you're supposed to as a Cherokee—even though there's a lot of bitterness for the losers, and the winners would really like to go around bragging and showing off. There's sure to be another rematch, so you don't want to push your luck too far. Usually the crowd breaks up before sunset and takes off for home.

You still gotta have that Victory Dance a week after a game before your conjure-man frees you up and while all the *gaktûn'-ta* that you paid attention to for the game still hold. That means you watch what you eat, and you can't get together with women until after the dance begins. Still, about all I remember of that Victory Dance thirty years ago is that afterward some of our team got pretty drunk and silly, and someone ran off with my girlfriend. But that's another story.

13 *Little Brother of War*

If Wolf-Town's captain, Twister, had continued his description of events following the defeat of Big Cove, he would have told of his role in the Victory Dance—the final episode in the Cherokee ball game cycle. Twister may not have been aware of the antiquity of the tradition, but that Saturday night at about ten o'clock, lined up with his team and handed a feather wand, he was symbolically transformed into a victorious Cherokee warrior recently returned from the warpath. Had he been born a century earlier, Twister would have held a scalp in his hand.

The obligatory Victory Dance to "free up" the ball players is but one of the rituals that make up the Cherokee lacrosse cycle. The many precautionary tactics practiced by players in training, the protective measures taken for them by the conjurer before the game, the ceremonial march to the field—all these actions suggest something serious, more to do with actual combat than with a simple ball game for amusement. Indeed, decoding the symbolism invested in this sport reveals the affinity of lacrosse and Indian warfare and provides a native North American example of ancient and universal relationships between game and battle. It was not by accident that on the prize table at Olympia the statue of Agon, the god of the games, stood immediately next to that of Ares, the god of war.

Not only were the rituals of Indian warfare and lacrosse the same but the two activities were conceived of as surrogates in Indian belief systems. This is explicit in the interchangeability of their terminology and in the various names assigned to lacrosse. The Creek frequently called the game *hótti icósi,* or "younger brother of war." Explained a former Creek player, James Hill: "Match game pretty near like war. Like United States make war 'gainst 'nother nation and United

States whip other nation, like U.S. whip Philippines.'' Hill used the fighting analogy in telling of the reconciliation of two communities that customarily played each other in lacrosse: "Okchai got tired of being beat and wanted to quit fighting, so they agreed to be 'friends' with Hilabi."[1]

While the common Cherokee term for the game is *a-ne-tsó*, another name frequently used by native speakers in the past was *da-na-wah' uwsdi'*, meaning "little war." Among various Cherokee slang expressions current in 1890, "Play ball against them" is said by Mooney to be a "figurative expression for a contest of any kind, more particularly a battle." In the first mention of Cherokee lacrosse in historical documents—an entry on 4 May 1714, by the South Carolina Board of Indians—is stated that the Cherokee invited the Yuchi to a game in order "to cut them off," suggesting a military ambush. Raymond Fogelson suggests (correctly, I believe) that the game challenge could have been a figurative declaration of war.[2]

The equation of lacrosse sticks to war clubs is apparent in the Creek legend of the scrofula-ridden child in search of Ûñtsaiyĭ', the gambler (see Appendix A, No. 6). His father hands him a war club, saying, "'Now you must play a ball game with your two elder brothers. . . .' He said a ball game, but he meant that the boy must fight for his life." The lacrosse stick/warfare relationship is embedded in a Menominee legend, in which a Thunderer informs "Uncooked," an Indian, that he will strike a tree with his lightning bolt, leaving behind black marks to show where to cut the wood in making lacrosse sticks (see Appendix A, No. 7). Creek games concluded as though a battle had been won: The winners ran to their goal and raced around it giving out war whoops and yells, while the scorekeeper shouted, "*Ilátitō' tō' tō'*," meaning "He is dead, dead, dead, dead." Such traditions are slow to die. In a game from the 1940s, just before tossing up the ball at midfield in the face-off, the Cherokee referee admonished the players of both teams: "We goin' play ball—only a small war, not a big war. Just run after the ball, not after people trying to hurt them."[3]

Southeastern tribes were not alone in conceiving of warfare as a game and calling it such in everyday language. In a boastful speech, a Winnebago chief, Little Priest, complained of the federal government's interference in his people's fighting traditions. Addressing an unidentified member of some western tribe, Little Priest explained:

> One of our favorite games is the game of war. . . . There was a time when we were a numerous people. Before our brother the white man came . . . I used to like to play that game with those of other tribes, but I never found any *men* to play with. All other Indians of

other tribes used to call me . . . elder brother. Because I was among
all the greatest warriors. Since our friends the white man came, I
have refrained from fighting. Things have changed now. We can no
longer play that game.[4]

Indian people used the color red symbolically in relating lacrosse
to warfare. In the traditional color scheme, red was associated not
only with war but also with success and winning. As is evident in the
myths and sacred formulas of the Cherokee, this color was attributed
to many spirit helpers—the Red Hawk, the Red Rattlesnake—while
anything to do with the enemy was designated black, the color of
death.

Red pigmentation was always applied to the equipment of those
about to do battle, whether in the woods or on the playing field. For
war paint, warriors of many tribes used vermilion, a highly prized
trade item; similarly, Creek ball players applied red paint to their
bodies before a game. Cherokee warriors would put red paint on
their bows, arrows, and war clubs, while coloring the white flag of
peace red in preparation for the warpath. For the same reason Yuchi
lacrosse sticks were painted red before being put on the ceremonial
scaffold the night before a game, "to symbolize their combative
function." In making the lacrosse ball, the Yuchi would insert a small
red cloth ball that had been conjured before sewing together the two
round pieces of soft deerskin covering that would conceal it.[5]

When lacrosse sticks are equated with war clubs, they are red
ones. The text of one Cherokee protective recitation called "What
those who have been to war did to help themselves," in which the
red/black imagery of winners/losers is also apparent, begins: "*Hayĭ!
Yû!* Listen! Now instantly we have lifted up the red war club.
Quickly his soul shall be without motion. There under the earth,
where the black war clubs shall be moving about like ball sticks in the
game, there his soul shall be, never to reappear." This formula was
spoken by the medicine man each of four consecutive nights before
Cherokee warriors set out on the warpath.[6]

The color red was also applied to articles of lacrosse dress, such
as feathers worn in the hair. For games as well as for battle, the
Cherokee conjurer's assistant would tie or fasten these to the participants; he would also paint their faces red with a substance made from
a certain soft stone that had been burned and pulverized. The
feathers—considered very sacred—had to be prepared by specialists.
Such feathers were requested by the seven principal war counselors,
gathered, and sent to the "sacred painter." The only distinctions
between preparations for war and the ball game in these matters were
that different prayers were recited during the body painting and

different people requested them. For "a general war" the war counselors asked them to be prepared; "in case of a small war expedition, or of a ball play, [the feathers] were painted at the request of the leader."[7]

All such attitudes toward the color red ultimately derive from its association with blood, the life-sustaining element. This connection helps to explain why Cherokee warriors and ball players alike were considered to be in a "red condition" for the entire cycle of their activities—susceptible to danger, injury, and even death—and why they continued their rituals after the principal event (battle/game) until they were "released" ceremonially by a conjurer through ritual purification. It also explains their fear and avoidance of menstruating women, who were also considered "unclean" and therefore dangerous because of their bleeding.

The ritual purification of Cherokee ball players after a game is nearly identical to the treatment accorded a returning war party two centuries ago. The warriors were said to be *u-ta-la'-wa-shu-hi'*, meaning in a "red" or bloody condition. (The term is also used to describe a state of anger.) Because those in battle had been in direct contact with death, had spilled blood and brought back scalps, they were in an unclean state; in this condition, they required purification. Alexander Longe, a trader among the Cherokee from 1711 to 1725, related how returning warriors were made to sit by the "war fire" and drink "physics" (cathartic liquids) for four days. On the fourth night they washed their clothes and bodies and passed their arms through the fire as a cleansing gesture. A similar need for purification was expressed by a Cherokee called "the Little Carpenter" in a letter to a British captain reporting on the Indians' successful fight against the French. He requested specifically that white shirts be made ready for the war party's return, when they would discard their bloody battle garments as a symbol of their cleansing.[8]

The Victory Dance—the final event in the purification of successful ball players—is unquestionably a vestige of the Scalp Dance of former times (Figure 56). Cherokee involvement in fighting virtually ceased after the Revolutionary War, and the forced removal of the Cherokee to Indian Territory (Oklahoma) in the early 1800s disrupted their society, throwing traditional culture into disarray. The Scalp Dance probably lay dormant, only to be revived under a less belligerent-sounding name at a later time in conjunction with the ball game cycle. Certain elements in the later version of the dance, however, relate it so closely with war practices reported on in the eighteenth century that the connection is unmistakable.

Take, for instance, Lieutenant Henry Timberlake's depiction of a returning war party in 1762. Bearing the four Shawnee scalps they

had brought back as war trophies, the warriors circled the "town-house" (council house) three times while sounding the "*Death Hallow*"—probably some sort of war whoop signaling a successful raid. They then retired inside, smoked, and recounted their various war deeds. In the course of a dance, each warrior in turn described his battle exploits, having first placed a donation on a buckskin for the privilege. At the conclusion of the dance, the donated items were distributed to the poor.[9]

In the Victory Dance of later times, as the line of ball players circled around the dance area emitting occasional war whoops, a master of ceremonies, or "dance driver," would point at one of the individuals with a stick and exclaim, "*Ka!*" All would cease dancing and gather behind the designated player as he recited his "exploits" in winning the game. This was concluded with loud whoops of approval, whereupon the dance resumed; the dance driver prepared to point out another, and so on until each had a turn to recite his accomplishments. The dance ended with the collection of the feather wands—what had formerly been scalps—and, in a gesture comparable to distributing booty to the poor, the rewarding of various ball game functionaries for their services. Players distributed food, goods, and money to the drivers, manager, women singers, conjurers, and others as expressions of appreciation.[10]

Figure 56 • Menominee sticks raised aloft as though they are scalp sticks. In the days of warfare, scalps brought back from battle were dried on small hoops and laced with rawhide thongs (not unlike lacrosse stick webbing) so that the lock of hair hung from the center of the ring. These hoops were then attached to long sticks and held aloft by women as they performed the Scalp Dance—a victory celebration.

Among southeastern tribes the purification rituals for returning warriors and the postgame activities of ball players share other aspects—the observation of sexual taboos, for instance. Having abstained from intercourse for three days before departure, Cherokee warriors were also required to maintain continence for another three days upon their return. Ball players were expected to follow similar restrictions. Isolation of the participants was another practice that warriors and ball players had in common. Instead of lingering on the field for postgame congratulations from their community, ball players went directly to the secluded spot on the river where their conjurer took them to water and cleansed themselves of the sweat, grime, and occasional blood of the game. This had its parallel in the isolation of returning warriors. A Chickasaw war party was sequestered in the townhouse for a period of fasting, singing, bathing, and taking emetics to purify themselves.[11]

Twister's narrative is filled with the sounds, gestures, and actions of men about to do combat. The piercing, warlike yell of the *talala* during the ball game dance as players line up facing the "enemy camp" (opponents' town), the brandishing of lacrosse sticks like weapons, the constant lookout for enemy "spies," the wearing of feathers in the hair—all suggest ball game preparations as a surrogate for wartime activities. The Creek, who undertook similar preparations for the game, carried the war imagery one step further: During their ball game dance, they tied the ball they would play with to a twig and inserted it in the ground, its end directed at the camp of the opposing team, as Swanton says, "much as cannon are trained on the enemy."[12]

The constant sound of the war whoop during games is noteworthy. In the southeast it was called a "gobble-whoop," in that the yell ends in a very throbbing, turkeylike gobble deep in the throat. The Yuchi said that it was in imitation of the wolf and used by a warrior when he took a scalp. The same cry was made whenever a Yuchi ball player scored a point: "When a player makes a goal he throws his body forward, elevates his elbows and gives the 'gobble' yell, a tremulous whoop also given as a scalp cry. This is a taunt."[13]

The march to the ball field also simulates earlier military practices. The direction taken is plotted by the conjurer, a scout is sent ahead to make certain "the path is clear"—that is, that no enemy has strewn magical substances on it—and four requisite stops are made at "resting places" to go to water. The players march single file without talking, and if they step on a twig, they are required to carry it with them to the ball field.[14]

Compare these practices with Buttrick's early nineteenth-century account of the Cherokee warpath. His information, collected from former warriors, is remarkably similar to the ball-play march:

> Ska-li-lo-ski [an important war officer] directed the march and the encampments, and ordered when to arise in the morning. In marching no one was allowed to speak on any vain or trifling subject, and especially must not talk about women. If in marching one broke a stick or twig without thinking of it, he must not let it fall, but keep it in his hand till they took up camp for the night. On encamping, it is said that the great warrior, now the Raven, went forward two days march and returned the same night [making sure "the path was clear"].[15]

Just as the river was sacred to the Cherokee, so was fire, and the small fire built the evening of the ball game dance was another important vestige from the days of warfare. Formerly, a small sacred fire was carried in a pot on the warpath, by either the chief warrior or the war priest. Great care was taken that it not be extinguished, for it was important to return with the fire for purification rites, when it was required by the conjurer at the morning sacrifice after the all-night vigil. At that time a meat offering was burned in the fire; if the fire died out, it was a sign of continuing trouble with enemies; if the fire consumed the meat, they could anticipate peace. Success in battle or even keeping the troops together depended on maintaining the sacred fire kindled in the pot. If the fire were to go out, noted Longe in his early-eighteenth-century account, "They all rome away but if the fire keeps in they presses on thire journey and when they ingeage the war king [leader] sits him down and keps a blowing the fire that they will have the beter of thire enemies."

Fire was widely used ceremonially and by conjurers for divination. Longe's account includes an incident that illustrates the veneration that Cherokee accorded the sacred element fire. Once Longe lit his pipe from the sacred council fire, whereupon an Indian grabbed the pipe from his mouth, emptied it immediately, and put out the smoldering ashes. Longe had unwittingly committed a great offense, as none of the sacred fire was to leave the building where it was kept burning.

Nearly two centuries later, Twister noted the care with which the ball game fire was prepared and later guarded, lest some of this sacred substance be stolen. One modern method of maintaining the ball game fire was to keep it in a lantern or in a "tote sack." Or the conjurer might have some of it in his pipe, in which case he could stand behind his team's goal and blow smoke to attract the ball toward it. Ball players feared that enemy spies could "steal" the ball game fire surreptitiously by casually lighting a cigarette from it to be taken back to their conjurer. Such an attempt was considered an act of desperation, indicating that the opposing team's conjurer, through divination, knew that his team's chances for winning were not good.[16]

Reviewing the history of Cherokee warfare, Fogelson stresses the *individualistic* nature of combat, which later found its expression in the ball game. In pre-contact times, Cherokee fighting, like that of many North American tribes, most often consisted of small-group skirmishes organized to avenge some wrong by a member of another tribe. Within the context of the lacrosse game, Cherokee are free to act out their personal predilections in physical battle. This seems to hark back to their former roles as warriors whose style of fighting was hand-to-hand combat. On the surface, the game might appear to be a contest between teams, but in actuality it is an outlet for *individual* performance. One need only consider the many wrestling contests into which the game seems to disintegrate, as players throw their sticks aside and "go at it" one-on-one.

Fogelson points out that in Cherokee lacrosse the rules were minimal and team coordination (in the modern sense) was lacking. Furthermore, any player who felt he had had enough was free to withdraw from the game. Fogelson compares this tendency toward an individual course of action to the days of Cherokee warfare. Joining a war party was voluntary, not mandatory; once on the warpath one was free to return home at any time he wished. The war chief led by example, not command, much like the center fighter/captain of a ball team served more to *inspire* his teammates than to call signals or decide on plays like a quarterback. A war speech before battle in 1840 reveals this fairly nonchalant attitude toward participation in a war expedition, giving priority to one's personal concerns: "If any of you have left a young woman you intend to marry and are troubled about her, now return. If any of you have left a wife and are fearful that some other man will sleep with her, now return. If any of you have left property of any kind, about which you are troubled, return and take care of it."[17]

Fogelson views the cessation of warfare at the end of the eighteenth century as a possible turning point in the development of the game in Cherokee culture. He offers the following tentative conclusions:

> The game may have taken on more of the attributes of real warfare. Games were probably fought with more deadly earnestness, since the ball play served as, perhaps, the only activity by which young

men could earn the sort of prestige and status formerly acquired on the war path. Large amounts of aggression formerly directed outward against Whites and other Indian tribes were now turned inward against fellow Cherokee of neighboring towns or political districts. The games took on a new seriousness.[18]

Thus the removal of warfare as an outlet for young men to vent the aggressive side of their nature only intensified their participation in lacrosse, which may help to explain why the game has survived among the Cherokee to the present.

Data supporting lacrosse as a war surrogate for other North American Indians are considerably sketchier, owing in part to their greater isolation and the much later documentation of their culture. Because the Cherokee game has continued to be played in a seemingly unbroken tradition, much of the traditional ceremonialism surrounding it is still intact, or at least the elders can still recall it. But elsewhere in North America—in the Upper Mississippi Valley, for instance—the game has completely died out, more than a generation ago in most cases. Still, there is evidence, however fragmentary, to suggest that at one time lacrosse functioned as a war surrogate for people of this region in much the way it did for the Cherokee—for example, the boasting of war exploits at the beginning of a Winnebago lacrosse match as a means of intimidating opponents (see Appendix A, No. 14).[19] When Francis B. Mayer witnessed lacrosse matches at Traverse des Sioux in 1851 between various bands of Dakota, each team, led by a chief (like the Cherokee), marched to the field "shouting loud whoops of defiance to their opponents."[20]

The frequent association of lacrosse with the Thunder spirits (var. Thunderbirds, Thunderers) elsewhere in the western Great Lakes area is another indicator that the game had warfare connotations. The Menominee lacrosse game was believed to be mimed warfare, the property of the Thunder spirits, who gave it to the Indians. Menominee games were ordered by a man whose guardian spirit was the Thunderbird and were played to honor him. Such men customarily possessed war bundles containing small packets of charms, which brought success in war to those who carried them. Such charms were also capable of restoring the wounded to health.

The making of a bundle was dream-dictated, and the items contained within its buckskin wrapping had special spiritual meanings known only to the bundle owner. A typical Menominee Thunderbird bundle contained both a miniature war club and a small carved lacrosse stick and ball, reflecting the Menominee belief that both war and lacrosse came from the Thunderers, who gave the Indians their first war bundle. It was said to contain a war club, and the Thunderers directed that the lacrosse stick be modeled after the weapon. The miniaturization of bundle objects symbolized that the owner had control over the activities these objects were associated with. If the bundle had a small war club, the owner would be a successful warrior; if it had a miniature lacrosse stick, he would have luck in the game. A Potawatomi "men's business" bundle from early-nineteenth-century Wisconsin Territory contains tiny versions of a canoe, a dance wand, a war club, and a lacrosse stick—all representative of activities associated with the realm of males (Figure 57).

Even though lacrosse is no longer played by the Ojibwe, its former close associations with aspects of war continue to emerge in the culture, however subtly. At summer powwows, it is common for older, "traditional" dancers to carry some item in their hand as they circle the dance arbor. Usually items are some sort of simulated weapon—a tomahawk or a war club, for example. (The event itself is directly descended from the Grass Dance, a warriors' society of the Plains.) Recently, I have observed "Porky" White, an elder from Leech Lake and a veteran, to carry a lacrosse stick. Leading the dancers in the "Grand Entry" of these powwows are flagbearers carrying American flags, Canadian flags, and those of veterans' organizations. But preceding them in the parade are men carrying "Indian flags"—long, curved stakes with a row of eagle feathers along the shaft. Such banners were once carried into battle as "coup sticks," said to be planted in the ground as a marker of the line behind which the warriors refused to retreat. In the summer of 1992 at Ojibwe powwows, an unusual Indian flag with its eagle feathers made its appearance. Painted red, its curved top had been brought around inside to butt against the shaft and buckskin thongs had been crossed at the center of the circle thus formed. When I scrutinized it closely I recognized it as a gigantic Great Lakes lacrosse stick!

War symbolism is also infused in the lacrosse games of the Iroquois. When Iroquois played lacrosse as a religious rite, there were seven men on each team, personifying the seven Thunder gods. They believed that lacrosse was played by these gods in the thunderhead and that the lightning bolt represented their ball. This is still practiced in many Iroquoian communities to heal the sick. When the great Seneca prophet Handsome Lake in 1815 was dying in a cabin at Onondaga, a lacrosse game was played for him. The popular belief is that the game was played in an attempt to cheer him up, or that he had requested it for personal amusement; I believe that it represented a desperate effort to save his life.[21]

Finally, it has often been suggested that Indians played lacrosse to keep themselves in shape for warfare. While lacrosse certainly provided physical exercise, it was not necessarily a training ground for

Figure 57 • Portrait of the explorer Beltrami in canoe with articles associated with "men's business" that he collected in 1823, probably from Ojibwe near the headwaters of the Mississippi River. Note that the war club and lacrosse stick lie together in the canoe bottom, while a war drum is propped in the prow. The stick is the same one pictured in Figure 20a.

fighters. Still, many of the best lacrosse players were from the ranks of warriors. William Stone learned from the mother of the player selected by Red Jacket to provoke violence in the game with the Mohawk that Iroquois warriors were chosen on the basis of their athletic skills as demonstrated in lacrosse games: "Mary Jemison states that these athletic games and exercises were practiced not only that their bodies might become more supple, or rather that they

Figure 58 • Eastern Cherokee player who appears to have been injured clutches himself. Possibly he has had the wind knocked out of him or been poked with the butt end of an opponent's stick.

might not be enervated, but that they might be enabled to make proper selection of chiefs for the councils of the nation and leaders for war."[22]

Precisely because of its warfare connotations, much has been made of the violent nature of American Indian lacrosse. Descriptions of the generally rough character of the game appeared early and have persisted over time, so that non-Indians harbor the impression that large numbers of players maimed opponents, leaving many dead on the field. Such impressions are only strengthened by chroniclers such as Peter Grant, who wrote that in Saulteaux rematches around 1804, "every object which might impede [players' forward movement] is knocked down and trod underfoot without mercy, and, before the game is decided, it is a common thing to see numbers sprawling on the ground with wounded legs and broken heads."[23] While severe injuries and even death did occur, many reports have been exaggerated simply to conform to the image of "the noble, savage warrior," unfettered by the artificial regulations of the modern field game.

A distinction should be made between accidental injuries resulting from the rough-and-tumble nature of the game and intentional wounds inflicted out of sudden anger, long-term group revenge, some personal grudge, or merely a desire to eliminate strong opponents. Until quite recently, Indian lacrosse players wore no protective gear—none of the shoulder pads or elbow guards of today's game—so they were constantly susceptible to bruises and dislocated joints (Figure 58). No helmets guarded against cracked skulls; no face masks prevented a freewheeling stick from bloodying a nose. Contact with the ground, sticks, and balls produced commonplace bruises on near-naked players, to the point that Baron Lahontan could remark on Huron play about 1700, "This game is so violent that they tear their skins and break their legs very often in striving to raise the ball."[24]

Any number of physical maneuvers that today would draw fouls were permitted: tackling, wrestling, tripping, charging, ramming, slashing, and striking with the stick. Some of these actions were to some extent controlled but with only minimal regulations (Figure 59). A Cayuga could use his stick to lift an opponent off the ground and dump him—the cause of many broken collarbones—or he could use his stick to strike another player, provided he had both hands on it at the time. Cherokee could do the same, but the sticks had to be held with one hand at each end—a rule usually ignored at the center-field toss-up action. Franklin Basina noted that the nature of the Great Lakes wooden ball made it especially dangerous: "My Uncle Tom Soulier, he got hit by the ball in the calf of the leg, and that goddam ball is carved out of a pine knot and still got pitch in it, it's kinda heavy. You get hit with that, well you're *hit!*" Whether it was a ball or a stick that caused it, Leonard Marksman, captain of the Bad River Big Bear team playing an exhibition match against the Chief Medicine Man team from the same Ojibwe reservation in 1948 "was hit on the head and knocked down. He was stunned for about 10 minutes but resumed play after that." Such injuries have been known to stop a game. Mississippi Choctaw today remember violent games of the past with so many injured that the games were called. In a 1947 Cherokee game, six players were hospitalized within the first fourteen minutes of play.[25]

As Perrot noted of the Huron, injured or fatigued players could

Figure 59 • Two Eastern Cherokee players prepare to go at it. Official on the right safeguards their sticks during the tussle.

take themselves out of a game and have substitutes put in, but care was taken that the original number on a side was never increased. To keep the teams at equal strength, the Cherokee retired an injured player's paired opponent when there was no substitute. When someone retired in a Creek game, the players threw down their sticks once again for counting to ascertain that the sides were still equal.[26]

Despite the lack of protective equipment, players nevertheless took measures to guard against the accidental injuries described. Some preparations were purely practical: Cherokee applied viscous oils to their bodies—eelskin, sassafras, or slippery elm—to help them slip out of an opponent's grasp. (According to Henry T. Malone, the body oils reduced somewhat the chances of injury: "Man-handling was somewhat difficult due to the use of slippery oils on the body, but even so, it was not uncommon for good players to be deliberately knocked unconscious.") Other ointments had magical protective powers: A decoction of devil's shoestring and beargrass rubbed on the body was believed to toughen a Cherokee player's limbs and enable him to spring back on his feet after being knocked down. Likewise, land tortoise blood was spread on limbs, the neck, and the back to provide sturdiness.[27]

Cherokee medicine men were consulted before a game to identify particularly weak players, so they could advise them to leave the game early, lest they tire easily and become susceptible to injury. Conjurers recited magical verbal formulas intended not only to protect their players but also to disable the opponents.[28]

• 227

Native doctors were always handy at the sidelines to apply herbal concoctions to injuries, sometimes effective enough that the player could return to action. The doctors also performed ritual healing actions over wounds. The Mexican Kickapoo in about 1905 used a sucking doctor to treat injuries inflicted by lacrosse sticks. Because the game was so rough, players received many blows that resulted in blood clots that needed extraction by this specialist, who used a sucking cup made of deer horn. Dakota Indians believed that the place where a spiritual leader's personal god or spirit resided within his body was particularly vulnerable. In a game about 1850, "Near the close of the play, VISIBLE-MOUTH, a young 'medicine-man,' received a blow from a ball club on his side immediately over the place where the Medicine-god lies in him, which felled him to the earth. It was said that the god was stupefied by the blow; but was soon reanimated by the wakon [magic] applications of the Medicine-men present."[29]

Broken collarbones were particularly common. Players were frequently tossed into the air by opponents, causing them to land headfirst on the ground. To avoid serious damage to the head or a broken arm, Cherokee players would instinctively hold their head to one side and extend their arms horizontally as they fell, but in doing so they risked breaking their collarbone. If that happened, to treat the fracture native doctors blew a decoction of poplar bark on the injured man's shoulder and breast and advised him to keep his arm suspended at a 45-degree angle in front of his chest until it healed.[30]

When the commercially made hard Indian-rubber ball replaced the Indian stuffed-deerskin ball in the late nineteenth century, a new potential for injury emerged on the lacrosse field. Because the Mohawk had to play Canadian teams by the latter's rules, they quickly learned to cope with this new piece of equipment, and many Iroquois began to develop their shooting skills to a high degree. Certain players became noted for their powerful shots. Discussions with Iroquois players today invariably lead to mention of Angus Thomas, a St. Regis Mohawk defenseman in both box and field lacrosse, whose legendary talents inspired the naming of a street on the reservation in his memory. Frank Benedict remembered as a small boy watching this remarkable player on the field: "The accuracy and the different styles of his shooting were so, that it stood out, and the strength of this individual and control of his shooting created a lot of fear with the goaltenders. He had one of the hardest shots in the league. Some of his shots, he'd hit the goaltender, and they'd be pushed back behind the goal-line."[31]

Thomas once accidentally killed another player with his famous "heavy shot," and after that he retired from lacrosse for a period. When he returned to the game, he once inflicted severe injury on Oren Lyons, at the time an Onondaga teenager playing goalie. As sportswriter Robert Lipsyte described his interview with Lyons, "Lyons's own eyes narrow as he remembers . . . [Thomas] came hurtling down the box at him. Oren stood his ground, determined to prove himself as good as his father [also a celebrated goalie]." The game was tied at 6–6 and in its final minutes. Thomas cranked up and took an underhand shot outside, striking the goalie and breaking three ribs. Lyons compares the blow to being hit on the chest by a baseball bat. The shot knocked him off his feet and into the net. There was no spare goaltender, and it took him fifteen minutes to recover sufficiently to stand again and finish the game. The wound left him powerless against four more goals by Thomas's team to win. Oren's son, Rex, blames part of his father's injury and the accidental death caused by Angus Thomas on the lack of protective gear available at the time: "[Thomas] did have a hard shot, and the pads weren't the state of the art they are now, you know, head-gear and stuff."[32]

These injuries, however serious, were accidental in nature, attributed to power and athletic skill. They were mainly forgiven (but not always forgotten). *Deliberate* injuries, on the other hand, could often lead to a game's suspension and ill feelings among players, such as the incident in the 1794 game between the Seneca and the Mohawk, which nearly led to war. The slashing of Jemison's face took place during a game. But there were magical ways of hurting an opponent by "witching" him before the game. W. David Owl, an Eastern Cherokee, told how a bucket of liquid brewed from the left hind leg of a rabbit could be sprinkled on the path that opponents would take to the ball game. If a player stepped on it unknowingly, he would get leg cramps when he was about to score. The practice owes its origin to the well-known legend: "In a ball-game long ago played between the birds and the animals, the rabbit's left hind leg was injured. Since that time the rabbit has never been able to use that leg. To this day he only leaves three tracks when he runs."

Some teams had reputations for playing "dirty." Yuchi ceremonial games pitted men of the Chief clan against the "traditionally mean" Warriors, who as late as 1900 still resorted to "foul play and violence." Run-ins during some games often provoked quarrels, and fights marred many others. Individual fisticuffs usually ran their course, as painter George Catlin put it: "Their stricks [*sic*] are dropped, and the parties are unmolested, whilst they are settling it between themselves."[33]

General free-for-alls were also not unheard of. A Creek game might last until dark unless fighting broke it up. Basil Hall did not stay for the whole Creek game he described in 1828 because the Indian agent had warned him that, often after a heated contest was over, players were still in such a high state of excitement "that they [fell] to in earnest, and [tried] the strength of their sticks on each others' heads." In one contest between the towns of Eufaula and Abihka in the early twentieth century, a general melee that lasted for three hours broke out at the first toss-up; the county sheriff and deputies were brought in but were unable to stop it. Mississippi Choctaw Jim Gardner was told by his grandfather, "They used to fight a lot at the stick games. The chief would set the game up and tell them not to fight, but they would fight anyhow. If two people started to fight, everybody would pretty soon be right in there fighting, too."[34]

Many scrapes in lacrosse games can be attributed to grudges, either personal or at a group level, such as family or clan. Walter Hoffman suggested that ill feelings between players were one cause of injuries in Ojibwe games about 1890, leading to blows with the stick to the arms or legs of a ballcarrier, often severe enough to force him to retire from action. In times of peace, animosity still ran high between tribes that had formerly engaged in warfare. During a peace meeting, the Yankton Dakota and Red River Ojibwe arranged a lacrosse game. While the game was going on, wrote historian William Warren, himself part-Ojibwe:

> One of the seven Dakota warriors who had survived the battle [against the Ojibwe] at Long Prairie, picked a quarrel with an Ojibway, by striking him for some trivial cause with his ball-stick. The blow was returned, and the fight would soon have become general, had not the young Wa-nah-ta, son of Shappa [head of the Yankton], rushed in, and forcibly separated the combatants, inflicting a summary punishment and scolding on his fellow Dakota who had commenced the fight.[35]

Ill tempers in games of other tribes have been reported into the twentieth century. An anonymous account of an Oklahoma Creek/

Cherokee game in the 1930s tells how a near-fight broke out when the Cherokee, badly out of practice, turned the tide after the Creek had scored several goals: "When those Cherokee boys caught on they got right in and won that game in a little while. Them old Creeks sure got mad. They just threw their ball sticks down and wanted to fight right now." Adair, an eyewitness to Chickasaw (possibly Choctaw) games in 1775, attributed violence to grudges between families. Fogelson once saw two brothers who "seemed to take special delight in belting each other all over the premises, both before and during the game."[36]

Deliberate rough play seems to have been less characteristic of Iroquois games. George Beers, in his *Lacrosse* (1869), berates the unnecessarily unruly behavior of Montrealers when they first took up lacrosse and contrasts it with the Mohawk style of play on the nearby Caughnawaga and Akwesasne reservations. Beers, wishing to rid lacrosse of slashing, swiping, spiked shoes, and other injury-inflicting aspects of early Canadian lacrosse, wrote that before any regulations were in place, "The best men were noted for maiming others and following the ball in raiding fashion, 'seeking whom they might devour.' That was in the days of no government [or rules], when [lacrosse] clubs were seriously considering . . . attaching surgeons, and purchasing club ambulances." Beers related witnessing a match at Caughnawaga, "a hard-fought game of an hour." The chief who had invited him admonished Beers in broken English on the Canadian manner of play: "You can't play Lacrosse like that. You smash heads, cut hands, make blood. We play all day; *no hurt, except when drunk.*"

Beers stresses that in the Mohawks' own games injuries were infrequent, and he insists that any rough play they exhibited had been learned from Canadians. Consequently, violence occurred only when the two races played each other. "Accidents" were particularly common near the goals, writes Beers, due to the Indians' habit of "bunching" whenever a goal was about to be scored: "They get very savage in such tussles. At an Indian match we got a stroke and a drag on the back of the left hand from an Indian's crosse, which opened a slit of an inch and a half in length, through which was afforded to the lover of anatomy a charming prospect of the articulation of the knuckles."[37]

If deliberate violence in the Indian game was a comparatively late development, as seems to be the case, it could be attributed to increasing encroachment of whites on Indian territories in the eighteenth and nineteenth centuries. During that period, the American frontier was expanding and the Indian land base was shrinking through removals and the creation of reservations. The Eastern Cherokee, instead of fostering national unity to confront this assault, simply intensified competition between their various towns, one of the principal outlets for which was the ball game, which invariably set off a chain of violence.[38]

Deaths did occur as the result of game injuries, but not by the hundreds, as imagined by many non-Indians today. Fatalities usually occurred under extreme circumstances. The playing was unusually vicious in an 1845 Tallulah versus Lufty game, with several hundred spectators and several thousand dollars' worth of livestock and property wagered. As Harry Morris, a mixed-blood Tallulah, was about to make the winning point for the west team, some Lufty Indians ran two horses in front of him in an attempt to cut him off. Morris, however, succeeded in running around one horse and jumping on the back of the other. Three players were said to have been killed; the number injured was so great and wounds so severe that many players had to remain at the ball field to recover—some as long as nine days.[39]

• 231

The cause of many deaths associated with lacrosse may have originated during play, but the deaths themselves usually happened outside the context of the game, usually as an aftermath of disputes. Such was the outcome of a Creek and Choctaw game played around 1790 to determine tribal rights to a large beaver pond. When the Creek were declared winners, the Choctaw attacked them with weapons of all sorts, warriors joined in the fray, and five hundred were dead by the next day. Another Creek-Choctaw game over territory between the Tombigbee and Black Warrior Rivers likewise ended in a battle. Seneca oral tradition relates that the war in 1654 in which they expelled the Erie from western New York originated in an Erie "breach of faith or treachery" during a lacrosse game that they had challenged the Seneca to play. In 1958 a Cherokee named Big Joe Toineeta, playing for Wolf-Town, was ambushed and murdered by his grudging brothers-in-law after he had finished a game against Big Cove. Although the killers were not from Big Cove, traditionalists on the reservation were convinced that the Big Cove conjurer had worked spells against Toineeta and that, once he walked onto the playing field, his fate was sealed.[40]

Despite the history of accidents, severe injury, and even death, Indian lacrosse players showed remarkable restraint. Furthermore, the game was *not* without rules against violence. Referees—usually respected tribal chiefs or elders—played a generally pacifying role in settling disputes on the field and defusing potentially explosive encounters. Even the earliest reports draw attention to their efforts. Bossu wrote of the Choctaw in 1759: "The players never become angry, and the old men, who act as referees, remind them that they are playing for sport and not for blood." When aggression on the field became excessive, a team's manager might impose penalties on, withdraw, or reprimand some player who was showing undue force. During a Choctaw game in the mid-nineteenth century, head butting was expressly forbidden; a violation of the rule could cost the offending team a five-goal penalty. Mohawk lacrosse in the Montreal area around 1860 was fairly restrained, and Indians were said to consider hitting another player "a mark of bad play." There were rules governing holding, tripping, throwing, or pushing; an infraction brought the game to a halt, and a face-off took place at the spot where the violation occurred. Continued disregard for the rules by the same Mohawk player "puts him in disrepute."[41]

Europeans were less impressed by the violence that they witnessed than by the lack of anger over injuries or losses. Almost all writers mention this "stoic" Indian characteristic. Bossu in 1759 noted that prospective rematches among the Choctaw helped soothe bad feelings: "After having played hard all day long, everyone goes home in glory or in shame. There is no bitterness as each one promises to play another day when the best man will win." Pope, in an early reference to Creek play, drew attention to the composure of wounded players: "A dislocated Joint or Fractured Bone is not uncommon: Suffer what they may, you'll never see an angry look or hear a threatening Word among them."[42]

The evenness of temper shown in the face of injury during a lacrosse game reflects in large part a characteristic Indian desire to demonstrate bravery. Iroquois traditionally viewed lacrosse as ideal training for youth, teaching them discipline as well as composure in the face of strife. Frances Eyman pointed to the schooling that Iroquois boys naturally receive as they participate in the game: "They learn to expend aggressive impulses within a ritualized pattern of behavior rather than in the murderous attacks of duel or war. They are trained away from the impulses of the 'burnt knives' [delinquents]." Mayer, witness to Dakota games in 1851, remarked on the generally controlled disposition shown by players: "No one is permitted to become angry or to take offence at any rough treatment he may receive."[43]

By the end of the nineteenth century, efforts apparently were made to reduce the level of violence in Indian lacrosse games. In this respect, the sport paralleled American football; the famous "flying wedge" inflicted so many casualties—the fall of 1905 saw eighteen football fatalities—that President Theodore Roosevelt summoned representatives of the big three Ivy League schools to demand an end to the brutality.

By midcentury, for example, attempts were under way to elimi-

nate the choking tactics described among the Cherokee in the early nineteenth century by observers such as I. P. Evans, who wrote that a stranger would shudder to see the violence on the field: "Before I witnessed an Indian ball play, I did not know that the vertebral column possessed as great a degree of flexibility as was demonstrated on such occasions. The principal respiratory tube is handled in such an uncourteous manner, that the jaws fly open involuntarily, followed by a protrusion of the tongue." An 1848 game in Qualla Town had two new restrictions, probably a result of pressure from the government and missionaries: property could no longer be bet on the game, and choking or breaking limbs was prohibited (Figure 60). The Mississippi Choctaw Jim Gardner recalled that fighting during games in his grandfather's time led to efforts to rechannel the aggression: "It was because of the fighting that they changed the way they played the stick game. The chiefs told the people not to fight. If they wanted to fight, he would make them wrestle; two falls. The first one

Figure 60 • A player from the Bears team on the Eastern Cherokee Reservation in a 1946 game chokes Captain Noah Powell of the Wolves, trying to force him to spit out the ball hidden in his mouth. The ballcarrier wears a sock on his right foot to protect an injury.

to fall twice was the loser, and the wrestling was over. Then they stood up and shook hands, and the chief told them not to fight anymore."[44]

Some elders by the beginning of the twentieth century were complaining that the game had lost its spark, becoming a mere shadow of lacrosse as they had known it. Older Choctaw considered the contemporary version a fad and said that players of the time lacked the strength, stamina, and skills of earlier ones. Claimed one, "[My father] hasn't seen good ball-players in a long time. . . . The old men say the players these days are not as strong as they were in the old days. They couldn't take the punishment they did. . . . It was a man's game then. If you weren't man enough, they wouldn't let you play." Recent games have become characterized by even tempers. Instead of flare-ups on the field, a jostled Cherokee player will control his feelings and wait for an opportunity to retaliate, catching his opponent off guard. In a game Fogelson watched in the 1960s, only four players retired from each team. In each case, he believed, the player left the game on instructions from the team conjurers rather than from fatigue or injury. In fact, the *only* injury he observed was the bruised arm of one Big Cove player, so slight that he remained in the game.[45]

Finally, there have been occasions in the recent past where Indian lacrosse has served two of its most traditional roles—that of healing and that of funneling group aggression into peaceable rivalry. During the violence on the St. Regis Reservation in the summer of 1990, an effort to bring the community back together centered on a new Mohawk lacrosse league, formed to reduce tensions and heal the social ruptures on the reservation. Ernie Mitchell was one of the principal organizers of this effort; a newspaper article described thusly how he and his colleagues went about creating teams and planning games: "Putting together a league at that point was a tricky business and [Mitchell] recalls being extremely careful in his planning. The first thing was to establish a non-contact rule and the second was to put a complicated draft system in place that ensured there wouldn't be some teams stacked with people from the pro-gambling faction and other teams stacked with antigamblers."

Ultimately the plan succeeded, but not without initial difficulties. The organizers, including Grand Chief Mike Mitchell, an anti-gambling leader, felt considerable hostility directed toward them. Given the rough nature of box lacrosse, they wondered if a noncontact league was feasible at all and feared that games might simply degenerate into fistfights. To guard against that, they established a rule against fighting and anyone who violated it was kicked out of the game and subject to a minimum three-game suspension.

In some of the early games, there was in fact considerable push-ing and shoving, and when the referees were not looking, a few lumps were taken and returned. But no really serious incidents erupted, and players seemed not to want to mix sports and politics. The minor leagues started up again, forcing parents of opposing factions to work together on behalf of their children. The rechannel-ing of aggression on the reservation was underscored by Mike Mit-chell: "I think that when the people see guys who used to be shoot-ing at each other playing lacrosse together, that sends a message to them that life is in the process of returning to normal."[46]

14 "It's a Toss-up"

Indian lacrosse was played on large, flat fields, their length determined by goals set up at either end. Plains and prairies offered particularly good natural fields. The trader Peter Pond, in present-day Wisconsin from 1773 to 1775, wrote of one such place, Prairie du Chien at the confluence of the Mississippi and the Wisconsin rivers, where the Indian camp extended for one and a half miles. It was particularly conducive to intertribal lacrosse games, which lasted three to four weeks each spring. There were always plenty to play and many to watch; Pond could count 130 canoes from the central trading post at Fort Michilimackinac.[1]

Generally, the size of the playing area vastly exceeded today's regulation lacrosse field, whose goals are but 80 yards apart on a 110-yard field; in most cases there were no defined sidelines. Whereas today's football field can accommodate a field lacrosse game and a hockey rink can serve for its box version, Indian games of the past ranged widely in all directions, as masses of players pursued the ball wherever it landed.

The distance between goals was invariably up for negotiation. The decision involved several factors, the most common having to do with the number of players. The Jesuit Pierre de Charlevoix reported as early as 1721 that Miami Indians in the area near present-day Chicago determined where to set the goalposts "in proportion to the number of players"; if eighty were to take part, the field would be "half a league"—roughly one and a half to two miles. Menominee claimed that "in the old days" their fields were one to two miles long, when "Indians used to be limber and tough, with good wind." By contrast, contemporary ritual games of the Onondaga may be played on fields from 75 to 430 yards long, depending on the number of participants.[2]

In some areas—particularly the western Great Lakes—a relatively consistent field length has been reported over long periods of time. Rarely were the fields of tribes living there less than a quarter of a mile long, and most have been reported as from a quarter to a half a mile; the Menominee field, according to one source, was a full mile or more, often a large clearing in a forest (Figure 61). Franklin Basina remembered from his youth on the reservation overlooking Lake Superior: "We always looked for a field, a meadow or something, a cow meadow, maybe five, six, seven acres at least. You know, an acre of land is a pretty good size piece of land." Hewitt implied that the same Mohawk field served as a general sports arena for "ball-playing, leaping, and vaulting, foot-racing, sparing, wrestling, etc."[3]

Many fields were created next to rivers or lakes. This explains why many towns bearing names that refer to the game are adjacent to water, such as La Crosse, Wisconsin, on the Mississippi River, formerly known as Prairie de la Crosse. The Winnebago had migrated there from Green Bay and established a large village. The topography was particularly conducive to playing the game there, hence the name given it by the French. Ball Club (lacrosse stick), Minnesota, on the Leech Lake Reservation, is the site of games once held on the exposed shorelines of Ball Club Lake whenever the waters receded sufficiently to provide a playing area. Mooney mentioned an ancient village, "*kanuga*" (the Cherokee word for the "scratcher" used ritually to prepare players), on the Pigeon River in Haywood County,

Figure 61 • A typical Indian lacrosse field during a Menominee game in Keshena about 1910. The sidelines are only barely marked with spectators. Players in the center are trying to score by hitting the single-post goal. The other end of the field must be at some distance, as the other goalpost is not visible.

North Carolina. He believed it was deserted before the historic period and probably abandoned because of its exposed location. In 1915, archaeologist George Heye, exploring some mounds on a farm on the east bank of the same river, concluded that they were not designed to be mortuaries and conjectured that they might have marked the ends of an ancient Cherokee lacrosse field. Such locations, adjacent to a river or stream, would have facilitated the Cherokee ball game ritual of "going to water."[4]

Tribes in the western woodlands often played next to lakes. In winter they simply took to the ice (Figure 62). Around 1880 Nett Lake Ojibwe from Minnesota played their Ontario relatives on frozen Rainy Lake on the Canadian border, inserting their goals on each side of a narrow part of the lake.

Today, where lacrosse is still alive on reservations, informal "pickup" games are played by teenagers just about anywhere—with buildings, roads, and woods serving as boundaries. In 1978 I watched a typical Sunday afternoon sandlot lacrosse game on the Onondaga reservation. A house and its front porch served as one side of the playing area; cars belonging to spectators formed another (Figure 63).

Since there were no real sidelines to a lacrosse field, the action could easily take players into the forest, like the Onondaga player against Hobart (see Prologue) or, in the case of a wooden (and floating) ball, into a lake, as happened in the taking of the British fort in 1763. From experience, William Warren verified that nothing got in the way when Ojibwe pursued the ball: "During the heat of the excitement, no obstacle is allowed to stand in the way of getting at

Figure 62 • Etching (1850) after *Ballplay of the Sioux on the St. Peters River in Winter,* an 1848 painting by Seth Eastman now in the collection of the Amon Carter Museum. It shows (Mdewakanton?) Dakota playing lacrosse on a frozen river or small lake. In the foreground a broken stick has been left behind. One player bends over to retrieve a dropped stick. Ballcarrier is pursued by two opponents about to come down on his stick to dislodge the ball. Pile of buckets, arrows, quivers, and clothes in the lower left foreground might be items wagered on the game.

[the ball.] . . . Let it fall in a high inclosure, it is surmounted, or torn down in a moment, and the ball recovered; and were it to fall into the chimney of a house, a jump through the window, or a smash of the door, would be considered of no moment."[5]

Although the width of a field was only minimally demarcated by spectators, the pursuit of the ball could take the players among or even beyond them. During a Cherokee game in North Carolina at the annual fall fair in 1992, I witnessed the ball land directly at the foot of an Indian fry bread concession stand. Half a dozen players immediately stormed it, scrambling to gain the ball. The counter was knocked over and the entire stand nearly demolished, but the players, oblivious to what stood in their way, continued to fight over the ball.

Given the ceremonial nature of lacrosse, ball fields were often oriented to the cardinal directions. The Ojibwe field, perhaps through some earlier association with the east-west axis of sacred objects—the medicine lodge, gravehouses, the ceremonial Big Drum—was laid out in relation to these cardinal points, even though the game lacked any religious overtones. Basina described Lake Superior fields of the early 1900s as arranged east to west and marked at intervals with small white flags—"just like a football field."[6]

While there were generally no side boundaries, a field's length was marked by the two goals. These were one of three types: a single post (the ball was to hit it or be thrown or carried past it), two upright poles (between which the ball was to be conveyed), or an enclosed area formed by a crossbar lashed near the top of two upright posts or—an exclusively Winnebago practice—made of a single arched pole like a croquet wicket. Data for most tribes show the consistent use over time of one of these types of goalposts. Most Iroquoian and southeastern tribes employed the two-pole variety, while in the Great Lakes area, tribes more frequently used the single post.[7]

The single post was a simple wooden pillar, frequently a section of a tree stripped of bark. A variation of this post—an exception to the customary southeastern goal—was the Mississippi Choctaw *aiulbi,* two posts or flat boards (four to six inches long) lashed or placed together to provide a combined one-foot striking surface (Figure 64). When two poles delimited the scoring area, fairly tall sap-

Figure 63 • An informal Sunday afternoon sandlot game on the Onondaga reservation, May 1978.

lings were selected, perhaps ten to fifteen feet high. The saplings were usually stripped of branches, but the Cherokee left the leaves on their eight-foot willow poles.

Of the enclosed goals, the crossbar type was the most frequent. Oklahoma Creek today use goals eight feet high with a four-foot crossbar lashed between the tops. Sometimes a string was attached across the top of the uprights instead of a crossbar, or, as in one Mohawk custom, marks were made at an agreed-upon height, and the player had to throw the ball below that point for a score. In place of poles, the Dakota occasionally improvised with two piles of blankets twenty feet apart.[8]

An unusual goal was a large pit on the Lac Court Oreilles Reservation, fifty to sixty feet in diameter, about ten feet deep; the two goals were located about three-quarters of a mile apart. Local residents asserted that one had only to throw the ball into the pit to score. (Guards stationed at the pits intercepted balls that were not lobbed high enough.) In winter, however, players from this reservation moved to a lake, set posts in holes in the ice about 100 yards apart, and let them freeze in place.[9]

Because the boundaries of the Indian field were vague or nonexistent, the impression is often conveyed that there were no rules, such as an "out of bounds," and consequently no one to call them. But there were, in fact, mechanisms for dealing with violations and officials appointed to carry them out. One of the several capacities of respected elders was officiating at lacrosse games. The same chief, coach, or medicine man might have the responsibility for lecturing players at midfield before the game, tossing up the ball, and retiring to the sidelines to referee and keep score. A good example is the Mississippi Choctaw referee, or *apisači*—selected by community leaders, usually from a pool of personnel trained in ritual. His responsibilities included tossing up the ball, watching for fouls and determining how to penalize them, and keeping score, for which he had a number of sticks to insert in the ground to represent goals scored.

The Cherokee had a special class of officials, called "drivers," to act as referees and call fouls. They carried long switches and (formerly) wore turbans as identification (Figure 65). Mostly they broke up wrestling matches that lasted too long or, if the progress of the game was impeded, took steps to break up a tangle of players and get the ball moving again: "The player is ordered to throw up the ball by the drivers who loom menacingly over him with their switches poised to insure immediate compliance." A driver would call a foul on a player if he was tied up but refused to give up the ball and had been warned before. Their switches were also used to point out where a ground ball lay, in case the players had lost track of it.[10]

Figure 64 • Mississippi Choctaw goal being scored by Robert Tubby in the late 1970s. The older style of *aiulbi* was constructed of twenty-foot split halves of a log put in the ground side by side. This contemporary version is made of a one-by-six plank, painted and wired to each upright of the goalposts on the football field where today's game is played.

• 244

Figure 65 • Two Eastern Cherokee "drivers" during an 1888 game between Big Cove and Wolf-Town. Their "uniform"—everyday dress and some sort of bandanna turban—distinguished them from the near-naked players.

Indian fans rarely argued over referees' decisions (or indecisions) in the way fans, players, and coaches complain vociferously about calls in the highly regulated sports of whites. That they did not disagree more often is particularly noteworthy given the minimal standardization of Indian lacrosse regulations and the frequent opportunity to contest decisions. Even when Cherokee play non-Indian American sports that *do* have more rules, they generally accept all refereed decisions.[11]

Long before the face-off evolved, Indian games almost universally began, once players were arranged on the field, with someone tossing the ball straight into the air at midfield (Figure 66). The same procedure set the ball into motion after each point was scored. Although the face-off of today's field lacrosse was ultimately adopted by the Iroquois from the Canadian version of the game, southeastern tribes such as the Creek and Choctaw continue today to use the toss-up. In a bow to tradition, the Iroquois, in ritual Cayuga games, even abandon the goal-cage for the two-stick goal of former times and use a toss-up at centerfield rather than a face-off.[12]

The person selected to toss the ball was meant to be impartial, and it was usually respected elders who were appointed. Many early sources state that it was "some old man," but more likely it was a distinguished person—a chief, a medicine man, a good speaker, or a specially selected referee. Formerly in the Menominee game the leader of one side removed the ball from his lacrosse bundle, tossed it in the air at midfield and gave out four loud whoops to inform the Thunderers (spirits) that the game was beginning, inviting their attendance. The only exceptional mode of setting the ball in play in the Great Lakes area was the Winnebago custom described by Wilbur Blackdeer. In their game, he says, there was a small mound of dirt a few inches off the ground at centerfield. Instead of tossing the ball *up* in the air, the referee would throw the ball onto the ground, and as it bounced back up, one of the centers would try to catch it with his stick.[13]

Before the toss-up, a speech at centerfield was commonplace, like the address of Joseph Brant before the 1794 game against the Seneca. The Cherokee "game director" gave a long speech admon-

• 245

Figure 66 • A fairly even distribution of players over the field of the Eastern Cherokee. Players (shirtless), officials in white shirts, and fully clothed spectators with hats before the start of a game in 1888.

ishing players to adhere to the rules and advising them not to waste too much time wrestling, then he suddenly tossed the ball into the air and dashed to the sidelines to escape the scramble. In the contemporary Oklahoma Creek game at the Green Corn Ceremony, the two teams march to centerfield, whereupon one of the two elders explains the rules of the game and calls for the game to begin. Wearing a ribbon shirt and a cowboy hat with the Creek eagle feather roach (ornamental headpiece) tied on its back, the elder walks back and forth between the line of players singing incantations. The players encircle him, whooping and yelling, and waiting for war whoops to signal that they should move into position for the toss-up. Suddenly and without warning, the elder tosses the ball up and runs quickly out of harm's way.

The element of surprise was essential to the toss-up. Lacrosse centers watched the referee intently for signs that he was ready to start the game, not unlike hockey centers today waiting for the puck to be thrown down on the ice. But he would deliberately try to divert their attention and throw the ball when they least expected it. Mooney wrote in 1890 that the Cherokee elder giving the preliminary speech stood at one end of the line of players, telling them the spirit of the sun was looking down on them and "urging them to acquit themselve[s] in the game as their fathers [had] done before them." He cautioned them to keep their tempers and ended abruptly "with a loud 'Ha! Taldu-gwǔ'! Now for the twelve [points needed to win]'" and threw the ball in the air.[14]

How today's face-off evolved as the standard means of starting a lacrosse game is not known. A description by Samuel Woodruff, an eyewitness to the Seneca-Mohawk game of 1797, gives evidence that something approaching a face-off had already been introduced to Iroquoian lacrosse before the end of the eighteenth century. To begin the game, fifty players from each side advanced to midfield, while ten men stationed themselves at each goal: "The match was begun by two of the opposing players, who advanced to the ball, and with their united bats raised it from the ground to such an elevation as gave a chance for a fair stroke; when, quick as lightning, it was sped through the air almost with the swiftness of a bullet. Much depends on the first stroke, and great skill is exerted to obtain it."

Morgan's *League of the Iroquois* describes the Mohawk game half a century later and shows the face-off to be more similar to the start of a hockey match. At about noon, the players were arranged in scattered groups covering the field. On either side of the center line at midfield were the center players, who formed two parallel rows facing each other: "The ball was dropped between the two files of players, and taken between the bats of the two who stood in the middle of each file, opposite to each other. After a brief struggle between them, in which each player endeavored, with his bat, to get possession of the ball, and give it the first impulse towards his own gate, it was thrown out, and then commenced the pursuit.'' By the time Hewitt described the game in *American Anthropologist* in 1892, the Iroquois face-off approached that of today's field lacrosse, the technique probably learned from playing regulation lacrosse against Canadian teams. The game began with the two captains holding their lacrosse sticks in the form of a Maltese cross: "[The ball is placed] mid way between the ends of the network on each club; then by a steady push each captain endeavors to throw the ball in the direction of the goal to which his side must bear it.''[15]

The one cardinal rule governing Indian lacrosse was the restriction against touching the ball with the hands. In fact, the Cherokee word for a foul, *ûwa'yi,* means "with the hand." Evidently this rule was almost universal on the North American continent. An old Iroquois regulation extended this restriction to the feet—a stipulation still observed in Cayuga ritual games but clearly disregarded by the time of the mid-nineteenth century. Still, touching with the hands in any way resulted in a penalty in Mohawk games, and the ball had to be set in motion again with a face-off at the point where the infraction occurred.[16]

The Eastern Cherokee game, on the other hand, played *mostly* with the double sticks, *did* permit handling of the ball under certain circumstances. Transfers of the ball by hand to a teammate's stick or from it were allowed. Transfers from hand to hand, however, resulted in a foul and a fresh toss-up at the point where the violation occurred. A player in trouble could deliberately pick up the ball to incur the foul and momentarily stop the action. Also allowed in the Cherokee game was carrying the ball by hand, provided the player had picked it up with his sticks. By 1943 Cherokee were playing with sticks until someone caught the ball in his hands and ran to the goal to score—the practice today. After a Cherokee team scores eleven points, it can discard its sticks entirely and continue playing only with the hands; the other team, if it has not reached eleven, must continue to play with sticks. (In Great Lakes games, contact of the ball with the hand permitted an opponent to strike the ballcarrier with his stick without incurring a foul but resulted in a new toss-up.)

Certain violent actions in southeastern games resulted in penalties. In the Choctaw game, for instance, anything except head butting was acceptable; that cost a team five points. New restrictions about 1848 on the older Cherokee game outlawed choking and breaking limbs or heads "when excited." When Beers drafted the first set of rules for non-Indian lacrosse in 1867, much of the violence that characterized the Indian game was curtailed; throwing sticks at another player, holding another player with sticks or hands, tripping, spearing, and threatening were now declared violations, as the game became more "civilized."

Regulations regarding substitutions have been fairly universal in Indian lacrosse. The rule of thumb was that each team on the field was to be at the same strength at all times. Substitutions were once allowed by the Iroquois—the platoon exchange of sixty players after every twenty minutes of play in the Seneca-Mohawk game of 1797, for example. But in the southeastern game, particularly among the Cherokee, *no* substitutions were permitted. Should a player become injured or too exhausted to continue, he could leave the game; but his opposite number on the other team had to quit as well. A player who had trouble keeping up with his opponent could change positions, though that rarely happened. Instead, he would voluntarily leave the game. This could result in gradual but drastic reductions in team size before the completion of a game. Fogelson cites a match in the mid-1930s in which Lloyd Sequoyah scored the winning goals for Big Cove against Yellow Hill as the sole remaining player on his team.[17]

Contrary to the Euro-American conception, Indians perceived the goal to be scored upon as *their* goal, not that of the opponents. Those guarding the goal tried to prevent the opposing team from penetrating their defense to "bring the ball home," as it were. This concept of "home goal" is reflected in Cherokee play, where each team's goal is put on the field as close as possible to the direction of the home community.[18]

The Great Lakes game, in which the single post was used for a goal, allowed three ways of scoring: one could strike the post with the stick containing the ball in its pocket, hit the post with a thrown ball, or simply run past the post with the ball. (Even in the Ojibwe "goal pits" at Lac Court Oreilles, the post at the bottom of the pit had to be hit for scoring.) If one missed the post, the ball would go past a foul line and be returned to centerfield for another toss-up. The Choctaw provide the only similar practice among southeastern tribes. The flat surface of the single post was to be hit by the ball, either thrown or carried in the racquet. Mississippi Choctaw today use one-by-six-inch lumber painted with decorations and wired to the uprights of football goalposts (see Figure 64). But all early reports of Choctaw games mention the double pole, although they do not always make clear whether a crossbar at the top defined the scoring area. Where there *was* a crossbar, the player apparently could score by hitting any part of the goal. Among the Creek, this might even be done from behind the goal (Figures 67a, b).[19]

Figures 67a, b • A goal being scored in an Oklahoma Creek game about 1938.

Sources on Cherokee "stickball" consistently agree that twelve goals were needed to win. The number twelve is specified in a ritual formula of the Cherokee ball play conjurer, Swimmer. The incantation was meant to be recited at the final stopping place before the game. It begins, "Listen! Now let me know that the twelve are mine, O White Dragonfly. Tell me that the share is to be mine—that the stakes [articles wagered] are mine. As for the player there on the other side, he has been forced to let go his hold upon the stakes. Now they are become exultant and happy. Yu!" One rule regarding scoring without actually reaching the goal was still in effect as recently as 1992. If the Cherokee ballcarrier suddenly breaks clear and is not chased by opponents, the point is conceded, and he is not required to run the full distance to the goal.[20]

In the Great Lakes region, usually two out of three points won the game. Saulteaux games of around 1800 were won in the "best of three heats," while the losers generally demanded a rematch the following day, a challenge that was rarely refused. Dakota games were also decided by two out of three "innings." Sources indicate, however, that Winnebago and Menominee games were played to four. This number suggests that informants may have referred to ritual games.[21]

Concerning the number of goals for a win, the Iroquois still distinguish between ceremonial and secular games. In secular games, apparently, the number of goals needed to win was simply agreed to by the teams in advance—usually an odd number—three, five, or seven. Sacred games had a fixed, ritually determined number of goals needed to win. Cayuga games played during midwinter ceremonies for some sick person were won with seven goals—the number seven having ritual connotations elsewhere in the game, e.g., seven paces between the two goalposts and seven players per side. Winning was really of no particular importance in these dream-dictated games, however; the fate of the patient was not determined by wins or losses, for the efficacy lay solely in the playing of the game itself. (The same attitude was held by the Menominee.) The winning side in some ritual games was even predetermined. Fox (Mesquakie) lacrosse was usually played at ceremonial adoption feasts for men, held to release someone in mourning. If the person in whose honor the feast was given belonged to the Tokan division of the tribe, then that side would win against the Kickos, and vice versa, if a Kicko were being adopted.[22]

Goals were traditionally tallied by special scorekeepers, like those of the Kickapoo, who used sticks, or those of the Texas Alabama, who made marks in the ground. The latter drew a straight line in the earth, making vertical marks on one side for goals scored by one team, on the other side for the other. The first to reach twelve goals won. Inserting sharpened pegs in the ground, however, was the more common practice.[23]

The number of goals needed for a win determined the length of Indian lacrosse games. There were brief games played by unevenly matched teams and others that lasted for days. The Ojibwe Frank Setter in the 1940s remembered games that went on for a week at Lac Court Oreilles, but on the same reservation Setter's contemporary, John Bisonette, said that games on frozen lakes lasted for only an hour. If the teams were equally skilled, the game might be stopped at dark and continued the next day. A Cherokee team might score the requisite twelve goals in twenty minutes or the game might last all day with no decisive outcome. If that were the case, the game might be called a draw or started again the next day. A quick-scoring Creek game witnessed by Swanton in 1913 lasted only an hour and a half, with a total of 36 goals, the west side beating the east 20–16.[24]

In historical accounts of lacrosse, one often reads of "innings," usually describing a goal's having been made and the teams' taking a break before resuming play. These "time-outs," which might last half an hour, were used for taking refreshments, awarding prizes, smoking, and general resting. During breaks in Great Lakes games, prizes were sometimes awarded for each goal scored. Menominee games were divided into four "innings." The gifts to be distributed to winners were divided into four parts, one part given for each period of play. Similarly, the Potawatomi played to five goals in games lasting at least three hours. The five prizes donated by the sponsor of the game (usually blankets and fabrics) were awarded at the end of each period, then donated by the scorer to some spectator—usually a relative.[25]

Accounts of games lasting more than a day usually indicate that a decisive win by one or the other team was simply prolonged or its conclusion postponed until some future date. But sometimes, if neither side had won by the end of the day, the team with the most points at that time might be declared the winner. Other factors extending the period of play were interruptions because of penalties, injuries, or fights.[26]

There are some indications that the "sudden-death" manner of determining a winner was used in Indian lacrosse. In lacrosse, as in other sports, officials were allowed to extend games to break a tie. This practice seems implicit in Stone's account of the Seneca-Mohawk game of 1797, where "the tally chiefs were allowed to check or curtail the count in order to protract the game." Because of the difficulty of scoring in the Ojibwe game, where a single "inning" might last an hour or more, the game could be terminated at the end of any inning through mutual agreement, the side with the greater number of points being declared the winner. Today's Mississippi Choctaw games consist of four twelve-minute periods, the team with the most points winning. In the case of a tie, however, the sudden-death rule extends the game. One of the longest games in recent times, the 1977 championship match between Pearl River and Bogue Chitto, went into overtime, lasting two and three-quarters hours before Pearl River won, 4–3.[27]

No matter how long an Indian lacrosse game lasted, the crowd typically erupted in celebration when the final goal was scored. Morgan wrote in his *League of the Iroquois:* "On the final decision of the game, the exclamations of triumph, as would be expected, knew no bounds. Caps, tomahawks and blankets were thrown up into the air, and for a few moments the notes of victory resounded from every side." It was fortunate, said Morgan, that the opposing teams and their fans were at some distance from each other: "Otherwise such a din of exultation might have proved too exciting for Indian patience." On the other hand, Indian people take lacrosse as seriously as Americans take baseball, and they like to forget losses. James Hill, a Creek from the town of Hilabi, provided anthropologist Mary Haas with full accounts of the many games his town had won in the past. But in relating all the preparations for a game that Hilabi lost against Pakantallahasee in 1905, Hill stopped abruptly when he came to describing the first toss-up. Explained Hill's daughter, acting as interpreter: "Maybe even today he didn't want to tell who won."[28]

15 *Montreal, 1866*

We may wish for the hereditary sagacity of the Indian, who plays mainly by instinct; as poor Tom in the "Mill on the Floss," envied the people who once were on earth, fortunate in knowing Latin without having learnt it through the Eton grammar; but the Indian never can play as scientifically as the best white players, and it is a lamentable fact, that Lacrosse and the wind for running, which comes as natural to the red-skin as his dialect, has to be gained on the part of the pale-face, by a gradual course of practice and training.

—*W. George Beers,* Lacrosse, *p. vii*

At four-thirty in the afternoon, Dr. William George Beers locked his dental surgery, put the keys in the pocket of his tweed jacket, and headed down Dorchester Boulevard in the direction of the Fox and Hounds to meet two Montreal Lacrosse Club teammates for the customary late-afternoon discussion of their favorite topic. The blustery wind caused him to wrap the scarf twice around his neck. It had been a busy day for the young dentist, with more than five tooth extractions, but his mind for the most part had been distracted by his principal mission, namely, completing his proposed rules for the game. With Canada's Confederation rapidly approaching, he and his friends wanted a finished document ready for debate in the national legislature; only then might their strategy to have lacrosse declared the national sport at the time of the Dominion's creation be successful.

Beers could aptly be described as more a lacrosse fanatic than a dentist, although the talented twenty-three-year-old would eventually go on to found and edit the first Canadian dental journal and become the dean of Quebec's first dental college. Imbued with passion for the game from the moment his father first took him at age six to Caughnawaga to see the early spring clan competitions of the Mohawk, the boy (like other Montreal youth) had been given a traditional Iroquois hickory crosse and had donned moccasins, stripped to the waist, and attempted to re-create the sport just as he had seen the Indians play it. He and classmates from the Phillip's School had spent many late afternoons tossing balls back and forth with their sticks and trying out various dodging and checking maneuvers that they had picked up watching Indian village matches across the water on the shores of Lac Saint-Louis.

As he grew older, however, Beers gave up "playing Indian" and began to develop more-ambitious plans for the game. He became obsessed with the need for some sort of controlled play, some codification that would stabilize the erratic nature of the Indian sport and at the same time standardize lacrosse to eliminate the petty squabbles over technicalities that characterized so many Canadian games. The general disorganization of game conduct had prompted him six years earlier to set forth some rules of play in a modest brochure, suggest specialized field positions beyond that of the goalkeeper, and assign names to the positions. Since then he had advanced considerably in his research, doubling his efforts to consult with the best players on the reserves and studying the Indian game intently. It is safe to say that he had attended as many matches at St. Regis and Caughnawaga as his dental practice would allow.

Beers looked back on the 1860 brochure with considerable misgivings—it was a product of his youth, he always maintained. He was still bitter that it had been published without his knowledge when he was out of town, and subsequently it was plagiarized by others attempting to write on lacrosse. He hoped that his current efforts would prove redemptive, and he was fortunate to enjoy the encouragement of friends like Dowd, Cushing, MacDonald, and the others helping to propel the club system to national recognition.

Following Dowd's directions, Beers turned a corner onto Mansfield and spotted a marquee with a painted fox hunt. This must be the entrance to the pub. Bracing himself against a sudden blast of wind and holding the brim of his hat with one hand, he lengthened his stride to reach the shelter of the pub. As he opened the door, he spotted Dowd immediately ahead of him sitting alone in a booth, smoking his pipe and reading the evening news. Beers hung his hat on a nearby rack and joined him, while casting a disparaging glance at the pipe. It was uncomfortable enough that Dowd had chosen a pub to meet in, but that he had taken up smoking again was clearly in violation of club rules. How could they hope to match the innately superior Indian lung power on the field if players didn't take training seriously? Beers might have to take the matter up with other members.

"Aha, back from St. Regis in one piece, I see!" chortled Dowd. "Repair any broken redskin fangs after the games?"

"Not really," replied Beers. "Too busy taking notes and asking questions. Besides, the Indians are fairly careful to avoid injuries when playing among themselves. See many more broken noses and missing teeth among palefaces after they're done playing us in a match."

Beers ordered tea and proceeded to tell Dowd about the games he'd watched at St. Regis over the weekend. "You know, I'm increasingly convinced that the secret to Indian wins over us is their persistency in checking. I doubt seriously that we'll ever be able to match the lung power they seem to be born with. When you see them play, wherever the ball falls there always seems to be a redskin within easy reach of it. Maybe it's magic."

Dowd interrupted him by sliding the folded newspaper across the table and pointing to a front page story on the Fenian raids. Beers, patriot that he was, had already signed up with the Victoria Rifles and enlisted members of the old Beaver Lacrosse Club to join him in forming Company 6. They were waiting for their marching orders to join others at the front. Country before lacrosse, thought Beers; lacrosse before pulling teeth. He returned the paper and continued his discourse on the Indian mode of play.

"They have no prearranged field configuration, like we want to see. That's one reason they can bunch so quickly in knots at the goals. You've seen them do that in defense *or* attack. I'm convinced it's a holdover from their ancient style of warfare—always as many as possible at the point of attack. You can see that, too, in the way they bear down in twos and threes on the dodger. Concentrated attack. Always. They never stop."

Dowd agreed. "It certainly makes it difficult for us to be posted independently on the field. Since they're always scattered with total disregard for our arrangement, it makes sense for our players to have more flexibility in positioning themselves, particularly when the Indian is constantly on the move to keep from being checked."

Beers glanced at the clock. "That bunching style of attack," he continued, "makes it essential to pick our goalkeepers for calmness in the face of action. You can't have some nervous Nellie at the flags facing a swarm of redskins bearing down on him." Beers spoke from experience. He had played this position for some time, and when he was seventeen his talents were rewarded when he was selected as one of the two goaltenders in the 1861 exhibition match before the Prince of Wales. "When you stand at the flags, and the Indians are frantically fighting your men for the ball, you really have to get into the action. And you need room to maneuver and not just stand there waiting for the rubber to keep you from the full use of your crosse. The redskins used to do that until their legs began to get banged up. Now they're more cautious. Give the man at the flags considerably more room."

"Have you noticed," asked Dowd, "that Indian goalkeepers seem to be getting better each year? Do you think they've started training certain players for the post like we do, or am I simply imagining this?"

"No," replied Beers, "you're undoubtedly right, although the Indians would have us believe otherwise. Only this weekend I was told by Big John Baptiste that once they adopted our flags for goals, they started defending the goal differently. Seems like special men were appointed to the task. But you still find Indians who refuse to admit this. They don't want us training goalkeepers. I guess they've been frustrated enough to wish we'd stop training for the position. But they've always taken advantage of our more inexperienced players. I can assure you it took me some time to learn how to defend against one of their favorite tactics in scoring. You've seen it, Dowd, I'm sure: One redskin will be carrying the ball or it will somehow be tacked up near to the flags." Beers started to move spare beer coasters into position on the table to simulate the flags and slid his hands, palms down, to represent Indian attackers. "Their 'home' starts closing in as a distraction, while a fielder will sneak up behind you, knowing you're totally focused on what's in front of you. All of a sudden the ballcarrier will throw a high curved ball over the flags to his fielder behind." Beers lifted one hand and arced his forearm over the coasters. "After he catches it, he immediately throws it back, dropping the rubber just within the crease. His teammates know that's what he'll do, so by bunching, they close in enough to hit the ball into your flags as soon as it lands."

Goalkeeping was but one of Beers's favorite lacrosse topics. He had done considerable research on Indian practices, despite the general paucity of published information. He had sieved through the historical literature on Indian culture and kept a notebook of the few kernels of information winnowed from his reading. What he had found was mostly the tidbits left behind by early settlers in North America, typically vague, often misleading, he felt, and exasperatingly lacking in detail. He had read Charlevoix on Miami lacrosse and Catlin's account of Choctaw games in the 1830s. But Beers's own experience with Indian consultants made him suspicious of the information that historians had published, for he knew Indians to be fond of hoodwinking outsiders when they asked questions. His attention to detail and accurate reporting was well known in the dental community, where he was particularly fond of exposing quackery. Beers was convinced that various of the legends shared with him on the reserves as accounts of the origins of lacrosse, fanciful and charming though they had been, were made up on the spot simply to satisfy his curiosity. Still, he put some faith in the descriptions given by Basil Hall of Creek lacrosse, and in Francis Parkman's account of the Ojibwe taking of Fort Michilimackinac during a game. And he considered himself fortunate to have at least a few reliable informants at Caughnawaga and St. Regis. Respecting young Beers as a player, they provided him with considerable information on the Mohawk game, although how far back the practices they described went was anyone's guess. Still, he always counted on friends like Morrison at Caughnawaga or Big John Baptiste, "master pilot of the Lachine Rapids," and accepted their word as gospel. With their information he could hope that the major work he was now preparing would at last provide the world with a publication elevating lacrosse to its proper place in history.

Always the historian, Beers continued to flesh out his discussion of goaltending for Dowd's edification. "What you see today on the Indian field is not what it always was. It's fairly clear that they've changed tactics since we introduced the flags. Any time on our fields, whenever a point's about to be won you'll notice the redskins have certain men either at or near the goal. That's why we need to train goalies. Now that the fields have been reduced in size from what the Indian once knew, the game has shifted from carrying the ball to throwing it accurately. So there's even more need for talented goalkeepers. Of course, the redskins have kept up with these developments." Beers slid the two coasters to either end of the long table. "In the old Indian game, when they had just a single post for a goal, there wasn't a real need for someone to be specially trained to guard it. In fact, when the playing field was a quarter mile or half a mile, you rarely saw anyone near the goal unless it was under attack. The size of the field and the number of players were the determining factors. But once the present-day goal was introduced, you began to notice Indian players assigned to be at the flags. Or at least near them."

Dowd finished his lager and motioned to the waiter for a refill. Beers, ever the tee-totaler, frowned and was about to lecture Dowd on the evils of alcohol. Readers of his book would soon learn that "lacrosse dislikes fellows who 'spree,' who make syphons of their œsophagi, and who cannot make better use of their leisure than to suck mint juleps through straws." Dowd, however, launched into another topic for Beers to consider in his writing before the author could berate him. "Shifting from a carrying to a throwing game seems crucial. I hope you'll deal with that in the book. It should help explain the change in the crosses we're now using. Not those old, loose-bagged Mohawk sticks we grew up with," said Dowd. "Maybe we could get more local woodworkers interested in turning out an improved version. We can certainly convince them that there's money to be made in this game."

"You're right," replied Beers, "and I do deal with the need for an improved crosse from the start." Nearly a decade of apprenticeship to Dr. Dickenson had exposed him to a number of advancements in the technology of dental surgery; there was no reason why the basic tool of lacrosse should not be equally refined. "The flat netting of the new crosses has certainly made catching different—turned it into a real art for a change. The network on those Indian sticks is really flimsy. Still, those Mohawks are famous for their catching ability, whether the crosse is bagged or not. Remember the match five years ago for the Prince of Wales? Of the twenty-five Indian players, only one used a crosse that wouldn't have passed the umpires' inspection, and still with that paltry network their catching was magnificent. It's probably because they use that sinking and rising motion in catching. If you've mastered that gracefully, it'll save on your netting and secure the ball better. We need to teach our beginners that once they master that movement, the various curves and sweeps on the follow-through will come naturally."

Dowd, who had been coaching a group of schoolboys on weekends, nodded in agreement. "My boys have gotten far enough along, so I've started them on some stick techniques that they probably haven't seen. Remember the old side throw that the first players of the Montreal Club used in passing?"

"That was definitely learned from the Indians. I wish more players would take advantage of it today," noted Beers.

Dowd didn't mind bringing the young dentist up to date on his own coaching prowess. "I show them how to grasp the butt with the right hand, as they usually do, then with the left hand around the collar or above it, put the ball on the top of the netting and throw from right to left. They can follow through with a full sweep, if they want, but I have them practice it with a jerk, which they seem to like better anyway." Dowd was very dedicated to promoting the game and spent most of his free time coaching interested youngsters. "They're getting pretty good at it. One in particular, young MacKenzie, picked it up right away. I think he has real potential."

"I hope you're drilling them in the overhead shot as well," said Beers. "Another technique we learned from the Indians. I'll admit it's a shot that's only needed in an emergency—like if you're being dogged by a checker and you haven't got time for something more graceful. But it's an important escape tactic. You see the Indians do it a lot—pick up the ball in front and send it right over their head." The waiter returned with Dowd's lager on his tray. Beers remembered his two Indian goalposts and quickly returned them to the center of the table. "Do you have them turn their head quickly to see where they will throw, or have they gotten good enough to respond to signals without having to look? Be sure to have them try to release the shot from the top rather than the center surface. You get a much more accurate aim that way."

"We've moved beyond pitching straight at the goal to trying some of those slow, curved Indian throws that are particularly effective if the sun is in the goalkeeper's eyes," said Dowd. "I think that was your suggestion, George, the last time you saw us at practice. With the new crosses they seem able to get a much higher trajectory."

"If you think the Mohawk crosse is inadequate for throwing, you should see what they play with out west. My friend Radiger brought me one back from the Garden River Reserve. He played with the Chippewas there once in a while and showed me how they scoop the ball off the ground. Their crosse has that small, round hoop at the end, you know, just slightly larger than the ball. They clamp the stick down over the ball and use a quick twist of the wrist to scoop it up, all in one motion. But throwing with that type of stick is different too, Radiger tells me. You have to kind of jerk the ball out, and it won't travel as far as when you throw it with an Iroquois stick."

Transforming lacrosse into a passing rather than a carrying game, the Canadians were stressing teamwork over the more individualistic style of Indian play. One consequence of this change was the need for heavier, longer crosses, with a more triangular shape and with more tightly woven gut netting than what the Mohawk produced. The various clubs were already promoting the manufacture of hickory crosses by non-Indian craftsmen in Montreal, testing them, accepting or rejecting them according to quality and performance. They felt that the new crosses helped in winning points as well, for they encouraged fast, hard-thrown shots to score—something the Indians were not used to. As throwing techniques improved and shots became more accurate, they reduced the distance between flags from seven feet to six feet in fairness to the goalkeeper. Indians, on the other hand, continued to win points, either by bunching and crowding at the flags or, when throwing, by using a slow, close shot or lobbing a curved ball to drop on the flags. Eventually, thought Beers, they too would see the advantages of rationally organized teamwork and would have to adapt the redskin game if they were to continue to compete successfully with the paleface.

"You see, there's nothing scientific about the old Indian game—nothing planned in the way of teamwork or strategy," he said. "It was totally a sport for individuals to show off their prowess. Each player wanted nothing more than a chance to carry the ball past the post and attract personal attention. Even Morgan writes about this in his history of the Iroquois. I've heard from Mohawk players that, when their grandfathers used the double pole goal, it was considered a great feat for an individual to carry the rubber on his crosse the length of the field. He'd have to escape every opponent and outplay the goalkeeper, then he'd be able to walk the ball right between the goalposts. They tell me that the team winning a point this way loved to taunt their opponents by yelling at them, 'Right on the crosse! Right on the crosse!' That meant the scorer didn't have to throw it or kick it in." Beers reached into his vest and pulled out his watch to glance at the time. He had a dinner engagement at six with Mary Elizabeth, whose parents, the Hopes, were in the city from Kingston to discuss plans for the impending nuptials. He still had an hour to spare, and Cushing hadn't arrived yet.

"But George, how do you get youngsters to realize that winning a point takes teamwork, when each of them by inclination wants to be the star? It's hard to explain to them that a point belongs to the whole team when, naturally, each player wants to take credit for having won it. You have to keep stressing that the ball needs to be moved from man to man down the field. That's the whole point in posting men to play *to* each other rather than hogging the ball, trying to get a reputation as a showy player. Also, too much time is wasted skirmishing over a ball simply to draw attention. That can really weaken a team's chances of keeping the ball moving in the right direction."

"Just keep stressing it, Mr. Trainer," said Beers. "Even the redskins know that, despite their individual playing style. When hard pushed, they quickly give up their egotism. That's certainly one of the reasons we kept losing to Indian teams, but I think the situation is improving. You see much more 'tacking' the ball these days by white teams."

Interrupting the discussion, Cushing joined them and waved to the waiter. "Well, George, what secrets did the savage mind divulge over the weekend? I hear St. Regis is really strong this year. Think they'll give us a run for our money?"

Beers leaned back. "You know, more club members should get down to their games. I

• 259

realize that the weekends when we're not playing get devoted to family matters, but there's still a lot to learn from the Indian. That's not to say they're all strong players, but I've never known one that couldn't manage a crosse well and probably outrun any of our members. It seems inborn with them. And the juveniles! Considering their age, it's amazing to watch even ten-year-olds—there was a group of them from Oka playing at St. Regis on Saturday. Fierce competition, I tell you! No, you can't beat the Indian for wind and endurance. What the primitive game must have been like a century ago! The physical condition of those savages must have been astounding. But learning is a two-way street, of course. Consider the cover-check. That was our creation, but the redskins quickly took it up. Remember? When we demonstrated it for the interpreter at Caughnawaga in 1859, none of their best players had ever seen it. Still, there are a number of their tricks we could stand to learn ourselves."

"But George," injected Cushing, "you yourself have always insisted that the greatest hindrance to the development of the sport has been Canadian players trying to imitate the Indian playing style down to the last detail. Surely civilized Canadians shouldn't play the game like the redskins do. It's one thing to admire their inherent talent at the sport, but what distinguishes us from them is our devotion to managing it, bringing it under control, giving it some orderliness. Maybe even someday we won't have to keep playing them."

"That's true, of course," admitted Beers. "One reason we don't follow their habit of allowing players to wander the field at will. But it's sheer folly to insist that our men never leave their positions when we're playing an Indian team. One of our greatest weaknesses *still* is the inability to anticipate where a thrown ball will land. Instead of standing around waiting to see where the rubber will end up, the Indian will instinctively be on the move the instant the ball leaves a crosse. It's uncanny how he can anticipate by the rise exactly where it will drop, and he'll be there to retrieve it. If you can't leave your position, you'll always give the Indian the advantage."

The front door of the premises slammed loudly behind a rather jolly group of men who had just entered. The Fox and Hounds was clearly not their first pub of the afternoon, and as they came closer Beers recognized Brown and several other former players for the Beaver Club. Brown appeared unshaven and slightly down in the mouth. Drink had taken its toll, thought Beers. He recalled hearing that Brown had recently lost his university teaching position. They smiled and nodded to each other, and Beers returned to his discourse on lacrosse training.

"One thing we *could* improve and take a lesson from the redskins on is the use of the feet in the game. Indians make much more use of their feet in close play than we do, particularly when they're around an enemy's goal. This is really frustrating to the goalkeeper and ties him up, while they're trying their damndest to kick the ball into goal. We need to train our homemen to use their feet more. Even though he's the last link to the goal, he's not always going to have luck with a straight-thrown shot from the front or sides, so the feet can sometimes come in handy. The redskins have some remarkable maneuvers, 'frisk-ing' with their feet. Just this weekend I saw a player from Oka who got the ball between his heels and jumped up with it. In mid-air he was able to kick it straight up behind him, turn as he landed on his feet and catch the ball in his crosse. It took his opponent totally by sur-prise; he was looking for it in another direction!''

Beers began to reflect on games of the past between his team and the Mohawks. He thought back to the exhibition match of August 1861 before the Prince of Wales, who was presented with a silver crosse mounted as a trophy while the band played ''Yankee Doodle'' and ''God Save the Queen.'' The game had followed a long, drawn-out exhibition match between Algonquian and Iroquoian Indians, with thirty per side. When the combined Montreal and Beaver clubs took to the field against Caughnawaga and St. Regis, the sides were reduced to twenty-five each, with Beers as one of the two goalkeepers. The score stood at 2–2, when Baptiste, the Indian captain, sensing that the Canadians were about to score, picked up the ball with his hand. The umpire awarded the match to the whites, but the Mohawks began to protest. To calm the situation the prince at once requested the Indian war dance that had been planned in his honor, so the field was cleared.

Canadian lacrosse had experienced erratic beginnings, and only now, Beers believed, was there an opportunity to crystallize the game in the name of Canada. Despite his young age, he was in the forefront of white efforts to civilize the Indian sport, dictate its rules, and promote its spread throughout the Commonwealth. The early Canadian lacrosse clubs emulated Indian play, each developing its own set of rules. This individualized approach resulted in nothing but insignificant and time-consuming bickering, since every game required lengthy negotiations to agree on the principles of play. Montrealers who had vis-ited nearby Indian villages had been well acquainted with the sport for some time. But it was not until Indian exhibition matches began to be brought to the city in 1834 to be played on the infield of the St. Pierre race course for the amusement of whites that any real audi-ences existed for lacrosse. The Montreal Club, which originated in 1839, got together a lacrosse team to play Indians—and lost consistently for a decade. When Beers was just thir-teen, the Montreal Lacrosse Club was formed by members of the disbanded Olympic Club. Beers was now positioned to coalesce the many and varied club teams that had emerged, as well as to capitalize on the rapidly growing national interest in the sport.

Cushing set down his mug and wiped his mustache with his shirtsleeve. ''You know, George, this game is really growing rapidly—all the more reason for your book to become available. Pretty soon it won't even look like an Indian game. They started up in Peel only last year, and already they have several clubs. It's mostly at the intervillage level, but they've been inviting Indian teams to come up from time to time. Mostly lose to them, as you might expect. We're starting to receive correspondence almost daily from all parts of Canada, from clubs forming of people who've never even seen the game but want to take it up. Your book should go a long way toward answering the sort of questions we're getting. Should the point or home never leave their assigned places? They really need a publication to help them get started. And, of course, when we start to 'export' the game, there are bound to be even more questions. Who's to know what kind of interest Johnson is going to spark when he takes the Caughnawaga team to England and France next year?" No one at the table could have predicted that Beers himself a decade later would also take the Mohawk team to the British Isles.

Beers sensed more than ever that he and his friends were watching a historic development in the world of sport unfold. "It's strange, but many of my friends who play other games are having a difficult time appreciating our passion for the primitive redskin sport. They're also amazed to see how quickly it's becoming popular. Half in jest, I tell them, 'Here's a game that can be played on snow or even on ice if you wear skates.' If they haven't played lacrosse, they have no idea how much power can be put into a shot. I have one friend who's so good at handball that he claims he can catch any ball thrown at him. So we put him at the goal, moved the flags about four feet apart, and lobbed a few shots at him as slowly as possible. He caught them, all right. Then we gradually got more serious with him. We moved out to about thirty feet from the flags and threw from the lower angle of the crosse. He couldn't stop the ball with his hands, so it bounced off his stomach. Then we came within twenty feet and increased the speed of the ball, throwing a shot at the ground a few feet in front of him. There was no way he could catch the ball in his hands, and it bounced up and struck him under the chin, making him yell in agony. That was enough to convince him."

"How close are you to finishing a draft of the rules?" asked Dowd. "Can you get them to us fairly soon? Your suggestion to form a national lacrosse association seems to be gaining in popularity with members of other clubs I've spoken to. Everyone's in favor of convening next year to discuss the rules and if possible to adopt them. As far as I know, all twenty-nine clubs have been contacted and asked to appoint delegates." These Montrealers could scarcely have anticipated that by the following year the popularity of the game would have increased the number of clubs to eighty. "Kingston was suggested to host the convention," added Cushing. "Most club presidents are eager to adopt a constitution. There's clearly sufficient political clout in Parliament on our side to forward the notion of a national game. Such moments in history are rare, to my knowledge."

"I'm nearly done with the first draft," Beers assured them. He wanted to finish before the wedding. "I've been working on it every evening for weeks. Obviously, I'd like the book to be in publishable form as well, so that the rules could be bound with it as an appendix. Maybe I can get something to you within the next few days."

Beers reached inside his jacket to retrieve a notebook from the pocket. "Actually, you two could expedite matters by reminding me of maneuvers I might have left out of my 'Dodging' chapter. I'm fairly well along in it." Thumbing through the notebook, he paused when he came to one page. "Let's see, I've pretty much covered its origins in the Indian game and listed the various types of the carried-dodge—turning on your own axis, the short-stop and turn-dodge, and so on. I'm well into the section on thrown-dodges and would like to complete it this week." Beers enumerated the various thrown-dodges he had already covered.

"What about mentioning what happens in a thrown-dodge when the checker strikes your crosse?" asked Cushing.

"Right," replied Beers and began to add to his notebook. "That certainly belongs in there. I need to stress that it increases the force of your throw and puts the checker momentarily more off guard than yourself. St. Regis players have a pretty version of this maneuver. Have you seen it? When the checker attempts to strike the dodger's crosse, he turns slightly to his right and, using his wrist, jerks the ball over the checker's stick, between it and the checker's body. While the ball's still in the air, he can pick it off neatly on the other side of the checker."

"Have you described what a dodger should do when a checker behind him strikes at the butt of his stick? Suggested that the dodger can pick it up again?" queried Dowd.

Beers flipped back a page. "Yes, I've already got that under Number Five. I also mention that the ball can be dropped at any angle or even thrown ahead quite a ways, if the dodger thinks he's running fast enough to get it in time." After a long pause in the conversation, when no further questions seemed to be forthcoming from his comrades, Beers closed the notebook and returned it to his pocket. "Well, gentlemen, that should do it for the time being. I appreciate your help, as always."

Finishing his tea, Beers decided it was time to join the Hopes for dinner. He was eager for it to be a relatively brief meal, as he wanted to return home to his manuscript. Cushing and Dowd could continue to discuss their favorite topic, but it had already been a long day, and Beers intended to get more of his "Laws of Lacrosse" down on paper before going to bed.

"We'll take care of it," said Cushing, as Beers, whose generosity was famous, began to reach for his *porte-monnaie* to pay for the refreshments. "You've more important matters to attend to," added Dowd, "so consider our small contribution in the interest of a noble cause."

Having said good night to Mary Elizabeth and her parents, Beers excused himself to retire for the evening. His fiancée, of course, was quite aware of the reason George had rushed through his dinner and skipped dessert entirely. Upon reaching his flat, he moved to his desk, lit the gaslight over it, opened his inkwell, and removed from beneath a pile of mail the folder containing his writings on lacrosse. The "Laws"—at least to the extent that he had recorded them—lay on the very top. The evening before, he had left off at Rule IX, Section 2, which defined three out of five games as the number to decide a match. After reading through the sections already put down on paper, he began to formulate his thoughts. Section 3, stating that captains would determine game time and postponements, and Section 4, on postponed or interrupted matches, came quickly to him, and he wrote them down. Then he paused, thinking he had forgotten something that should logically follow. Suddenly it occurred to him and he added Section 5, designating that periods of rest between points should be between five and ten minutes long. Beers was tired, but he felt compelled to continue. He paused again, thinking carefully of something he might have missed. He knew how the regulation should read, but was this the proper place for it? Beers drew a deep breath as he removed the pen from the inkwell and painstakingly began to record the rule that would irrevocably change lacrosse history by depriving its indigenous creators of proper recognition and participation for more than a century.

Beers wrote down Rule IX, Section 6: "No Indian must play in a match for a white club, unless previously agreed upon."

The ink dried quickly. He closed the folder and retired for the night.

"Lo, the Poor Mohawk!"

The present game, improved and reduced to rule by the whites, employs the greatest combination of physical and mental activity white men can sustain in recreation. And is as much superior to the original [Indian game] as civilization is to barbarism, base ball to its old English parent of rounders, or a pretty Canadian girl to any uncultivated squaw.

—W. George Beers, Lacrosse, *pp. 32–33*

After more meetings to complete and refine the first set of lacrosse regulations, everything went as Beers had planned. On the same day that the Dominion of Canada came into being, 1 July 1867, the topic of lacrosse was purportedly debated in parliament and the sport was proclaimed Canada's national game.[1] The convention met in Kingston on 26 September to form the national association, amend Beers's rules, and adopt a constitution. The Montreal dentist—the Bob Scott of his time—saw his book, together with his "Laws of Lacrosse," published in 1869 by Dawson Brothers in Montreal as well as by the New York firm W. A. Townsend and Adams "with the sanction of the National Lacrosse Association of Canada."

Indian teams were now required to play by the new rules when facing Canadians. Ironically, on the very day of Canada's creation, the Dominion lacrosse title—at that time the equivalent of world championship—was taken by Caughnawaga, who defeated the Montreal Lacrosse Club 3–2. Five months later the title changed hands—Indian hands, that is—when St. Regis beat Caughnawaga for a purse of $60. The first attempt at a national tournament was held in 1868, when twelve teams played on the grounds of the Brant Lacrosse Club in Paris, Ontario, with Beers officiating all games. St. Regis retained its title, beating Prescott, Ontario, 2–0 in just under two hours. It was not until the following year that the title went to Canadians, and then only through default. When the St. Regis team declined to play off a 2–2 tie with the Montreal Lacrosse Club, Montreal claimed the title; their new championship was later confirmed by delegates to the association's national convention.[2]

Meanwhile, the sport was attracting increasing numbers of spectators, both at home and abroad. The Six Nations team beat Toronto 3–2 in September 1867 at the Toronto Cricket Club before a crowd of four thousand. The event sparked a lacrosse boom in that city—it soon boasted thirteen new clubs with six hundred members—and inspired a local musician to compose a sprightly new dance tune, "The Lacrosse Gallop."[3] Johnson's tour of Europe with the Mohawk team in 1867 was a great success, as was Beers's with the Caughnawaga nine years later. Indians were given maximum exposure, playing before Queen Victoria in the Crystal Palace and at the World's Fair in Paris. As in Toronto, initiation to this new sport led to the creation of local teams; following the Mohawk visit, three English clubs were started and the English Lacrosse Association formed in 1868.

Lacrosse was gaining attention in the United States as well. With the Civil War at an end, there was opportunity for Canadian Indian teams to travel for exhibition play south of the border. In 1867 Indians were brought to Saratoga Springs, New York, to give demonstration games at the height of the racing season. In October the same year the Six Nations team played a match in conjunction with a baseball tournament at Van Renssalaer Park in Troy, New York. After an Indian explained the game to the spectators in broken English, his team appeared on the field wearing feathered bonnets and brightly colored tights. The following day, eight Six Nations players beat an equal number of whites. The local newspaper reported that "thousands gained admission and several hundred saw the game from the hills to the east," while assuring its readership that the Indians had been paid for their services.[4] Nor was Iroquois lacrosse the only Indian form of the game being toured. Although Beers was under the impression that the sport had died out in the United States, in the summer of 1868 a former colonel, S. N. Folsom, brought teams of Chickasaw and Choctaw Indians to Cincinnati and other midwestern cities. Playing their double-stick version of lacrosse, these southern Indians had mostly been assembled from the recently disbanded Confederate Army.[5]

Why were Indian lacrosse teams being toured throughout the last half of the nineteenth century? The answer is twofold: First,

there was an earnest desire on the part of white aficionados to spark interest in the sport and see it taken up by non-Indians, and second, not only were Indians the best players to demonstrate the game but they were an attraction in themselves. While the frontier was still advancing westward to the Pacific, Indians became something of a curiosity—particularly in Europe. They drew large crowds and inspired "sensational" newspaper reports of their exhibition games in England and other countries. Advance billing helped mount excitement among a public who eagerly awaited their first live exposure to athletes from the wilderness abroad (Figure 68). *The Illustrated London* in 1876, for instance, anticipated that "a team of Canadian amateurs and twelve picked Iroquois Indians . . . ought to attract immense crowds in London." The highlight of the 1876 tour was a command performance before Queen Victoria after tea on 26 June in a game played on turf next to the walls of the Italian garden. The Indian captain, Big John Baptiste, in ceremonial Iroquois dress, placed his tomahawk at the queen's feet and gave a long address in Mohawk, referring to the monarch as "Our Great and Good Mother." He presented her with an Iroquois basket, and she reciprocated with a medal for Baptiste and autographed photographs of herself for each of the players.[6]

At that time, Indian troupes touring for whatever reason clearly had racist undertones. Indians were still considered "savages," and as showpieces they were meant to portray themselves to fit the ste-

Figure 68 • Catlin's engraving of Indians in a canoe racing against an English crew at Saint-Cloud. Paddlers were part of a troupe of nine Ojibwe taken to England by Canadian entrepreneur Arthur Rankin in 1843.

reotype. Having Indian lacrosse players on tour was part of the same phenomenon that inspired Bill Cody to organize his "Wild West Show" or Frederick Burton to compose a "Hiawatha" theater musical and bring costumed Garden River Ojibwe to tour Europe as its performers. Even George Catlin, as early as 1843, became involved in using Indians in Europe for promotional purposes. A group of Ojibwe brought to London by Canadian entrepreneur Rankin were hired by Catlin, who enlisted them to dance before Queen Victoria at Windsor Palace and to replace his troupe of English actors. The latter had been posing in *tableaux vivants*—brief costumed episodes, such as "Foot War Party on the March" and "Treaty of Peace"—to attract attendance at Catlin's Indian Gallery in London. (Their appearance was short-lived after the English press accused both Rankin and Catlin of exploiting the Indians.)

That Euro-Americans considered the Indian version of lacrosse to be "untamed," that Beers could write that "it had its first existence in [the Indian's] wild brain," and that the very nature of the Indian game was close to warfare—all these factors engendered excitement and attracted crowds whenever the Indians played. Here white audiences could see with their own eyes a genuine primitive, violent sport. And to make certain that the Indian players fit European expectations, tour promoters invariably saw that they wore feathered headdresses, moccasins, and other stereotypical costuming for the game. Frequently the players had to perform double duty by concluding their entertainment with a "war dance" (Figure 69).

To comprehend fully why Beers and his colleagues took lacrosse in the direction that they did, one must understand the climate of belief prevalent among Euro-Americans at the time. Americans were continuing to push west as part of their notion of a "Manifest Destiny," and with Canadian independence from England in 1867, many of the same sentiments prevailed north of the border. What a unique moment in history it would be to have an indigenous game declared the Canadian national sport on the very day that the Dominion came into being!

This was also a time when the Darwinian theory of evolution held sway, however it was distorted for social purposes. Just as other organisms could be shown to be at various stages of development, a belief in a graduated hierarchy of man, from "primitive" to "civilized," characterized most Euro-American attitudes toward peoples of other races, their practices, their arts, their belief systems, and even their games. Beers applied the evolutionary concept to sport in general. Citing Greece in Homer's time and England when Caesar landed, he could write that the early history of all countries "shows their recreations to have been of a rude and barbarous nature." Thus

CANADIAN LACROSSE TEAMS.

PATRONS:
His Excellency the EARL OF DUFFERIN, Governor-General of Canada.
His Grace the DUKE OF ABERCORN, Lord-Lieutenant of Ireland.
Lord GEORGE HAMILTON, M.P.   Sir GARNET WOLSELEY, K.C.B.
General LYSONS, Q.M.G.   Sir JOHN ROSE, Bart.
&c., &c., &c.

THE

CANADIAN GENTLEMEN AMATEURS

AND

IROQUOIS INDIANS

(Twelve on each side) will play their

FIRST PUBLIC MATCH IN LONDON OF THE

CANADIAN NATIONAL GAME OF LACROSSE

AT THE

SURREY C. C. GROUND,

KENNINGTON OVAL,

ON

WHIT-MONDAY, JUNE 5,

Commencing in the Morning at 11.30 & in the Afternoon at 4.

Play at Old Deer Park, Richmond, June 6th; Brighton, 7th &
8th, on County Cricket Ground; Prince's, 9th; Sandown Park,
Esher, 14th; Lord's Ground, 17th of June.

THE INDIANS WILL DANCE THE "GREEN CORN" DANCE, &c.

Admission to each Match, One Shilling.   Pavilion, 1s. extra.
Vauxhall Station (L. and S. W. R.) is within Five Minutes' Walk of the Oval.

Figure 69 • London poster advertising forthcoming matches on the 1876 tour led by George Beers, in which "gentlemen amateurs" from the Montreal Club would play Caughnawaga Indians. Such exhibitions from abroad were intended not only to spread the sport but also to encourage English to emigrate to thinly populated Canada.

• 269

it followed that, in the case of lacrosse, "civilization tamed the manners and habits of the Indians" to the point where the game was "gradually divested of its radical rudeness and brought to a more sober sport." While he and his teammates admired the physical prowess evident in the Indian style of play, they nevertheless believed that the native version of the game remained at a primitive level:

"Only a savage people could, would or should play the old [Indian] game; only such constitutions, such wind and endurance could stand its violence." That such views still hold sway is reflected as recently as 1989 in the Canadian Lacrosse Association's "position paper," whose authors could write: "Canada is the product of an evolution which began with the Natives and was molded by the European settlers. It took the combined efforts of these people to open this country to development."[7]

In drawing up the new "laws" of lacrosse, the Montrealers also reflected another prevailing current of thought. This time was also the age of rapid scientific advancement, and "progress," whether economic or social, was paramount in the plans of all Euro-Americans. Only "rational" and "scientific" approaches to any problem would produce the optimum solutions. Such ideals are tacitly reflected in the following typical passage from Beers's book: "To improve Lacrosse, and not detract from its native merits, we must agree to the systematic conformity, intended in the regulations which guide the game. Unscientific play in any game has sometimes been more effective than its antithesis, as poor shots have sometimes made bull's-eyes when champions have missed altogether; but the more head-work put into such a game as Lacrosse, the more beautiful and less rough it will become."[8]

Everything about the Indian game seemed to Beers and his compatriots to be irrational, unscientific, impromptu, or otherwise lacking in organization. They objected, for instance, to the absence of clearly defined boundaries on the Indian field. Although goalposts, lines, or flags marked its ends, there were no sidelines to further demarcate the field and indicate "out of bounds." Thus Beers could complain in his book about Lac la Pluie Ojibwe games, where players "do not scruple to jump over the fences and run through the ground crops if their ball . . . is driven in that direction."[9]

The Montrealers also disdained the Indian mass attack and wished instead to substitute a dodging and passing game that relied more on teamwork and the rational decisions of a team captain. This preference is clear throughout Beers's discussion of lacrosse techniques. Take, for instance, his treatment of dodging, which includes the following passage: "Our laws allow any strength of attack at one dodger, but it is the custom among the St. Regis Indians not to interfere between two adversaries, unless at goal; so that the dodger has only one opponent at a time to avoid. This Indian play would not answer for our small fields and our improved game. We prefer trusting to the common sense of the men, and the directing genius of a Captain."[10]

The Canadians also objected to the emphasis that Indians placed on individual play. They felt that the bagged net of the Indian crosse simply encouraged show-offs to hog the ball and run the length of the field to score. Teamwork required more passing, and accurate passing meant using sticks with tighter webbing. Thus, in the Canadians' final judgment, if the Indians wished to continue playing white teams, they would simply have to conform to the new game— which is exactly what happened.

But what of Rule IX, Section 6, disallowing Indian participation on white clubs unless agreed upon? There is no indication that such agreement was ever even attempted; there is, in fact, sufficient evidence that it was never intended to be reached. The rule was a blatant, segregationist "separate but equal" clause, which would eventually and effectively bar Indians from participation in international lacrosse competition for more than a century.

Why did the nascent white lacrosse community wish to exclude Indians from the game in this manner? There is some suggestion that the whites actually believed Indian players to be superior, so any team, including their own, that included Indians would be at an advantage. Recognition of Indian talent is reflected in the makeup of many early games between the two races in which white teams were allowed more players on the field than the Indians, presumably to enable them thus to match the strength of their opponents. When the Caughnawaga team gave their command performance before Queen Victoria, she noted that the Indians were playing with thirteen men versus Montreal's fourteen. When the Montreal Amateur Lacrosse Association (MALA) was requested in 1895 to bring a white and an Indian team to Chicago, the secretary was instructed to reply favorably, that "we would be pleased to go & bring along an Indian or another team provided they would pay all Railroad & Hotel expenses for both teams & cost of Indian team which would be about $1.50 a day each man While they were away & that the Indian would be satisfyed to travel 2nd class. Our team would consist of 15 men and the Indian 13."[11]

The Chicago request and similar entries in the association's minutes books make it clear that not only were Indians second-class citizens—Chicago could get them to ride "for cheap"—but they needed to be paid for their time away from home. This important distinction between white and native players ultimately was used to exclude Indians from the lacrosse world: whites were considered amateurs, and Indians professionals because they had to be paid for their services. It mattered not that most white lacrosse players of the time, like Beers, came from the ranks of dentists, lawyers, doctors, merchants, and the like, and the game served principally as a pastime for them. Meanwhile, faced with poverty and unemployment on the reservations, most Indians *had* to charge fees, if for nothing else than to pay for their travel to games—a mere pittance of an expense for white, middle- and upper-class "club" sportsmen.

The problem of defining professional and amateur continues to plague the sports world (viz. the Olympics), but in lacrosse it was a sufficient weapon to exclude the originators of the sport from any further involvement in its development. In 1880 the National Lacrosse Association of Canada ruled that only amateurs could play, effectively barring Indian teams from further competition in national championships, which they had been winning consistently. Relegated to playing at the inter- and intratribal level, the Indians stoically formed their own Indian World Championship—a competition mostly between St. Regis and Caughnawaga.[12] Eventually Indian historians, having found no Indian lacrosse players mentioned in the Canadian Lacrosse Hall of Fame, decided to put on a "Tribute Night," complete with a ceremonial dinner and individual awards—some of them posthumously—to the championship team of the 1930s.[13] Despite these events, white teams received the most press coverage, as they still do. The game was now effectively theirs; they had invented its rules, were in control of its spread, and were given exclusive attention.

After the association's decision in 1880 to consist solely of amateurs, the temptation arose for small towns to employ Indian "ringers" on their teams in order to have a crack at beating clubs from the large cities. When the small town of Cornwall, adjacent to St. Regis, kept winning the Canadian championship from 1887 to 1891 against teams from Toronto and Montreal, it was suspected that the town's team was illegally recruiting Indian players from the nearby reserve. Although nothing is officially recorded about the practice, there is much in oral tradition to confirm it. The ringers chosen were those particularly with non-Indian facial features, preferably sporting a mustache and possessing some fluency in English. (Most Indians at the time did not meet this requirement.) If a ringer was suspected, opposing teams would hire a native "snitch" to approach him in the locker room and speak directly to him in Mohawk. If he showed signs of understanding what was said or inadvertently responded in his native tongue, he would be removed from the roster. But because Cornwall enjoyed beating the large city clubs, their fans kept quiet about the presence of Indians on their team. Two of the most successful Cornwall ringers, Jake Cook and Tom Sam, learned to become wary of the locker-room saboteurs from their reserve.[14]

Mohawk lacrosse historians have found French surnames in Mohawk annals from that period that are extremely rare and show no evidence of true French ancestry. They suggest that the presence of such names as Papineau, Beauvais (Bova), and Beroux (Bero) were possibly cover names for Mohawk ringers.[15] It is conceivable that just such a person was "Leroux," a topic for discussion by the lacrosse association in 1890. The association's minutes for 11 June 1890 state that the board of directors of the Montreal Amateur Athletic Association (MAAA) "would like to see us push the protest re Leroux of Cornwall Lacrosse Club. The secretary was requested to secure proof if possible and push the matter through." The minutes for 16 July show that "McIndoe read an affidavit from Mr Solomon Angus declaring that Leroux of the Cornwall team had played on several occasions for money." He was subsequently charged with being a professional, but by the 4 November meeting the charges were dropped for insufficient evidence.

Weeding out Indian ringers from the Cornwall team continued to be a problem for this "amateur" association. An entry in the minutes book for 5 June 1895 reads: "Mr D Patterson informed the meeting that he had protested White of the Cornwall team as being an Indian." The matter was tabled, but on 19 June it was voted to initiate the protest, since the game had been a tie. On 17 July it was noted that "Mr Fridley reported that the match with Cornwall was declared null & void, but that the Cornwalls were given two weeks to prove White was not an Indian."[16]

To comprehend the zeal devoted to exposing ringers, it is important to understand what the terms "amateur" and "professional" meant when the Montreal Amateur Athletic Association came into being. The definition of "amateur" appears in Article V ("Membership") of the association's constitution and reads: "An amateur is any person who has never competed in any open competition, or for a stake, or for public money, or for admission money, or under a false name, or with a professional, for a prize or where gate money is charged; and who has never at any period of his life taught or assisted in the pursuit of athletic exercises as a means of livelihood."

The belief in "excellence in sports for their own sake" reflected the mores and social values of the Victorian era. The obsession with this notion is apparent in the sportswriting of the period. The *Toronto Star* of 25 May 1880 called professionalism "the evil" and proclaimed that "its hateful presence has fully declared itself." Over the next few decades, however, not only would this idea erode but the lacrosse world itself would become sharply divided over the issue.

Because money was at the root of it, the dues charged lacrosse club members were ostensibly used to defray whatever expenses were incurred in the various competitions. Beyond that, of course, the funds helped to underwrite the costs of fancy clubhouses, training gymnasiums, the best playing fields and their upkeep, annual banquets, and similar activities of athletic clubs. Still, under the official distinction, Indians were judged to be "professionals" because they accepted money to play; thus they were excluded, first from competing for the Canadian championship, then from international competition. In the opinion of Mohawk Frank Benedict, "They used that as a leverage to ban the best Indian players out of competition. They classified them as professionals. Back in those days, what type of employment did the native or Indian people have? They had no means of a salary or creating any wages for them to be able to participate or compete in any organized lacrosse, so they had to receive funds from somebody or somewhere to be able to play. All this was used against them."[17]

Sportswriter Robert Lipsyte, in interviewing Iroquois Nationals coach Oren Lyons, found him to echo similar sentiments: "To young Oren and his teammates, this was part of the systematic policy of stealing lands from Indians, of denying their culture, of eradicating their nations. They were taught by their elders that any money accepted by Indian teams was used to pay for trips to tournaments. The rich white teams never had such financial problems; they could afford the growing Anglo-American cult of 'amateurism,' embodied in the Olympic movements." (Indian people are mindful of the inherent racism behind Jim Thorpe's losing his two Olympic gold medals in 1913 when it was discovered that he had once played a baseball game for money.) In this sense, Indian lacrosse players of the time were not unlike their lower-class counterparts in ancient Greece, who lacked both time and money to gain the higher-level training needed to enter the world of Greek sport.[18]

No one contests the fact that Indians accepted and even "charged" money to play. In fact, considerable bartering took place when matches with Indians were arranged. MALA minutes book entries for May 1887, for example, show the sort of financial negotiating that went on—each side holding out for less or more money than the Indians would be paid. On 4 May is reported: "A letter was read from the Secy of the Caughnawagas asking for sixty dollars for the match on 24th May. the secretary was instructed to answer in reply that we had their acceptance for fifty dollars, and to say that we would see that the rates by G.T.R. would not be higher than formerly, and to wire us in reply."

The next week the club was notified that the Indians would not accept less than $60. The secretary was told to answer the Indians, saying that since they refused the $50 offer, the match was off. That motion was carried, as was one to invite the Shamrocks to play in their stead. By 18 May the Indians had caved in to the pressure and agreed to play for $50 but were told other arrangements had already been made. The day following the game with the Shamrock Club a minutes book entry shows "the Amount received from Shamrocks was $177.67 which was very satisfactory, it being more than Indian matches generally brought."

Despite the amateur ruling on playing where gate money was charged, this matter was simply ignored, even though compared to today's ticket prices the amounts being charged were fairly small. Nor do the minutes books try to hide the fact that fees were collected from the general public to attend matches. On 18 August 1886 is entered: "It was decided to engage the Indians for next Wednesday night at 5 oclock. Also for Saturday afternoon. Mr. Woods was requested to notify Mackay to be on hand Saturday at 4 oclock to take charge of gate & charge 25 cents admission to non-members attending match." On 4 August 1897, membership was notified that the British Medical Association requested an exhibition match on 3 September "with indians preferred, and expenses of same." The Montreal Lacrosse Club requested $125 to defray the Indians' expenses, but also asked to be able to charge at the gate. Furthermore, there were different levels of admission fees. Entered in the book for 20 April 1887: "Mr. Lloyd asked to notify boxholders about rent." By 1909 the association was charging 50 cents general admission, 75 cents for grandstand, and $1 for chairs.

Reading through the annual minutes books, one cannot fail to notice a steady rise in the amount of money the so-called amateur teams were receiving for games. An entry for 18 July 1894 notes the reception of a letter from Victoria Lacrosse Club of British Columbia, who "would like our team to visit the coast this fall & that he thought they could give us $1200 for 2 matches in Victoria & $800.00 for 2 matches, one in Vancouver & the other in New Westminster." Annual lacrosse budget requests to the MAAA were also increasing. The appropriation for 1899, which included the expenses of a trip to New York, was $1,000. By 1909 the budget was considerably higher, including $4,500 for "salaries," which probably included the expense of a trainer, and $800 for travel. Minutes books after 1900 mention the signing of contracts with club players. By 1908 the average Canadian "amateur" player could make $100 a season, while "stars" could make $1,000. A famous player for the New Westminster Salmonbellies, "Cyclone" Taylor, was earning nearly $2,000.[19]

Clearly, a crisis had arisen in the lacrosse world over the issue of professionalism. In the late 1890s the National Amateur Lacrosse Association had become so factionalized that some clubs broke away to form the National Lacrosse Union of professionals, soon to be followed by the creation of a second professional league, the Dominion Lacrosse Union. This left the Canadian Lacrosse Association as the sole amateur group. At the turn of the century, Canadians were club jumping and committing other infractions of amateur ethics, as is evident from the increasing number of rules on residency, rosters, and player eligibility. Because of professionalism, by 1920 the Montreal Lacrosse Club, in effect the "founder" of the game, had been so heavily penalized that it was no longer able to compete in any league.[20]

If the restrictions against playing for money or where gate charges were made went so unobserved, what about the other aspects of "amateurism" defined in the 1880 statement? The definition also declares that amateurs were ineligible to play for prizes, but that rule soon went by the boards. "Prizes" were evidently interpreted as individual cash awards, so did not exclude trophies. Even before Beers's book had been published, T. J. Claxton of Montreal had donated four poles and flags worth $250 for competition among the city clubs. The "Claxton Flags," as they were known, bore the motto Our Country—Our Game and set a precedent for further championship awards. In 1901 Lord Minto, Governor General of Canada, donated a silver cup for senior amateur championship, though soon the Minto Cup was usurped by the professional leagues as their trophy.[21]

While prizes were being awarded to all-white teams in Canada, Indian players continued their traditional game relatively unnoticed, although *not* without problems from outside their culture. Throughout the nineteenth century Indian lacrosse in many places came under attack from both church and state. Government interference and prohibition were prompted mostly by the violence provoked by gambling on lacrosse matches. For the most part, the game was viewed by Indian agents and other government officials as an innocent pastime; it posed no real threat to the plans of Euro-American society eventually to assimilate Indians into the "melting pot." Nevertheless, there were complaints that lacrosse represented part of a "heathen" proclivity of Indians that they should abandon because such activities interfered with the government's agenda to bring them into "civilization." Andrew Barnard complained to the governor of North Carolina in 1840 over the influx of mixed-blood Cherokee coming in from Georgia: "[They] are forming Settlements, building townhouses, and Show every disposition to keep up their former manners and customs of councils, dances, ballplays, and other practices, which is disgusting to civilized Society and calculated to corrupt our [local Indian] youth, and produce distress and confusion among all good thinking people."[22]

But missionary objection to lacrosse, even in Father Le Mer-

cier's time, was far more adamant and had more severe consequences. In Iroquois country the church played a role in changing
the nature of the game. In 1752, when the St. Regis Mission was
founded by a Jesuit with Caughnawaga Mohawk, the game was still
firmly rooted in the Indian religious belief that lacrosse, or *tewaarathon* in Mohawk, was a gift of the Creator. As the relationship
between lacrosse and the Creator began to disintegrate under the
pressure of Christian teachings, the game became increasingly a secular pastime. But missionaries were still unhappy about its effect on
attendance at church services. In the St. Regis Mission Records of
Letters for 1808, for example, the complaint is noted that "the
Indians could not be persuaded to return to church on sunday afternoons for vespers and benediction because they were always more
interested in a rough game called 'lacrosse.' "[23]

The same charge was made elsewhere in North America,
although usually combined with exhortations against the evils of
gambling, drink, and associated vices. From about 1880 to 1900, for
instance, there was intense proseltyzing among the Mississippi Choctaw by both Baptist and Catholic clergy. They attempted to discour-
age Indian participation in native dances and lacrosse games, which
they regarded as disruptive to church attendance. As sports historian
Kendall Blanchard wrote: "Church leaders of the period [1800s]
argued that their programs provided ample opportunity for social
interaction and thus negated the need for the *toli* [lacrosse] matches.
Also, it was felt that the influence of the local Whites, their whiskey,
and their frequent attempts to sexually solicit and abuse native
women, had so corrupted the stickball contest that it had become
morally degrading in and of itself."[24] Lacrosse among Oklahoma
Choctaw fared somewhat better; nevertheless, the laws of the Choctaw General Council prohibited matches on Sunday.

Eastern Cherokee were also harassed by missionaries over their
ball games. In a journal of the Brainard Mission is a complaint about
a truant Indian boy (6 July 1822), who "appears to be in a great
degree ignorant of the evil of ball play." Moravian missionaries
seemed concerned about the gambling involved. Wrote one:
"Around Springplace [mission in northwestern Georgia] the evils in
connection with the frequent ball-playing among the Cherokees
were especially marked. The game, innocent enough in itself, was
generally attended with much bad behavior, drunkenness and licentiousness. At one such game in 1825, not far from Springplace,
Schmidt estimated the crowd in attendance at about 3,000, and he
had information, on good authority, that the bets made during the
game aggregated $3500." After a period of some inactivity, about 1898
the Cherokee resumed their traditional stickball matches and other

former customs, much to the dismay of the superintendent of Quaker schools.[25]

Opposition to Indian lacrosse by church and state in the nineteenth century was based on the perception of it as "immoral" (gambling) and "uncivil" (the game's violence). But the large majority of Indian players invariably belonged to the so-called traditional segment of Indian society that did *not* convert to Christianity, conform to white notions of "civilization," or join "the melting pot." As a consequence, they were subject to the racial stereotyping that the larger society conveniently used for all its "backward," lower-class citizens, be they African American, Appalachian, European immigrant, or Native American.

Such racial stereotyping was attended with derogatory terminology that, in the case of lacrosse, persists today. We can perhaps excuse Beers and his contemporaries for its explicit use more than a century ago. Given their perception of the Indian's place on the evolutionary ladder, expressions like "paleface" and "redskin" to distinguish the races, or words such as "squaw" and "buck" to refer to Indian gender were commonplace. To them, native people were just a lower-class, disenfranchised segment of humanity. (In a succession of reports in the MALA minutes books from August through September 1897, the recorder almost consistently wrote "indians" beginning with the lowercase "i.")

One derogatory code name for Indian people of the time was the expletive "Lo." It derived from the expression "Lo, the poor Indian!," created by poet Alexander Pope in 1733 and subsequently meant to depict the socioeconomic plight of American Indians, albeit demeaningly.[26] The word made its way into sportswriting when lacrosse was just beginning to gain attention. The *New York Herald* described a game in 1869, saying it resembled shinny and noting that "the way the 'Lo's' handle their 'crosses,' run and toss the ball is really marvelous and well worthy of being witnessed." The custom of naming non-Indian athletic teams "redskins" or "braves" began early in lacrosse; the first white team in the United States, founded in December 1867 in Troy, New York, called itself the Mohawk Lacrosse Club. Forced to travel to Canada to find teams to play against, they were usually severely beaten. Reporting on their performance, the *Montreal Gazette* commiserated with the young, inexperienced American team by punning, "Lo, the poor Mohawks."[27]

Has any progress been made in the area of racial slurring? Nearly all of the many former and present Indian lacrosse players interviewed cite instances of blatantly racist remarks from white opponents, directed either at them personally or at Indians in general. As recently as 1991, a young Onondaga who was playing in a summer indoor league tells that his Indian coach at the time had chosen, for one game, to join his non-Indian assistant coach on an otherwise all-white team playing the Iroquois: "They're all in their huddle, and they're getting ready for the game, right? We're all down warming up, and he comes up to us after the game. He says, 'I can't believe it, I can't believe what I heard in there. When they were warming up, [the assistant coach] forgot that I was there, and said, "Come on, let's beat this bunch of fucking Indians," you know. "Let's beat these fucking redskins."'' My coach said he just stood straight up and just forgot that he was standing there."[28]

As in other sports, racial epithets obviously surface in the heat of the action. Rex Lyons explains how he and his cousin Kent arrived at the name Wagon Burners for their popular Syracuse rock band. During a particularly one-sided game against a Montreal team, where the Indians were routing the Canadians, the Montreal goalie lost his temper: "We were crushing them. Things were getting pretty rowdy, tempers were flaring, and we were winning. But we were good sports about it, and the goalie was just getting so frustrated that he finally lashed out with 'You ain't nothing but wagon burners anyway.' He said, 'I'll get you, you fucking wagon burner' to my cousin Scott. These guys were so pissed off, you know. It was done with full rage. If it was a knife, it would have killed us, that's what he had thrown. But you know, it's just like being in the way; somebody throws something bad at you, you turn it around and use it for something that's useful [e.g., the name for an Indian rock band]."[29]

Some Indian players have sensed racial sentiments even from teammates. When Emmett Printup entered Syracuse University, there were three other Indian players on the team, but by his senior year they had graduated. As he quips, "I was the only Indian, the only [red]'skin of the Orange."[30] His affability generally earns him friends among lacrosse players of all races. Still, he recalls a remark once directed at him by a teammate, which seemed to suggest that, as an Indian player, Emmett was disadvantaged: "It was a weird kinda like prejudice. I remember one time, like Jimmy Olson [pseudonym], you know he's a big time scorer in NCAA in Division I that I played with at SU. I remember we were sitting around, we were shooting around at the net, just Jimmy and I, you know, after practice, just passing the ball back and forth, 'cause we were playing on a power play. We were shooting around, and he looks over to me and he goes, 'Too bad you're Indian,' or something like that. Kinda sensing that it was like, hell, you could probably be starting and playing the whole game if maybe you weren't. That's what I kinda picked up from that."[31]

The college experience alone can be intimidating to young Indian players who have not already dropped out of school. Many enter college seeing lacrosse careers as a way to break out of the certain poverty that otherwise awaits them in reservation life. When it was pointed out to Onondaga Freeman Bucktooth that no Indians had played at nearby Syracuse for some time, he painted a bleak picture. Bucktooth explained his Indian view of the relationship between education and lacrosse talents: "I believe myself if it weren't for sports, I probably may have never finished high school. I would have dropped out and started working, but what I'm trying to do now [coaching on the reservation] is give back to a sport what it gave me. It kept me in school and gave me two years of higher education and a better outlook on life."[32]

Even with a chance at higher education, Indian players often experience the feeling of isolation on a mostly white campus. Said one Tuscarora player, "No one from my family has ever gone to college, not even my cousins. Everyone usually becomes ironworkers right away. No, I always wanted to get a college education, and lacrosse was like a bonus. It was hard putting up four years, because you know when you first start out, you feel like you shouldn't be there; you feel different, and it doesn't help when people, like even when coaches act racial, like little sly things that you pick up on."[33]

Social issues totally outside sports can inflame anti-Indian sentiment and adversely affect otherwise friendly competition on the field. Frank Benedict noted how the violence in the wake of the Oka confrontation in 1990 simply made a bad relationship worse: "There's a lot of racism and dissention against the Mohawk communities, and it's even affected our athletic and sports programs, where a lot of the French teams will not play against the Mohawks. . . . We've always gotten along, but the racism has always been there, but just lately [following Oka] it has really come out."[34]

Even in supposedly friendly tournament competitions, sometimes Indian teams today have the perception that they are not particularly welcome. These sentiments were voiced by players for the Iroquois Nationals who, in the 1990 Lacrosse World Cup, for the first time in more than a century were permitted to play in international competition. One Indian player remembers the experience: "Like when we were in Australia, [the USA team] acted like we didn't belong there. They were the ones that voiced it the most; they thought that we played the game in such a manner that they didn't like it. They thought we played dirty, you know, because our style of playing was different, and they were frustrated. But they beat us pretty easily, but physically I think we came out on top and with more dignity, because they were doing a lot more whining and crying about things. They were the ones that stepped in the racial slur kinda zone there, and they were apologetic afterwards, and after everybody got together they felt bad."[35]

Despite the large numbers of Indian people playing lacrosse today throughout North America, two distinct worlds of lacrosse have emerged: that played mostly on reservations by Indians and that played by "the Lacrosse community." The Great Lakes game is virtually extinct. Southeastern lacrosse is still a vital part of native culture and ceremonialism, but whites have never taken up the double-stick game. The Iroquois play mostly box, but the fastest-growing version of the game is unquestionably men's field lacrosse, and since 1880 it has been dominated by Euro-Americans, with minimal Indian participation. It is this community that controls the rules and regulations, manufactures and sells the equipment, and financially supports the institutions where field lacrosse is played. For the most part, its members are only minimally aware of or are indifferent to the history of this major contribution of the American Indian to world sport. Thus it is with a certain mixture of cynicism and bitterness that Indian people view the lacrosse power structure.

To begin with, Indians feel that, despite being the originators of lacrosse, they receive little if any recognition for this accomplishment. In their minds, a white player with a plastic stick might just as well assume that L. L. Bean invented the canoe. As Mohawk researcher Ernest Benedict sums it up: "Much has been written in the record books about the accomplishments of our White brothers who admired, learned and helped develop the game into its present forms, field and box lacrosse. We appreciate their contributions, but feel that we have been pushed out of the way of recognition. We will be pushed no longer."[36]

Nevertheless, Indian players recognize that the better white lacrosse players have at least some appreciation for the Indian tradition. As Emmett Printup puts it: "If you're into it, you know everything about the product you're getting, like playing lacrosse. If you're really into lacrosse, you know how it started."[37] Many younger Indians today take pride in lacrosse as part of their heritage. Ansley Jemison, a Seneca playing at the high school level, is typical (Figure 70). He grew up on the Allegany Reservation, where lacrosse, along with many other Seneca traditions, had been lost for a long time following the removal of his people to Salamanca, New York, because of the construction of the Kinzua Dam. Though his grandfather had played on the Cattaraugus Reservation, it was not until his family moved near Rochester that Ansley had any real exposure to the sport. Because the high school in his new hometown had no lacrosse program, he chose instead to attend Canandaigua Academy,

Figure 70 • Ansley Jemison, Seneca player for Canandaigua Academy and tenth-generation descendant of Mary Jemison.

despite the commute. The only Indian in the academy, he takes special pride in his lacross activity and supplements his annual spring training with summer practice for the Iroquois Junior Nationals. Jemison knows that many of his teammates are ignorant about the origins of the game: "Some of the coaches tell them, but it's not part of the teaching. It's really not part of the game. In a way it *is* part of the game, 'cause we're the ones that started it, but when you teach the game of lacrosse, you kind of, like, lose the values of it, 'cause now it's a sport. Before it was a sport for fun, it had a lot more meaning, a lot more traditional value."[38]

Despite pride in their lacrosse heritage, Indians are weary of having mere lip service paid them when it comes to the game. The $10 Canadian coin minted for the 1976 Olympics, for instance, depicted Indians of the past playing lacrosse. But the Canadian Lacrosse Association was upset only that lacrosse per se was excluded from the games, not that the Indian role was reduced simply to a historical logo. Indians are resentful that they continue to be exploited in this way for their publicity value in such international arenas, while at the same time they are blocked from active participation. In 1986, for example, Canada prevented the Iroquois attempt to play in the quadrennial World Games in Toronto, arguing that it would cost too much logistically and would require printing new tickets.[39]

There is also some Indian hostility toward the so-called Baltimore clique. Because much of the college field game developed in the Maryland area, the proximity of such teams as Navy, Maryland, and Johns Hopkins and the presence of some of the major equipment outlets led naturally to locating the Lacrosse Hall of Fame in Baltimore. Consequently, Indian players would probably agree with the following sardonic observation: "Though the game was played by Indians for centuries, there is a feeling in the lacrosse community that Johns Hopkins [University] people like to think they invented the game, or at least perfected it." A recent review of Bob Scott's well-known "how-to" book on lacrosse in *Maryland Magazine* called it "a message to the outside world from the cosmic center of the sport." And Indian stickmakers resent the claims of lucrative Baltimore plastic stick manufacturers that without their product the sports world would see the eventual demise of lacrosse.[40]

Indian sensitivity over the attention Baltimore receives as the mecca of lacrosse has been ameliorated somewhat in recent years through the sincere efforts of the Lacrosse Foundation to restore proper recognition to the Indian game. The foundation has begun to redress past inattention to the Indian contributions to lacrosse through its promotional video, magazine articles, accessioning of Indian sticks for its collections, and the 1992 commission of a large bronze casting of two historic Indian players, prominently displayed on the front lawn next to the Johns Hopkins field. And in 1993, Oren Lyons was elected to the Lacrosse Hall of Fame—the second Indian out of 201 inductees to be so honored. (The first was a Cherokee from Carlisle Indian School, elected in the early 1900s.)

But Indians properly question whether the lip service they receive is truly sincere. The coauthor of a book on lacrosse, a former coach and player, was interviewed in 1985, with the following write-up by the reporter: "Lacrosse is not, to him, just another sport. It is the game that was on this continent before we were, a gift from the Indian nations. . . . If Indian magic has mostly disappeared in these latter days, it lives, he feels, on the lacrosse field. He puts it this way: 'When a lacrosse game takes place, a great spirit moves over the battleground and gives a magic touch to the battle weapon—the lacrosse stick—granting it the power to do unbelievable deeds.' " While one cannot doubt the sincerity of these remarks, they seem curiously romantic by comparison with the text that he coauthored some twenty years earlier: Indian games were preceded by "all manner of pagan rites"; the "squaws" played a prominent role in pre-game rituals; and contact with women was taboo before a game, because Indians were "so superstitious." And the question is raised: "How came the Indians to fashion a racket? No one will ever know. They were not very inventive."[41]

True, we will never know the origin of the Indian lacrosse "racket," but surely it is one of the most inventive pieces of sports equipment in the world's history. If racism is evident in other areas of lacrosse, the fate of the wooden stick is but another example of it. In the white man's obsession to "improve" the game, he came to judge the Indian crosse to be as inferior as the people who had carefully handcrafted it for centuries. Having learned the game from the Mohawk, rewritten the rules, and successfully excluded Indians from playing in international competition, Euro-Americans had effectively seized the game for themselves. There was one unfinished piece of business, however. The one essential piece of equipment for the game, the stick, was still for the most part manufactured by Indian craftspeople. By the end of the twentieth century, this, too, would have been taken from Indian hands and the stick industry would be essentially dominated by whites. The replacement of the traditional Iroquois hickory stick with its plastic counterpart in the men's field game effectively marked the final step in non-Indian control and development of the sport.

The reputation for the quality of Mohawk sticks spread as the game was taken up by increasing numbers of players, and Akwesasne (St. Regis) sticks became valued trade items among various tribes of the northeast. When the popularity of the game reached beyond Indian communities to non-Indians beginning in the mid-nineteenth century, small family units were hard-pressed to meet the increased demand for sticks. Extended families and even friends joined forces in cooperative ventures to increase production.

At the time, sports equipment manufacturers were increasingly aware of a new market in lacrosse gear, and by 1880 almost all equipment was available commercially. For example, the Lacrosse Emporium on West King Street in Toronto offered sticks at under $1 apiece, but single-netted Grand River sticks, presumably from the reserve, cost as much as $1.75. Even though Canadians were turning to nonnative stickmakers, entries in the MALA minutes books of the 1880s and 1890s suggest that sticks were still coming from the Indians. Frank Lally, for example, an outstanding non-Indian goaltender before he entered the business, was only beginning to supply them, but the relatively low price of his sticks at the time and certain MALA entries asking the services of Montrealers for gutting suggest that Lally may have been sending them unstrung Mohawk frames. Clearly, purchases from Indian stickmakers continued to be part of the seasonal request for funds submitted to the directors of the association. On 17 May 1893, "The account from P. De Lorimier St. Regis 1 doz Lacrosse Sticks $12.55 was passed."[42]

Despite the exclusion of Indians from white teams, contacts with the Indian community by virtue of stick purchases were numerous. But it was not long before white entrepreneurs found the Mohawk "assembly line" method of stick production appealing and entered the business themselves. Lally, for example, invited "Matty" White, a bilingual Mohawk and gifted stickmaker, to his home to make sticks. Lally's brother, a lacrosse referee, became interested; together they formed the Lally Company, which, through Matty's encouragement, attracted Mohawk stickmakers as employees. Though serving principally as an outlet, the company began to refuse sticks made outside the factory, or it would bargain to purchase them at a reduced rate.

The only other commercial outlet at the time was Lantry Brothers in Hogansburg, New York. Since lacrosse was gaining popularity in the United States, many Mohawk began to sell their products to Lantry Brothers, despite the necessity of covert transportation across the border and the frequent interception of goods by the United States Customs agents (for the sticks were subject to duty).[43] During Prohibition the number of border guards was increased, and agents even hired Indian informers—much like the locker-room spies of Beers's day—who were paid the value of the goods seized. Under these circumstances a stickmaker stood to lose his entire inventory—a full year's work—in one stroke.[44]

Ultimately, the largest producer was Colin Chisholm, whose factory was on Cornwall Island. With markets in Toronto and promotional samples shipped to the United States, by 1931 the factory was filling large orders, as the game became more widespread not only in the United States but also throughout the British Commonwealth.

Combining modern factory technology with traditional stringing of the frames overnight in Mohawk homes, the Chisholm enterprise was a most successful venture. By the late 1960s Akwesasne Mohawk stickmakers were crafting 72,000 sticks annually for Chisholm and satisfying 97 percent of the world's demand. Roy Simmons relates how Chisholm, shrewd Scotsman that he was, kept his Mohawk workers from wandering off: "I can vividly remember going up there in the middle of winter, and they were carving like crazy, because Mr. Chisholm was smart enough, he wouldn't buy any fuel for the wood-burning stove that kept them warm. They had to rely on the shavings from carving, and if they slacked on their carving, then they didn't have fuel for the fire; they got cold. So to keep themselves warm they carved like crazy to keep the fire stoked."[45]

As field lacrosse became more and more popular, Chisholm suddenly found a major distributor in Baltimore. The owner of a sporting goods store, Peck Auer, entered into a business arrangement with Chisholm that began to funnel Chisholm sticks to the major American universities now playing the sport. Simmons describes the exclusive agreement between maker and distributor: "[Auer] would buy them sanders and drill presses or whatever it took to make these sticks, and he fronted the money for the equipment. But in return he was guaranteed an exclusive, so that nobody would be in competition with him. If you wanted a lacrosse stick, Auer would wholesale or retail it to you, but he owned them, so in essence he really controlled the sport."

As a former Syracuse player himself, Simmons reminisces about visits with the team to the Howard Street store to pick through the new Chisholm sticks: "Mr. Auer would open up the third floor where all the sticks were. But as a result of them being in Baltimore, the sole output of the one piece of equipment that you need, Maryland and Johns Hopkins and Navy, being in close proximity to Howard St. would get there first, and they would cut open the bundles, and they'd be knee-deep in sticks all over the floor. And they would go through and pick out the best ones. . . . And so we'd get the second shot, and there were a lot of bent and twisted sticks, and some of them were too thick and too heavy and the handles were a little off. But it was always fun as a kid to be able to have your pick of five or six hundred sticks, the new spring batch, so to speak."[46]

The Chisholm factory flourished until a disastrous fire burned it to the ground in 1968—a blow from which it never fully recovered. Through frantic efforts, 85 percent of the blanks stockpiled for curing were saved. Still, the fire created an enormous shortage on the market, since Chisholm had become the world's principal manufacturer.[47]

In the wake of the Cornwall fire, the introduction of the plastic, mold-stamped stickhead by W. H. Brine Company of Boston in the spring of 1970 was fortuitous. It is clear that, after Auer's earlier monopoly, Brine had made arrangements with Chisholm for exclusive distribution rights in the United States—in effect now controlling the wooden stick market. In a form letter dated 22 December 1971 and sent to every known field lacrosse coach, Brine informed them that, because of the "tremendous" reception of their new plastic stick, "as a result we decided this past October to cease our operation of the wooden stick plant in Cornwall, Ontario." The rest of the letter spelled out how Brine would "remainder" the existing supply of wooden sticks until it was depleted. Thus with one mass mailing, Brine dictated the future of the men's field lacrosse stick, just as Beers had established the rules of the game 104 years earlier. Whereas one deprived the Indian from participation in the international arena, the other put uncounted numbers of native stickmakers out of work, hastening the decline of yet another centuries-old American Indian craft.

Most of today's field lacrosse players have rarely even seen, let alone played with, a wooden lacrosse stick, and they are usually bewildered upon first encountering one. Roy Simmons keeps a number of older sticks in his Manley Fieldhouse lacrosse office: "Kids coming in now look at my collection of wooden sticks, and they say, 'My God! These must be ancient!' And I say, 'No, '50s, early '60s.' Well, that's still before they're born. And they pick it up and say, 'Well, this is one-sided, you know, and it's not balanced, and this is too stiff. How could you catch the ball?' And I said, 'Well, you caught the ball and caught it quite well, I think.' But you couldn't get a kid today to pick up a wooden stick, 'cause it wouldn't lay right in his hands."[48]

Despite the disappearance of the individual stickmaker, since 1970 small, family-run production units have managed to maintain successful wooden lacrosse stick businesses, which offer employment to reservation residents. Wes Patterson of the Tuscarora Reservation in western New York employs some twenty people full time, adding high school students to his workforce in the busy summer season, and Frank Benedict of Akwesasne (St. Regis) continues a brisk business of his own, with relatives and friends forming the core of his shop labor force on the site of the old Chisholm plant. But with the plastic manufacturers controlling the field lacrosse market, Patterson, Benedict, and others like them are reduced to supplying sticks to the vastly smaller world of box lacrosse and women's field lacrosse, whose players continue to use the traditional wooden stick.

Should the men's field lacrosse community lament the passing of the wooden stick? There are some who feel strongly that the loss to the game is significant. The arguments on both sides of the issue need reviewing. Those who favor the plastic stick—mostly non-Indian players—prefer the lighter weight of an aluminum shaft and plastic head and find it more manageable. The heavier wooden stick is viewed as clumsier to handle. Furthermore, they argue, wooden sticks can be dangerous and inflict serious injury. Finally, because no two hand-carved sticks are exactly alike, they stress the difficulty of finding a backup stick identical to their main stick.

The nub of the argument favoring the wooden stick, according to Frank Benedict, has to do with the sort of game being played today, which diminishes the role of the defenseman: "In the transition of the game in field lacrosse, everybody seems to be emphasizing or specializing in offense. The question is, what about defense? There's two parts to the game, and on the defensive part of it the wooden stick can be used as a good defensive tool to maintain and control the attack and the midfield."

Benedict acknowledges that part of the "intimidating factor" of the wooden stick is the discomfort of being struck with one, but he minimizes the severity of the wounds inflicted: "The only injuries you can receive from the wooden stick is the bruises are probably a little more severe. It stands from nature; the wooden stick is slightly heavier and more rigid [than the plastic stick]."[49]

Kent Lyons, an Onondaga who played for the Iroquois Nationals in Australia during the World Cup games of 1990, recalls subtle racial slurs directed against the Indian team, prompted, he feels, by the Nationals' use of wooden sticks: "Yeh, it was terrible. But what did they blame it on? They blamed it on the wooden stick. That was their whole gripe, because all our defensemen had the six-foot-long Patterson [Tuscarora-made] wooden sticks. An interesting note: None of those sticks came back from Australia, either! Well, the Japanese were looking at them pretty good, too."

On the other side of the argument, plastic heads are easily broken and can inflict serious injury if they are. Behind the scenes in the rear of sporting goods stores are boxes upon boxes containing broken and mangled plastic heads. Benedict's son, Owen, a starter on his college team, gave an example of the potential danger of the plastic head. In a game played during his 1992 season, "one of our attackmen was in the process of beating a man when he broke his [plastic] stick, and when he shot the ball towards the net, his stick hit the defenseman in the cage, in his mask, and a piece of his stick went right through the mask and sliced the defenseman's face open right beneath the eye, with blood all over the place."

Benedict also argues that although the wooden stick may be heavier than the plastic one, there are certain advantages to it. Neither type of stick has a deep pocket, but a hard pass caught with the wooden stick, he argues, will not bounce out of the stick, so it is easier to catch and cradle the ball, whereas the frame of the plastic stick cups the ball only loosely: "The other key factor in the wooden stick is also the feel of the ball, whereby an individual can have more confidence in himself when he has a natural feeling in control of the ball because of one solid, single-grain frame, versus the two artificial pieces that make up the plastic stick."

Kent Lyons echoes Benedict's remarks about the "natural feel" of the wooden stick: "I mean you pick up a plastic stick and it's the same thing everywhere." He also agrees about the diminished role of defensemen. When he tried out for one professional team, he was told to abandon his wooden stick if he wished to make the team. "You have to use the plastic stick, you know, it's all supplied [by the manufacturer]. And the thing is, it's a cross-checking game and a slashing game; it takes the defense away and it's turning the game into a high-scoring spectator sport."

The universal feel of plastic sticks raises the question of individuality, which Indian people feel is inherent in the wooden stick. As Frank Benedict puts it, even though no two hand-carved sticks will be identical, still there is one in the pile just made for the particular player: "The wood stick is a personalized stick, and normally [a player has] to go through possibly two or three dozen to find a stick that is suitable to him because of the different feel, the different weight, the different balance, but within that two or three dozen somewhere in there his name is on it. . . . The plastic sticks are all the same; all there is is a choice of color."[50]

Benedict feels the built-in obsolescence of plastic sticks is attributable to profit-hungry manufacturers, who are constantly changing the design or color of the stick heads: "You know darned well that these kids are willing to try anything, so anything that the manufacturers do to change the design or color, everything is pointed at the market and increase in volume of sales. The life cycle of the stick will only last so long. The plastic is so adaptable, and the manufacturers have had a heyday, and they are constantly changing the design to improve the game or to have more control without any consideration to the other producers, where the sidewalls either have taken different shapes, or the thickness of the sidewalls to give it more ball control or make it very hard to dislodge a ball from the defensive point of view."[51]

The adaptability of the plastic head is freely acknowledged even by non-Indian players. Despite regulations governing width of the stick's head, shape, ball retention, and such, players freely work the easily pliable plastic to suit individual purposes. In so doing, they risk penalties if referees in their random stick checks catch them with an illegally shaped plastic head. (Referees become suspicious of players who are scoring frequently.) According to Joe Callahan, attackman at Georgetown University in the early 1990s, "Players will work hard at pinching the head, making it skinnier at the top by forcing the corners to pinch in. With the plastic you can bend it a little bit, bag it more so that it will shoot better. You create a little funnel, with no room for error. They'll tie the head together, put it in the oven to remold it, then in the refrigerator to cool it back down."[52] Indian players are aware of these practices and view the regulations as merely part of a larger conspiracy to eliminate the wooden stick. Remarked Rex Lyons: "You can tell it's just a corporate thing, because the referees . . . half the guys that use the plastic sticks, they all bent their heads in anyways, so they're not following that regulation anyway. You know the rule is just there for probably the reason that it makes the wooden stick hard to get made."

Does the wooden stick have any future in the men's field game? As of this writing, Frank Benedict has applied for an NCAA rule change that would accommodate a new wooden model he has developed through experimentation. The new design of his hickory stick is much lighter—only two ounces heavier than the plastic stick—and smaller. It is easier to handle than the old wooden stick, and he claims that there is even greater feeling and control of the ball. Like the plastic stick, the head of his new model is universal, the only difference being a short or long shaft available in the defenseman's stick. In requesting the rule variance, he is only asking for a fair chance to share the lucrative men's field stick market. He also insists that the price of his new wooden stick can compete with the current price of the plastic stick. Benedict's request to the NCAA rules committee to grant him a variance on the six-and-a-half-inch measurement rule—from its present reading "from inside the walls" at the spoon end to "from outside to outside"—was tabled in the June 1993 meeting. A subcommittee was appointed to review all stick measurements and make proposals at the 1994 rules committee meeting.

Beyond commercial considerations, from the Indian standpoint there is a spiritual aspect to the traditional wooden lacrosse stick. Rex Lyons, whose grandfather, a renowned goalie, was buried clutching his trusted Onondaga lacrosse stick in his hands, puts it this way: "What I was taught, it all comes from the stick. The reason you use a wooden stick is because in the center of that tree is what they call a heart, the heart of the tree, and that's your link between the natural world and what you're doing."[53]

In 1990 a milestone in the history of lacrosse was reached when the Iroquois Nationals traveled to Perth, Australia, to compete in the lacrosse World Games. This marked the first time that Indians had been accepted for official international competition in more than a century. Although the team failed to win any matches, it was a symbolic victory for them. As one team member said, "Some people were disheartened because they thought we were expected to win one, at least one. But actually, when you think about it, we did win something, because we participated in it. That was a big win itself."[54]

The World Games were established by the international lacrosse community principally because the sport has been systematically excluded from the Olympics. Actually, lacrosse did enjoy a short career in the Olympics as part of the 1904 St. Louis and 1908 London events, since in those days the host country determined the program. But when the game moved outside America and the Commonwealth, lacrosse was dropped.

Historical events and social changes adversely affected the chances of lacrosse's being accepted for Olympic status. Despite being the "national sport," the Canadian game actually experienced a decline beginning in the 1900s. The summer season was short, and as more urbanites acquired vehicles, they departed the large cities for summer vacation spots. Also, baseball was beginning to compete seriously with lacrosse in Canada, and football was making inroads as well. (An entry for 3 April 1895 in the MALA minutes books noted, "Mr Whyte suggested shortening the season so that it would not interfere with football.") The split in the lacrosse community over the amateur/professional issue fragmented efforts to promote the game, and World War I had a disruptive effect on sports in general.

In 1925 attempts were made to re-create the Canadian Lacrosse Association. But probably the one development that most seriously affected the game for whites and Indians alike was the emergence of box lacrosse in the 1930s. From that point on, two worlds of lacrosse evolved—the Canadian, which completely abandoned the field game in favor of the box game, and the American, which continued to promote and develop field lacrosse. Most Indian players took up box lacrosse, and that was one reason the Iroquois Nationals had difficulties in the 1990 World Games—they were used to a different style of play.

Box lacrosse was the invention of promoters desiring to capitalize on the many indoor rinks available in Canada, as hockey rapidly caught on. Contemplating potential revenue from idle rinks, they combined aspects of Canada's two most popular sports—lacrosse and hockey—and created indoor lacrosse, or boxla, as it was known for a while. It was a totally new game, emphasizing speed and action; with its ruggedness and absence of rules against slashing, cross-checking, and offsides, the game was a far cry from the gentlemen's club sport envisioned by George Beers seventy years earlier. It had the same blue-collar appeal that violent contact sports, like hockey and professional football, continue to exhibit. By the mid-1930s box lacrosse had become the official sport of the Canadian Lacrosse Association.

Meanwhile, Indian teams continued to play competitively against each other, usually on a national or a reservation level, but in the early 1970s the Iroquois decided to form their own box league. It was from this organization that the impetus arose to create a "national" Iroquois team that would include players from all six nations. The development was also partly an outgrowth of a period of Indian activism, which reflected much of the social unrest of the Vietnam era. Still, the formation of a national team in 1983 followed the ancient pattern of Indian alliances in putting together teams for "great" games of the past. According to Oren Lyons, this new national unity of Iroquois was a natural expression of their traditional lifestyle: "When you talk about lacrosse, you talk about the lifeblood of the Six Nations. . . . The game is ingrained into our culture and our systems and our lives. . . . There are two times of the year that stir the blood . . . in the fall, for the hunt, and now [in spring] for lacrosse."[55]

Lyons, a Faithkeeper at Onondaga and a former Syracuse player, together with Rick Hill and Wes Patterson from Tuscarora, were the principal founders of the Iroquois Nationals (Figure 71). The intent from the beginning was to gain official recognition from the non-Indian amateur lacrosse community and become eligible to compete in the World Games. Lyons functioned simultaneously as coach and political voice for the cause. The best Iroquoian players were recruited from high schools and colleges, and they traveled considerable distances to practice together. In the fall of 1985 they toured England, winning three of five games and playing the English national team to a tie. In 1986 they competed against the Australian national team.

But once again Indian players faced the same problem that had led to their exclusion in 1867. Financial support was needed for uniforms, travel, equipment, and the like. With promotional videotapes, Lyons and Hill went to corporations for help, but they were often met with skepticism. Remembers Lyons's son: "It was hard to sell. It sounded pretty good, you know, but we were just so new. We were untested."

When the Australian 1990 trip was being planned, each player had to raise his own $1,200 for travel to the event. Organizers had to skimp in putting together practice sessions by relying on the traditional pattern of Indian hospitality. Said one, "The way that we cut

expenses was, wherever the practice was held, that community would feed the players. I think the only thing that we'd actually get would be gas mileage, and that would be it, and then we'd be fed there, just to cut some corners. Everybody was just scraping every last penny." But the funds were ultimately forthcoming, and the Iroquois Nationals traveled bearing Iroquois, not American or Canadian, passports.

One of the symbolic high points of the trip was the customary performance of national anthems for each country represented. Apparently this matter had been overlooked before the team arrived, but a Seneca member of the team suddenly came forward with a traditional Indian Flag Song that he had on tape and offered the team its use. Another player describes the pride he felt the first time it was played, even though he was unfamiliar with the song: "We needed this national anthem, and this guy says, 'Here's my song, would you use it? I'd like you to use it if you want to.' It turns out that's the one we used, but it was pretty weird to hear our national anthem, so-to-speak, in its earliest form, because who knows if it's going to be the one for all time? We had a tape of it, everybody had a tape. It was pretty powerful the first time just to be standing there [when it was played]." Kent Lyons summed up his emotions when the Iroquois players stood at attention before the game: "To hear that anthem and then to see the purple flag with the [Indian] insignia on there. That's really where I understood then, at that point, what had been going on and where I was actually standing and being part of history."[56]

Figure 71 • The Iroquois Nationals in Los Angeles for the Jim Thorpe Memorial Games, a special event preceding the 1984 Summer Olympics. In front, from left: Sid Hill (Onondaga), flag-bearer; Dave Bray (Seneca), in jersey; Lee Lyons (Onondaga), in traditional dress; Greg Tarbell (Mohawk), in jersey; Coach Oren Lyons (Onondaga), in vest. Lee Lyons holds an Iroquois headdress that the team donated to the International Lacrosse Federation.

The acceptance of the Iroquois Nationals by the lacrosse community marks a turning point in the history of Indian lacrosse. Tom Hayes, coach at Rutgers University and vice president of the Lacrosse Foundation, as early as 1986 declared that the Nationals were not only up to international standards of play but were of symbolic importance to the sport: "They add something to the pageantry of the game. This is an original American game. Not to have original Americans playing it is ludicrous."[57]

The successful creation of the Iroquois Nationals has also sparked a Junior Nationals team composed mostly of Indian high school players who train together in the summer. Their inspiration for joining identifies them with the Nationals and provides a much-needed goal for many. Kent Lyons remarks: "Some of the older kids, they don't even wait for me to talk to them, they're already coming to me, 'Kent, what's the next thing happening? Is the Nationals still going?' They're all over, they really want to be part of it."[58] Ansley Jemison credits his experience with the Junior Nationals for rapidly increasing the skills that he brings to his high school team. He had already trained with the Junior Nationals on longstick defense even before starting Canandaigua Academy as a freshman: "I think I had a few more advantages over a lot of guys coming out this year because I played for the Iroquois National Junior Team, and it was just like playing two seasons in one year."[59]

These newly established Indian teams still face the difficulties of the players' living considerable distances from each other throughout New York State. Communication between them is difficult, and travel for practices is both time-consuming and expensive. Whatever problems still face the Iroquois Nationals, the team is definitely a focal point for Indian pride and could serve as a model for an Indian lacrosse revitalization elsewhere in North America, as Indian people continue to take their social and cultural matters into their own hands. The rise of Indian lacrosse among the young people may go a long way toward solving the problems faced by Indians in white schools, the lack of respect for their culture and history coupled with racism and an expectation of failure. For Oren Lyons the experience with the Iroquois Nationals addresses these problems and returns the game to those who originated it: "This team is so important because it's a place where we can prove ourselves without all those [non-Indian] rules jammed at us. . . . When they say you've got to be an American college boy to be an all-American at lacrosse, that's a subtle way of controlling and directing us."[60]

Niagara-Wheatfield High School, 1991

I was returning from research on the Six Nations Reserve in Ontario for a program on contemporary Indian music for the Smithsonian's annual Festival of American Folklife. With time to spare before flying from Buffalo back to Washington, I contacted my friend Emmett Printup, who at the time was the varsity lacrosse coach at Niagara-Wheatfield High School, directly across the road from the Tuscarora Reservation where he grew up. We had known each other since his graduation in 1985 from Syracuse University, where he had been the last Indian to play for Coach Simmons.

Although I had never seen Emmett play for Syracuse, he had subsequently joined the Washington Wave of the Major Indoor Lacrosse League franchise together with his Syracuse teammate Brad Kotz, and the two of them continued to play until the Washington franchise became defunct as a result of poor game attendance. Because he stayed overnight at my house whenever he had a game, I had an opportunity to have Emmett examine the old and poorly documented Iroquois lacrosse sticks in the Smithsonian collections. Thus began a continuing friendship, centering around the game, and together we started to formulate plans for including Indian lacrosse as part of a folklife festival program which I was to curate in 1989. That program would focus on the issues of access to and continuity of Indian culture.

Lacrosse was a perfect example of the Indians' loss of recognition for something that once had been solely theirs—a contribution to the sports world not overlooked but instead usurped by non-Indians. I felt that it was important to remind visitors to the festival that lacrosse was an Indian game, so we planned to construct a lacrosse box in the middle of the National Mall and invite two Iroquois teams to give demonstration matches. There were two points that I wished to make in team selection: First, Indian kids grow up playing lacrosse as naturally as inner-city youth grow up playing basketball, and second, it was traditional among Indian people for community or national teams to play their counterparts. We invited two teams made up of nine- and ten-year-olds—one from Tuscarora to be selected and coached by Emmett, the other from Onondaga—Bossy Bucktooth's "Washington Bunch." Their competitions on the Mall were successfully complemented by Mohawk Frank Benedict and his family, who demonstrated traditional Iroquois stick making.

Emmett had since married and fathered Emmett, Jr., who was already familiar with his dad's stick and his passion for the game (Figure 72). He often brought his young son to high school practices and admonished him to keep his eye on the ball and make sure he didn't get trampled by the action. "Like if the defensemen are doing shots and full clear passes, whatever group's near my child, I have him watch the balls that go his way," Emmett laughed. "So they all get to play goalie for a little bit here and there, depends what line they're in, or what line he's in."

As we drove north from Buffalo that afternoon, I talked with Emmett about his lacrosse career. Compared with other Indian kids, he was a latecomer to the sport. Whereas most Indian children start playing pickup games on the reservation as toddlers, Emmett didn't start until he was thirteen, when his aunt took him to Canada to watch his cousin Jimmy Bissell play. Unlike Emmett, Jimmy had started as a lacrosse player when he was four or five. And unlike most other Tuscarora, neither Emmett's father nor his grandfather had played the game. His father had in fact been forbidden to play, for the grandmother associated lacrosse with general boozing and so she directed him to baseball and track.

Emmett began his career in a Canadian summer box league, but it was at Niagara-Wheatfield High School that he mastered the field game. After three years on the varsity squad he earned all-American honors his senior year—which was enough for Syracuse to invite him to try out. His relocation from western New York, however, demanded some changes in his playing techniques. "Since the game was fairly new in the area, the field-stick skills weren't as polished as, say, in the Syracuse or Rochester area. In the western New York league, everyone's just starting to learn the field game, so there weren't really any left-handed or right-handed players yet. It was difficult for me to adjust, but I got going, the left-handed started coming around for me. There's a big difference in the strategy of each game. Field's more open. Box lacrosse is a grind-it-out game; field lacrosse is a finesse, running game."

I broached the subject of Emmett's different coaching experiences—Indian teenagers on the one hand, who made up about 75 percent of the team at Niagara-Wheatfield, and white kids at the private Park School in Buffalo, on the other. The principal difference, as he saw it, was that whites picked up lacrosse in school because it was the "in" thing; on the reservation the game was simply a natural part of everyday life: "It's just like smiling; playing lacrosse and smiling are brothers on the reservation." But there were inequities, he

Figure 72 • Emmett Printup and his son relax with Emmett's stick.

found: "Indians have such raw talent. They have a natural niche for lacrosse but they don't really push themselves physically to get to the best shape they can be in. You know, when some do do that, they just stand out from all the players. At Niagara-Wheatfield you get a lot of Indians that just want to come out and play, 'cause they've been fooling around with their sticks their whole lives. They do have good stickwork, but some rely on the stick rather than 'the wheels.' In box that can work sometimes, but hardly ever in field. The only difference with the white kids is that they always wanted to learn. They just want to keep working at the sport and get better, because this was their first experience with lacrosse. It was a new toy for them. The native kids already had that toy; some just didn't want to take it that much farther. The native kids that *do* go on to college, the situation reverses roles for them."

Here Emmett spoke from his personal experience at Syracuse. "You don't see hardly any native players out in your major schools anymore. There are so many great native box players around, but they just don't have any desire for further education. The one that does decide to take his box talents to that caliber is a real treat to watch. At the same time, he's there because he wants to be there, he's in shape, he likes to play ball, so he could be a power. I say 'could' because it comes down to politics. Playing time reflects where you come from; the greater the field reputation, the greater the playing time. It's a shame, because box players could and will have a big influence on the field game in the future. I know it."

Emmett left the Washington Wave after two seasons—principally because it paid so little and the commute from Buffalo usually ate up his earnings. He was forced to supplement his income by trying different businesses that he either started or worked for—some nonprofit and not from choice. He tried everything from T-shirt printing to advertising, then eventually the tax-free cigarette business on reservations. Soon Emmett returned to the high school where he had played, first as assistant lacrosse coach, then as head coach.

We entered the locker room about three-thirty and headed for his small office. The assistant coach was filling out scouting reports, and Emmett immediately asked him: "Hey, Scott. Any of the kids get into trouble at school today? Anybody that didn't show up or missed classes? We gotta be at full strength on Friday when we butt heads with Orchard Park." Scott replied that most of the team were already dressing for practice and that he knew of no particular problems aside from one lingering injury that still needed a week or so to heal. "OK, then let's get Travis and Wayne to run out and tell the guys we got to get on the practice field in ten minutes. And we gotta try to scrape up some practice balls, find out where the rest of the balls are. Have the captains take the boys around the park a couple of times for a warmup, and we'll meet over by the tennis courts for line drills."

A few latecomers were hurrying to dress as we left the locker room. Emmett looked in the direction of the junior varsity field to make sure the coach had all his team there and was running practice. The varsity had returned from their laps, so Emmett ordered them into lines for the requisite stretching. "All right, guys, bring it on over here, let's go." Wayne and Travis positioned themselves in front and began to lead the exercise. "Oh, oh, Tom, see a couple of guys over there—look like they're dogging? Kinda need to be pushed down a little bit. C'mon, let's get into it, guys, we got a big game—Orchard Park's in first place, and they really knocked the heck out of the team that we played last week. We barely beat them, so let's get pumped up."

After the stretching, Coach Printup blew his whistle to call the team around him for further instructions (Figure 73). "Hey, Travis, take the attack behind the goal, let's get some line drills going. And Wayne, take the middies in the middle, and Lance, take the defense just past midfield. Let's get some line drills going here." Turning to me, he added, "I'll get the balls and warm up the goalie—seems to be my specialty." Having witnessed Emmett's shot hundreds of times, I was concerned for the goalie's safety. With his huge upper torso, he had a real power shot when he got cranked up—it was once clocked at 94 miles per hour. He assured me that he would take it easy on his goalie but needed to move out to midfield to determine how "warm" he was.

Following fast-break drills, Emmett would go over scouting reports with the team. "Talk to the guys when they're still in line and tell them what this Orchard Park player likes

Figure 73 • Printup and the varsity Niagara-Wheatfield lacrosse team, spring 1989.

to do, give certain jersey numbers, what hands they are, righty or lefty. This way they kinda judge what they're going to do on the field and how they're going to defend against the other team."

It was time for scrimmaging. He began by pitting his first attack line against his first defense. "All right, let's get it going, c'mon, let's get the ball hot, let's do some hitting and clean contact." He grinned at me. "The boys like to scrimmage. Friends or not, they like to hit each other. Wakes them up a little bit."

A couple of players seemed less than enthusiastic about scrimmage. "What do you do with laggards?" I asked. Emmett was quick to respond. "When I see someone dogging it, I usually send them around 'the jungle.' The jungle's around the football field, around the outer fence, and there's thorns in the path." He laughed, "You never know what's back there, and there's dens near the path, and you don't know what kinda animal. A bear could probably come out of those holes, who the hell knows. When you come through there, it's like torture; you gotta use your stick to defend yourself running around the path. It's all the way around the whole stadium, the whole football field. It was a popular form of punishment when I was in high school, 'cause there were a lot of us knuckleheads that played on that '81 team. I really believe all lacrosse players have a little 'King of the Jungle' in them, and everybody in general has a little lacrosse player in them, so I just yell, 'Hey, so and so, take a jungle!' When they come back, they're a little peppier."

Looking over the team, I was reminded of the racial mix that made up the high school and how the players' roster reflected it. There were descendants of Italian immigrants alongside Tuscarora Indian kids clearly of mixed ancestry, some bearing Irish names like McKie or Sheehan. Certain players bore distinctly Indian features and had unusually dark complexions for Tuscarora. Having migrated from their former homelands in North Carolina in the early eighteenth century, the Tuscarora were the last nation to join the Iroquois Confederacy, in about 1722; they are generally more fair-skinned than their Seneca, Onondaga, or Mohawk compatriots—so much so that other Iroquois sometimes jokingly refer to them as "the Sun-Screen People."

Printup's co-captains were certainly from the reservation. Travis Kilgour, in particular, was a really impressive player, and I asked Emmett about his future. He replied, "Travis has a great opportunity to be a superstar in the field game. His strengths are his size—he's about six foot three, weighs about 235. And he can play both right- and left-handed, which is hard to find coming from western New York. He's pretty much my utility man. He's a great attackman, but I put him on midfield 'cause we were very shallow. And one game I put him in at goal, late in the second half, 'cause he got hurt in the leg and couldn't run. I couldn't afford to have him out. So at 235 pounds and a great stick, not to forget six feet three inches tall, it was the only move. He only let one goal in that quarter. His future? I think maybe he's looking at going to community college, then to Nazareth where his brothers Rich and Darris played briefly. Someone's just gotta give him a shot, come practice, and try out for their team, see how he likes the university setting. But physically he's got it down."

Scrimmage was nearly over, so we started to walk out on the field. Emmett turned from me and, looking straight ahead, continued to extol Travis's talent. "Yeah, he's my utility man; someone's just gotta give him the shot." Rather wistfully he added, "Too bad he's an Indian."

APPENDIX A

Lacrosse Legends

Lacrosse occurs in a surprisingly large number of traditional American Indian legends. It may be the focus of the story—a moral lesson, a historical or etiological explanation—or it may simply be part of a string of episodes involving the protagonist. A reading of some of these rich and colorful tales will illustrate the place of lacrosse in Indian life.

One must always be cautious in accepting the accuracy of published versions of Indian legends. Early collectors of texts in oral tradition often abbreviated, embellished, "cleaned up," or otherwise changed what was told them. The legends certainly lost much in translation from the original Indian language into English, and it is nearly impossible to communicate the style of a storyteller's delivery in print. (The linguist William Jones attempts to do so in No. 9 below.) Because no two narrators would give identical renderings, collectors sometimes combined several versions to provide what they considered "the full tale." With these caveats in mind, the reader may enjoy considering the following stories.

NO. I (EASTERN CHEROKEE)

According to a Cherokee myth, the animals once challenged the birds to a great ball play. The wager was accepted, the preliminaries were arranged, and at last the contestants assembled at the appointed spot—the animals on the ground, while the birds took position in the tree-tops to await the throwing up of the ball. On the side of the animals were the bear, whose ponderous weight bore down all opposition; the deer, who excelled above all others in running; and the terrapin, who was invulnerable to the stoutest blows. On the side of the birds were the eagle, the hawk, and the great *Tlániwă*—all noted for their swiftness and power of flight. While the [birds] were preening their feathers and watching every motion of their adversaries below, they noticed two small creatures, hardly larger than mice, climbing up the tree on which was perched the leader of the birds. Finally they reached the top and humbly asked the captain to be allowed to join in the game. The captain looked at them a moment and, seeing that they were four-footed, asked them why they did not go to the animals where they properly belonged. The little things explained that they had done so, but had been laughed at and rejected on account of their diminutive size. On hearing their story the bird captain was disposed to take pity on them, but there was one serious difficulty in the way—how could they join the birds when they had no wings? The eagle, the hawk, and the rest now crowded around, and after some discussion, it was decided to try and make wings for the little fellows. But how to do it! All at once, by a happy inspiration, one bethought himself of the drum which was to be used in the dance. The head was made of ground-hog leather, and perhaps a corner could be cut off and utilized for wings. No sooner suggested than done. Two pieces of leather taken from the drum-head were cut into shape and attached to the legs of one of the small animals, and thus originated *Tlameha,* the bat. The ball was now tossed up, and the bat was told to catch it, and his expertness in dodging and circling about, keeping the ball constantly in motion and never allowing it to fall to the ground, soon convinced the birds that they had gained a most valuable ally.

They next turned their attention to the other little creature; and now behold a worse difficulty! All their leather had been used in making wings for the bat, and there was no time to send for more. In this dilemma it was suggested that perhaps wings might be made by stretching out the skin of the animal itself. So two large birds seized him from opposite sides with their strong bills, and by tugging and pulling at his fur for several minutes succeeded in stretching the skin between the fore and hind feet until at last the thing was done and there was *Tewa,* the flying squirrel. Then the bird captain, to try him, threw up the ball, when the flying squirrel, with a graceful bound, sprang off the limb and, catching it in his teeth, carried it through the air to another tree-top a hundred feet away.

When all was ready, the game began, but at the very outset the flying squirrel caught the ball and carried it up a tree, then threw it to the birds, who kept it in the air for some time, when it dropped; but just before it reached the ground the bat seized it, and by his dodging and doubling kept it out of the way of even the swiftest of the animals until he finally threw it in at the goal, and thus won the victory for the birds. Because of their assistance on this occasion, the ball player invokes the aid of the bat and the flying squirrel and ties a small piece of the bat's wing to his ball stick or fastens it to the frame on which the sticks are hung during the dance.[1]

NO. 2 (OJIBWE)

Down the hill there was a village with all kinds of wigwams. One of them was pretty long; it must have been a *midewigan,* a Medicine Dance lodge. Pretty soon an old lady came out of the long wigwam and came running up to the fire. She didn't expect to see anyone there, but then she saw Wak-ayabide and could see his guts in plain sight. She saw his teeth too. She was scared and ran back down the hill and jumped into the wigwam. She nudged her old man. "I've seen a *manido* [spirit] by the fire. His guts and teeth are in plain sight; he's naked."

The old man, who was the chief, said, "There's a stranger by the woodpile."

His son, a clever boy, jumped up and said, "Well, well. It can't be my brother-in-law."

Some other old fellows said, "Here, here, young man; don't talk that way. That's a *manido*. If you talk like that, he'll come and kill us some day. Be careful. A *manido* has come to us, so we'd better be good to him."

Some kids said, "I wouldn't call him *manido*. His guts are in plain sight."

The old man said, "Be good to that man! Don't talk like that!"

The young man had three sisters. His name was Madjikiwis. He said, "I'm going to go and look at my brother-in-law." He took up his [war] club. It had a big ball at the end of it; when he picked it up, sparks flew all over the room. That's how powerful he was. There was thunder and lightning.

When he got to Wakayabide, he said, "My friend, I want you to have a new home. When we go into the wigwam, there's a heavy-set woman; that's my sister. The next one is a medium-sized woman. The next is a smaller one. I'll give you the smallest. I want you to be my brother-in-law. When you go into the wigwam, go to my sisters. Pay no attention to what people say. When you get to the first one, the fat one will say, 'Stop here and sit down; I'm the one you're going to marry.' Just keep right on going. The next one will say the same thing. She'll want you to sit next to her. But keep right on going to the smallest one. That's the sister I want you to marry. All right, get up and follow me."

He got up. People all came and stared at them. The little kids shouted, "Do you call him *manido* with his guts and teeth in plain sight? I don't call him *manido*."

The old fellows said, "Here, here. You be quiet. *Manido* will fix you after a while, if you talk like that."

When they came to the doorway, the young chief went to his place, and the other man turned the way he'd told him to go. The man came to the big fat woman. She said, "Sit down here; that's where you're supposed to sit." He kept right on going. The second one said, "So you've come to me now. Sit right here with me." He kept on until he came to a little tiny woman. She said nothing, and he sat right down.

He looked around at all the things hanging up that Madjikiwis owned. When his brother-in-law hung up his club, he saw the sparks fly out.

His wife started to teach him: "We have all kinds of games here. I want you to be careful. The people here are dangerous. They kill each other. You won't live very long if you play in any of their games."

The three sisters were going with some men, powerful men. Everybody heard that Madjikiwis had a new brother-in-law, so they all wanted to see him. The first man who came said, "I've come to see my brother." He was a great big tall man. There was a great big rock inside the wigwam. This man came and sat on the rock. He was carrying a big tobacco pouch. He talked to the man: "I'm glad you've come; I'm glad to see you. We have a lot of fun here, lots of games. We'd like you to play with us." Then he said, "Now I'm going to show you my power." He picked up the big rock—solid rock—and tossed it up and down. He walked to the man, playing with it to scare him. He almost dropped it. Then he set it down. He said, "That's my power. That's the kind of man I'd be if I stayed with that woman."

Wakayabide filled up his pipe with tobacco. Then he tightened the cord on his bow. He had to get his revenge. This man was naked. Wakayabide was going to shoot him between the legs. He wasn't going to hurt him, just graze him. He pulled the bow, and the arrow just grazed him. The man took his tobacco and ran outside. Outside you could hear him laughing: "Ha ha ha! I've found a man who's better than I am. I give up! He's a *manido*. I won't bother him anymore."

The next day another man came to see him. The first man that had come in was a grizzly bear. The next one who came in was a polar bear. Wakayabide found out that those people changed into animals. This man said, "I've come to see my brother." He had a tobacco pouch and a long pipe too. He sat on the big rock there. He said, "I've got to show you my power." He scratched the stone, and you could see flames springing out of it. It didn't bother those people. They just sat there. Rocks flew around. Then he said, "That's how I'd be if I knew I'd have that woman." Then he sat down to fill up his pipe.

Wakayabide got his bow and arrows out and shot this man by the head, just shaved his skull. Then that man jumped up and ran out. Outside he laughed: "My brother is a better man than I am. I'll give up, and I won't bother him anymore."

There was one more visitor, who came the next day: a human being this time, a well-built fellow. His wife knew about what would happen and told him: "The men that go [have sex] with me are going to try out your power. Be careful. Say nothing to anybody."

This man came in. When he raised the curtain of the wigwam, a flood of water came in—red clay water. That's the power he had. The current was strong. Wakayabide was just about to float away, when his wife grabbed him and tied him with a sash and held him. He could hardly get his breath. He was near drowning when the water went down. It dried in no time. The other people in there didn't even feel it. They just sat there. It was nothing to them. Then the man sat on the rock, filled up his pipe, and said, "That's the kind of man I'd be if I married this woman."

Wakayabide got out his bow and arrows again. This time he shot the rock right in the center. He said in his mind, "A little piece of rock will be in that man's body." That's what happened.

That man said, "I can't beat that man! He's too good for me. I give up!"

Three men had tried to drive that man out, but they couldn't do it. He had too much power.

The next day, early in the morning, there was an announcer going around the village. I suppose the wigwams were in a circle. He announced: "Today we have a lacrosse game. Madjikiwis' brother-in-law must play too."

Wakayabide's wife said, "Be careful! I don't want you to go. They'll kill you."

The man laughed. "They can't kill me. I'll go and look on, anyway. If I don't play, I'll look on."

Madjikiwis was losing the game all the time. He lost all of his clothing. He wanted his brother-in-law to play for him. That's what he had figured before, although he hadn't said so.

Everybody was out in the field. Wakayabide stood with his bow and arrow, watching. Pretty soon one of the fellows, the grizzly bear, came over to him. "Here, brother." He gave him a lacrosse stick.

"I don't know how to play. I can't play."

"No, no. You must play."

"All right, I'll try."

He took the lacrosse stick. This man had left his belt in the wigwam, so the wolf wasn't there. Out in the woods the wolf had told him never to leave the belt and always take it along.

The ball was coming. His partner said, "Grab the ball and run!"

He grabbed the ball with his club and ran for the goal. The other man followed. Instead of taking the ball away, the bear jumped on his bare back and tore his skin to the bone. He dropped dead right there. When the game was over, there was no Wakayabide coming home. They must have cut him up into pieces and shared the meat.

The woman was worrying about him. She asked people where he was, but they didn't tell her. That night all the families feasted on that meat. The man's wife was worried. She couldn't sleep. The wolf knew that something was wrong with his master. He started to howl inside the belt. The woman heard that noise. She kept quiet and listened. It sounded like a wolf howling. At first it was like a wolf way off in the woods. Then she saw that it was coming from the belt. She found a little pocket there. She opened it and found a tiny dog. She set it on the ground. She knew right away that it belonged to that man.

The dog shook and began to grow. Then he dashed outside right away. He ran all over town. He got all the bones and put them together in the shape of a man. There was one joint he couldn't find—the elbow. He ran all over but couldn't find it. Then he saw smoke going up out in the woods. There was a young woman living by herself out in the woods (in a seclusion hut for menstruating girls). She had a piece of meat too—the elbow. The dog ran over there. The woman had the bone he was looking for. He sat by the doorway, looking at the woman, wishing for her to throw the bone down. She chewed and kept saying, "My, my! that tastes good. I can't stop chewing." She saw the dog and said, "I guess he wants that bone. I won't give it to him, though; it tastes too good." The dog moved a little nearer, but she said, "Go outside! I want that bone myself."

The dog got tired of waiting, so he jumped at her, grabbed the bone, and dashed off. Now he had all the bones in the shape of a man. Then he hollered. The bones humped together. He hollered again. Flesh came on the bones. He hollered again. Then his eyes opened up.

The people were surprised to hear that dog holler. One of the old fellows, who was trying to make the young people behave, said, "I wouldn't be surprised if that man is coming alive again."

When the wolf hollered the fourth time, Wakayabide's breath began to come. The wolf said, "You didn't listen to me, my grandchild, so I came to save you. That's what happens when you don't listen. Get up now. We'll go home." His wife was glad to see him again. She said, "I found that little dog in your belt. He's saved your life. Always take him along now."

The next day the announcer went around again. "Today we have another lacrosse game. Madjikiwis' brother-in-law ought to play too."

His wife said to him, "Don't go. They'll kill you again."

He said, "No, I want to go." He wanted to get his revenge on that fellow who had killed him.

That morning he put on his belt and went out. He was looking for that fellow he'd played with the day before. "Hey, brother," he said, "come here. I want to play with you."

The bear said, "Oh, fine!"

The ball came up. The bear said, "I'll show you how to play!" He took the ball. Wakayabide followed him with two arrows in his hands.

They used to play for a live person. That's how they got their food, their meat. They ate each other.

Wakayabide jumped on the bear with his two arrows and buried them in his skin. He tore the bear to pieces with the arrows and killed him. Then he walked away. The other people cut up the bear and cooked him. They passed the meat around to all the families. He had some of it too. It tasted good, nice and fat.

That man came alive again the next day too. He was a powerful man.[2]

NO. 3 (EASTERN CHEROKEE)

This story, a variant of No. 1, depicts in some detail the plight of the rodents and how they were converted into bats by the birds:

The [ceremonial ball game] dance was over and they were all pruning their feathers up in the trees and waiting for the captain [the Eagle] to give the word when here came two little things hardly larger than field mice climbing up the tree in which sat perched the bird captain. At last they reached the top, and creeping along the limb to where the Eagle captain sat they asked to be allowed to join in the game. The captain looked at them, and seeing that they were four-footed, he asked why they did not go to the animals, where they belonged. The little things said that they had, but the animals had made fun of them and driven them off because they were so small. Then the bird captain pitied them and wanted to take them.

But how could they join the birds when they had no wings? The Eagle, the Hawk, and the others consulted and at last it was decided to make some wings for the little fellows. They tried for a long time to think of something they might do, until someone remembered the drum they had used in the dance. The [detachable rawhide] head was of ground-hog skin and maybe they could cut off a corner and make wings of it. So they took two pieces of leather from the drumhead and cut them into shape for wings, and stretched them with cane flints and fastened them on to the forelegs of one of the small animals, and in this way came *Tla'meha*, the Bat. They threw the ball to him and told him to catch it, and by the way he dodged and circled about, keeping the ball always in the air and never letting it fall to the ground, the birds soon saw that he would be one of their best men.[3]

NO. 4 (OJIBWE)

Once Wenebozhoo turned himself into a caribou and laid down and made believe he was dead. All fall and winter birds and animals came and ate from [his carcass]. But the turkey buzzard knew that Wenebozhoo was a spirit, so he stayed up in a tree until just bones were left, and not much meat. He thought Wenebozhoo was surely dead now, so he flew down and the only meat that was left was around the anus. He started eating that until his head was all inside. Then Wenebozhoo closed his anus and caught the head of the turkey buzzard inside. He then got up and walked to the village where the Indians were playing lacrosse. He asked if he could join, and they said, "Sure." While he was playing, he tripped and fell and the turkey buzzard slipped out and got away, but in the process his head and neck were scraped, so that is why the buzzard has a red and scabby neck today. He also smells because of that.[4]

NO. 5 (EASTERN CHEROKEE)

In addition to its appearance in animal and historical legends, lacrosse shows up in stories otherwise filled with magical occurrences and moral lessons. For example, around 1823 Haywood was told that in the distant past, lacrosse was played by the Cherokee only during a full moon because the moon presided over the game as a tutelary spirit.

In the time of Te-shy-ah-Natchee, two chiefs made a ball-play, at which all the red people attended, men, women, and children. The contest between the parties was very severe for a long time, when one of them got the advantage by the superior skill of a young man. His adversary on the other side, seeing no chance of success in fair play, attempted to cheat, when in throwing the ball, it stuck in the sky and turned into the appearance which the moon hath, to remind the Indians that cheating and dishonesty are crimes. When the moon becomes small and pale, it is because the ball has been handled by unfair play.

NO. 6 (CREEK)

An extraordinary lacrosse match occurs within the context of a long, fantastical story about a great gambler named Ûñtsaiyĭ', who whenever he loses can metamorphose and thereby make his escape. The episode is used to prove the bravery of a young man in his travels and provides insight into the close relationship between lacrosse and warfare. Born in the east and said to be a son of Thunder, the child from birth is afflicted with scrofula sores, which cover his body. He begins a journey to seek a father who can cure him. When he finds him, the father has the son boiled with certain roots and thrown into a river. When his wife finally retrieves the boy from the water, he has been miraculously cured of scrofula, and his skin is clear.

On the way home [the wife] told him, "When we go in, your father will put a new dress on you, but when he opens his box and tells you to pick out your ornaments, be sure to take them from the bottom. Then he will send for his other sons to play ball against you. There is a honey-locust tree in front of the house, and as soon as you begin to get tired strike at that and your father will stop the play, because he does not want to lose the tree."

When they went into the house, the old man was pleased to see the boy looking so clean, and said, "I knew I could soon cure those spots. Now we must dress you." He brought out a fine suit of buckskin, with belt and headdress, and had the boy put them on. Then he opened a box and said, "Now pick out your necklace and bracelets." The boy looked, and the box was full of all kinds of snakes gliding over each other with their heads up. He was not afraid, but remembered what the woman had told him, and plunged his hand to the bottom and drew out a great rattlesnake and put it around his neck for a necklace. He put down his hand again four times and drew up four copperheads and twisted them around his wrists and ankles. Then his father gave him a war club and said, "Now you must play a ball game with your two elder brothers. They live beyond here in the Darkening land, and I have sent for them." He said a ball game, but he meant that the boy must fight for his life. The young men came, and they were both older and stronger than the boy, but he was not afraid and fought against them. The thunder rolled and the lightning flashed at every stroke, for they were the young Thunders, and the boy himself was Lightning. At last he was tired from defending himself against the two, and pretended to aim a blow at the honey-locust tree. Then his father stopped the fight, because he was afraid the lightning would split the tree, and he saw that the boy was brave and strong.

After his father had armed him with secrets on how to win, the boy was then sent east to gamble against the famous Ûñtsaiyĭ'.[5]

NO. 7 (MENOMINEE)

A tradition of the origin of lacrosse among the Menominee was related to the ethnomusicologist Frances Densmore in the early 1920s by Mitchell Beaupre, as follows.

A man named Ac'kĭnĭt (Uncooked) had a dream. He had been hunting in the woods all winter and had a great deal of game hanging up. As it was time for sugar making, he thought he might as well stay for the sugar camp. The snow was deep. One night there was a severe storm, and the wigwam was bright with the lightning. Suddenly Ackinit heard a voice say, "Ackinit, go on top of the bluff where you killed the deer. We have left something there for you to show your friends every spring." Ackinit's oldest boy was about 6 years old and had never been in the deep woods with his father. Ackinit wanted to take his first child with him, so he told his wife about the voice that said "Something has been left for you on top of the bluff where you killed two deer."

Ackinit and his son traveled about 3 miles, then he said to the little boy, "Do you see that place? There is no snow up there. I brought you to carry what we find."

The boy said, "What shall we look for?" His father replied, "Medicine."

When Ackinit and his son reached the top of the bluff they found a big nest full of feathers. They were out of breath when they reached the top, and Ackinit saw the feathers shaking like snow that is blown by the wind. He stepped softly because the motion looked as though something alive was in the nest. Looking in, he saw a green egg, and a voice said, "Keep this and show it to your people every spring." The little boy carried the egg back to the sugar camp.

This egg was left by the Thunderers, who said, "We want tobacco. We live among the rocks, but your people have earth and can raise tobacco. Each person who comes to see this egg must give a little tobacco."

The next year, when they heard the first thunder, Ackinit called the people together and showed the egg. He collected tobacco and tossed it into the air for the Thunderers and talked about his dream.

After Ackinit died, the egg was in charge of his grandson, Wecananak- wut, who kept it in his medicine bag and showed it every year. Mitchell Beaupre said he had seen it many times and that it was about the size of a duck's egg. It was in the feathers, which once were white but had become yellow with age. Wecananakwut collected a great heap of tobacco and passed it around, both men and women smoking while he talked about Ackinit and his dream. He said, "We will have a lacrosse game tomorrow, and if I am telling the truth you will hear the Thunderers coming to their game." The weather was clear when they began the game, but soon they could see a little cloud next to the horizon, and by the time they made a goal there was thunder and rain. Then Wecananakwut always said, "Don't be afraid. We gave tobacco to our grandfather yesterday and he has come to the game." (Beaupre said that Wecananakwut always said "grandfather," but he meant the Thunderers.)

The informant said that the first lacrosse ball was made in imitation of the egg found by Ackinit, in accordance with the instructions of the Thun- derers. The inside was of basswood twine, wound solid, and the outside was made of the hide of the black squirrel.[6]

NO. 8 (MENOMINEE)

Now it happened that the beings above challenged the beings below to a mighty game of lacrosse. The beings below were not slow to accept the game and the goals were chosen, one at Detroit and the other at Chicago. The center of the field was at a spot called Kē'sosāsit ("where the sun is marked," [on the rocks] near Sturgeon Bay on Lake Michigan. The above beings called their servants, the thunderers, the eagles, the geese, the ducks, the pigeons, and all the fowls of the air to play for them, and the great white underground bear called upon the fishes, the snakes, the otters, the deer, and all the beasts of the field to take the part of the powers below.

When everything was arranged, and the two sides were preparing, Mä'näbus happened along that way. As he strolled by, he heard someone passing at a distance and whooping at the top of his voice. Curious to see who it was, Mä'näbus hastened over to the spot whence the noise emanated. Here he found a funny little fellow, like a tiny Indian, no other, however, than Näkuti, the sunfish. "What on earth is the matter with you?" queried Mä'näbus. "Why haven't you heard?" asked Sunfish, astonished. "Tomorrow there is going to be a ball game, and fishes and the beasts of the field will take the part of the powers below against the Thunderers and all the fowls, who are championing the powers above." "Oh ho!" said Mä'näbus, and the simple Näkuti departed, whooping with delight. "Well, well," thought Mä'näbus, "I must see this famous game, even if I was not invited."

The chiefs of the underworld left their homes in the waters and climbed high up on a great mountain where they could look over the whole field, and having chosen this spot they returned. Mä'näbus soon found their tracks and followed them to the place of vantage which they had selected. He judged by its appearance that they had decided to stay there, so he concluded that he would not be far away when the game commenced. Early next morning, before daybreak, he went to the place, and, through his magic power he changed himself into a tall pine tree, burnt on one side. At dawn, he heard a great hubbub and whooping. From everywhere he heard derisive voices calling "Hau! Hau! Hau!" and "Hoo! hoo! hoo!" to urge on the enemy. Then appeared the deer, the mink, the otters, and all the land beings and the fishes in human form. They arrived at their side of the field and took their places and all became silent for a time. Suddenly the sky grew dark, and the rush of many wings made a thunderous rumbling, above which rose whoops, screams, screeches, cackling, calling, hooting, all in one terrific bable [*sic*]. Then the thunderers swooped down, and the golden eagles, and the bald eagles, and the buzzards, hawks, owls, pigeons, geese, ducks, and all manner of birds, and took the opposite end of the field. Then silence dropped down once more, and the sides lined up, the weakest near the goals, the strongest in the center. Someone tossed the ball high in the air and a pell mell mêlée followed, with deafening howling and whoopings. Back and forth surged the players, now one side gaining, now the other. At last one party wrested the ball through the other's ranks and sped it toward the Chicago goal. Down the field it went, and Mä'näbus strained his eyes to follow its course. It was nearly at the goal, the keepers were rushing to guard it and in the midst of the brandished clubs, legs, arms, and clouds of dust something notable was happening that Mä'näbus could not see. In his excitement he forgot where he was and changed back into a man. Once in human shape he came to himself, and, looking about, noted that the onlookers had not discovered him. Fired by his lust for revenge he promptly took his bow, which he had kept with him all the time, strung it, and fired twice at each of the underground gods as they sat on their mountain. His arrows sped true, and the gods rushed for the water, falling all over themselves as they scurried down the hill. The impact of their diving caused great waves to roll down the lake toward the Chicago goal. Some of the players saw them coming, rolling high over the tree tops. "Mä'näbus, Mä'näbus!" they cried in breathless fright.

At once all the players on both sides rushed back to the centerfield to look. "What is the matter?" said everyone to everyone else. "Why it must have been Mä'näbus, he's done this, nobody else would dare to attack the underground gods." When the excited players reached the center of the field they found the culprit had vanished. "Let's all look for Mä'näbus," cried someone. "We will use the power of the water for our guide." So the players all waded into the water, and the water rose up and went ahead of them. It knew very well where Mä'näbus had gone.

In the meantime Mä'näbus was skipping away as fast as he could, for he was frightened at what the consequences of his rashness might be. All at once he happened to look back and saw the water flowing after him. He ran faster and faster, but still it came. He doubled, he zigzagged, he dodged, but still it came. He strained himself to his utmost speed and it gained on him. On, on, lead the chase, further, and further away.[7]

NO. 9 (OJIBWE)

Once upon a time, as the story goes, there lived some first-born sons; in a town they dwelt; exceedingly large was the town where they were. All sorts of things they did in the way of games; as often as the days came round, they played at games. Now, once (one of) the first-born announced that there would be a ball-game. Whereupon truly began they to get ready for the contest.

Now, another first-born (and his friends) did a little differently. Half of them were on one side to play ball (against the other half). One of the first-born took out the ball which they were to use, blue was the color of the ball. Thereupon said the first-born: "Towards the east will I play for goal," he said. "And you," he said to them against whom he was to play, "toward the west." Accordingly they picked out the men that were fleet of foot. On the morning of the next day they began (playing). And when they started the ball going, it was a long while before any one could make a goal. Along in the afternoon was when (one of the first-born) was being beaten by Winter-Wind. At last was the first-born being beaten, for Winter-Wind had made a goal on the side toward the west. And when the first-born was beaten, he was addressed by Winter-Wind saying: "Well, therefore have I beaten you," was the first-born told. "As soon as ever the wind blows from the east, then will foul weather hang aloft in this sky for the rain to fall. Therefore such is what I have won from you," he was told.

And that is what happens. When the wind blows from the east, then that is a sign for a bad day. It is because the first-born was once beaten in a contest.

He was not pleased to be beaten. Over again did the first-born wish to play. "Come, let us have another game!" said the first-born.

"Very well," he was told by Winter-Wind.

On the morrow they then took their places for another game of ball. "Towards the north will I play for goal," said the first-born. "And you, Winter-Wind, towards the south do you play for goal," he said to Winter-Wind.

So when they began playing, they were cheered on by the yells of them who were watching them. All day long against them they carried the ball back and forth and all around. Red was the color of the ball. When it was getting well on towards the evening, then again was the first-born being beaten. At length again did Winter-Wind make a goal at the end towards the south. Thereupon once more was the first-born addressed: "Well, therefore again have I beaten you," he was told. "As soon as ever the wind blows from the north, then will all your youths flee away, but of me will my youths not be afraid."

Now, there were all the birds that fly about in the air, it was they that were in the contest. All the birds of summer with whom the first-born played were the ones that feared the winter. This, then, was the first-born told at the time: "I am Winter-Wind. Not from me would flee my youths."

They are the birds that pass the winter here; it was on their side that Winter-Wind played. And that is how it came to pass that some of the birds go south in the winter-time; and some do not go away, for they were the youths of Winter-Wind.

So thereupon the first-born gave up (the contest), whereas they then lived together again.[8]

NO. 10 (SENECA)

When the old man came home he said to his son, "I thank you for outrunning your enemy; there has never been anyone to outrun him; all have been beaten. Since the wager was heads, you can take his life whenever you wish." The son asked the man whether he had done his best. "No," said he, "I used about half my strength." "Very well," said the man; "he has another game to propose. He will never stop proposing trials of strength, skill, or speed until he has taken your life. To be beaten this time makes him very angry; in two days he will challenge you to play ball with him." "All right," replied the man, "I am ready to meet him."

In two days they saw the chief coming, and as he entered the lodge, he said: "I am sick for a game of ball, and I challenge you to play a game against me; you won in one game, so now try another. I will wager all I have, and if you win, you shall be chief in my place." The man replied: "I also am sick from lack of amusement and I accept your challenge. I have never met the man who could beat me in a game of ball. But give me time. You have come unexpectedly, and I must make a ball club." "Very well," said the chief, going away.

The bent ball club the hunter hung up to season, and the old man made strings; the next day they netted the club. They were ready just in time to go to the ball ground. The time appointed for the game was at midday, and the old man and woman said, "We shall now start." "Very well; I shall come soon," said the adopted son. Then the little dog said, "Let it be our eldest brother who shall take part in this game." So the man removed his garments, and the dog put them on; there he stood, looking just like the man. The little dog said, "We shall surely win the game." The hunter and the other dogs went to the woods to hunt, while the dog-man went to the ball ground.

The chief was on the spot watching impatiently for the man. At last he saw him coming, with his long hair tied back; he carried his club well and looked splendid. The old man, supposing it was his son, said: "Now, you must use all your strength and must not be beaten." The dog-man saw that his antagonist was walking around in the crowd, with a very proud and haughty manner. The dog-man seemed very mild and without strength enough for the game.

Seeing that it was time to begin, the people fell back and gave room to the players. When the word was given the players came forward, and the chief said: "I will take my place on this side." "No; you shall not," said the other: "You gave the challenge, and I will choose my place." The chief had to yield, the dog-man choosing the side the chief wanted. They then began to play. "Now," said the little dog to the hunter in the woods, "our brother has begun the game, which will be a very close contest." Soon he said: "The chief's ball has missed the goal; they play well; our brother has caught and sent the ball back. Oh! now he has won an inning. They will play one more inning." All at once he called out: "They have begun again. It is a very close game. Our brother is having all he can do. We may be beaten, however." Then he called out: "*Owe! Owe!* Our brother has won the game. You are chief, and all the old chief has is ours."

As the dog-man had won two straight games, he caught the chief by the hair and cut his head off. Many of the people thanked him. They said that the old chief had never spared them; that when he had been the loser he had always given the people up to slaughter and saved his own life. The winner seemed to have won many friends among those who witnessed the game. The little dog said: "Now we shall go home." They had been there but a short time when the ball player came in; giving back the man's garments, he immediately became a dog again.

When the old people came into the lodge, they thanked their son, saying: "You have done more than anyone else was ever able to do before. You are the chief now." As they praised their son they did not know that it was a dog that had done the work.

The next morning the little dog said: "Let us go to live in the chief's lodge." So the hunter, with the old man and his family, moved into the new lodge. All the old chief's things had been left in their places, as they were part of the wager. Now, as the dogs were so full of orenda [power], he became a great chief and had much power and influence among the people.

[The narrator of the foregoing story said: "It is true that whenever a person loves a dog he derives great power from it. Dogs still know all we say, only they are not at liberty to speak. If you do not love a dog, he has power to injure you by his orenda."]9

NO. 11 (SENECA)

The old mothers now cautioned their children again to take great care and make no missteps. Now the youngest one thought of some bear's fat they had in the lodge, and the idea came to her that the only way they could kill the Head was by use of this. After the Head had eaten the first girl and was chasing the others through the lodge the bear's oil began to boil. As they threw the boiling oil, it singed and burned the Head, killing it (the animated Head was merely the skull with long projecting teeth).

All wishing to give thanks, the mothers said: "We ought to have a game of ball. Your brother is free. It is our duty to give thanks. The ball shall be this Head." Picking up the Head, she carried it out, calling in a loud voice, "Here, warriors! is a ball you can have to play with." Soon a great crowd of people came together with their netted clubs and began to play. All the players were wild beasts of the woods. The man stood near and saw the wild beasts playing ball with his wife's head. All tried to get the ball, and in this way they wore it out.

The dog now came up to his master and told him that his wife was dead; and when it said: "Your wife is dead," his strength seemed to leave him; his arms dropped down, and he was sad. The invisible brother said: "You feel grieved; for my part I am glad I do not see why you should be sad; she would have devoured you if they had not killed her. Now there is nothing to harm us. Your old uncle has gone back to his own home and will not trouble us now that he has eaten your wife's flesh." He added: "Your children are living in this direction (pointing westward); be of good courage, and go after them. I shall return. You will continue in one direction with your dogs until you reach the boys. You need never fear to suffer such hardships again." So saying, he went home, and when the brother looked after him he had disappeared.10

NO. 12 (SENECA)

There was a very poor little old woman, who lived in the woods. She was so destitute that she was nothing but skin and bones. She dwelt in a smoky little lodge and cried all the time, both day and night. Her robe of skins was so old and dirty that one could not tell without difficulty of what material it was made. She had seven daughters, six of whom were carried off one after another by hostile people, while the seventh died.

The daughter who died had been buried some time when one night the old woman heard crying at the grave. Going to the grave with a torch, she found there a naked baby. The child had crawled up out of the grave through a hole in the earth. Wrapping the baby in her blanket the old woman took it home. She did not know, she did not even suspect, that her daughter was with child when she died.

The little boy grew very rapidly. When he was of good size the old woman came home one day from gathering wood but could not find him. That night it stormed, with thunder and lightning raging. In the morning the child returned to her. His grandmother asked, "Where have you been, my grandson?" "Grandmother," said he, "I have been with my father; he took me to his home." "Who is your father?" "Hinon is my father; he took me home first, then we came back and were all about here last night." The old woman asked, "Was my daughter, your mother, in the grave?" "Yes," said the boy, "and Hinon used to come to see my mother." The old woman believed what he said.

As the boy grew up he used to make a noise like that of thunder, and whenever Hinon came to the neighborhood he would go out and thunder, thus helping his father, for he was Hinon Hohawaqk, the son of Hinon.

Some time after this the boy asked his grandmother where his six aunts were, and the grandmother answered: "There are an old woman and her son, whose lodge is far away; they live by playing dice and betting. Your aunts went one by one with a company of people, and played dice (plum pits); being beaten, their heads were cut off. Many men and women have gone to the same place and have lost their heads." Hinon Hohawaqk answered, "I will go, too, and will kill that woman and her son." The old woman tried to keep him home, but he would not remain with her. He told her to make two pairs of moccasins for him. He was very ragged and dirty, so she made the moccasins and got him the skin of a flying-squirrel for a pouch.

Setting off toward the west, soon he came to a great opening where there was a large bark lodge with a pole in front of it, and on the pole a skin robe. He saw boys playing ball in the opening, and going on a side path, he heard a great noise. After a while the people saw him, whereupon one of them said, "I do not know where that boy comes from." The old people were betting and the boys were playing ball. Soon an old man came up to Hinon Hohawaqk and gave him a club; he played so well that the old man came again, saying, "We want you to play dice; all the people will bet on you." A bowl was placed on an elk skin lying under the pole. The woman and her son were there and the other people stood around. Hinon Hohawaqk answered, "I do not know how to play the game." The old man replied, "We will risk our heads on you;" so he followed the old man. He saw a white stone bowl as smooth as glass. The old woman was sitting there on the elk skin, ready to play, and Hinon Hohawaqk knelt down beside the bowl. She said, "You play first." "No," answered he, "you play first." So she took out her dice, which were round and made from plum stones, and blowing on them, cast them into the bowl, which she shook, at the same time calling out, "Game! game!" The dice flew up into the air, all becoming crows and cawing as they went out of sight. After a while they came down, still cawing, and resumed the form of plum stones as they settled in the bowl. The old woman had three plays to make a count of seventeen. She threw three times but got nothing. Then Hinon Hohawaqk in order to win took dice out of his pouch of flying-squirrel skin. The old woman wanted him to use her dice, but he would not touch them. Placing his dice in the bowl, he shook, whereupon the dice, becoming ducks, flew upward. They went very high, and all the people heard them as they rose; when they touched the bowl again they were plum stones, and scored 10. Then Hinon Hohawaqk shook the bowl again, calling, "Game! game!" while the old woman called out, "No game!" Back came the dice, scoring another 10. He cast the third time and scored 10 more. He had won. Then he called the people to see him cut off the heads of the old woman and her son. "No," said the old woman, "you must play again. Here is my son; you must play ball with him, and if he loses we shall both forfeit our heads." At this Hinon Hohawaqk asked the old man what he thought. The people, seeing how skillful he was, said "Play!" whereupon he went to the ball-ground, ragged and looking poor. There were but two playing, one on each side. Hinon Hohawaqk jumped, knocking the club far out of his opponent's hand. Then the old woman's son ran for his club, but before he could get it back Hinon Hohawaqk had sent the ball through the goal posts. This was repeated seven times and Hinon Hohawaqk won the game. "Now," said he to all the people, "you can have the heads of the old woman and her son." The two heads were cut off, and the boys played with the old woman's head over the whole field.[11]

NO. 13 (SENECA)

Without further parleying they started forward. As they traveled along they saw that the trees of all kinds were very large and tall, and that they were in full bloom; there trees were of surpassing beauty. The travelers were greatly surprised to learn that the flowers supplied the light of that world, and they also observed that all the beasts and animals and birds possessed exceptionally fine bodies and presence. They remarked, too, that they had seen nothing during their journey thither so wonderful and strange. They saw with astonishment also the exuberance of the growing grasses and plants, among which they beheld in rich profusion the fruited stalks of the strawberry plants, which were as tall as the grasses. During their entire journey thither never had they found such large, luscious berries.

Having gone some distance into the new country they were surprised to see in the distance a great multitude of human beings, who were assembled on the heath, which was the playground of that people; they appeared to the travelers to be occupied with games of amusement. Dehaenhyowens, the leader of the band, said, "What is to be done now, my friends, seeing that we have arrived at the dwelling place of strange human beings, and that we have nothing with which to defend ourselves should they attempt to do us harm?" Thereupon, Gaenhyakdondye said: "We have indeed made an agreement, as you know, that we should forsake our kindred and our lives in order to accomplish the purpose of this expedition. You know that each of us volunteered by 'notching the rod' to carry out that agreement. If we are to die here, we can do nothing to avoid such an end; we must not break our resolution and compact to follow the path of the sun to the last. The only thing that is certain in the case of our death is that our careers would end here." His brother, Dehaenhyowens, replied, "The matter stands even as you have stated it; so then let us go forward to meet this people." At this they started toward the place where they saw a great multitude assembled. In a very short time the anxious travelers came to a standstill not far from the others. Looking around, they saw that the inhabitants of the settlement were in readiness to witness a game of lacrosse, and that the players were even then standing in their accustomed places.

In a short time the game commenced, and the vast multitude drew near as interested spectators. As soon as it was fairly under way there arose a great tumult; there was shouting and loud cries of excitement and approbation caused by the varying fortunes of favorite players. The great multitude rejoiced, and the new arrivals were greatly delighted with what they saw.

At this time one of the players exhibited great rudeness in his manner of playing, striking right and left with his netted club without regard to other players who might be injured by his recklessness. Thereupon a person from the crowd, going up to him, said: "Do thou cease acting so rudely; thy manner is too violent, because one who is rejoicing does not act thus. So do not act thus again." Then the players at once resumed the game, playing as they never had played before. In a short time, however, the player who had been cautioned to be more mild in his methods of play exhibited again his violence toward his playmates. At once the man who had before reprimanded him went up to him again and said, "Assuredly, I forbade thee acting again so rudely as thou hast done, yet thou hast disobeyed my request. Now thou shalt rest for a time. Thou art too unkind and head-strong." Thereupon, seizing the ball player by the nape of the neck and by the legs and lifting him up bodily, he bore him away. Not far distant stood a very large tree. Thither the man carried the ball player, and having arrived near the tree, he cast the youth against its trunk. Headforemost his body penetrated the trunk, part of his head coming out on the opposite side, while his feet still protruded on the nearer side. Then the man quietly returned to the ball ground, and play was resumed. The game was continued until one of the sides had scored the number of points requisite to win, and then the players again mingled with the crowd. Then the man who had imprisoned the rude player in the tree released the prisoner, with an admonition to be more mild in his methods in the future. On his return to the multitude the man told them that it was time for them to return to their several homes, and they dispersed.[12]

NO. 14 (WINNEBAGO)

The WañgEre'gi and the Mane'gi people were to play lacrosse. So the Wañg-Ere'gi took an invitation stick and attached some tobacco to it and sent it to the Mane'gi people. Thus they fixed a day for the contest. The contest was to be in four days. In the meantime both sides were to get ready, for some might be without balls or sticks, etc. Then the WañgEre'gi said: "We are the fleeter and will therefore go and look for food." When they returned the leader of the WañgEre'gi said again, "We are the fleeter and will therefore win from our opponents. In addition to that we are holy and for that reason we will be strengthened in the coming contest." Then the leader of the Mane'gi said: "I will first pour tobacco and then I will arise with the blessing of life which was bestowed upon me and through which I know my men will be strengthened." Then they arranged the goals, i.e., the *wak'a'rani,* and arranged for the points. Then they took an emetic and went into a vapor-bath in order to strengthen themselves. The goals were now standing far apart from each other. Then the people who were to play gathered on the field and two men from each side began to tell their war exploits. First, one of the WañgEre'gi men told how he had cut off an enemy's head; how proud his sisters had been at receiving the gifts and how they had danced in the Victory Dance. "With such a man you will have to play," he shouted to those on the other side. Then a man from the Mane'gi said, "I also am a brave man. I did with the enemy as I pleased. Once when an enemy had been killed between the firing lines, I rushed for him and in the midst of bullets I cut off his head. With such a man you will have to fight," he shouted to those on the other side. Then he gave a whoop and the ball was thrown into the air and they began to play lacrosse. Those who first succeeded in putting the ball through the *wak'a'rani* four times would be declared the winners. All day they played and in the evening they stopped. Lacrosse was the favorite game among the Winnebago. This is all.[13]

Indian Lacrosse Stick Making

The following descriptions of three contemporary lacrosse stickmakers who are still producing traditional wooden sticks by hand will give some idea of the technology involved. Like all native craftspeople, probably no two stickmakers follow exactly the same procedure, so the steps involved, the materials and equipment used must be taken as being general, although typical. Also, it will be noted, Indian craftsmen have readily accepted modern technology to facilitate production; in so doing, however, they have adapted it to suit their needs in characteristic Indian fashion: Whereas once abrasive stones may have been used to smooth carved surfaces, today belt sanders are used (Figure 74). By far the most detailed study of lacrosse stick making is by Mitchell R. Childress (1992). His meticulous description of the methods of Wood Bell, a Neshoba County, Mississippi, Choctaw maker of the traditional *kapocha* (ballsticks) not only suggests the antiquity of the craft but attempts to re-create the pre-contact mode of manufacture.

THE SOUTHEASTERN STICK

The characteristic construction of contemporary southeastern sticks is well exemplified by the stick-making methods of Tema Tiger, a Creek (Muskogee) member of the Fishpond Ceremonial Ground near Okema, Oklahoma. Tiger learned his craft from his father and, like all stickmakers, is dedicated to keeping the tradition alive. As he put it, "A lot of things we'd seen with our own eyes and we thought that's the way they done it, so that's the way we've been carrying it on." Noting the antiquity of making lacrosse sticks this way, Tiger stated, "That [art of stick making] comes from way beyond the sunrise, the older people had said." (Catlin's illustrations of Choctaw sticks confirm that the tradition goes back more than a century and a half.) The seriousness with which Tiger assumes his responsibility in carrying on the role of stickmaker is reflected in his wearing a red kerchief knotted

Figure 74 • Kevin Patterson, a Tuscarora, uses a band saw to remove bark from a dried lacrosse blank before it is carved, as part of a demonstration of Iroquois lacrosse stick making at the annual Festival of American Folklife at the Smithsonian Institution in 1976.

around his neck when he works on sticks. Creek (and certain other tribes) traditionally wear such scarves for play; the color red, previously associated with warfare, is still an integral emblem of combat.

In making his *tokon'he* (crooked sticks), Tiger uses modern tools, as do all contemporary stickmakers. By no means does this imply that the same result was not achieved before European contact and trade. The tasks accomplished today with shaped metal tools were formerly performed with implements of stone, bone, wood, or other natural substances. Indian people were quick to adapt the technology of Europeans to their own needs, thereby expediting certain laborious tasks and precluding the need to make replacements for tools that broke easily or wore out. Metal pails clearly had a longer life span than those of birch bark, and metal blades used to split wood did not break so often as those of sharpened stone or bone. The new tools probably did make the manufacture of lacrosse sticks easier and less time-consuming. Tiger believes that his ancestors used flint rock to smooth their sticks; today he uses commercial sandpaper. The deerhide once used for lacing has been replaced, he says, "by white people's leathers."

Ordinarily Tiger makes a stick in half a day, but when pressed he can turn out two pairs in a day. First, he selects a hickory log about four feet long, splits it in half lengthwise, then examines the grain in each piece to determine the "good" half—the one that will better withstand further splitting. Using two old ax blades, he begins to divide the better half down the middle of the bark side, alternately driving the blades the length of the wood, so that the second acts as a wedge to free the first. To make sure the

V-shaped blank will curve well when bent, he pulls off a splinter and attempts to tie a knot in it. If successful, he continues work on that section.

With an ax, Tiger then removes the bark from his blank, peeling off any loose strands of wood. The blank is inserted in a vise, and he begins to use a spokeshave, or drawknife, to shave down and remove parts of the wood. With a pencil and ruler he measures six inches from the end of the blank, makes a mark, then measures an additional sixteen inches, which must be thinned to form the cup. In whittling, he generally draws the knife toward him but occasionally uses it back and forth to smooth the work. Finally, he rounds off the edges of the sixteen-inch portion, which will form the cup when bent back upon itself (Figure 75).

Further variation in the stick making of southeastern tribes has been documented. The Creek, after tapering the thin end, steamed it for pliability, then turned the ends to one side or the other to accommodate a specific player. For the right-handed player, the tapered end was turned to the right, then bound onto the handle, as is the practice of Tema Tiger; for the left-handed player, the reverse process was used. To effect the lip of the cup, the Creek applied heated lard to the top, then inserted that end into a crack in the wall or the floor, and bent it slightly to angle the cup's end. The Choctaw used long deerhide strings to lash the tapered end to the handle, but shorter raccoon-skin cords for the webbing, since the latter were less expensive by ten cents.[1]

THE GREAT LAKES STICK

To obtain a round pocket, the stickmaker proceeds not unlike his southern counterparts. Whereas hickory is the wood of choice in the south, Great Lakes craftsmen, like Franklin Basina, almost always select white or black ash for strength, absence of knots, and easy carving. Basina described his selection of wood and manner of working it as follows: "Most of the sticks were made of white ash, second growth . . . some guys made them out of ironwood and some were of oak. But most of them were made out of white ash, because white ash is easier to work, and there's a trick to that. Now, when I go get a white ash, I gotta see that it's straight grain, so when you split it and it runs. Now when I cut my width and my lacrosse stick, I scrape all the bark off, except where I make the turn. I take the bark off, but I'm very careful [in the space] from the bark to the wood, there's a slimy substance in there, you know that. I leave that on, so when it comes to bend it, the slimy substance, after it helps you, so you don't break [the wood]. That slimy stuff holds it there until it's bent, and after it dries out, then I scrape that off and take it off. A lot of guys don't do that, that's why they have a helluva time to bend that. When you bend it, it's kinda brittle-like, but that slimy stuff holds that brittle."

Basina collects his wood when the trees are sapping, when he can notice frost coming out of the tree. That ensures that the "slimy" layer will still be in the wood. In wood that is cut later in the summer, much of the slime will have dried. He selects ash eight inches "on the stump," cutting his log

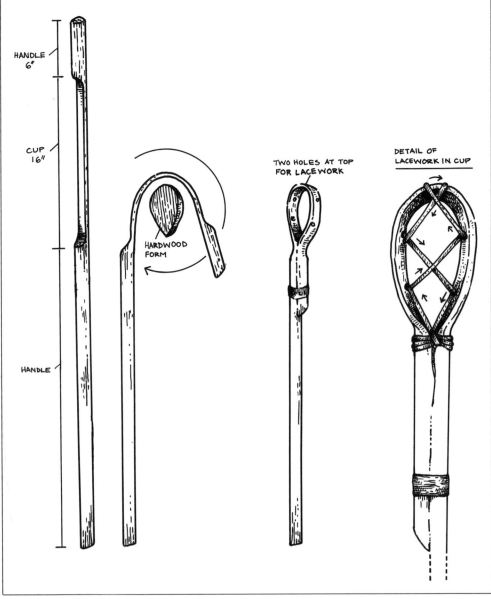

Figure 75 • Stages in the construction of the southeastern lacrosse stick, as practiced by Tema Tiger (Oklahoma Creek).

about fifty inches long. ("I got enough to play on, you gotta cut it off, to have enough timber. I don't want to cut it too short, see.") First he splits the log in half, then again in half, and again, making enough blanks for eight sticks.

The blank is whittled and the end to be bent tapered to about a quarter inch in thickness and made about one and a half to two inches wide. This stick is roughed out into a rectangular form, about one and a half by three-

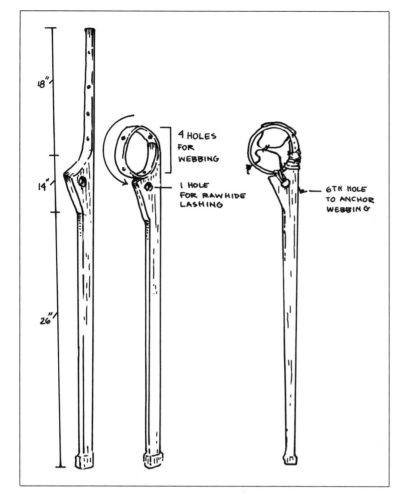

18"

14"

26"

4 HOLES
FOR
WEBBING

I HOLE
FOR RAWHIDE
LASHING

6TH HOLE
TO ANCHOR
WEBBING

Figure 76 • Construction of the traditional Great Lakes lacrosse stick, following the practice of Franklin Basina (Red Cliff Ojibwe).

quarters inches, later to be rounded with a knife. (Some Great Lakes makers, like Basina, carve a rectangular bulbous end at the bottom of the handle; others leave them plain and the stick purposely long, in order to let the player cut the stick to his desired length.) As the stick nears the pocket, it widens abruptly, from the one-and-a-half-inch handle at a point about 26 inches from the butt end of the stick. This provides a curved inner surface to accommodate about four and a half inches of the tapered end, which, while it is pliable, is curled back inside the body of the stick and lashed to it (Figure 76). Basina acknowledges that, even with the protective help of the "slime," he steams his wood as he bends it ("Well, yeah, I do. You're damned sure I don't want to go out in the woods and get some more!").

Like the webbing of the southeastern stick, that of the Great Lakes variety is minimal, rarely more than a simple cross of two thongs tied together. Basina uses tanned buckskin of leather because it is soft and flexible, but he believes his people formerly used moose- or deerhide: "Deerhide's all right, but you gotta use the neck of the deer. That's where his hide is the thickest . . . from the back of his ears down to his shoulders, that's the part. It's awful thick." Several holes are drilled into the cup end of the stock—three along the bent portion, one diagonally from the shaft through the part of the bend that is anchored against the butt of the shaft, and a larger one just below the bend where the shaft widens. With a single strand of leather, Basina knots it and begins to thread from the diagonal hole outside the shaft, comes through to about the middle of the pocket, ties it in a knot to itself, and brings it across one of the outside holes. The thong is then brought around the outside of the cup to the next hole, threaded through, brought into the knot, then threaded through the other outside hole and knotted. The curve is easily secured by lashing it to the shaft with rawhide in two places—one for about two inches at the very end of the tapered section, and the other through the large drilled hole and over the bent portion immediately above it.

THE IROQUOIS STICK

The following technology of Iroquoian stick making is based on the practice of Louis Jacques, a Mohawk living at Onondaga, and his son Alf and describes essentially the technology of other Iroquoian tribes, such as the Mohawk or Tuscarora, regarding choice of wood, methods of preparing it, carving, and stringing. Information about lacing was provided by Frank Benedict, a Mohawk stickmaker at Akwesasne.

The Jacqueses, like all Iroquois, prefer hickory for their sticks. In selecting trees, they look for straight ones, with bark that shows no knots in it. The smoother the bark, the better. In hickory with knots, the grain will twist and be unsuitable for a lacrosse stick. Trees have to be cut when there is no sap in the bark; otherwise, when the bark is pulled off, the wood will break. Therefore trees are selected after they have lost their leaves and the sap has completely run out.

After the hickory has been split into wooden blanks, these are steamed for bending in a mold. The Jacqueses use an improvised enclosed fireplace in their yard that has a rear chimney to create a draft as well as a side opening that produces the steam needed to make the wood pliable. While steaming, the fire is kept stoked from a large pile of wood and bark shavings from stick carving. The end portion of the blank that needs bending to form the crook of the stick is inserted in the steam hole until the wood has become sufficiently pliable for them to bend it in the mold.

To form the gross shape of the stick's crook, the Jacqueses use a metal plate (Figure 77) fastened to one side of a vertical post about three feet from the ground. The plate itself has two round metal tubes and a vertical metal stop welded to it. With these three permanent fulcrums on the plate, each of the three bending operations is accomplished. (Some Iroquois stickmakers use a similar fulcrum plate fixed horizontally to a table for the same purpose.) The stick with its bark intact is removed from the steam hole in the fireplace and the steamed portion, which has previously been spokeshaved to

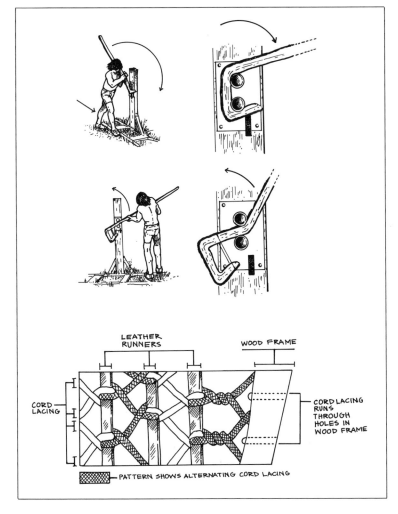

LEATHER
RUNNERS

WOOD FRAME

CORD
LACING

CORD LACING
RUNS
THROUGH
HOLES IN
WOOD FRAME

PATTERN SHOWS ALTERNATING CORD LACING

Figure 77 • Sketches of Alf Jacques forming bends in the Iroquois lacrosse stick. Lacing according to the practice of Frank Benedict Akwesasne (Mohawk).

taper slightly in a V-shape, is inserted (northeast to southwest) between the lower tube and the vertical fixture, the tip of the crook extending perhaps four inches beyond the vertical. The stickmaker, using the unsteamed end, which will become the shaft or handle of the stick, simply brings the stick, bark side out, pushing it around and outside the two tubular pieces and pulling it down over the top one. (With the fulcrum plate fixed to a table, the stickmaker performs these motions horizontally.) This procedure forms the basic crook of the stick, but it must be held in that shape to dry for ten months or more. A heavy piece of wire tied into a thin oval is then slipped from the butt end of the handle down to where the crook—still in the mold—has been formed. The wire is slipped over the hook end of the crook, which holds this shape and allows for the stick to be removed from the mold. The maker wiggles the stick free, then inverts it and reinserts it (southeast to northwest) between the two tubes. By pushing down on the handle, he puts tension on the crook where it is held together by the wire, so that the bend in the crook is brought in even tighter (the second bending operation), forming the desired nearly triangular shape.

The final bend—where the crook terminates and the straight shaft begins—is also effected on the metal mold. The stick is once more inverted and inserted (southwest to northeast) between the two tubes, so that a point about fifteen inches from the top of the triangle rests inside against the top tube. The maker then pushes the handle as straight up as he can to effect the final bend, which will be at the throat of the stick. The stick at this point is ready to be put away to dry and hold its shape. When the wood has dried completely, the wire is removed and the crook will hold its shape naturally.

When the dried stick is ready to be carved, the maker is seated on a horse bench that has a pivoting wooden clamp, which he manipulates by foot, much like a loom treadle. The first procedure is to remove the bark from the outside of the crook. Using a spokeshave, or double-handled drawknife, the carver starts at the throat and begins to slice off the bark, drawing the shave toward him. Once he gets a good "run" going with his carving, by the time he reaches the first bend at the top of the crook, he is usually able to pull the remainder of the bark layer off by hand. In this way that section of bark comes off in one long piece. Once it is removed, he inverts the stick in the clamp and begins to shape the end of the crook, but shaving away from him toward its tip. The stick can be inserted in any position and held with the wooden clamp, so the carver continues to turn the stick, rounding and thinning the crook until the head of the stick is nearly complete in form. Then the butt end of the stick is cut to the desired length, the bark shaved off, and the shaft thinned. In using the drawknife, a number of techniques are possible—for instance, one hand can hold one handle beneath the stick with the thumb hooked over the crook to anchor that end of the handle and use it as a sort of fixed pivot point, while the other end is free to carve at various angles and depths.

Once the stick has been roughed out, it is sanded (usually mechanically), and the holes to accept the four or five rawhide "runners" are drilled along the top of the spoon and at the throat, where the runners will be pulled through and tied (loosely, for the player's occasional adjustments). Holes are also drilled at the tip of the crook and along the inside of the crook to secure the gut-wall and thread the clockcord webbing. The stick is then lacquered for protection and is ready to receive the various strings of rawhide, catgut, and clockcord that make up the webbing.

While Alf does most of the carving, his father, Lou, does the stringing. (In many Iroquois communities, lacing is a task commanded by women.) After the runners and the gut-wall are in place, two strands of rawhide are twisted horizontally across the top of the spoon at intervals of about an inch, then near the throat to form the base of the pocket. Wherever they cross a runner, they are twisted around it, binding the gut to the vertical rawhide. Interwoven clockcord forms the bulk of the webbing. It is strung in such a way that it weaves in and out of the runners, being turned around it each time, then run at a different angle.

Frank Benedict uses (usually) four leaders or "runners" made of commercial leather on his sticks. These are put on before it is laced and anchored at the spoon end by slits cut in them, so that the runner is brought back around the shaft and through the slit. Each runner comes the length of the stick through its own hole at the throat, where it is brought through and tied in a half-hitch, so that the player can adjust the tension on it. The gut-wall is also made of four strands of twisted *babiche* (cowhide), forming the main runners. Then from five to seven vertical rawhide "posts" are interwoven with the runners to form the wall. The wall is attached to the frame of the stick with leather ties so that it, too, can be adjusted for tension. In lacing, the person stringing uses a long single strand—these days of nylon in various colors, although formerly it was thin-cut sheep-gut. With one continuous string, the worker begins at the top of the stick and, using two runners at a time, weaves down to the throat, then comes back up. The second string is then woven into the third in the same manner, and so on (Figure 77).

Notes

PREFACE

1. The only indication of "damage" to the stick is a small area of the rawhide webbing near the end of the crook that has been replaced with tanned-leather thongs. The wooden frame, however, shows little signs of use.

2. A. Frances Eyman, "Lacrosse and the Cayuga Thunder Rite," passim. Marshall J. Becker, "Lacrosse: Political Organization in North America as Reflected in Athletic Competition," p. 55, offers a better analysis. For the use of dogs as ritual intercession, see Thomas Vennum, Jr., "The Ojibwa Begging Dance."

3. Roger Wulff, "Lacrosse among the Seneca," p. 21.

4. Frank G. Speck, *Midwinter Rites of the Cayuga Long House*, p. 152.

PROLOGUE

1. The Onondaga name for lacrosse. The orthography used was provided by Hanni Woodbury (personal communication, 20 March 1992). Spellings of Indian words throughout the text are as they appear in the sources. Except for certain proper names, Ojibwe spellings in Chapter 6 conform to the Nichols-Nyholm system. Fox orthography for the word "lacrosse" was provided by Ives Goddard (personal communication, 28 September 1992).

CHAPTER 1

1. Reuben G. Thwaites, ed., *The Jesuit Relations and Allied Documents: Travels and Explorations of the Jesuit Missionaries in New France, 1610–1791*, 10:185, 187. Translations from *Jesuit Relations* have been edited slightly to make them more readable. I have also changed the translation "country" (from the French "*paye*") to read "countryside" or "territory" to avoid the implication that a sorcerer could issue orders affecting the *whole* of Huronia. His power probably extended only to his village or, at most, to the surrounding area or tribe (Conrad Heidenreich, personal communication, 12 August 1992).

2. Thwaites, *Jesuit Relations*, 10:187.

3. Ibid., 13:131.

4. Gabriel Sagard, *The Long Journey to the Country of the Hurons*, p. 143. The original translation uses "tonsure" in place of "shaven crown of the head."

5. Ibid., p. 120.

CHAPTER 2

1. William J. Baker, *Sports of the Western World*, p. 11. Few among today's Olympics audiences are aware that the games derived from ancient religious cults. With the spread of Christianity, such rituals were suppressed, and at the end of the fourth century the religious rites associated with the Olympics were dropped. Forcibly deprived of their original purpose,

the games quickly declined, not to be revived for 1,400 years.

2. James Mooney and Frans M. Olbrechts, *The Swimmer Manuscript: Cherokee Sacred Formulas and Medicinal Prescriptions*, pp. 91–92.

3. Compare *Tewaarathon (Lacrosse): Akwesasne's Story of Our National Game*, pp. 19ff., with Stewart Culin, "Games of the North American Indians," pp. 578–79.

4. John R. Swanton, *Myths and Tales of the Southeastern Indians*, p. 23; see also p. 187 for a Tukabachee Creek variant.

5. Raymond Fogelson, "The Cherokee Ball Game: A Study in Southeastern Ethnology," pp. 15ff.

6. Robert E. Ritzenthaler, Field Notes and Papers, collected from Frank James. For a variant from the same reservation narrated by Delia Oshogay, see Victor Barnouw, *Wisconsin Chippewa Myths and Tales*, p. 90.

7. M. Carolissa Levi, *Chippewa Indians of Yesterday and Today*, pp. 167, 169. No source is given.

8. Walter James Hoffman, "The Menomini Indians," p. 131.

9. Robert E. Ritzenthaler and Pat Ritzenthaler, *The Woodland Indians of the Western Great Lakes*, p. 42.

10. John Haywood, *The Natural and Aboriginal History of Tennessee*, p. 285.

11. John R. Swanton, "Social Organization and Social Usages of the Indians of the Creek Confederacy," pp. 54–61.

12. William Jones, *Ethnography of the Fox Indians*, pp. 109–10.

13. Robert E. Ritzenthaler, *The Potawatomi Indians of Wisconsin*, pp. 163–64; Ritzenthaler and Ritzenthaler, *Woodland Indians*, p. 110.

14. Frances Densmore, *Menominee Music*, pp. 37–39. See Thomas Vennum, Jr., *Wild Rice and the Ojibway People*, p. 5.

15. The half red/half blue may have been associated with drumhead decor. See Thomas Vennum, Jr., *The Ojibwa Dance Drum: Its History and Construction*, pp. 201ff.; Densmore, *Menominee Music*, pp. 37–39.

16. Lewis Henry Morgan, *League of the Ho-dé-no-sau-nee or Iroquois*, p. 280; Robert E. Ritzenthaler, "Kickapoo Vocabulary," pp. 21–22; see also Fogelson, "Cherokee Ball Game," p. 29.

17. Frank G. Speck, *Midwinter Rites of the Cayuga Long House*, pp. 117–18.

18. Truman Michelson, "Notes on Fox Mortuary Customs and Beliefs," p. 38.

19. Densmore, *Menominee Music*, p. 40.

20. J. N. B. Hewitt, "Iroquois Game of La

Crosse," p. 191; See also I. P. Evans, cited in Fogelson, "Cherokee Ball Game," p. 40; John Witthoft, cited in ibid., p. 114.

21. Fogelson, "Cherokee Ball Game," pp. 51–52.

22. Mooney and Olbrechts, *Swimmer Manuscript*, pp. 91–92.

23. Rev. George White, *Historical Collections of Georgia*, p. 671.

24. Swanton, "Social Organization," pp. 462–64.

25. Felipe A. Latorre and Dolores L. Latorre, *The Mexican Kickapoo Indians*, p. 301; John H. Payne Papers, p. 36, cited in Fogelson, "Cherokee Ball Game," p. 99; Edward D. Neill, *Dakota Land and Dakota Life*, pp. 281–82.

26. Swanton, "Social Organization," p. 462.

27. John R. Swanton, "Religious Beliefs and Medical Practices of the Creek Indians," p. 492; Fogelson, "Cherokee Ball Game," p. 100.

28. Levi, *Chippewa Indians*, p. 342, n. 3.

29. Alanson Skinner, *Material Culture of the Menomini*, p. 367; Johann G. Kohl, *Kitchi-Gami, Wanderings round Lake Superior*, p. 89.

30. Fogelson, "Cherokee Ball Game," p. 98; James Mooney, "The Cherokee Ball Play," p. 114.

31. Fogelson, "Cherokee Ball Game," pp. 125, 98.

32. Swanton, "Social Organization," pp. 462, 465.

33. Frank G. Speck, *Ethnology of the Yuchi Indians*, p. 86; Seymour Feiler, *Jean-Bernard Bossu's Travels in the Interior of North America, 1751–1762*, p. 304.

34. John Lawson, *History of North Carolina*, pp. 35–36. See also Mooney, "Cherokee Ball Play," pp. 116–17.

35. Levi, *Chippewa Indians*; Kendall Blanchard, *The Mississippi Choctaw at Play: The Serious Side of Leisure*, pp. 30, 67–68.

36. Swanton, "Social Organization," pp. 462–65.

37. Speck, *Ethnology of the Yuchi Indians*, p. 87; Franklin Basina, interview transcripts, pp. 10–11. *Jiibik* is a shortened form of *ojiibik*, meaning "root" (usually medicinal). It is used by English-speaking Ojibwe as slang to indicate something magical.

38. Hoffman, "Menomini Indians," pp. 127–28.

39. Freeman Bucktooth, Jr., interview transcript, p. 9.

40. Peter Jones, *History of the Ojebway Indians*, plate opposite p. 145; Skinner, *Material Culture*, pp. 310–11.

41. See Vennum, "Ojibway Drum Decor: Sources and Variations of Ritual Design," passim.

42. Speck, *Ethnology of the Yuchi Indians*, p. 115.

43. Paul Radin, "The Winnebago Tribe," p. 73; Levi, *Chippewa Indians*.

44. Swanton, "Social Organization," p. 462;

Alanson Skinner, *Social Life and Ceremonial Bundles of the Menomini Indians,* p. 57.

45. James Mooney, *Myths of the Cherokee,* pp. 422, 425–26. See also James Mooney, *Sacred Formulas of the Cherokee,* p. 325.

46. Lawson, *North Carolina,* pp. 237–38.

47. Mooney, *Swimmer Manuscript,* p. 70; Fogelson, "Cherokee Ball Game," pp. 61ff.; Frank Speck and Leonard Broom, *Cherokee Dance and Drama,* p. 53.

48. Speck, *Ethnology of the Yuchi Indians,* pp. 115ff.

49. Fogelson, "Cherokee Ball Game," pp. 61–62. For scarification practices of the Creek, see Basil Hall, *Travels in North America in the Years 1827 and 1828,* pp. 293–94.

50. Fogelson, "Cherokee Ball Game," p. 67.

51. Ibid., pp. 62, 66. See also Jack Frederick Kilpatrick and Anna Gritts Kilpatrick, "Notebook of a Cherokee Shaman," p. 115.

52. Fogelson, "Cherokee Ball Game," pp. 66–67, Appendix B, "Ball Game Ethnobotany"; see also Mooney, *Myths,* pp. 425–26, for the use of smallrush in place of great bulrush for the same purpose.

53. James Davidson, "Enemies Become Teammates to Promote Healing," p. A16.

54. Roy Simmons, Jr., interview transcript, p. 3; James Tabor, "Molding Talent," p. 12.

CHAPTER 4

1. John Lawson, *History of North Carolina,* p. 186; Edward D. Neill, *Dakota Land and Dakota Life,* p. 280; Peter Grant called the favorite game of the Saulteaux about 1804 "hurdle," noting that even old men play it ("The Saulteaux Indians about 1804," p. 337).

2. Martyr, cited in John R. Swanton, "Early History of the Creek Indians and Their Neighbors," p. 45; Jonathan Carver, *Travels through the Interior Parts of North America in the Years 1766, 1767, and 1768,* p. 363. Bossu noted that the Choctaw "play a game similar to our tennis and are very good at it" (Seymour Feiler, *Jean-Bernard Bossu's Travels in the Interior of North America, 1751–1762,* p. 169).

3. See James Mooney, *Myths of the Cherokee,* p. 454; Roger L. Wulff, "Lacrosse among the Seneca," p. 16.

4. William H. Maddren, "Lacrosse," p. 370. Lacrosse histories were also appended to cricket manuals.

5. Alexander M. Weyand and Milton R. Roberts, *The Lacrosse Story,* p. 3. See, e.g., William J. Baker, *Sports in the Western World,* p. 71; Marshall J. Becker, "Lacrosse: Political Organization in North America

as Reflected in Athletic Competition," p. 53; Dave Laubin, "Lacrosse: 'Little Brother of War,' the Indians Called It," p. 37. Nancy B. Martel ("Little Brother of War," p. 49) and Milton Roberts (*Brine's Lacrosse Guide and Almanac,* p. 1) attribute the crozier analogy to the Jesuit Jean de Brébeuf.

6. Edwin M. Duval, personal communication, 28 December 1991.

7. Weyand and Roberts, *Lacrosse Story,* p. 4.

8. The Ojibwe word can be broken down linguistically as follows: *baag* ("hit")/*a'* (by an instrument)/*adow* ("ball, or clot")/*e* (abstract final) (John Nichols, personal communication, 12 November 1992). In Fox (Mesquaki) the same word is used for baseball (Truman Michelson, "Notes on Fox Mortuary Customs and Beliefs," p. 384). *Pa:kah* had more the connotation of tapping, or patting (as one would a horse), but (ironically) *not* forcefully (Ives Goddard, personal communication, 28 September 1992). The Onondaga word is found in old texts and is broken down as follows: *de* (dualic)/*hun* (masculine plural)/*tshigw* ("fist, or rounded object")/*a* (morpheme joiner)/*'e* ("hit")/*s* (habitual aspect) (Hanni Woodbury, personal communication, 20 March 1992). Incorrect explanations appear in W. M. Beauchamp, "Iroquois Games," p. 273; Robert Lipsyte, "Lacrosse: All-American Game," p. 44; Frank G. Speck, *Midwinter Rites of the Cayuga Long House,* p. 117.

CHAPTER 5

1. Frances Densmore, *Chippewa Customs,* p. 119; W. Vernon Kinietz, *Chippewa Village: The Story of Katikitegon,* fig. 35; Edward D. Neill, *Dakota Land and Dakota Life,* p. 281.

2. Alanson Skinner, *Material Culture of the Menomini,* p. 67; Johann G. Kohl, *Kitchi-Gami, Wanderings round Lake Superior,* p. 89.

3. Jonathan Carver, *Travels through the Interior Parts of North America in the Years 1766, 1767, and 1768,* p. 364; William L. Stone, *Life of Joseph Brant—Thayendanegea,* p. 448; Col. Landmann, *Adventures and Recollections of Colonel Landmann, Late of the Corps of Royal Engineers,* pp. 85–86; Peter Grant, "The Saulteaux Indians about 1804," p. 337; W[illiam] G[eorge] Beers, *Lacrosse: The National Game of Canada,* p. 31.

4. Seymour Feiler, *Jean-Bernard Bossu's Travels in the Interior of North America, 1751–1762,* p. 304; Kendall Blanchard, *The Mississippi Choctaw at Play: The Serious Side of Leisure,* p. 34; Raymond Fogelson, "The Cherokee Ball Game: A Study in Southeastern Ethnology," pp. 99–100.

5. Felipe A. Latorre and Dolores L. Latorre, *The Mexican Kickapoo Indians*, pp. 301–3; Frances Densmore, "Choctaw Music," p. 128; Starr, cited in John R. Swanton, "Source Material for the Social and Ceremonial Life of the Choctaw Indians," p. 151. Frances Densmore, *Menominee Music*, pp. 37–38.

6. William Bartram, *Travels through North and South Carolina, Georgia, East and West Florida*, p. 398; I. P. Evans, cited in Fogelson, "Cherokee Ball Game," p. 41; Carver, *Travels*, p. 364. George White in the mid-nineteenth century described Cherokee sticks as "two wooden spoons, curiously carved, not unlike our large iron spoons" (Rev. George White, *Historical Collections of Georgia*, p. 670). Buttrick described Cherokee lacrosse sticks as "wove with some deer skin, same as the snow shoes of the Northern Indians" (cited in Fogelson, "Cherokee Ball Game," p. 39). Mrs. W. Wallace Brown wrote of Abanaki sticks "with stripes of hide after the manner of snow shoes" (*Some Indoor and Outdoor Games of the Wabanaki Indians*, p. 45).

7. James Mooney, "The Cherokee Ball Play," pp. 106–7. See also p. 120.

8. Fogelson, "Cherokee Ball Game," pp. 97–98. The position one played also determined the length of the Mississippi Choctaw stick. See Blanchard, *Mississippi Choctaw*, pp. 33–34.

9. Fogelson, "Cherokee Ball Game," p. 98; John R. Swanton, "Social Organization and Social Usages of the Indians of the Creek Confederacy," pp. 459–60.

10. James H. Howard and Victoria Lindsay Levine, *Choctaw Music and Dance*, pp. 34–35.

11. See, e.g., Carver, *Travels*, p. 364.

12. See Stewart Culin, "Games of the North American Indians," p. 568, fig. 752. Hoffman claimed that the Mississaugas, or eastern Ojibwe living in Ontario about 1800, used the same serrated pattern (Walter James Hoffman, "The Menomini Indians," p. 135). Blackdeer, personal communication, 19 September 1991; Beers, *Lacrosse*, p. 13 (illustration, p. 11); Franklin Basina, interview transcripts, p. 2; Skinner, *Material Culture*, p. 339.

13. A. Frances Eyman, "Lacrosse and the Cayuga Thunder Rite," pp. 16–18.

CHAPTER 7

1. George Copway, *The Traditional History and Characteristic Sketches of the Ojibway Nation*, p. 52; William L. Stone, *Life of Joseph Brant—Thayendanegea*, p. 447; Horatio B. Cushman, *History of the Choctaw,*

Chickasaw, and Natchez Indians, pp. 131–35; Kendall Blanchard, *The Mississippi Choctaw at Play: The Serious Side of Leisure*, p. 71.

2. Charles Lanman, *Letters from the Alleghany Mountains*, p. 101.

3. Raymond Fogelson, "The Cherokee Ball Game: A Study in Southeastern Ethnology," p. 126; Lanman, *Letters*, p. 101.

4. Buttrick, cited in Fogelson, "Cherokee Ball Game," p. 38.

5. Blanchard, *Mississippi Choctaw*, p. 34; Basil Hall, *Travels in North America in the Years 1827 and 1828*, p. 305.

6. Perrot, cited in Stewart Culin, "Games of the North American Indians," p. xl.

7. Blanchard, *Mississippi Choctaw*, p. 34.

8. Marinus Willett, *A Narrative of the Military Actions of Colonel Marinus Willett*, p. 110; Starr, cited in John R. Swanton, "Source Material for the Social and Ceremonial Life of the Choctaw Indians," p. 151; George Catlin, *North American Indian Portfolio*, p. 11.

9. Blanchard, *Mississippi Choctaw*, pp. 36–37.

10. Frank Speck, *Ethnology of the Yuchi Indians*, p. 88; *Literary Digest*, p. 59, cited in Fogelson, "Cherokee Ball Game," pp. 152–60.

11. Alexander Henry, *Travels and Adventures in Canada and the Indian Territories between the Years 1760 and 1776*, p. 85; Copway, *History and Sketches*, p. 51.

12. Fogelson, "Cherokee Ball Game," pp. 159–60.

13. Jonathan Carver, *Travels through the Interior Parts of North America in the Years 1766, 1767, and 1768*, p. 363; Reuben G. Thwaites, ed., *The Jesuit Relations and Allied Documents: Travels and Explorations of the Jesuit Missionaries in New France, 1610–1791*, 15:155; Pierre de Charlevoix, *Journal of a Voyage to North America*, p. 12.

14. Seymour Feiler, *Jean-Bernard Bossu's Travels in the Interior of North America, 1751–1762*, p. 170; John R. Swanton, "An Early Account of the Choctaw Indians," p. 68; University of South Dakota American Indian Oral History Project, tape 279A, pp. 2, 4; Edward D. Neill, *Dakota Land and Dakota Life*, p. 281; Alanson Skinner, *Social Life and Ceremonial Bundles of the Menominee Indians*, p. 53; J. N. B. Hewitt, "Iroquois Game of La Crosse," p. 191.

15. Roger Williams noted that Rhode Island Indian summer "football [soccer]" in 1643 was played "upon some broad sandy shore, free from stones, or upon some soft plot, because of their naked feet, at which they have great stakings [bets], but seldom quarrel" (cited in William J. Baker, *Sports in the Western World*, p. 70). See also Cushman, *History of the Choctaw, Chickasaw, and Natchez Indians*, p. 130.

16. Thwaites, *Jesuit Relations,* 10:187.

17. Cited in Fogelson, "Cherokee Ball Game," p. 28.

18. Blanchard, *Mississippi Choctaw,* p. 39.

19. Lanman, *Letters,* p. 102; Swanton, "Choctaw Indians," p. 140.

20. Cited in Blanchard, *Mississippi Choctaw,* p. 135.

21. Lewis Henry Morgan, *League of the Ho-dé-no-sau-nee or Iroquois,* p. 282.

22. Will C. McKern Papers; James Mooney, *Sacred Formulas of the Cherokee,* p. 396.

23. Blanchard, *Mississippi Choctaw,* pp. 32, 109; Robert Lipsyte, "Lacrosse: All-American Game," p. 44.

24. Blanchard, *Mississippi Choctaw,* p. 109.

25. James Mooney, "The Cherokee Ball Play," p. 118.

26. James Mooney, *Myths of the Cherokee,* p. 369.

27. Johann G. Kohl, *Kitchi-Gami, Wanderings round Lake Superior,* p. 88; Edmund Schwarz, *History of the Moravian Missions among Southern Tribes of the United States* (Bethlehem, Pa.: Times Publishing Co., 1923), p. 177, cited in Fogelson, "Cherokee Ball Game," p. 31; Mooney, "Cherokee Ball Play," p. 107.

28. Fogelson, "Cherokee Ball Game," p. 54; Stone, *Life of Joseph Brant,* p. 447; Henry T. Malone, *Cherokees of the Old South: A People in Transition,* p. 31; Blanchard, *Mississippi Choctaw,* p. 130.

29. Robert E. Ritzenthaler, Field Notes and Papers.

30. Neill, *Dakota Land and Dakota Life,* pp. 281–82.

31. Walter James Hoffman, "Remarks on Ojibwa Ball Play," p. 135.

32. Stone, *Life of Joseph Brant,* p. 447; Morgan, *League of the Iroquois,* p. 282.

33. Copway, *History and Sketches,* pp. 49–50; William H. Gilbert, Jr., "The Eastern Cherokee," p. 269; John H. Payne Papers, 6:64.

34. Rev. George White, *Historical Collections of Georgia,* p. 670; H. S. Halbert, cited in Swanton, "Source Material," p. 149; George E. Starr, cited in Culin, "Games of the North American Indians," p. 603.

35. Fogelson, "Cherokee Ball Game," pp. 146–47.

36. Perrot, cited in Culin, "Games of the North American Indians," p. xi; Elisabeth Tooker, *An Ethnography of the Huron Indians, 1615–1649,* p. 116.

37. Blanchard, *Mississippi Choctaw,* pp. 109–10.

38. Tooker, *Ethnography of the Huron Indians,* p. 116; Capt. Bernard Romans, *A Concise Natural History of East and West Florida,* p. 80; Thwaites, *Jesuit Relations,* 10:81.

39. Thwaites, *Jesuit Relations,* 10:81; Ruth Landes, *The Mystic Lake Sioux,* p. 45.

40. Cushman, *History of the Choctaw, Chickasaw, and Natchez Indians,* pp. 131–35; Blanchard, *Mississippi Choctaw,* p. 40.

41. Henry T. Malone, *Cherokees of the Old South: A People in Transition,* p. 134; Schwarz, *History of the Moravian Missions,* cited in Fogelson, "Cherokee Ball Game," p. 31.

42. Kohl, *Kitchi-Gami,* p. 88.

43. Halbert, cited in Swanton, "Source Material," pp. 24–25.

44. Blanchard, *Mississippi Choctaw,* p. 41.

45. Ibid., pp. 41–42.

46. Lanman, *Letters,* p. 100.

47. John H. Payne Papers, 6:212.

48. Fogelson, "Cherokee Ball Game," pp. 184–85.

CHAPTER 8

1. Basil Hall, *Travels in North America in the Years 1827 and 1828,* p. 302.

2. Kendall Blanchard, *The Mississippi Choctaw at Play: The Serious Side of Leisure,* p. 68; James Adair, cited in John R. Swanton, "Social Organization and Social Usages of the Indians of the Creek Confederacy," pp. 456–57; George Catlin, *Letters and Notes on the Manners, Customs, and Condition of the North American Indians,* 2:124.

3. Blanchard, *Mississippi Choctaw,* p. 37; Raymond Fogelson, "The Cherokee Ball Game: A Study in Southeastern Ethnology," p. 154.

4. I. P. Evans, cited in Fogelson, "Cherokee Ball Game," p. 42; Charles Lanman, *Letters from the Alleghany Mountains,* p. 103; Fogelson, "Cherokee Ball Game," p. 154.

5. Fogelson, "Cherokee Ball Game," p. 155.

6. Walter James Hoffman, "The Menomini Indians," p. 128. See also Thomas L. McKenney, *Sketches of a Tour to the Lakes,* pp. 180–81.

7. Peter Grant, "The Saulteaux Indians about 1804," p. 337; Col. Landmann, *Adventures and Recollections of Colonel Landmann, Late of the Corps of Royal Engineers,* p. 86; Franklin Basina, interview transcripts, p. 5. See also Mayer's Dakota sketches (Figure 28); Wilbur Blackdeer, personal communication, 19 September 1991.

8. Johann G. Kohl, *Kitchi-Gami, Wanderings round Lake Superior,* p. 89; Ernestine Friedl Papers; Robert E. Ritzenthaler, Field Notes and Papers; George Copway, *The Traditional History and Characteristic Sketches of the Ojibway Nation,* p. 51. For Miami skills, see Pierre de Charlevoix, *Journal of a Voyage to North America,* p. 104.

9. Basina, interview transcripts, p. 8.

10. Jonathan Carver, *Travels through the Interior Parts of North America in the Years 1766, 1767, and 1768*, p. 365; Fred Jones, interview transcripts, University of South Dakota American Indian Oral History Project, pp. 14–15. See also Grant, "Saulteaux Indians," p. 337; Walter James Hoffman, "Remarks on Ojibwa Ball Play," p. 134. Although teamwork was of some importance to the Potawatomi, the fastest runners usually scored the most goals (Robert E. Ritzenthaler, *The Potawatomi Indians of Wisconsin*, p. 164).

11. Baron Louis Armand Lahontan, *New Voyages to North America*, cited in Stewart Culin, "Games of the North American Indians," p. 589; Landmann, *Adventures and Recollections*, pp. 86–87.

12. Basina, interview transcripts, p. 8; Landmann, *Adventures and Recollections*, p. 87.

13. J. N. B. Hewitt, "Iroquois Game of La Crosse," pp. 190–91. For example, Smith's description of the Canadian Wyandot game says little more than that a player catches the ball and runs with it while opponents are in pursuit. If he is overtaken, "he give the staff a stroke, which causes the ball to fly out of the net; then they have another debate for it." Smith noted that a player could throw the ball fifty to sixty yards (James Smith, *An Account of the Remarkable Occurrences in the Life and Travels of Col. James Smith*, p. 84).

14. Lewis Henry Morgan, *League of the Ho-dé-no-sau-nee or Iroquois*, pp. 285ff.

15. Linley Logan, personal communication, 5 March 1992.

16. Morgan, *League of the Iroquois*.

17. See, e.g., W[illiam] G[eorge] Beers, *Lacrosse: The National Game of Canada*, pp. 79–80.

18. Cited in William Perkins Bull, *From Rattlesnake Hunt to Hockey: The History of Sports in Canada and of the Sportsmen of Peel 1748 to 1974*, p. 376.

CHAPTER 10

1. See John C. Ewers, "George Catlin, Painter of Indians and the West."

2. George Catlin, *Letters and Notes on the Manners, Customs, and Condition of the North American Indians*, 2:37.

3. Ibid., 1:2; Ewers, "George Catlin," p. 485.

4. William H. Truettner, *The Natural Man Observed: A Study of Catlin's Indian Gallery*, p. 64. See also Ewers, "George Catlin," p. 499, for "shortcuts" in Catlin's Mandan paintings and Audubon's comments on them.

5. Ewers, "George Catlin," pp. 493–94.

6. Catlin, *Letters and Notes*, 2:139.

7. Ewers, "George Catlin," p. 500.

8. John Francis McDermott, *Seth Eastman: Pictorial Historian of the Indian*, p. 105.

9. Harold McCracken, *George Catlin and the Old Frontier*, p. 138.

10. In Catlin's 1844 version of *Ball-play of the Choctaw—Ball Up*, he has colored some of the players white, presumably to imply that teams were so distinguished. (His 1844 *Portfolio* text supports the practice.) This distinction does *not* appear in the earlier versions of the scene, where players are dressed identically, nor does he mention it in *Letters and Notes*. It is my belief that Catlin encountered this practice among the Dakota in 1835 and later transferred it to the Choctaw.

11. Catlin, *Letters and Notes*, 2:126.

12. E.g., Alexander M. Weyand and Milton R. Roberts, *The Lacrosse Story*, p. 8; Justin Cobb, "The Evolution of the Rules of Lacrosse," p. 9; Nancy B. Martel, "Little Brother of War," p. 49. Elsewhere on the playing field in the background of the 1844 lithograph are two other women with whips about to lash players. Their intended victims, however, are not clutching others but are running alone.

13. Catlin, *Letters and Notes*, 2:126; George Catlin, *North American Indian Portfolio*, p. 11.

14. Starr, cited in Stewart Culin, "Games of the North American Indians," p. 604; see also Horatio B. Cushman, *History of the Choctaw, Chickasaw, and Natchez Indians*, pp. 184–90.

15. See Thomas Vennum, Jr., *Wild Rice and the Ojibway People*, pp. 174–75.

16. Catlin, *Letters and Notes*, 2:123.

17. Seymour Feiler, *Jean-Bernard Bossu's Travels in the Interior of North America, 1751–1762*, pp. 100–103.

18. Halbert, cited in Cushman, *History of the Choctaw, Chickasaw, and Natchez Indians*, pp. 131–35.

CHAPTER 11

1. Bossu, cited in Stewart Culin, "Games of the North American Indians," p. 599; Starr, cited in ibid., p. 603.

2. George Catlin, *Letters and Notes on the Manners, Customs, and Condition of the North American Indians*, 2:134–35; Edward D. Neill, *Dakota Land and Dakota Life*, p. 281. See also William W. Warren, *History of the Ojibway People*, pp. 202–3.

3. Francis B. Mayer, *With Pen and Pencil on the Frontier in 1851: The Diary and Sketches of Frank Blackwell Mayer*, pp. 149–50.

4. W[illiam] G[eorge] Beers, *Lacrosse: The National Game of Canada,* p. 85.

5. James Mooney, *The Sacred Formulas of the Cherokee,* p. 308.

6. Marinus Willett, *A Narrative of the Military Actions of Colonel Marinus Willett,* p. 109.

7. Lewis Henry Morgan, *League of the Ho-dé-no-saunee or Iroquois,* p. 284.

8. John Lawson, *History of North Carolina,* p. 202.

9. Letter of D. Huntington, cited in Emma Lewis, "Art and Artists of America: Henry Kirke Browne, N. A.," p. 428.

10. Robert E. Ritzenthaler, "Kickapoo Vocabulary," p. 39; Albert B. Reagan, "Some Games of the Bois Fort Ojibwa," p. 276; A. Frances Eyman, "Lacrosse and the Cayuga Thunder Rite," p. 19.

11. Catlin's large color paintings of the Choctaw game seem to show the exposed skin of some players more lightly colored than others. Since he learned that Sioux used white clay on players of one side, he may have added this detail to suggest similar distinctions between Choctaw teams.

12. Robert E. Ritzenthaler, Field Notes and Papers, pp. 22–23; Robert E. Ritzenthaler and Pat Ritzenthaler, *The Woodland Indians of the Western Great Lakes,* p. 111.

13. Frank G. Speck and Leonard Broom, *Cherokee Dance and Drama,* pp. 51, 55. See also Alanson Skinner, *Social Life and Ceremonial Bundles of the Menomini Indians,* p. 57; Frank G. Speck, *Ethnology of the Yuchi Indians,* pp. 86–87; Basil Hall, *Travels in North America in the Years 1827 and 1828,* pp. 297–98, 303.

14. John R. Swanton, "An Early Account of the Choctaw Indians," p. 43; Raymond Fogelson, "The Cherokee Ball Game," p. 109. For more on feather symbolism, see Victoria Lindsay Levine, "Feathers in Southeast American Indian Ceremonialism," pp. 5, 8.

15. Fogelson, "Cherokee Ball Game," pp. 104–5; Speck and Broom, *Cherokee Dance and Drama,* p. 57.

16. Jerry Wolfe, personal communication, 8 October 1992.

17. J. N. B. Hewitt, "Iroquois Game of La Crosse," p. 191; John R. Swanton, "Social Organization and Social Usages of the Indians of the Creek Confederacy," p. 465; Fogelson, "Cherokee Ball Game," p. 109.

18. Fred Jones, interview transcripts, University of South Dakota American Indian Oral History Project, tape 156, p. 15; James Howard, *The Plains-Ojibwa or Bungi,* p. 72.

19. Eyman, "Lacrosse and the Cayuga Thunder Rite," p. 19.

20. Franklin Basina, interview transcript, p. 9.

21. William Perkins Bull, *From Rattlesnake Hunt to Hockey: The History of Sports in Canada and of the Sportsmen of Peel 1748 to 1974,* p. 355; Beers, *Lacrosse,* pp. 220–21, 230–31.

22. MAAA, Minutes Books, 14 July 1909, p. 214.

23. Swanton, "Social Organization," pp. 297–98, 460.

24. Kendall Blanchard, *The Mississippi Choctaw at Play: The Serious Side of Leisure,* p. 29. For the Menominee practice, see Walter James Hoffman, "Remarks on Ojibwa Ball Play," p. 127.

25. Reuben G. Thwaites, ed., *The Jesuit Relations and Allied Documents: Travels and Explorations of the Jesuit Missionaries in New France, 1610–1791,* 10:187; Seymour Feiler, *Jean-Bernard Bossu's Travels in the Interior of North America, 1751–1762,* p. 169; Jonathan Carver, *Travels through the Interior Parts of North America in the Years 1766, 1767, and 1768,* p. 364.

26. Ritzenthaler and Ritzenthaler, *Woodland Indians,* p. 110; Robert E. Ritzenthaler, *The Potawatomi Indians of Wisconsin,* pp. 163–64; Skinner, *Social Life and Ceremonial Bundles,* pp. 55–57; Frances Densmore, *Menominee Music,* p. 37.

27. Frank G. Speck, *Ethnology of the Yuchi Indians,* pp. 117–18; Eyman, "Lacrosse and the Cayuga Thunder Rite," p. 18. The teams do not necessarily have to represent opposite moieties.

28. Freeman Bucktooth, Jr., interview transcript, p. 3.

29. Paul Radin, "The Winnebago Tribe," pp. 72–73, 142. The Iroquois likewise divide clans into earth and sky creatures. See Morgan, *League of the Iroquois,* p. 281.

30. William N. Fenton, *The Iroquois Eagle Dance: An Offshoot of the Calumet Dance,* p. 138.

31. Mooney, "Cherokee Ball Play," p. 107; Reagan, "Some Games of the Bois Fort Ojibwa," p. 275; Basina, interview transcript, p. 3.

32. Neill, *Dakota Land and Dakota Life,* p. 281; George Copway, *The Traditional History and Characteristic Sketches of the Ojibway Nation,* p. 52.

33. Swanton, "Social Organization," pp. 251, 256–58, 463; Mary R. Haas, "Creek Inter-town Relations," pp. 479ff.

34. Blanchard, *Mississippi Choctaw,* pp. 117, 120.

35. William L. Stone, *Life of Joseph Brant—Thayendanegea,* pp. 447–48. See also William W. Warren, *History of the Ojibway People,* p. 202, who asserts that a hundred per side played at Fort Michilimackinac in 1763. Numbers playing in "great games" tend to become inflated over time. Those who read of hundreds of lacrosse players pitted against equal

numbers should be reminded that in one account five hundred years after the event, the Olympic athlete Milo is claimed to have led 100,000 Krotons against 300,000 Shibarites (Michael B. Poliakoff, *Combat Sports in the Ancient World: Competition, Violence, and Culture,* p. 118).

36. Catlin, *Letters and Notes,* 2:135.

37. Alexander McFarland Davis, *Indian Games,* p. 90. The general impression of large teams persists. For example, lacrosse historians Alexander M. Weyand and Milton R. Roberts have written: "In the early days, teams seldom consisted of less than a hundred players, and sometimes the number ran to over a thousand" (*The Lacrosse Story,* p. 6).

38. Fogelson, "Cherokee Ball Game," pp. 28–29, 48. Mooney, "Cherokee Ball Play," p. 129.

39. For Cherokee team makeup, see Fogelson, "Cherokee Ball Game," pp. 139–42.

40. *Tewaarathon (Lacrosse): Akwesasne's Story of Our National Game,* p. 37.

41. Fogelson, "Cherokee Ball Game," p. 141.

42. Hoffman, "Ojibwa Ball Play," p. 135; Jones, cited in Stewart Culin, "Games of the North American Indians," p. 573.

43. Culin, "Games of the North American Indians," p. xl; Thomas L. McKenney, *Sketches of a Tour to the Lakes,* pp. 180–81.

44. Timberlake, cited in Fogelson, "Cherokee Ball Game," p. 22; Hoffman, "Ojibwa Ball Play," p. 135; Paul Buffalo, University of South Dakota American Indian Oral History Project, tape 344, p. 12.

45. Fogelson, "Cherokee Ball Game," p. 56. The practice of some tribes regarding team membership eliminated rematches. Early rival Creek teams belonged to opposite political divisions in the community. Should one team beat the other four successive times, the loser was forced to change affiliation by joining the winner's division, effectively preventing the teams from playing against each other again (Haas, "Creek Inter-town Relations," p. 481).

46. Thwaites, *Jesuit Relations,* 15:179; William H. Gilbert, Jr., "The Eastern Cherokee," p. 268; Radin, "Winnebago Tribe," p. 72. See also Feiler, *Bossu's Travels,* p. 309.

47. Gilbert, "Eastern Cherokee," p. 268.

48. Hoffman, "Ojibwa Ball Play," p. 133; Blanchard, *Mississippi Choctaw,* p. 29.

49. Radin, "Winnebago Tribe," p. 73; Hewitt, "Iroquois Game of La Crosse," p. 191.

50. Blanchard, *Mississippi Choctaw,* p. 7.

51. Perrot, cited in Culin, "Games of the North American Indians," p. xl; Swanton, "Social Organi-

zation," p. 465; Lawson, *North Carolina,* p. 33. Examples of Cherokee pregame speeches are given in Fogelson, "Cherokee Ball Game," p. 136.

52. William Bartram, *Travels through North and South Carolina, Georgia, East and West Florida,* pp. 298–99.

53. Walter James Hoffman, "The Menomini Indians," p. 127.

54. Basil Hall, *Travels in North America in the Years 1827 and 1828,* pp. 298–300. Because of the elaborate and time-consuming preparations, Creek towns usually played only once a year. During Haas's fieldwork (1938–39), however, many of the ceremonies before games had been given up, and towns were playing several games each year (Haas, "Creek Inter-town Relations," p. 480).

CHAPTER 13

1. Mary R. Haas, "Creek Inter-town Relations," p. 483.

2. John H. Payne Papers, p. 61; James Mooney, *Myths of the Cherokee,* pp. 384, 433; Raymond Fogelson, "The Cherokee Ball Game: A Study in Southeastern Ethnology," pp. 2, 21.

3. Mooney, *Myths of the Cherokee,* p. 313; John R. Swanton, "Social Organization and Social Usages of the Indians of the Creek Confederacy," pp. 426, 459, 461; Frances Densmore, *Menominee Music,* p. 37; Witthoft, cited in Raymond Fogelson, "The Cherokee Ball Game: A Study in Southeastern Ethnology," p. 153.

4. Will C. McKern Papers, Winnebago notes.

5. Swanton, "Social Organization," p. 460; Fogelson, "Cherokee Ball Game," p. 208; Frank G. Speck, *Ethnology of the Yuchi Indians,* pp. 86–87.

6. James Mooney, *Sacred Formulas of the Cherokee,* pp. 388–89.

7. John H. Payne Papers, pp. 202–3, 287.

8. Longe, cited in David H. Corkran, "The Sacred Fire of the Cherokees," p. 25.

9. Samuel C. Williams, ed., *Lt. Henry Timberlake's Memoirs,* pp. 92–93, 112–13.

10. Frank Speck and Leonard Broom, *Cherokee Dance and Drama,* p. 64; Fogelson, "Cherokee Ball Game," pp. 177, 180.

11. Cf. John H. Payne Papers, 4:62–63, for proscriptions against contact with females.

12. Swanton, "Social Organization," p. 461.

13. Speck, *Ethnology of the Yuchi Indians,* pp. 85, 88.

14. Fogelson, "Cherokee Ball Game," p. 127.

15. John H. Payne Papers, 3:62–63.

16. Longe, cited in Corkran, "Sacred Fire," pp. 22–23, 25. Fogelson, "Cherokee Ball Game," pp. 115–16.

17. John H. Payne Papers, cited in Fogelson, "Cherokee Ball Game," p. 215, n. 1.

18. Fogelson, "Cherokee Ball Game," pp. 232–33. See also ibid., pp. 16–18.

19. Paul Radin, "The Winnebago Tribe," p. 73.

20. Francis B. Mayer, *With Pen and Pencil on the Frontier in 1851: The Diary and Sketches of Frank Blackwell Mayer,* p. 152.

21. Anthony F. C. Wallace, *The Death and Rebirth of the Seneca,* p. 319; A. Frances Eyman, "Lacrosse and the Cayuga Thunder Rite," p. 19.

22. William L. Stone, *Life of Joseph Brant—Thayendanegea,* p. 445, n. 1. Games as war surrogates were certainly not exclusive to North American Indians. In the Renaissance Italian *giuco del ponte,* armored participants clashed on a bridge, attempting to force their opponents to retreat from its center.

23. Peter Grant, "The Saulteaux Indians about 1804," p. 337.

24. Baron Louis Armand Lahontan, *New Voyages to North America,* p. 18.

25. Eyman, "Lacrosse and the Cayuga Thunder Rite," p. 15; Franklin Basina, interview transcripts, p. 5; *Ashland Daily Press,* 2 August 1948, p. 7; Kendall Blanchard, *The Mississippi Choctaw at Play: The Serious Side of Leisure,* pp. 37–38; Fogelson, "Cherokee Ball Game," p. 3. See also *Tewaarathon,* p. 104.

26. Swanton, "Social Organization," p. 463.

27. Fogelson, "Cherokee Ball Game," pp. 136–37; Henry T. Malone, *Cherokees of the Old South: A People in Transition,* p. 31.

28. Fogelson, "Cherokee Ball Game," pp. 130–31.

29. Felipe A. Latorre and Dolores L. Latorre, *The Mexican Kickapoo Indians,* p. 301 ("Today's Kickapoo declare that not a single male would be alive if they had continued to play with rackets, so heated did tempers become during the game"); Edward D. Neill, *Dakota Land and Dakota Life,* pp. 281–82.

30. James Mooney and Frans M. Olbrechts, *The Swimmer Manuscript: Cherokee Sacred Formulas and Medicinal Prescriptions,* p. 71.

31. Frank Benedict, interview transcript, p. 5.

32. Robert Lipsyte, "Lacrosse: All-American Game," p. 65; Rex Lyons, interview transcript, p. 1.

33. W. David Owl, "Cherokee Indian Ball," p. 6; Speck, *Ethnology of the Yuchi Indians,* p. 86; George Catlin, *Letters and Notes on the Manners, Customs, and Condition of the North American Indians,* 2:126.

34. Basil Hall, *Travels in North America in the Years 1827 and 1828,* p. 306; Blanchard, *Mississippi Choctaw,* p. 39.

35. Walter James Hoffman, "Remarks on Ojibwa Ball Play," p. 134; William W. Warren, *History of the Ojibway Nation,* pp. 358–59. See also Catlin, *Letters and Notes,* 2:137. In July 1835, Catlin visited Fort Snelling, where Sioux and Ojibwe were encamped on opposite sides of the fort, trying to work out their differences through the Indian agent. For two weeks they had been dancing and playing lacrosse together amicably, "only to raise the war-cry and tomahawk again, when they set upon their hunting grounds."

36. Cited in Fogelson, "Cherokee Ball Game," p. 236; Adair, cited in Swanton, "Social Organization," p. 457; Fogelson, "Cherokee Ball Game," p. 152; Owl noted that Eastern Cherokee "grudge matches" often set off sideline fights ("Cherokee Indian Ball," p. 7).

37. W[illiam] G[eorge] Beers, *Lacrosse: The National Game of Canada,* pp. 44, 177–78, 205, 241.

38. Fogelson, "Cherokee Ball Game," p. 231.

39. C. R. Harwood, cited in Fogelson, "Cherokee Ball Game," p. 43. Fogelson conjectures that the Indian accounts of this game may have exaggerated the number of injuries and deaths over time.

40. H. S. Halbert, cited in Horatio B. Cushman, *History of the Choctaw, Chickasaw, and Natchez Indians,* pp. 131–35; Lewis Henry Morgan, *League of the Ho-dé-no-sau-nee or Iroquois,* p. 280, n. 1; Fogelson, "Cherokee Ball Game," p. 155. John R. Swanton, "Source Material for the Social and Ceremonial Life of the Choctaw Indians," p. 148.

41. Seymour Feiler, *Jean-Bernard Bossu's Travels in the Interior of North America, 1751–1762,* p. 170; Blanchard, *Mississippi Choctaw,* pp. 34–35; Beers, *Lacrosse,* pp. 177–78.

42. Feiler, *Bossu's Travels,* p. 170; Pope, cited in Swanton, "Social Organization," pp. 458–59.

43. Eyman, "Lacrosse and the Cayuga Thunder Rite," p. 19; Mayer, *Pen and Pencil on the Frontier,* p. 158. Complaints about the new direction of gambling were not unlike those heard today, as bingo parlors and casinos spring up on Indian reservations, ostensibly as a source of nontaxable revenue for the tribes. Since many of these enterprises are initiated and run by white entrepreneurs from the outside, allegations, as yet unproven, of "mob" control are not uncommon. Despite short-term financial gains and the employment they offer, these gambling halls have been detrimental to both the traditional culture and the personal financial condition of reservation residents. Many have become "bingo junkies,"

squandering their monthly Indian Relief checks in the casino or its adjacent cocktail lounge.

44. I. P. Evans, in John H. Payne Papers, 6:214; Charles Lanman, *Letters from the Alleghany Mountains*, p. 100; Blanchard, *Mississippi Choctaw*, p. 39.

45. Fogelson, "Cherokee Ball Game," p. 35.

46. Mitchell, cited in James Davidson, "Enemies Become Teammates to Promote Healing," pp. A14, A16.

CHAPTER 14

1. Reuben G. Thwaites, ed., *Journal of Peter Pond, 1740–1775*, pp. 339–41.

2. Pierre de Charlevoix, *Journal of a Voyage to North America*, pp. 103–4; Frances Densmore, *Menominee Music*, p. 38; Freeman Bucktooth, Jr., interview transcript, p. 9.

3. Franklin Basina, interview transcripts, p. 11; J. N. B. Hewitt, "Iroquois Game of La Crosse," p. 189.

4. Paul Buffalo, University of South Dakota American Indian Oral History Project, tape 344, p. 12; James Mooney, *Myths of the Cherokee*, p. 479; George G. Heye, "Certain Mounds in Haywood County, North Carolina," p. 185.

5. William W. Warren, *History of the Ojibway Nation*, p. 203. In this passage, Warren echoes earlier writers on Ojibwe culture, such as John Long, who remarked, "*Playing at ball*, which is a favourite game, is very fatiguing," and Alexander Henry, who noted that "the game of baggatiway . . . is necessarily attended with much violence and noise" (Long, *Voyages and Travels of an Indian Interpreter*, p. 52; Henry, *Travels and Adventures in Canada and the Indian Territories between the Years 1760 and 1776*, p. 85).

6. Basina, interview transcripts, p. 4.

7. Paul Radin, "The Winnebago Tribe," p. 72. In games of the Shuswap and Thompson Indians in British Columbia, the goals were marked variously— with wooden pegs, stakes about three feet high, stones, or even lines scratched in the ground; James A. Teit, *The Thompson Indians of British Columbia*, p. 277; James A. Teit, *The Shuswap*, p. 564. William Jones's term "hoop wickets" for the goals of the Shawnee may have meant something similar to the Winnebago goal (Jones, cited in Stewart Culin, "Games of the North American Indians," p. 573). Densmore is the sole author to claim that the Ojibwe used the double posts with a crossbar—all others report the single post, although some mid-nineteenth-century illustrations show the eastern

Dakota using the former (Frances Densmore, *Chippewa Customs*, p. 119). Beers reports that the Iroquois had a single tree or pole as a goal and gives the word for it, *Iorhenoketo-ohikta* (W[illiam] G[eorge] Beers, *Lacrosse: The National Game of Canada*, p. 6).

8. J. N. B. Hewitt, "Iroquois Game of La Crosse," p. 189; Walter James Hoffman, "Remarks on Ojibwa Ball Play," p. 135.

9. Robert E. Ritzenthaler, Field Notes and Papers. The only similar goal described was in the Abanaki game, where two rings or holes were dug into the ground; one knocked the ball into the hole to score (Mrs. W. Wallace Brown, *Some Indoor and Outdoor Games of the Wabanaki Indians*, p. 45).

10. Kendall Blanchard, *The Mississippi Choctaw at Play: The Serious Side of Leisure*, p. 35; Raymond Fogelson, "The Cherokee Ball Game: A Study in Southeastern Ethnology," pp. 143–46, 154.

11. Fogelson, "Cherokee Ball Game," p. 156.

12. A. Frances Eyman, "Lacrosse and the Cayuga Thunder Rite," p. 19.

13. Densmore, *Menominee Music*, p. 39; Blackdeer, personal communication, 19 September 1989.

14. Mooney, "Cherokee Ball Play," p. 130.

15. William L. Stone, *Life of Joseph Brant—Thayendanegea*, p. 449; Lewis Henry Morgan, *League of the Ho-dé-no-sau-nee or Iroquois*, pp. 284–95; Hewitt, "Iroquois Game of La Crosse," p. 191; Beers, *Lacrosse*, p. [97].

16. Fogelson, "Cherokee Ball Game," p. 145; Morgan, *League of the Iroquois*, p. 284; Beers, *Lacrosse*, p. 136; Eyman, "Lacrosse and the Cayuga Thunder Rite," p. 19. For the use of the feet, or "frisking," see Beers, *Lacrosse*, p. 185. For exceptions, see Felipe A. Latorre and Dolores L. Latorre, *The Mexican Kickapoo Indians*, pp. 302–3, and David I. Bushnell, *The Choctaw of Bayou Lacomb, St. Tammany Parish, Louisiana*, p. 20. The Louisiana Choctaw played *only* with the hands, but the game was nearly extinct in 1909 when Bushnell visited.

17. Charles Lanman, *Letters from the Alleghany Mountains*, p. 103; William H. Gilbert, Jr., "The Eastern Cherokee," p. 269; Fogelson, "Cherokee Ball Game," pp. 145–46.

18. John R. Swanton, "Social Organization and Social Usages of the Indians of the Creek Confederacy," p. 464; Fogelson, "Cherokee Ball Game," p. 142.

19. Joseph Casagrande Papers; Jonathan Carver, *Travels through the Interior Parts of North America in the Years 1766, 1767, and 1768*, p. 364; George Copway, *The Traditional History and Characteristic Sketches of the*

Ojibway Nation, p. 50; Basina, interview transcripts, pp. 3–4; Blanchard, *Mississippi Choctaw*, p. 67. James Smith says Wyandot carry the ball over a line to score (*An Account of the Remarkable Occurrences in the Life and Travels of Col. James Smith*, p. 84).

20. James Mooney, *Sacred Formulas of the Cherokee*, pp. 395–97; Lanman, *Letters*, p. 102; Fogelson, "Cherokee Ball Game," pp. 31, 144. William H. Gilbert, Jr., "The Eastern Cherokee," p. 269.

21. Peter Grant, "The Saulteaux Indians about 1804," p. 337; Hoffman, "Remarks on Ojibwa Ball Play," p. 135; Ritzenthaler, Field Notes and Papers; Densmore, *Menominee Music*, p. 37; Radin, "Winnebago Tribe," p. 72.

22. Morgan, *League of the Iroquois*, pp. 283–84; Hewitt, "Iroquois Game of La Crosse," p. 190; Eyman, "Lacrosse and the Cayuga Thunder Rite," pp. 18–19; Densmore, *Menominee Music*, p. 39; William Jones, *Ethnography of the Fox Indians*, p. 109, n. 67.

23. Latorre and Latorre, *Mexican Kickapoo*, p. 303; Swanton, "Social Organization," pp. 461, 464; Fogelson, "Cherokee Ball Game," p. 137.

24. Ritzenthaler, Field Notes and Papers; Fogelson, "Cherokee Ball Game," p. 144, n. 1; Swanton, "Social Organization," p. 466. See also Morgan, *League of the Iroquois*, pp. 286–87;

25. Walter James Hoffman, "The Menomini Indians," p. 127; Robert E. Ritzenthaler, *The Potawatomi Indians of Wisconsin*, p. 164; Robert E. Ritzenthaler and Pat Ritzenthaler, *The Woodland Indians of the Western Great Lakes*, p. 110.

26. Robert E. Ritzenthaler, "Kickapoo Vocabulary"; Copway, *History and Sketches*, p. 54; Blanchard, *Mississippi Choctaw*, p. 40.

27. Stone, *Life of Joseph Brant*, p. 448; Blanchard, *Mississippi Choctaw*, p. 69.

28. Morgan, *League of the Iroquois*, p. 287; Mary R. Haas, "Creek Inter-town Relations," p. 481, n. 10.

CHAPTER 16

1. In 1989 Canadian sportswriters paid a flurry of attention to the question of whether lacrosse was in fact ever officially made "the national sport" of Canada, when the Canadian Lacrosse Association admitted that it could find no record of the parliamentary debate that Beers had hoped for. See, e.g., Milt Dunnell, "Should Lacrosse Be Named National Game?" *Toronto Star*, 20 May 1989; Roy McGregor, "Lacrosse Group Plays Hardball with a Myth," *Ottawa Citizen*, 29 May 1989; Archie McDonald column in *Vancouver*

Sun, 20 May 1989. It is possible that the evidence was destroyed in the Parliament fire of 1916.

2. Alexander M. Weyand and Milton R. Roberts, *The Lacrosse Story*, pp. 20–22.

3. Ibid., p. 17.

4. Ibid., pp. 24–27.

5. Ibid., p. 27.

6. *Illustrated London*, 6 May 1876.

7. W[illiam] G[eorge] Beers, *Lacrosse: The National Game of Canada*, pp. [7], 32; CLA position paper.

8. Beers, *Lacrosse*, p. 183.

9. Ibid., p. 30.

10. Ibid., p. 162.

11. MALA Minutes Books, 28 August 1895, pp. 107–8.

12. Mohawk researchers describe the Indian pride in these early "Indian Cups"; see *Tewaarathon (Lacrosse): Akwesasne's Story of Our National Game*, p. 47.

13. Ibid., p. 97.

14. Ibid., p. 50.

15. Ibid.

16. MALA Minutes Books, 1895, p. 93.

17. Frank Benedict, interview transcript, p. 8.

18. Robert Lipsyte, "Lacrosse: All-American Game," p. 61. See Michael B. Poliakoff, *Combat Sports in the Ancient World: Competition, Violence, and Culture*, p. 131.

19. CLA position paper, p. 7.

20. Justin Cobb, "The Evolution of the Rules of Lacrosse," p. 40; CLA position paper, p. 7.

21. CLA position paper, pp. 5–6. Likewise, in 1910 Sir Donald Mann, chief architect of the Canadian Northern Railway, donated a cup of solid gold. The Mann Cup was to be awarded to the national amateur senior championship winner.

22. Barnard, cited in John R. Finger, *The Eastern Band of Cherokee Indians 1819–1900*, p. 68.

23. *Tewaarathon*, p. 3.

24. Kendall Blanchard, *The Mississippi Choctaw at Play: The Serious Side of Leisure*, p. 169.

25. Cited in Raymond Fogelson, "The Cherokee Ball Game: A Study in Southeastern Ethnology," p. 31; Finger, *Eastern Band of Cherokee*, p. 174.

26. Pope's expression appeared in his "An Essay on Man" (1733) and began, "Lo, the poor Indian! whose untutored mind . . ."

27. Cited in Weyand and Roberts, *Lacrosse Story*, p. 25.

28. Kent Lyons, interview transcript, p. 10.

29. Rex Lyons, interview transcript, pp. 9–10.

30. Emmett Printup, interview transcript, p. 1.

31. Ibid., p. 2.

32. Freeman Bucktooth, Jr., interview transcript, pp. 3–4.

33. Anonymous personal communication.

34. Benedict, interview transcript, p. 7.

35. Anonymous personal communication.

36. *Tewaarathon,* p. [vi].

37. Printup, interview transcript, p. 2.

38. Ansley Jemison, interview transcript, p. 3.

39. Dunnell, "Should Lacrosse Be Named National Game?"

40. Dave Sell, "Syracuse: Another Shot," *Washington Post,* 29 May 1989, p. C4. See Mark Kram, "Stick Shift," p. 56.

41. Weyand and Roberts, *Lacrosse Story,* pp. 8, 6, 5.

42. Other gear was also on the market. The association received a letter in May 1890 from Spalding Bros. of New York, offering lacrosse shoes for $3 a pair. The company was requested to send a sample pair for the next meeting, at which time the membership would compare them with samples submitted by Smardon City.

43. For the ordeal of "smuggling" sticks across the border, see *Tewaarathon,* pp. 106–7.

44. Ibid., pp. 108–9.

45. Roy Simmons, Jr., interview transcript, p. 1.

46. Ibid., pp. 1–2.

47. *Tewaarathon,* pp. 120ff.

48. Simmons, interview transcript, p. 5.

49. Benedict, interview transcript, p. 5.

50. Kent Lyons, interview transcript, p. 10; Benedict, interview transcript, p. 5.

51. Benedict, interview transcript, passim; Lyons, interview transcript, passim.

52. Callahan, personal communication, 20 August 1992.

53. Rex Lyons, interview transcript, pp. 3, 5–6. Manufacturers of the plastic stick are discreet about their volume of sales. Industry directories, however, show that one of the largest plastic stickmakers, Wm. T. Burnett Company of Baltimore, has annual sales in excess of $20 million (Mark Kram, "Stick Shift," pp. 54–59).

54. Kent Lyons, interview transcript, p. 6.

55. Lipsyte, "Lacrosse," p. 29.

56. Kent Lyons, interview transcript, pp. 3–6.

57. Hayes, cited in Lipsyte, "Lacrosse," p. 44.

58. Kent Lyons, interview transcript, pp. 8–9.

59. Jemison, interview transcript, p. 2.

60. Oren Lyons, cited in Lipsyte, "Lacrosse," p. 29.

APPENDIX A

1. James Mooney, "The Cherokee Ball Play," pp. 108–9. For another version, see James Mooney, *Myths of the Cherokee,* p. 286.

2. Victor Barnouw, Lac du Flambeau, 1944, collected from Sam Whitefeather; see Victor Barnouw, *Wisconsin Chippewa Myths and Tales,* pp. 142–48. For other versions, see Henry Schoolcraft, *The Indian in his Wigwam* [1848], p. 106, and Walter James Hoffman, "The Menomini Indians," pp. 182–96.

3. James Mooney, *Myths of the Cherokee,* p. 286.

4. Robert E. Ritzenthaler, Field Notes and Papers.

5. Mooney, *Myths,* pp. 311–15.

6. Frances Densmore, *Menominee Music,* pp. 36–37.

7. Alanson Skinner and John V. Satterlee, *Menomini Folklore,* pp. 255–57.

8. William Jones, *Ojibwa Texts,* pp. 167–71. Collected from J. B. Penesi, Fort Williams, Ontario.

9. J. Curtin and J. N. B. Hewitt, "Seneca Fiction, Legends and Myths," pp. 234–36.

10. Ibid., pp. 294–95.

11. Ibid., pp. 372–74.

12. Ibid., pp. 611–13.

13. Paul Radin, "The Winnebago Tribe," pp. 72–73. Told by member of the Bear clan.

APPENDIX B

1. John R. Swanton, "Social Organization and Social Usages of the Indians of the Creek Confederacy," pp. 675, 459.

Bibliographic Note

No American team sport has received as little attention from historians as the game of lacrosse. Widely played throughout North America in a variety of forms long before Europeans arrived, the game nevertheless remains one of the most poorly documented American Indian traditions. Early accounts by missionaries and explorers are scant, vague, and often misleading. Not until the nineteenth century was lacrosse described in any detail; when Canadians took up the game and declared it their "national sport" in 1867, attention was permanently diverted to its non-Indian development. And authors of the few books and articles published on lacrosse since then pay little more than lip service to the people who invented the game.

James Mooney was the first to provide an in-depth look at Indian lacrosse, as played by the Eastern Cherokee, in an article published in *American Anthropologist* (1890). Stewart Culin in his classic *Games of the North American Indians* (1907) undertook to assemble, tribe by tribe, what was known of their lacrosse traditions, taking into account all published and manuscript sources as well as providing illustrations of lacrosse equipment in museum collections. (Culin's general approach has been updated, though not enlarged, by Joseph Oxendine's *American Indian Sports Heritage* [1988]). More-recent sports scholars, focusing on aspects of Native American games, have taken a fresh look at lacrosse. Kendall Blanchard's study of Mississippi Choctaw sports (1981) includes much valuable data on their ball game and places present practices in historical context; Raymond Fogelson's unpublished doctoral thesis on Eastern Cherokee ball play (1962) is by far the most comprehensive study of any game of one North American tribe. Rich in interpretation, it is the first to accord Indian lacrosse its rightful place in the annals of American sport. Peter Nabokov (1987) gives similar attention to Indian running traditions. As interest in the anthropology of sport continues to grow, we may expect to find long-overdue recognition given to the sports of this continent's first inhabitants.

Because Indian lacrosse is so poorly documented, we shall probably never have a definitive history of the game. Delving into the sketchy historical literature, I realized that the gaps in our composite knowledge could be filled only by those who own the story. Increasingly I relied on Indian friends—players, coaches, stickmakers—to help me interpret what seems perplexing in the historical record. Their many valuable interviews are cited throughout my text. Most lacrosse enthusiasts harbor stereotypes, albeit honorable ones, of the Indian game, so I have tried to correct the record and balance exaggerated impressions with as much factual information as I could assemble.

The question concerning the geographic distribution of lacrosse remains unanswered. The map shows a large blank area in the region of the Ohio River Valley, reflecting our generally poor understanding of the history and customs of peoples living in that region when Europeans first arrived. They may or may not have played some form of lacrosse; we simply have no information. The map should also indicate that I have not been able to find lacrosse played much farther west than the Mississippi River. Tribes playing the game in present-day Oklahoma had mostly been resettled from the east, and lacrosse was part of their tradition; those in Kansas and Iowa brought lacrosse from their former homelands in the western Great Lakes woodlands. In many cases, there are insufficient data to determine much about games that are now extinct but that seem to resemble lacrosse in what scant description we have. For instance, other than the eastern bands of Dakota, who probably learned the game from their neighboring Ojibwe, lacrosse seems not to have been played among tribes of the Great Plains. But in Alice Fletcher's late nineteenth-century study of Omaha culture, she describes a ball game that used curved sticks; the game has several features in common with lacrosse elsewhere. Still, she does not provide sufficient data to indicate whether it was lacrosse or a form of field hockey (the ball is said to have been rolled on the ground, suggesting the latter), and my best Omaha information does not support their having played lacrosse. Some Plains tribes may once have known the game but discontinued playing it. A mid-nineteenth-century source, F. V. Hayden, in 1862, for example, gives a word in the "Shyenne [Cheyenne]" language that means "a ball club, with a hoop at the end to hold the ball as it is thrown" (p. 295).

Isolated instances of games resembling lacrosse have been cited for tribes on the West Coast (for the Shuswap and Thompson people, see James A. Teit's *The Thompson Indians of British Columbia* [1900] and *The Shuswap* [1909]; for the Pomo, see Stephen Powers, *Tribes of California* [1976]). But the reports are relatively late in the literature, and the game could by that time have been imported, invented, or even copied. (Canadians were already playing field lacrosse in British Columbia before the end of the nineteenth century.) The data for these games are difficult to interpret. Culin, for example, speaks of the Pomo's using a network bat that reflects the weaving technology of California tribes of the area, but he states that the ball is not thrown or hit but rather pushed or shoved along on the ground, suggesting some type of field hockey. There were also tribes playing what I take to be degenerate forms of lacrosse, indicating that the game was dying out at the time fieldwork was conducted. Such were the Louisiana Choctaw when visited by Bushnell in 1908. Many southeastern tribes had another, perhaps older, ritual game using a single post with some effigy affixed to its top. Men using lacrosse sticks played against women using their hands; they hit the post at certain marked places to score. Some tribes who had this game also played true lacrosse (Oklahoma Creek continue to play both in the Green Corn Ceremony); others, like the Apalachee, played only the single-post game (see John H. Hann's *Apalachee: The Land between the Rivers* [1988]).

The narrative chapters are my own fictional creations. Intended to enliven the text, they bring into play the elements of Indian lacrosse that are considered in the more analytical chapters. In casting these episodes in narrative form, I have relied on the recorded ethnologies of the people involved. For more detailed accounts of the settings I would refer the reader to the same sources that inspired my imagination. The best summary backgrounds and up-to-date bibliographies of the northeastern and Great Lakes tribes in my text are found in the *Northeast* volume of the *Handbook of North American Indians*, edited by Bruce Trigger (1978). Unfortunately, the *Southeast* volume in the series has yet to be published, but I would refer the reader to the many excellent and detailed essays of John R. Swanton, mostly published by the Bureau of American Ethnology.

Those interested in the experience of missionaries among the Huron are recommended to the more than seventy volumes of the *Jesuit Relations*, edited by Reuben G. Thwaites (1896–1901), one of the largest and earliest published sources in American anthropology. For the comings and goings of Father Le Mercier and his fellow missionaries, the Reverend Arthur Jones (1909) provides a scrupulous accounting. Reliable ethnographies of the Huron are provided by Elisabeth Tooker and Bruce Trigger; the latter's *The Huron: Farmers of the North* (1969) is certainly recommended. For background on the 1794 confrontation between the Mohawk and the Seneca, the reader will find rich material in William Stone's biographies of Joseph Brant (1838) and Red Jacket (1841), as well as in Mary Jemison's account of her captivity among the Seneca (Seaver 1856). The tragedy of the Iroquois loss of their lands at the time of the national game between the Seneca and Mohawk and the continuing unsolved problem is aptly covered in *Iroquois Land Claims*, edited by Christopher Vecsey and William A. Starna (1988). The story of the capture of Fort Michilimackinac has been told often, but one should begin with Alexander Henry's own account. Though not an eyewitness, he was the trader in hiding whom Makoons would have liked to capture but who escaped to tell his tale some forty years after the event. William Warren (1885) supplemented Henry's information with accounts from the oral history of the Ojibwe, and Francis Parkman (10th rev. ed., 1908) gives the capture a lively treatment, putting it in the context of the entire Pontiac campaign.

George Catlin continues to fascinate us, but for critical assessments of the man and his work one should consult the analysis of John Ewers (1956) and especially the insightful study by William Truettner, *The Natural Man Observed: A Study of Catlin's Indian Gallery* (1979), which interprets Catlin less from an anthropological side than from the perspective of a cultural historian. Raymond Fogelson's dissertation on Eastern Cherokee stickball and

James Mooney's photographs were my inspiration to make Twister and his team come alive. The dissertation deserves publication and a wider audience; that I relied heavily on its general analysis of lacrosse as a war surrogate should be apparent in my text. Finally, I would unhesitatingly recommend George Beers's *Lacrosse* (1869) to anyone interested in the game. Not only does it tell the full story of why lacrosse is played the way it is today in the non-Indian world, but the book contains a wealth of information on the Mohawk game of the period. It is a remarkable achievement for a twenty-three-year-old dentist, and Beers's wonderfully whimsical style of writing at times is sheer enjoyment.

Lacrosse has at last begun to be documented by those who invented the game. *Tewaarathon* (1978) is a commendable history of Mohawk lacrosse as researched and written by St. Regis residents. One hopes that other tribes will follow their example while there is still time to gather the recollections of elders who played in their youth.

With these sources to rely on, one can better judge the many brief pieces on Indian lacrosse that continue to make their way into magazines and journals. My own book, in a sense, reflects the combined literature and our general knowledge of American Indian lacrosse. It is a mixture of fact and fiction.

Bibliography

Adair, James. *The History of the American Indians.* London, 1775.

Atwater, Caleb. *The Indians of the Northwest.* Columbus, 1850.

Baker, William J. *Sports in the Western World.* Rev. ed. Urbana and Chicago: University of Illinois Press, 1988.

Baraga, Frederic. *A Dictionary of the Otchipwe Language.* Cincinnati, 1853.

Barnouw, Victor. *Wisconsin Chippewa Myths and Tales.* Madison: University of Wisconsin Press, 1977.

Bartram, William. *Travels through North and South Carolina, Georgia, East and West Florida.* Philadelphia, 1791.

Basina, Franklin. Interview transcript, 10 September 1990. Archives of the Center for Folklife Programs and Cultural Studies, Smithsonian Institution.

Beauchamp, W. M. "Iroquois Games." *Journal of American Folklore* 9 (1896): 269–77.

Becker, Marshall J. "Lacrosse: Political Organization in North America As Reflected in Athletic Competition." *Expedition* 27 (1985): 53–56.

Beers, W[illiam] G[eorge]. *Lacrosse: The National Game of Canada.* New York: W. A. Townsend and Adams, 1869; Montreal: Dawson Brothers, 1869.

Benedict, Frank. Interview transcript, 3 June 1992. Archives of the Center for Folklife Programs and Cultural Studies, Smithsonian Institution.

Benedict, Owen. Interview transcript, 3 June 1992.

Archives of the Center for Folklife Programs and Cultural Studies, Smithsonian Institution.

Blanchard, Kendall. *The Mississippi Choctaw at Play: The Serious Side of Leisure.* Urbana, Chicago, and London: University of Illinois Press, 1981.

Brine, W. H. *Brine's Lacrosse Guide and Almanac.* Milford, Mass.: W. H. Brine Company, 1982.

Brown, Mrs. W. Wallace. *Some Indoor and Outdoor Games of the Wabanaki Indians.* Vol. 6, sec. 2 of *Transactions of the Royal Society of Canada.* Montreal, 1889.

Bucktooth, Freeman, Jr. Interview transcript, 2 May 1991. Archives of the Center for Folklife Programs and Cultural Studies, Smithsonian Institution.

Bull, William Perkins. *From Rattlesnake Hunt to Hockey: The History of Sports in Canada and of the Sportsmen of Peel 1748 to 1974.* Toronto: George J. McLeod, Ltd., 1934.

Bushnell, David I. *The Choctaw of Bayou Lacomb, St. Tammany Parish, Louisiana.* Bureau of American Ethnology Bulletin no. 48. Washington, D.C.: Government Printing Office, 1909.

Canadian Lacrosse Association. Position paper, 1989.

Carver, Jonathan. *Travels through the Interior Parts of North America in the Years 1766, 1767, and 1768.* 3d ed. 1781. Reprint. Minneapolis: Ross and Haines, 1956.

Casagrande, Joseph. Papers. Anthropology Section of the Milwaukee Public Museum.

Catlin, George. *Letters and Notes on the Manners, Customs, and Condition of the North American Indians.*

2 vols. London: Tosswill and Myers, 1841. Reprint. Minneapolis: Ross and Haines, 1965.

———. *North American Indian Portfolio*. London, [1844].

Charlevoix, Pierre de. *Journal of a Voyage to North America*. Vol. 3. London: R. and J. Dodsley, 1761.

"Cherokee Stickball." *Life Magazine,* 11 November 1946, pp. 90–92.

Childress, Mitchell R. "Choctaw Ball Racket Manufacture." *Tennessee Anthropologist* 17, no. 2 (1992): 93–109.

Cobb, Justin. "The Evolution of the Rules of Lacrosse." Master's thesis, Springfield University, 1952.

Copway, George. *The Traditional History and Characteristic Sketches of the Ojibway Nation*. London: C. Gilpin, 1850.

Corkran, David H. "The Sacred Fire of the Cherokees." *Southern Indian Studies* 5 (1953): 21–26.

Creek Nation Communication Center, producers. Videotape. *Little Brother of War*. Produced by Gary Robinson, photographed by Gary Robinson and Scott Wearingen. 1982.

Culin, Stewart. "Games of the North American Indians." In *Twenty-fourth Annual Report of the Bureau of American Ethnology, 1902–1903,* pp. 1–846. Washington, D.C.: Government Printing Office, 1907.

Cuoq, J. A. *Lexique de la Langue Algonquine*. Montreal, 1886.

———. *Lexique de la Langue Iroquoise*. Montreal, 1882.

Curtin, J., and J. N. B. Hewitt. "Seneca Fiction, Legends, and Myths." In *Twenty-eighth Annual Report of the Bureau of American Ethnology, 1911,* pp. 37–819. Washington, D.C.: Government Printing Office.

Cushman, Horatio B. *History of the Choctaw, Chickasaw, and Natchez Indians*. Greenville, Texas: Headlight Printing House, 1899.

Davidson, James. "Enemies Become Teammates to Promote Healing." *Toronto Globe and Mail,* 6 June 1992, pp. A14, A16.

Davis, Alexander McFarland. *Indian Games*. Bulletin of the Essex Institute, vol. 17. Salem, Mass., 1886.

Densmore, Frances. *Chippewa Customs*. 1929. Reprint. St. Paul: Minnesota Historical Society Press, Borealis Books, 1979.

———. "Choctaw Music." In *Bureau of American Ethnology Bulletin no. 136*. Anthropological Papers, no. 28, pp. 101–83. Washington, D.C.: Government Printing Office, 1943.

———. *Menominee Music*. Bureau of American Ethnology Bulletin no. 102. Washington, D.C.: Government Printing Office, 1932.

Draper, David E. "Occasions for the Performance of Native Choctaw Music." In *Selected Reports in Ethnomusicology,* vol. 3, no. 2, edited by Charlotte Heth, pp. 147–73. Los Angeles: University of California, 1980.

Ducatel, J. J. "A Fortnight among the Chippewas of Lake Superior." In *The Indian Miscellany*, edited by W. W. Beach. Albany: J. Munsell, 1877.

Duval, Edwin M. Personal communications, 28 December 1991 and 1 June 1992.

Ehle, John. *Trail of Tears: The Rise and Fall of the Cherokee Nation*. New York: Anchor Books/Doubleday, 1988.

Ewers, John C. "George Catlin, Painter of Indians and the West." In *Annual Report of the Smithsonian Institution for 1955,* pp. 483–528. Washington, D.C.: Government Printing Office, 1956.

Eyman, A. Frances. "Lacrosse and the Cayuga Thunder Rite." *Expedition* 6 (1964): 15–19.

Feiler, Seymour, trans. and ed. *Jean-Bernard Bossu's Travels in the Interior of North America, 1751–1762*. Norman: University of Oklahoma Press, 1962.

Fenton, William N. *The Iroquois Eagle Dance: An Offshoot of the Calumet Dance*. Bureau of American Ethnology Bulletin no. 156. Washington, D.C.: Government Printing Office, 1953.

Finger, John R. *The Eastern Band of Cherokee Indians, 1819–1900*. Knoxville: University of Tennessee Press, 1984.

Fletcher, Alice C. *Indian Games and Dances with Native Songs*. Boston: C. C. Birchard and Company, 1915.

———. "The Omaha Tribe." In *Twenty-seventh Annual Report of the Bureau of American Ethnology, 1905–1906,* pp. 17–654. Washington, D.C.: Government Printing Office, 1911.

Fogelson, Raymond. "The Cherokee Ball Game: A Study in Southeastern Ethnology." Ph.D. diss., University of Pennsylvania, 1962.

Frazier, Alex. "George Catlin and Choctaw Lacrosse." *Lacrosse,* March 1990, pp. 50–52.

Friedl, Ernestine. Papers (June 1942). Anthropology Section, Milwaukee Public Museum.

Gilbert, William H., Jr. "The Eastern Cherokees." In *Bureau of American Ethnology Bulletin no. 133,* pp. 169–414. Washington, D.C.: Government Printing Office, 1943.

Grant, Peter. "The Saulteaux Indians about 1804." In *Les Bourgeois de la Compagnie due Nord-Quest,* edited by Louis R. Masson, pp. 337–40. Quebec, 1890.

Haas, Mary R. "Creek Inter-town Relations." *American Anthropologist* 42 (1940): 479–89.

Hall, Basil. *Travels in North America in the Years 1827 and 1828.* Vol. 3. Edinburgh: Cadell, 1829.

Hann, John H. *Apalachee: The Land between the Rivers.* Gainesville: University of Florida/Florida State Museum, 1988.

Hayden, F. V. "Contributions to the Ethnography and Philology of the Indian Tribes of the Missouri Valley." *Transactions of the American Philosophical Society* 12 (1862): 274–320.

Haywood, John. *The Natural and Aboriginal History of Tennessee.* Nashville: George Wilson, 1823.

Heidenreich, Conrad E. "Huron." In *Handbook of North American Indians,* edited by William Sturtevant. Vol. 15, *Northeast,* edited by Bruce Trigger, pp. 368–88. Washington, D.C.: Smithsonian Institution Press, 1978.

Henry, Alexander. *Travels and Adventures in Canada and the Indian Territories between the Years 1760 and 1776.* New York: I. Riley, 1809.

Hewitt, J. N. B. "Iroquois Game of La Crosse." *American Anthropologist* 5 (1892): 189–91.

Heye, George G. "Certain Mounds in Haywood County, North Carolina." In *Holmes Anniversary Volume, Anthropological Essays,* compiled by Ella Leary, pp. 180–86. Washington, D.C., 1916.

Hoffman, Walter James. "The Menomini Indians." In *Fourteenth Annual Report of the Bureau of American Ethnology to the Secretary of the Smithsonian Institution, 1892–1893,* pp. 11–328. Washington, D.C.: Government Printing Office, 1897.

——. "Remarks on Ojibwa Ball Play." *American Anthropologist* 3 (1890): 133–35.

Howard, James H. *The Plains-Ojibwa or Bungi.* Anthropological Papers of the South Dakota Museum, no. 1. Vermillion, S.D.: South Dakota Museum, University of South Dakota, 1965.

Howard, James H., and Victoria Lindsay Levine. *Choctaw Music and Dance.* Norman and London: University of Oklahoma Press, 1990.

Jemison, Ansley. Interview transcript, 27 March 1992. Archives of the Center for Folklife Programs and Cultural Studies, Smithsonian Institution.

Jones, Arthur E. *"8endake Ehen"; or, Old Huronia.* Fifth Report of the Bureau of Archives for the Province of Ontario. Toronto, 1909.

Jones, Peter. *History of the Ojebway Indians.* London, 1861.

Jones, William. *Ethnography of the Fox Indians.* Bureau of American Ethnology Bulletin no. 125. Washington, D.C.: Government Printing Office, 1939.

——. *Ojibwa Texts.* Edited by Truman Michelson. Publications of the American Ethnological Society, vol. 7, pt. 2. New York: G. E. Stechert and Company, Agents, 1919.

Kane, Paul. *Wanderings of an Artist among the Indians of North America.* London, 1859.

Kilpatrick, Jack Frederick, and Anna Gritts Kilpatrick. "Notebook of a Cherokee Shaman." *Smithsonian Contributions to Anthropology* 2, no. 6 (1970): 83–125.

Kinietz, W. Vernon. *Chippewa Village: The Story of Katikitegon.* Cranbrook Institute of Science Bulletin 25. Bloomfield Hills, Mich., 1947.

Kohl, Johann G. *Kitchi-Gami, Wanderings round Lake Superior.* London: Chapman and Hall, 1860.

Kram, Mark. "Stick Shift." *Warfield's,* March 1990, pp. 54–59.

Kurath, Gertrude P. *Dance and Song Rituals of the Six Nations Reserve, Ontario.* National Museum of Canada Bulletin 220, no. 4 (1968).

Lahontan, Baron Louis Armand. *New Voyages to North America.* Vol. 2. London: H. Bonwicke, T. Goodwin, M. Wotton, B. Tooke, and S. Manship, 1703.

Landes, Ruth. *The Mystic Lake Sioux.* Madison: University of Wisconsin Press, 1968.

Landmann, George Thomas. *Adventures and Recollections of Colonel Landmann, Late of the Corps of Royal Engineers.* Vol. 2. London: Colburn and Company, 1852.

Lanman, Charles. *Letters from the Alleghany Mountains.* New York: Geo. P. Putnam, 1849.

Latorre, Felipe A., and Dolores L. Latorre. *The Mexican Kickapoo Indians.* Austin and London: University of Texas Press, 1976.

Laubin, Dave. "Lacrosse: 'Little Brother of War,' the Indians Called It." *Canadian Geographic,* October-November 1984, pp. 36–43.

Lawson, John. *History of North Carolina.* 1714. Edited by F. L. Harris. 3d ed. Richmond: Garrett and Massie, 1937.

"The Legacy of Lacrosse." In *Realm of the Iroquois,* edited by editors of Time-Life Books, pp. 113–21. Alexandria, Va.: Time-Life Books, 1993.

Levi, M. Carolissa. *Chippewa Indians of Yesterday and Today.* New York: Pageant Press, 1956.

Levine, Victoria Lindsay. "Feathers in Southeast American Indian Ceremonialism." *Expedition* 33 (1991): 3–11.

Lewis, Emma. "Art and Artists of America: Henry Kirke Brown, N. A." *Graham's Magazine,* April 1854, p. 428.

Lipsyte, Robert. "Lacrosse: All-American Game." *New York Times Magazine,* 15 June 1986, pp. 29–68.

Logan, Linley. Personal communication, 5 March 1992.

Long, John. *Voyages and Travels of an Indian Interpreter.* London, 1791.

Lyons, Kent. Interview transcript, 4 July 1992. Archives of the Center for Folklife Programs and Cultural Studies, Smithsonian Institution.

Lyons, Rex. Interview transcript, 4 July 1992. Archives of the Center for Folklife Programs and Cultural Studies, Smithsonian Institution.

McCracken, Harold. *George Catlin and the Old Frontier.* New York: Dial Press, 1959.

McDermott, John Francis. *Seth Eastman: Pictorial Historian of the Indian.* Norman: University of Oklahoma Press, 1961.

McKenney, Thomas L. *Sketches of a Tour to the Lakes.* Baltimore: Fielding Lucas, Jr., 1827.

McKern, Will C. Papers. Anthropology Section, Milwaukee Public Museum.

Maddren, William H. "Lacrosse." In *Lawn Tennis: Its Past, Present, and Future,* by J. Parmly Paret, pp. 415–19. New York and London: Macmillan, 1904.

Malone, Henry T. *Cherokees of the Old South: A People in Transition.* Athens: University of Georgia Press, 1956.

Martel, Nancy B. "Little Brother of War." *Mid-Atlantic Country,* April 1986, pp. 49–50.

Mayer, Francis B. *With Pen and Pencil on the Frontier in 1851: The Diary and Sketches of Frank Blackwell Mayer.* St. Paul: Minnesota Historical Society, 1932.

Michelson, Truman. "Notes on Fox Mortuary Customs and Beliefs." In *Fortieth Annual Report of the Bureau of American Ethnology,* pp. 351–496. Washington, D.C.: Government Printing Office, 1919.

Montreal Amateur Athletic Association. Minutes Books. Public Archives of Canada.

Mooney, James. "The Cherokee Ball Play." *American Anthropologist* 3 (1890): 105–32.

———. *Myths of the Cherokee.* Nineteenth Annual Report of the Bureau of American Ethnology, pt. 1. Washington, D.C.: Government Printing Office, 1900.

———. *The Sacred Formulas of the Cherokee.* Seventh Annual Report of the Bureau of American Ethnology, 1885–1886, pp. 307–95. Washington, D.C.: Government Printing Office, 1891.

Mooney, James, and Frans M. Olbrechts. *The Swimmer Manuscript: Cherokee Sacred Formulas and Medicinal Prescriptions.* Bureau of American Ethnology Bulletin no. 99. Washington, D.C.: Government Printing Office, 1932.

Morgan, Lewis Henry. *League of the Ho-dé-no-sau-nee or Iroquois* [Rochester, 1851]. Edited by Herbert M. Lord. New York: Dodd, Mead and Co., 1904.

Nabokov, Peter. *Indian Running: Native American History and Tradition.* 2d ed. Santa Fe: Ancient City Press, 1987.

Neill, Edward D. *Dakota Land and Dakota Life.* Collections of the Minnesota Historical Society, vol. 1. St. Paul, Minn., 1872.

Nichols, John D. Personal communication, 12 November 1992.

Ofield, Jack. "Lacrosse Stick Maker." Video. Bowling Green Films, New Pacific Productions, n.d., c. 1978.

O'Grady, Michael A. "The Aboriginal Ball Game of the Southeastern United States: Its Forms, Distribution, and Origin." Master's thesis, Harvard University, 1991.

Olbrechts, Frans. Papers. National Anthropological Archives, Smithsonian Institution.

Owl, W. David. "Cherokee Indian Ball." *The Cherokee One Feather,* 5 October 1988, pp. 6–7.

Paret, J. Parmly. *Lawn Tennis: Its Past, Present, and Future.* New York and London: Macmillan, 1904.

Parkman, Francis. *The Conspiracy of Pontiac.* 10th rev. ed. Boston: Little, Brown, 1908.

Payne, John H. Papers. 14 vols. Newberry Library, Chicago, n.d., c. 1830.

Peckham, Howard H. *Pontiac and the Indian Uprising.* Princeton: Princeton University Press, 1947.

Perrot, Nicolas, "Memoir of the Manners, Customs and Religion of the Savages of North America." In *The Indian Tribes of the Upper Mississippi and the Region of the Great Lakes,* vol. 1, edited and translated by Emma Helen Blair, pp. 24–272. Cleveland: Arthur H. Clark Company, 1911.

Pistorius, Alan. "Lacrosse." *USAIR,* March 1985, pp. 69–82.

Poliakoff, Michael B. *Combat Sports in the Ancient World: Competition, Violence, and Culture.* New Haven and London: Yale University Press, 1987.

Powers, Stephen. *Tribes of California.* Berkeley and Los Angeles: University of California Press, 1976.

Printup, Emmett. Interview transcript, 28 March 1992. Archives of the Center for Folklife Programs and Cultural Studies, Smithsonian Institution.

Quimby, George I. *Indian Life in the Upper Great*

Lakes, 11,000 B.C. to A.D. 1800. Chicago: University of Chicago Press, 1960.

Radin, Paul. "The Winnebago Tribe." In *Thirty-seventh Annual Report of the Bureau of American Ethnology, 1915–1916,* pp. 35–560. Washington, D.C.: Government Printing Office, 1923.

Reagan, Albert B. "Some Games of the Bois Fort Ojibwa." *American Anthropologist,* n.s., 21 (1919): 264–78.

Ritzenthaler, Robert E. Field Notes and Papers. Anthropology Section, Milwaukee Public Museum.

———. "Kickapoo Vocabulary." Anthropology Section, Milwaukee Public Museum.

———. *The Mexican Kickapoo.* Milwaukee Public Museum Publications in Anthropology, no. 2. 1956.

———. *The Potawatomi Indians of Wisconsin.* Milwaukee Public Museum Bulletin 19, no. 3 (1953).

Ritzenthaler, Robert E., and Pat Ritzenthaler. *The Woodland Indians of the Western Great Lakes.* Garden City, N.Y.: Natural History Press, 1970.

Romans, Capt. Bernard. *A Concise Natural History of East and West Florida.* New York, 1775.

Sagard, Gabriel. *The Long Journey to the Country of the Hurons.* Edited by George M. Wrong. Translated by H. H. Langton. Toronto: Champlain Society, 1939.

Schoolcraft, Henry. *Historical and Statistical Information respecting the History, Conditions, and Prospects of the Indian Tribes of the United States.* Pt. 5, p. 277. Philadelphia, 1851–57.

Seaver, James E. *Life of Mary Jemison: Deh-he-wä-mis.* 4th ed. New York and Auburn: Miller, Orton, and Mulligan, 1856.

Sell, Dave. "Syracuse: Another Shot." *Washington Post,* 29 May 1989, p. C4.

Simmons, Roy, Jr. Interview transcript, 26 March 1992. Archives of the Center for Folklife Programs and Cultural Studies, Smithsonian Institution.

Skinner, Alanson. *Material Culture of the Menomini.* Indian Notes and Monographs, no. 20. New York: Museum of the American Indian, Heye Foundation, 1921.

———. *Social Life and Ceremonial Bundles of the Menomini Indians.* Anthropological Papers of the Museum of Natural History, vol. 13, pt. 1 (1913), pp. 1–165.

Skinner, Alanson, and John V. Satterlee. *Menomini Folklore.* Anthropological Papers of the Museum of American History, vol. 13, pt. 3 (1913), pp. 217–546.

Smith, James. *An Account of the Remarkable Occurrences in the Life and Travels of Col. James Smith.* Cincinnati, 1870.

Speck, Frank G. *Ethnology of the Yuchi Indians.* Publications of the University Museum, vol. 1. Philadelphia: University of Pennsylvania, 1909.

———. *Midwinter Rites of the Cayuga Long House.* Philadelphia: University of Pennsylvania Press, 1949.

Speck, Frank G., and Leonard Broom. *Cherokee Dance and Drama.* Norman: University of Oklahoma Press, 1983.

STONE, WILLIAM L. *Life of Joseph Brant—Thayendanegea.* Vol. 2. New York: Alexander V. Blake, 1838.

———. *The Life and Times of Red-Jacket, or Sa-go-ye-wat-ha.* New York and London: Wiley and Putnam, 1841.

Swanton, John R. "An Early Account of the Choctaw Indians." *Memoirs of the American Anthropological Association* 5 (1918): 53–72.

———. "Early History of the Creek Indians and Their Neighbors." In *Bureau of American Ethnology Bulletin no. 73,* pp. 207–86. Washington, D.C.: Government Printing Office, 1922.

———. *Myths and Tales of the Southeastern Indians.* Bureau of American Ethnology Bulletin no. 88. Washington, D.C.: Government Printing Office, 1929.

———. "Religious Beliefs and Medical Practices of the Creek Indians." In *Forty-second Annual Report of the Bureau of American Ethnology, 1924–1925,* pp. 473–672. Washington, D.C.: Government Printing Office, 1928.

———. "Social Organization and Social Usages of the Indians of the Creek Confederacy." In *Forty-second Annual Report of the Bureau of American Ethnology, 1924–1925,* pp. 22–472. Washington, D.C.: Government Printing Office, 1928.

———. "Source Material for the Social and Ceremonial Life of the Choctaw Indians." In *Bureau of American Ethnology Bulletin no. 103,* pp. 1–282. Washington, D.C.: Government Printing Office, 1931.

Tabor, James. "Molding Talent." *Pursuits,* Winter 1988, pp. 8–17.

Teit, James A. *The Shuswap.* Memoirs of the American Museum of Natural History, vol. 4, pt. 7. New York: G. E. Stechert, 1909.

———. *The Thompson Indians of British Columbia.* Memoirs of the American Museum of Natural History, vol. 2. New York: American Museum of Natural History, 1900.

Tewaarathon (Lacrosse): Akwesasne's Story of Our National Game. North American Indian Travelling College, 1978.

Thwaites, Reuben G., ed. *The Jesuit Relations and Allied Documents: Travels and Explorations of the Jesuit Missionaries in New France, 1610–1791.* 73 vols. Cleveland: Burrow Brothers Company, 1896–1901.

———, ed. *Journal of Peter Pond, 1740–1775.* Collections of the Wisconsin State Historical Society 18 (1908).

Tooker, Elisabeth. *An Ethnography of the Huron Indians, 1615–1649.* Bureau of American Ethnology Bulletin no. 190. Washington, D.C.: Government Printing Office, 1964.

———. "Iroquois since 1820." In *Handbook of North American Indians,* edited by William Sturtevant. Vol. 15, *Northeast,* edited by Bruce Trigger, pp. 449–65. Washington, D.C.: Smithsonian Institution Press, 1978.

Trigger, Bruce G., ed. *Northeast.* Vol. 15 of *Handbook of North American Indians,* edited by William Sturtevant. Washington, D.C.: Smithsonian Institution Press, 1978.

Truettner, William H. *The Natural Man Observed: A Study of Catlin's Indian Gallery.* Washington, D.C.: Smithsonian Institution Press, 1979.

University of South Dakota American Indian Oral History Project, Part 2, *New York Times* Oral History Program. Microfiches of typed transcripts of tape interviews. Sanford, N.C.: Microfilm Corporation of America, 1979.

Vennum, Thomas, Jr. "The Ojibwa Begging Dance." In *Music and Context: Essays for John M. Ward,* edited by Anne Shapiro, pp. 54–78. Cambridge, Mass.: Department of Music, Harvard University, 1985.

———. *The Ojibwa Dance Drum: Its History and Construction.* Smithsonian Folklife Studies, no. 2. Washington, D.C.: Smithsonian Institution Press, 1982.

———. "Ojibway Drum Decor: Sources and Variations of Ritual Design." In *Circles of Tradition: Folk Arts in Minnesota,* pp. 60–70. St. Paul: Minnesota Historical Society Press, 1989.

———. *Wild Rice and the Ojibway People.* St. Paul: Minnesota Historical Society Press, 1988.

Wallace, Anthony F. C. *The Death and Rebirth of the Seneca.* New York: Alfred A. Knopf, 1970.

Warren, William W. *History of the Ojibway Nation.* St. Paul: Minnesota Historical Society Press, 1885.

Weyand, Alexander M., and Milton R. Roberts. *The Lacrosse Story.* Baltimore: H. and A. Herman, 1965.

Wheelock, Thomas B. *Journal of the Company of the Regiment of Dragoons.* Public Documents of the U.S. Senate, 23d Cong., 2d sess., 1834. Vol. 1.

White, Rev. George. *Historical Collections of Georgia.* New York: Pudney and Russell, 1854.

Willett, Marinus. *A Narrative of the Military Actions of Colonel Marinus Willett.* New York, 1831.

Williams, Samuel C., ed. *Adair's [1775] History of the American Indians.* New York: Promonton Press, 1986.

———, ed. *Lieut. Henry Timberlake's Memoirs, 1756–1765.* Johnson City, Tenn.: Watauga Press, 1927.

Wolfe, Cheri L. " 'Something Tells Me This Feeling about the Land Is the Old Choctaw Religion': The Persistence of Choctaw Culture in Mississippi since 1830." In *Persistence of Pattern in Mississippi Choctaw Culture,* edited by Patti C. Black, pp. 10–27. Jackson: Mississippi Department of Archives and History, 1987.

Wulff, Roger L. "Lacrosse among the Seneca." *Indian Historian* 10 (1977): 16–22.

Illustration Credits

Map: Illustration by Joan Wolbier.

Figs. 1, 2a, and 2d: Photographs courtesy of University Museum, University of Pennsylvania.

Fig. 2b: Photograph by Thomas Vennum, Jr., courtesy of Charles Trudell, Spooner, Wisconsin.

Fig. 2c: Photograph courtesy of Anthropology Department, National Museum of Natural History, Smithsonian Institution.

Fig. 3: Photograph by Thomas Vennum, Jr.

Fig. 4: Photograph by Jeff Tinsley, courtesy of Archives of the Center for Folklife Programs and Cultural Studies, Smithsonian Institution.

Fig. 5: Photograph by David G. Noble, courtesy of David G. Noble.

Figs. 6, 7, 8, and 9: Photographs courtesy of Rare Book Collection, National Library of Canada/Collection des livres rares. Bibliothèque nationale du Canada.

Figs. 10, 44, 56, and 61: Photographs by S. A. Barrett, courtesy of Milwaukee Public Museum of the County of Milwaukee.

Fig. 11: Photograph by Dean Loomis, courtesy of *Life* magazine, © Time Warner Inc.

Figs. 12, 27a, 27b, 67b, and 67c: Photographs by Eugene Heflin, courtesy of National Anthropological Archives, Smithsonian Institution.

Figs. 13, 16, 23, 35b, 36b, 46, 47, 48, 49, 50, 51, 52, 53, 54, 55, 58, 59, 65, and 66: Photographs by James Mooney, courtesy of National Anthropological Archives, Smithsonian Institution.

Fig. 14a: Photograph by M. R. Harrington, courtesy of National Museum of the American Indian, Smithsonian Institution.

Figs. 14b, 37a, and 64: Photographs by Edward John, courtesy of Kendall Blanchard.

Fig. 15: After an illustration in Frank G. Speck, *Ethnology of the Yuchi Indians,* p. 121.

Figs. 17, 18, 21a, 21b, and 40: Photographs courtesy of National Museum of Natural History, Smithsonian Institution.

Fig. 19: Photograph by Carole Thompson, © 1981.

Fig. 20a: Photograph by Franco Zaina, courtesy of Laboratorio di Ricerca e di Documentazione Antropologica, Bergamo, Italy.

Figs. 20b, 20c, 37b, and 37c: Photographs courtesy of National Museum of the American Indian, Smithsonian Institution.

Fig. 22: After an illustration by Victor Hogg, courtesy of Mackinac State Historic Parks, Michigan.

Fig. 24: Photograph from Churchill Collection, courtesy of National Museum of the American Indian, Smithsonian Institution.

Figs. 25, 38a, and 45: Photographs courtesy of National Anthropological Archives, Smithsonian Institution.

Fig. 26: Photograph by P. Framer, courtesy of Archives of the Center for Folklife Programs and Cultural Studies, Smithsonian Institution.

Figs. 28a, 28b, and 38b: Photographs courtesy of Edward E. Ayer Collection, Newberry Library, Chicago.

Fig. 29: Photograph courtesy of Thomas Gilcrease

Institution of American History and Art, Oklahoma, Tulsa, Oklahoma.

Fig. 30: Photograph by Alanson Skinner, courtesy of Milwaukee Public Museum of the County of Milwaukee.

Figs. 31 and 42: Photographs by Fred R. Wolcott, courtesy of Onondaga County Parks, Office of Museums.

Figs. 32a, 32b, 33, and 68: Photographs courtesy of National Museum of American Art, Smithsonian Institution.

Figs. 34, 35a, and 36a: Photographs by Victor Krantz, courtesy of National Museum of Natural History, Smithsonian Institution.

Fig. 39: Photograph courtesy of Library of Congress.

Fig. 41: Photograph courtesy of Notman Photographic Archives, McCord Museum of Canadian History.

Fig. 43: Photograph by Martin G. Schneckenberger, courtesy of Buffalo Museum of Science.

Figs. 57 and 62: Photographs courtesy of Minnesota Historical Society.

Fig. 60: Photograph from *Life* Magazine, 11 November 1946.

Fig. 63: Photograph by Leland Torrence, courtesy of Archives of the Center for Folklife Programs and Cultural Studies, Smithsonian Institution.

Fig. 69: Photograph courtesy of Montreal Amateur Lacrosse Association and Public Archives of Canada.

Fig. 70: Photograph by Peter Jemison, courtesy of Peter Jemison.

Fig. 71: Photograph courtesy of Iroquois Nationals.

Figs. 72, 73, and 74: Photographs by Thomas Vennum, Jr., courtesy of Archives of the Center for Folklife Programs and Cultural Studies, Smithsonian Institution.

Figs. 75, 76, and 77: Illustrations by Daphne Shuttleworth.

Index